For James Ratcliffe
Hope you enjoy.
All Best,
Gerald Smart
11/1/87

Can't Help Singin'

Can't Help Singin'

THE AMERICAN MUSICAL ON STAGE AND SCREEN

Gerald Mast

THE OVERLOOK PRESS • Woodstock • New York

First published in 1987 by
The Overlook Press
Lewis Hollow Road
Woodstock, New York 12498

Library of Congree Cataloging-in-Publication Data

Mast, Gerald, 1940-
   Can't help singin'.

   Bibliography: p.
   Includes index.
   1. Musical revue, comedy, etc.—United States.   2. Moving pictures,
   Musical—United States—History and criticism.   I.-Tltle.
ML1711.M39   1987   782.81'0973   87-7986
ISBN 0-87951-283-0

BOOK DESIGN BY BERNARD SCHLEIFER

Printed in the United States of America

Acknowledgments

Let me also take this opportunity to acknowledge the contribution of those with whom my conversation has been both literal and current. So many friends and colleagues have taken the time and trouble to offer their encouragement, their insight, and their expertise. I'm not sure whether they kept me from falling on my face or putting my foot in my mouth, but they sure tried. So much in this book has benefited from their advice, suggestions, corrections, and exhortations. Robert Ashenhurst, Lauren Berlant, Bruce Kawin, and Joe Savage read through the entire manuscript, as laborious a task for them as it was helpful to me. Susan Bernard, Deborah Baker, and Don Hunt worked mightily to get the manuscript in shape at the Overlook Press. George Feltenstein of Films Incorporated, Jack Lusk of MGM/UA, and Charles Silver of the Museum of Modern Art graciously screened prints of films for me so I could check both their details and my memories. Mary Corliss of the Museum of Modern Art, Lisa Onofri of the Museum of the City of New York, and Dorothy Swerdlove, curator of the Billy Rose Theater Collection of the Lincoln Center Library of the Performing Arts, made it possible for me to gather the book's many production stills. Bill Cullum did a magnificent job of turning my blurry frame blow-ups into visually coherent images. Finally, B. Y. Sitterly did his usual everything from provoking ideas to correcting sentences. To all of you I am supremely grateful.

Contents

In Some Secluded Rondaydoo

My mother tells me I sang before I spoke.

If I can't help singing, I might as well take lessons—which I began at the age of five. My conservatory was a 1918 Hollywood imitation-Victorian mansion on Sunset Boulevard, directly across the street from Charlie Chaplin's studio, a 1918 Hollywood imitation-Tudor village. Rubens Musical Workshop, the name of the Victorian mansion, founded by Maury and Gladys Rubens early in the years of the singies (commonly known as the talkies), was one of the most famous Hollywood akademies for musikal komedy kiddies (like Bobby Breen and Jane Withers). By the age of eight I was a regular on the Rubens's local television show, Sandy Dreams, *every Saturday at six—in the days when a television show traveled from coast to coast on a DC-6 as a blurry 16mm kinescope.*

The Sandy Dreams *formula was very simple, built around ten-year-old Sandy. (Played by Susan Lucky, she later danced Louise in the film of* Carousel *and the mayor's daughter in the film of* The Music Man *before she died of a drug overdose.) Every week Sandy dozed off to meet her circle of childhood friends in a half-hour dreammusical set in some exotic location—like a country farm or county fair. We Rubens kiddies then decorated the dream with appropriate musical numbers plucked from popular shows and films: "It's So Peaceful in the Country," "I Wanna Go Back to the Farm," or "Don't Fence Me In," "Come Ye to the Fair," "Heigh Ho, Come to the Fair," or "Our State Fair." Billy Barnes hadn't yet written "Too Long at the Fair" or you can bet that Sandy would have warbled it just before she awoke to end the show.*

The most suggestive or ferocious love lyrics of these songs were dutifully cleansed for us kiddies. I never could figure out what a "rendezvous" was in "Cocktails for Two," which I sang in some dream or other. I don't think Sandy dreamed us into a cocktail bar; perhaps we kiddies went to a chic party. My emendation, "In some secluded rondaydoo," made perfectly good sense to me.

I played Gerald the Intellectual, one of those monstrous adult ideas that turn unknowing kids into parodies of cultural stereotypes. You knew I was an intellectual because I wore glasses and said "indubitably" as often as they could ram the word into the script. I was in inevitable and indubitable pursuit of my intellectual girlfriend, Anita. You knew she was an intellectual because she wore glasses and said "precisely" at least as often as I said "indubitably." One Halloween I wooed her in the guise of a ghost (draped with indubitable white sheet, glasses over the eye holes), crooning, "I Don't Stand a Ghost of a Chance with You." In the light of film history and present experience, I suppose Gerald the Intellectual was a vague custardization of Harold Lloyd's "Glass Character," performing in a weekly (and weakly) kiddie tab version of The Wizard of Oz.

Indubitably.

In the decades since Sandy closed her dream shop I have spent a lot of time with musicals—watching them on stages and screens, performing in them and directing them, listening to them on original cast and soundtrack recordings, listening to jazz and pop versions of the songs that come from them. But I have never written about them: about what they are and why I, like so many others, have spent so much time with them. How does one engage in analytical conversation about a subject that seems simultaneously so vital and so ephemeral? Musicals seem both beneath and beyond intellectual conversation: important to us while they pretend to be unimportant to anyone. Conversing seriously about musicals means exploring this paradox.

This book is dedicated to those with whom I began this conversation, even when it wasn't at all clear that a conversation had begun. To my mother, who dutifully drove me to lessons and rehearsals. To my father, who took me to my first musical at the age of five, The Desert Song, *his eternal favorite. To my sister, who showed me that performance could be easy and not just hard work. To Gladys Rubens, who showed me that musicals were produced less by talent and inspiration than sheer force of will. To Mabel Mohrman, who showed me how a graceful accompanist helps a singer understand a song. To Buddy Herrick, who tried to teach me to tap dance. To the Ashenhursts—Bob, Nancy, and Ruth—who combined a love of musicals with a thorough knowledge of their styles and traditions. To Bob Applebaum and Steve Brown, the most promising and talented creators of songs and scores with whom I worked. To Heery Lynn and Harry Knight, with whom I argued and shouted and laughed. To Napier Wilt, the only professor who showed me how to take the frivolous products of popular culture seriously. To Peter Burnell, who taught me the meaning of performance for performers. And to all the kids at* Sandy Dreams—*wherever you may be. This book is for all of us, expecially those no longer here to participate in the conversation.*

Will It Be Bach that I Hear,
Or Just a Cole Porter Song?

OVERTURE

If we have been taught anything at all about art, music, drama, or poetry, it is that musicals are essentially frivolous and silly diversions: lousy drama and lousy music. While most intellectuals are willing to admit that Fred Astaire, Cole Porter, George Gershwin, and Gene Kelly were pretty good at what they did, it's what they did—the musical comedy song and form, the genre as a whole—that doesn't seem valuable, either artistically or socially. As Jane Feuer notes in her study, *The Hollywood Musical*, "Musicals seem particularly resistant to analysis; peel away the tinsel and you find the real tinsel underneath."[1]

What does it mean to *musicalize* a story: to tell a tale in which music is not only possible but necessary, where the world not only accommodates singing and dancing but demands them? Why tell a story with music at all? How do you get the songs into the story, and vice versa? What kinds of stories require which kinds of songs? Which songs are sung, which danced, which sung and danced? What constitutes the success or value of a single number or a whole musical? What are the relevant differences and similarities between stage and screen musicals? How do musicals reflect or avoid the larger problems and aspirations of American life? And how can I convince anyone about the interest of these questions—at least anyone who has not already memorized the lyric to "There's No Business like Show Business?"

The musical is no different from any other art. Its goal is to make external and physical the internal and imaginary, to make tangible the intangible, to translate thought and feeling into concrete form so they can be perceived by and, therefore, shared with another. In the same way that writers use words, painters use pigments, and composers use sounds, the creators of musicals use singing and dancing. Musical numbers, no less than

1

television beams and celluloid projections, are media of transmission. Folks in musicals can't help singing because their singing mirrors and transmits the emotions they can't help feeling.

Americans take musicals for granted because we do them so well and like them so much. Because they are so close to us, we simultaneously take their enjoyment and dismiss their art. The ruse that musicals are supremely unimportant is the masquerade that gives them their power to move and amuse. The game allows both their creators and their audiences to pretend that musicals don't matter. A musical paradoxically proclaims its own worthlessness and the importance of its worthlessness. To take the musical seriously is a self-conscious act of cultural subversion, in which musicals themselves are often consciously engaged.

What then is a musical? Obviously, a musical is a show or movie with musical numbers. But then, some shows with musical numbers are not musicals—or are not thought to be. Shakespeare's comedies are unthinkable without music. Restoration comedies weave songs into the dialogue scenes. Brecht's plays seemed to be musicals when Kurt Weill composed their songs (*The Threepenny Opera* and *The Rise and Fall of the City of Mahagonny*) but not when Paul Dessau or Hanns Eisler composed them (*Mother Courage and her Children* or *The Good Person of Setzuan*). *The Blue Angel, Morocco* (and almost every other Marlene Dietrich film), *She Done Him Wrong, Duck Soup, It Happened One Night, Casablanca, To Have and Have Not, Fort Apache, Rio Bravo, The Man Who Knew Too Much, Bonnie and Clyde, Butch Cassidy and the Sundance Kid*, and *Annie Hall* are just a few examples of familiar films with musical numbers that no one thinks of as musicals.

It isn't simply that there isn't *enough* music in them. Their musical numbers, however interesting in themselves and relevant to the whole, are simply not the reason one goes to it in the first place. A play or film is a musical if its primary entertainment value and investment lie in the musical numbers themselves. The numbers could survive without the script and do—as record albums, popular songs, and excerpts in compilation films. The script could not and does not survive without the numbers. At least forty-five minutes of every rehearsal hour is invested in the numbers of a musical show—teaching the songs and staging to the principals and chorus, then polishing them to perfection. In films, this investment translates into both time and money. While actors arrive on a set to shoot dialogue with little or no rehearsal (often none until the day of shooting), musical numbers must be carefully planned in advance. The set must be designed for the movement of both dancers and dancing camera, the music prerecorded in laborious sessions with singers and full orchestra, the choreography both devised and rehearsed before anyone steps before a camera on a set. Vincente Minnelli was able to direct an entire dialogue comedy, *Father's Little Dividend*, in twenty-two shooting days, while just the ballet of *An American in Paris* was in rehearsal and preproduction design.

Although the book for a musical play or film might be serviceable at worst and pleasant, moving, astute, or funny at best, the value of the musical is proportional to the value of its musical numbers. The real service that the book performs is to provide slots for the most lively, imaginative, and meaningful musical numbers. A "good book" finds a good reason for its musical numbers—not the other way around. In musicals, the musical parts do not generate the whole, contrary to the usual Aristotelian procedure: the whole provides an excuse and a meaning for the musical parts. Because musicals are far more costly and far more difficult to do than nonmusicals, why bother to do a musical at all if the musical numbers are not worth doing?

Both film and stage musicals are entertainment fabrics woven from the warp of numbers and the supporting woof of not-numbers. Both arose from the same Entertainment tradition that combined theatrical conception, popular song, and performance virtuosity. Those who spun the best scores for stage musicals usually spun the best songs for filmusicals. Those who wore them best on stage wore them best in movie musicals when they went West—as Astaire did in 1932, Kelly did in 1942, Julie Andrews and Barbra Streisand did in the 1960s, and Liza Minnelli did in 1972. The Golden Age of the original movie musical—roughly 1930 to 1955—coincided with the Golden Age of the Broadway stage musical—when George Gershwin, Jerome Kern, Cole Porter, Richard Rodgers, Irving Berlin, Harold Arlen, and many others created their very best stage scores while writing film scores at the same time. Both the stage and movie musicals thrived as separate, competitive equals, each convinced of its superiority to the other, each attempting to deny the importance of the other—rather ironic denials since the disputants had been or still were on both sides of the argument.

To speak of the numbers that underlie both musical plays and films is to speak of their "songness," the complex interplay of lyric and music, word sound and musical sound, verbal idea and musical idea that marks the best American film and theater songs. Dorothy Hammerstein liked to point out that Jerome Kern did *not* write "Ol' Man River"; Kern wrote "Dum dum dum dum" while her husband, Oscar, fitted the familiar words on the dums. The dums of Kern simply can't keep rolling along without the river of Hammerstein. The best American songs that propel the best American musicals are simply incomplete as words or as tunes.

Two simple examples, both apparently artless and easily taken for granted, suggest this musical-verbal whole. The musical line of Cole Porter's "You're the Top" (from *Anything Goes*) leaps up, to its top note, on every repetition of the word, "top." How effective could the song have been if the musical line dropped to its bottom note on "top?" And "top" is a monosyllable, dominated by its crisp initial and final consonants. How effective would the song have been if Porter had written "You're the tops," ascending with that hissing sibilant? We'd get no kick from "You're the Top" without a singular top on the singular top note of each musical line.

In Rodgers and Hammerstein's familiar "A Wonderful Guy," from *South Pacific*, the hard, alliterative consonants of the opening line, "corny" and "Kansas," fall precisely on the downbeat of two successive measures. However interesting Rodgers's waltz and Hammerstein's simile, the two join in a musical-verbal conjunction that conveys the emphatic joy of the singer at that moment. Hammerstein knew that the anapests ("corny as," "Kansas in") were verbal equivalents of the waltz, which he emphasized with the crackling alliteration. Kansas is actually not very corny in August: Kansas is the wheat state and Iowa is the corn state. If you imagine "I'm as corny as Iowa in August," you can hear the poetic, musical, and dramatic reasons for Hammerstein's agricultural stretcher.

Americans hear and, consequently, understand these verbal-musical bundles automatically; the words and music of the best American film and theater songs fit so snugly that their conjunction seems "natural." Only by pulling words and music apart does one hear careful art coyly masquerading as simple nature. Many non-English-speaking peoples don't appreciate musicals because the lyrics of songs are either incomprehensible or ineffective in translation (whether sung in the native language or, worse, appearing as printed words at the bottom of a film frame). Such translations destroy the careful conjunction of word and music that produced the song in the first place.

American musicals, of course, are not the only kind of entertainment whose value rests on its musical sections. Musicals exist in a historical and cultural paradigm that includes other familiar forms: opera, operetta, vaudeville, variety, burlesque, music hall, minstrel show, medicine show, the circus. All describe theatrical entertainments that combined musical performance with sections of story telling or joke telling or some other nonmusical performance. The musical vaguely seems an aesthetic middle ground among them—born from an unlikely marriage of nineteenth-century opera and variety entertainments. Its potential types move in opposite directions, toward one of its two parental poles: either toward opera (or its "light" equivalent, operetta), the European theatrical piece that integrated drama and music, song and story; or toward the minstrel and medicine show, a variety of individual musical acts, comic sketches, and performance specialties. The two opposite tendencies still describe Broadway musicals—a *Sweeney Todd* tending toward opera (it has entered the repertory of the New York City Opera), an *Ain't Misbehavin'* or *Sophisticated Ladies* tending toward the minstrel show, and a *Company* or *A Chorus Line* as curious and conscious hybrids of the two opposite book and revue types.

A musical also seems an economic and cultural midground. Opera, at least in twentieth-century America, has been primarily intended for and attended by the most educated and affluent classes. The cultural distance of the fixed texts in the opera repertory, the incomprehensible languages in which those texts are usually performed, the cost of a ticket, and the rituals of attending a performance—particularly codes of dress—all suggest an elite cultural activity. At the opposite end, the cheapest and most accessible forms of variety entertainment were primarily intended for and attended by the lowest economic and least educated: the music hall for working-class English males; the burlesque for working-class, urban American men. These were not polite family entertainments. The raucous amusement on stage mirrored the frequent drinking and solicitation in the audience. Variety and burlesque shows were extensions of "the whorehouses and dance-halls of the red-light districts . . . [with] roots in the transience of male life in the nineteenth century and in the Victorian double standard."[2]

The musical (whether in its American or English forms, its French form of *opéra-bouffe* or its Viennese form of operetta) was very much a polite family entertainment. Lighter, more in touch with current cultural issues, more pleasantly amusing than opera, it could appeal to a wide spectrum of more and less educated, more and less affluent. It has been primarily devised for and attended by the great middle—the urban bourgeoisie of the nineteenth and twentieth centuries. Not for nothing have the plots of musicals been built around conflicts of social class—frequently resolved by a meeting of opposites in the middle.

Because musicals so clearly inhabit this middle ground between past and present, rich and poor, high and low, they cause cultural consternation when they refuse to stay there. Take the 1935 reaction to *Porgy and Bess*. Was this musical thing a genuine opera or merely a musical in opera drag? Its creators (George and Ira Gershwin and DuBose Heyward) called it a "folk opera," which was either a paradox or an oxymoron (since, in 1935, operas neither came from nor went to the "people"). What was at stake in this argument? Merely the entire catalog of prejudices against the maturing American popular arts of this century, viewing them in vulgar opposition to past accomplishments rather than as a vital evolution from them. It reflected a nostalgic preference for the ancient over the modern, the European over the American, the difficult over the pleasurable, the elite over the popular. It shrouded aesthetic objects in an aura of sanctity that derived from their absolute lack of contact with any issues of contemporary life.

Like the other popular arts, musicals participate in the major cultural debates that shape the thought (and, therefore, the events) of their time. It may have seemed escapist for a 1943 Broadway audience to enjoy a hick musical about Oklahoma settlers at the turn of the century. But the underlying cultural question of *Oklahoma!* was what makes a country of immigrants and settlers into a "people," what makes a neutral expanse of land into the spiritual entity we call a state. As a metaphoric return to the founding of America itself, *Oklahoma!* participated in the wartime debate by attempting to define who *we* were as opposed to who *they* were—the menace *we* were fighting. Perhaps one reason that many critics believed *Porgy and*

Bess couldn't be an opera was that it was so obviously relevant to vital contemporary issues.

Musicals are time capsules. They preserve a vision of the past and from the past in its original, pristine condition while seeming perpetually fresh and new on each rehearing. Cole Porter's "You're the Top" is a catalog of cultural values in 1934—the acknowledged excellence, in their respective categories, of Shakespeare sonnets and Bendel bonnets, of the National Gallery and Garbo's salary and cellophane. Stephen Sondheim's "I'm Still Here" (Follies, 1971) is a capsule history of American fads and crazes, from getting the heebie jeebies over Beebe's bathysphere, through strumming ukuleles and singing the blues, to rest cures, religion, and pills. Like "I'm Still Here," the history of the American musical is a history of twentieth-century American culture as a whole.

A musical is what twentieth-century America came to call the sort of thing that eighteenth- and nineteenth-century Europe called opera. Musicals have enjoyed the same kind of popularity in our century as Mozart and Verdi in theirs. "Opera" describes a particular form of music drama bound to a particular time and place; even those few twentieth-century composers who have successfully injected modernist musical constructions into that historically bound dramatic form (Benjamin Britten, Virgil Thomson, Alban Berg) have been unable to escape the aroma of the pretentious, the elitist, and the academic. Opera companies, productions, and recordings preserve the past and reinterpret it, just as museums preserve paintings and repertory theater companies preserve Sophocles, Shakespeare, and Ibsen. But in so far as musical drama continues as a living form and force in the twentieth century, it lives as musical shows and films. Porgy and Bess has come to the Metropolitan and to Glyndebourn, Candide, Sweeney Todd, and South Pacific have come to the New York City Opera, and singers of opera—Ezio Pinza, Georgio Tozzi, Eileen Farrell, Leontyne Price, Jessye Norman, Barbara Hendricks, Marilyn Horne, Kiri Te Kanawa, Teresa Stratas—have come to American theater songs.

Born in a cultural, economic, and artistic middle ground between opera and burlesque, the American musical on both stage and screen has simply refused to know and keep its place. Its success and vitality lie in that refusal.

$\mathcal{2}$

Before the Ball

AMERICAN MUSICAL THEATER
BEFORE AMERICAN MUSICALS
(1866–1900)

According to critical consensus and traditional thinking, the first American musical was *The Black Crook*, which opened in New York City on September 12, 1866. According to the same consensus and thinking, the first fully "mature" American musical was *Show Boat*, which opened in New York on December 27, 1927. The dates alone imply that for half its history the American musical remained a juvenile, growing slowly and gropingly, in search of its forms, aims, and directions. This contrast between the great quantity of early theatrical production and low quality of early theatrical achievement results in the murky impression of a nineteenth-century theatrical ocean, dotted with unfamiliar islands—shows, composers, lyricists, librettists, and stars whose names, titles, even showstopping songs are unremembered and, by implication, unmemorable.

Of course, Americans know just as little about the nonmusical theater of the same period—not even the names of America's most respected playwrights before Eugene O'Neill.[1] The musical shows and nonmusical plays have suffered the same fate and for the same reason. Although their texts have been preserved as printed books, manuscripts, and copyrighted scores, those theatrical blueprints are incapable of reproducing the excitement, energy, style, and interest of those theater pieces for their contemporary audiences. This historical impression is a reminder that one reason we can appreciate the musical plays and films of the last sixty years is that their texts have been preserved on materials that suggest not only their formal outlines but their performance energy. We have phonograph recordings and motion pictures, not merely printed texts and still photographs.

Despite the unfamiliarity of these early musical shows, many features that were to define the mature musical, whether on stage or on film, were locked into the form in its beginning. Take, for example, that first musical

7

hit, *The Black Crook*. Its birth resulted from a compilation of disastrous accidents that, as with so many later musicals, just happened to turn out well. When one of New York's many devastating theater fires of the nineteenth century destroyed the Academy of Music on East 14th Street, a French ballet troupe lost a home for its scheduled performances of *La Biche au bois*.[2] The troupe's impressarios, Henry C. Jarrett and Harry Palmer, began negotiations with William Wheatley, manager of Niblo's Garden, a theater at the corner of Broadway and Prince Street specializing in spectacular entertainments. Wheatley was preparing to mount a flamboyant adaptation of the Faust legend that had been lifted from Carl Maria von Weber's *Der Freischütz* by a hack American melodramatist, Charles M. Barras. Wheatley agreed to shove the ballet troupe into his Faust story. He then commissioned some original songs, engaged several specialty acts and singers, and invested an enormous sum for the time, $50,000, in mounting the production. The result was a show that ran five and a half hours—for 475 performances, one of the longest runs of the century, at a time when an original New York run of even a hundred performances was quite remarkable. At the height of its popularity, three different productions of the show ran simultaneously in New York and dozens of touring companies took it to large and small American towns and cities. Revived throughout the century in New York and the provinces, *The Black Crook* survived until well into the twentieth century, when the small-town playhouse became its movie house.

The Black Crook was a show that had everything: melodrama, romance, comedy, dance, songs, specialty acts, spectacular scenic effects, elaborate costumes, and legs, legs, legs. Of course, it didn't have them all in a very unified way; and it was common for revivals of the show to add or drop musical numbers, to add new specialty acts (jugglers, contortionists, animal acts, whatever), to drop or add dances at will. The book was as invariable as the legs—a comic variant of the Faust story: a painter named Rudolph trades his soul for his art but is saved by the love of a pure woman. Any sort of musical, comedic, or novelty number could be thrown into that book—and was. Ironically, the plot of one of the last great Hollywood studio musicals, *The Band Wagon* (1953), explores the very difficulty of turning the Faust legend into a musical—a reference, perhaps, to the very beginning of a musical tradition that the film senses is near its end. The only way that *The Band Wagon* could turn *Faust* into a musical hit was to dump the book and do the numbers; *The Black Crook* did pretty much the same.

What meaningful aesthetic could "explain" this kind of show? The answer is the weaving of entertainment diversity and variety into a dramatic unity. *The Black Crook*, like most musical shows to follow it for fifty years, was longer on the diversity than the unity. Songs were rarely conceived as intrinsic to the book (most songs were rarely "conceived" as anything at all) and could be added or dropped at will. Shows imported from England or

A newspaper advertisement for the original New York production of *The Black Crook*

France received an injection of interpolated musical material in New York. The young Jerome Kern spent a ten-year Broadway apprenticeship writing new songs for other composers' scores. New specialty acts and new stars brought their own musical numbers with them, sticking them into a show wherever they might fit (or not fit). A star like Blanche Ring would sing her trademark number, "Rings on Me Fingers, Bells on Me Toes," in every show in which she was featured, even when the remainder of the score was by Victor Herbert. Well into the 1920s a star like Al Jolson would bring his own specialty numbers to shows with scores by composers no less important than Sigmund Romberg and George Gershwin. Another 1920s star, Cliff Edwards ("Ukulele Ike"), specified in his contract that he would appear on stage precisely between 10:00 and 10:15 to perform his ukulele specialty. Even George and Ira Gershwin figured out a way to accommodate him in *Lady, Be Good!* (1924). Not until the 1920s did it become standard practice for songs in a musical show to be written specifically for the characters and situations in that show by a single composer or composer-lyricist team. One obvious way to achieve diversity within unity was to conceive the show's songs as a whole, unified, dramatic score, inseparable from the book, rather than a miscellaneous series of musical numbers to be added to or subtracted from the book at will.

The American stage musical matured by steady attention to a paradoxical problem: to preserve the diversity, the variety necessary for an enjoyable musical entertainment while weaving that diversity into some kind of pattern so that the diversity at least *seemed* a dramatic unity. This aspiration was not without traditional models, particularly in the English-language theater. An obvious ancestor of *The Black Crook* was the greatest of Faust plays in English, Christopher Marlowe's *Doctor Faustus*, which was also very much a diverse entertainment within a unified conception. Scenes of Faustus's tragic confrontations with Mephistopheles alternate with low-comic scenes between the company clowns, who reduce conjury to gibberish, Satanism to acrobatics.[3] The artist Rudolph, like the scholar Faustus, had his inevitable comic servant who mucked about with his master's tools. The most famous English architect of this theatrical model was Shakespeare, who could write a low-comic porter or gravedigger into his deepest tragedies and write comedies with such diversities as the romantic struggles of entangled noble lovers, the fantastic imagery of sprites and fairies, the low comedy of the mechanicals, as well as singing and dancing. Because the English theater ignored both the spirit and the letter of the "laws" of neoclassical unity that dominated the French theater, Shakespeare's comedies became prototypes of musicals. It is hardly surprising that American musical shows unified their diverse entertainment by reverting to the Shakespearean model. Nor is it surprising that Shakespeare's comedies provided the books for some very successful musicals.

Like most American musicals to follow it, *The Black Crook* built its unified diversity exactly as Shakespeare did—on a multistrand plot, derived from Roman New Comedy, with at least two independent lines of action.[4] One strand followed the romantic enganglements of one or two pairs of high-born, poetically inclined lovers, the other the romantic entanglements of mock lovers—more vulgar or common, more openly and brazenly funny than the romantic pairs. The obstacle to the eventual union of these embattled couples could be either external, internal, or both. External obstacles were societal prohibitions, whether a law forbidding the marriage of citizens from two specific cities, a father's vow about his son's or daughter's intended, or a mistake about either the gender or the identity of the beloved. Internal obstacles were psychological barriers between the two lovers—presumptions about one another's needs, intentions, or moral character that could only be overcome by time and companionship. In the multistrand *Much Ado About Nothing*, one pair of lovers is separated by an initially external obstacle (Claudio's mistaken vision of the man on Hero's balcony) and the other (Beatrice and Benedick) by their internal resistance to one another. Both obstacles are defects in "vision"—either literal seeing or figurative insight. In *As You Like It*, however, external and internal barriers weave into a single complex problem for the romantic lovers (Rosalind and Orlando), leaving the courtiers, the clowns, and the country-folk to parody romantic activity on several social levels.

By the end of the nineteenth century, the Shakespearean multistrand plot had become so standard in the musical theaters of Vienna, Paris, London, and New York that virtually every musical show was engineered for a pair of noble lovers (the leading lady and leading man) and a pair of comic lovers (the soubrette and the comic). The romantic couple could talk—and sing—about romantic things while the comic couple could do— and sing about—comic things. In shaping an entertainment diversity, the multistrand plot also built certain assumptions about class and gender into the very structure of the musical show. The key difference between Shakespeare's high and low characters was birth, the differences of mind produced by the assumed inherent distinctions between masters and their servants, noblemen and tradesmen, courtiers and peasants. Nineteenth-century musical shows, particularly those of European origin or setting like *The Black Crook*, could preserve these class differences, for there was no shortage of European princes, dukes, counts, countesses, and marquesas, attended by their inevitable maids, valets, and retainers. As American musical shows grew increasingly uncomfortable with these external distinctions of class and birth, they found a more internal distinction of mind and spirit, based on assumptions about gender, to separate the high and low lovers.

The romantic lovers were distinguished by their "higher aspirations"; her eye was fixed on true romance, his on a worthy partner—the romantic extension of his manly, often military vocation. While the leading man and lady gazed heavenward (often quite literally in songs transporting them toward the stars), the comic and soubrette remained firmly rooted to the earth. In typical American fashion, the soubrette and comic were not servants but pals of the romantic leads. Unlike his valorous friend, the leading man, the comic is a cowardly klutz, inept at every pursuit except avoiding the soubrette's openly lustful and aggressive pursuit. While the romantic leading man woos a properly reticent leading lady, the soubrette energetically chases the comic until she catches him, since both her sexual appetite and strategic vigor far exceed his. By the 1920s, the soubrette had become an explicit example and exponent of Elinor Glyn's "It," the open female exhibition of sexual aggression and intention. But the division of the classes into the romantically spiritual and the comically lustful began early in American musical theater, as early as *Evangeline* (1874), the second great native hit of American musical theater, and *Adonis* (1884), the third, which surpassed *The Black Crook*'s original run with its 603 performances.

Although late-nineteenth-century American musical theater felt the influence of both Viennese operetta and French *opéra-bouffe*, the strongest bond tied New York to London, where the multistrand plot originated. Throughout the century, the American musical remained a British colony, even more in its musical shows than nonmusical plays. The first play written by a playwright born in America, Royall Tyler's *The Contrast* (1787), predated *The Black Crook* by eighty years.[5] Until about 1915, English musical shows set the standard by which any American upstart was judged. This standard of taste and value was confirmed by the international triumph of the Gilbert and Sullivan satiric operettas, beginning with *H.M.S. Pinafore* in 1878, the single biggest musical hit of the century in America and perhaps the single most influential show at shaping the future of native American musicals. Though Gilbert and Sullivan were the most celebrated and accomplished British creators of musical theater in the late-nineteenth century, they were not alone; the romantic operettas of Ivan Caryl and Lionel Monckton and the lavish productions, beautiful chorines, and sharp satire of George Edwardes's Gaiety Shows were considered far superior to the native American competition.

Sometime around World War I, the tide between London and New York shifted. Along with American musicals, American movies, songs, poetry, drama, and fiction all came of age at the same time for the same reason. When American fighting forces went "Over There," spreading American economic and political influence globally, American cultural and artistic forces accompanied them. The British continued to contribute to the musical theater of both New York and London—whether performers, from Beatrice Lillie to Twiggy, or composers, from Noël Coward to Andrew Lloyd Webber. But London had become the province and Hollywood-Broadway the capitals of musicalized narrative. The strongest bond still ties New York to London: the British musical remains the only non-American musical theater to have maintained an international cultural presence through-out the twentieth century.[6] Although one reason for this shared presence is our shared language, another is our shared heritage of the multistrand plot.

If one source of *The Black Crook*'s success was its theatrical variety, another was its spectacular visual production. Audiences of the late nine-teenth century delighted at displays of dazzling stage effects, made possible by the increasing mobility of theater machines and the increasing fluidity of stage lighting from oil to gas to electricity. David Belasco, the most successful and important American theatrical figure from 1890 to 1915, was also the American writer-producer who most successfully combined theatri-cal plots with dazzling visual effects. The most spectacular of all stage effects was the "transformation," the audience's witnessing elaborate changes of scene before its very eyes. This theatrical predecessor of the cinematic dissolve was all the more magical for its apparent dissolving of concrete and heavy stage material into the ether of solid stage space. *The Black Crook* imported its spectacular transformation scenery from London at a cost of $15,000. Scenes shifted from a raging storm at sea to a vast fairy grotto to a "wild pass" in the Harz Mountains.

The spectacular scenic production of *The Black Crook* established a convention of visual opulence and inventiveness that has remained constant for both stage and film musicals. For over a century, musicals have generally been more visually elaborate (i.e., expensive) than nonmusical plays and films. The elaborate display of sets, costumes, color, and light add even more entertaining diversity to a musical that might distract from the concentrated intensity of a nonmusical play or film. The ultimate early demonstrations of visual opulence were the yearly shows at the enormous

A poster for the Kiralfy Brothers' revival of *The Black Crook* promises scenic delights.

five-thousand-seat Hippodrome Theater, which opened in New York in
1905. For fifteen years, the Hippodrome mounted an annual musical
extravaganza on a stage that approached the size of a New York City block
and accommodated a *corps de ballet* of two hundred, four hundred chorus
girls, one hundred chorus boys (a revealing disproportion), plus assorted
elephants, camels, horses, and llamas. The extravaganza came as close as
the musical theater ever would to P. T. Barnum's circus (and the last show
ever to play the Hippodrome, Billy Rose's *Jumbo*, in 1935, literally was a
circus). The Hippodrome alternated its lavish production numbers with
specialty acts that ranged from the renowned ballerina Anna Pavlova to the
notoriously free-spirited swimmer Annette Kellerman. Busby Berkeley, the
obvious descendant of the Hippodrome tradition, directed the water ballets
of Kellerman's filmusical biography for MGM in 1949, *Million Dollar Mermaid*. Its dazzlingly choreographed and photographed aquacades may have
overstated the possibilities of the vast Hippodrome stage (as Berkeley's
musical sequences overstated the possibilities of any stage), but Berkeley
compensates with his nostalgic affection for the lavish Hippodrome style, to
which the film (and Berkeley's entire career) pays tribute.

Over a century after *The Black Crook* musicals still treat their audience to
"transformations," although the single push of a button now sets the
computerized scenery and lights into choreographic motion. Musicals have
always cast the newest stage technologies as performers in the show itself:
from the first elaborate uses of electric light (the stage of the Hippodrome
used over five-thousand incandescent instruments), to the self-propelled
modular scenic units of the 1960s, to the completely automated and
computerized sound, light, and scenic systems of the 1970s, to the laser
light-show of *Sunday in the Park with George* (1984). Among the most
important members of the creative team for a stage or film musical have
always been its set and costume designers; the history of American theater
design is inseparable from the designers of American musicals: Joseph
Urban, Norman Bel Geddes, Oliver Smith, Boris Aronson, Cecil Beaton,
Jo Mielziner, Edith Head, Tony Walton, Theoni V. Aldridge, Robin
Wagner, John Napier. In film the names are perhaps less familiar: Hans
Dreier (Paramount's great designer of the 1930s who created the Art Deco
worlds of the Lubitsch musicals), Carroll Clark (who turned Fred Astaire's
choreographic conceptions into visual patterns at RKO), Irene Sharaff (who
spun the characters and costumes for the *American in Paris* ballet out of her
head while listening to Gershwin's music), Cedric Gibbons (who presided
over MGM's art department in the 1940s and 1950s).

The Black Crook prefigured still another pattern for future musicals. We
can draw a clear distinction between musicals set in some foreign or exotic
place or time—call it Operettaland—and those set in the here and now of
contemporary America. *The Black Crook*, draped in the costumes of some
vaguely Middle European duchy (with a Count Wolfenstein among its

dramatis personae), carried its audience to Operettaland. So did many of the nineteenth century's biggest musical hits. In *Humpty Dumpty* (1868), a vehicle for the forgotten musical star, George L. Fox, we traveled to Nurseryland; *Evangeline* (1874), vaguely adapted from the Longfellow poem, roamed the globe from Africa to the wild West; *Adonis* (1884), the story of a beautiful male statue brought to life (prefiguring both *One Touch of Venus* and the use of the Pygmalion myth in *My Fair Lady*), traveled the cosmos between earth and heaven; *Wang* (1891) sailed to a place purporting to be Siam. The most famous of all the early leg shows, *Floradora* (1900), draped the shapely limbs of its "Floradora Girls" in the exotic grass skirts of the Philippines. *The Sultan of Sulu* (1902) carried a modern American to yet another island in the Philippines; as in so many musicals set in wildly exotic places between the Spanish-American War and the end of the Teddy Roosevelt presidency, the solid American flexed his imperialistic muscles to teach some homiletic lesson to the nasty natives. Aided by superior moral strength and the superior military strength of the United States Navy or Marines, these "big stick" shows lead directly to Rodgers and Hammerstein's *South Pacific* and *The King and I* as well as Stephen Sondheim's *Pacific Overtures*.

Other musicals burlesqued these flights to Operettaland. In *The Mikado* (1885) and *The Gondoliers* (1889), Gilbert and Sullivan debunked cultural impressions of exotic places like Japan and Venice, based not on any earthly reality but on the stage fantasies of musical comedies: that gondoliers have only two appetites, for loving and singing; that gentlemen of Japan exist not in social reality but only in artistic fancy—on many a vase and jar. Contemporaneous with the Gilbert and Sullivan parodies were specifically American responses to Operettaland, often explicit burlesques of it. Set in contemporary America, these musical farces observed American urban ethnic types confronting topical American problems.

Standing firmly on contemporary urban soil were the shows written by Edward (Ned) Harrigan, with scores by David Braham, starring Harrigan and his comic partner, Tony Hart. The Harrigan and Hart series began with *The Mulligan Guards Ball* (1879), although *Old Lavender* (1877) and other one-act musicals preceded this full-length hit. Harrigan starred as stage Irishman Dan Mulligan, appealing to New York's large Irish immigrant community. The boyish, diminutive Hart spun playfully around Harrigan in multiple character roles—pranksterish kiddies, blackface mammies, seductive sirens, battle-axe mamas, and other drag ideas. Harrigan's likable strength and broad Irish humor, Hart's imaginative impersonations, and Braham's agreeable (if unmemorable) music sustained the series for almost two decades, until Hart went insane from the syphilis that killed him. The Harrigan and Hart shows led directly to the modern American musicals of George M. Cohan, just after the turn of the century. Cohan would acknowledge his debt to Harrigan with one of his most famous songs,

Weber and Fields in a publicity pose and (*below*) a burlesque of exotic Orientalia from the stage of Weber and Fields Music Hall

"H-A-Double R-I-G-A-N," in *The American Idea* (1908). That title alone reveals both Harrigan's and Cohan's distaste for Operettaland and preference for contemporary American life.

Harrigan and Hart were succeeded by a very different comic team of urban immigrants. Joe Weber and Lew Fields built musical shows by burlesquing other hit shows with their trademark "Dutch humor." "Dutch," a bowdlerization of *Deutsch*, actually meant Yiddish. Nothing could knock the romantic stuffing out of Operettaland royalty as a prince with a Yiddish accent. Nothing could deflate the fancy costumes of Operettaland as calling them fancy-schmancy, feeling the texture of the very nice material, and asking how much it cost a yard. Musicals set in contemporary America were inextricably bound to America's immigrant and ethnic populations. The shift from Harrigan and Hart's Irish-American dialect to Weber and Fields's German-Jewish accents and grammar (or lack of it) mirrored the contemporary shift in American immigration patterns—from the Irish, who came in large numbers after 1849, to the Jews, who began to arrive in large numbers in the 1880s. The fashions of American musicals were mirrors of social forces in surrounding American life. Two other teams of Dutch comedians, the Rogers Brothers and the Howard Brothers, copied the Weber and Fields pattern of punning malapropisms, suggestive mispronunciations, and parodic deflations in the same period. Weber and Fields, who opened their own Music Hall in 1896, maintained their popularity and leadership in Dutch humor for over fifteen years, until the enmity of the two partners dissolved the team.

Like the Harrigan and Hart series, the Weber and Fields style lasted much longer than the performing team itself. Lew Fields was the father of Herbert Fields—who would write the books for musicals of Cole Porter, Irving Berlin, and Rodgers and Hart—and Dorothy Fields, America's most distinguished woman lyricist—who would write songs with Jerome Kern, Sigmund Romberg, Jimmy McHugh, Arthur Schwartz, and Cy Coleman. Lew Fields himself would produce a half-dozen 1920s Rodgers and Hart musicals on Broadway. The zany style of Weber and Fields comedy, its lunatic pace of anarchic spoof and irreverent nonsense, only occasionally interrupted by some relevant plot point or irrelevant musical number, would be recaptured and reincarnated a generation later in the movies. The anarchic films of the Marx Brothers descend directly from the Weber and Fields Music Hall. The two earliest Marx films, *The Cocoanuts* (1929) and *Animal Crackers* (1930), filmed virtually as they had been performed on the Broadway stage, are our best surviving records of Weber and Fields musical insanity and inanity. Like many turn-of-the-century musicals, these two Marx films slap together a series of comic dialogue routines based on puns, malapropisms, and mispronunciations (like "Why a Duck?"), specialty numbers (Groucho's loony song, Chico's piano solo, and Harpo's harp number), some theatrical parody (for example, of Eugene O'Neill's *Strange*

Interlude), and a few chorus numbers, all of them loosely hanging on a slender string of melodramatic plot that no one could care less about anyway. No better Weber and Fields parody of Operettaland nonsense can be found than the Marx Brothers *Duck Soup* (1933), set in the mythical kingdom of Freedonia and ending with a parodic musical war to end all Operetta wars.

The most successful and influential nineteenth-century musical show set in contemporary urban America was neither one of a series nor one associated with a star or team of stars. Charles Hoyt's *A Trip to Chinatown* (1891) was a musical farce that toured New York City's high and low spots, culminating in a downtown restaurant where various squabbling romantic couples would be properly sorted out and paired up by a young widow. Sound familiar? The scene was deliberately recreated in three later shows and films set in the late nineteenth century—Thornton Wilder's *The Matchmaker*, its musical adaptation (Jerry Herman's *Hello, Dolly!*) and its movie parallel (Charles Walters's *The Belle of New York*). The farcical comedy of *A Trip to Chinatown* and its three big song hits, "The Bowery," "Reuben, Reuben," and "After the Ball" (the latter two interpolated well after the show's opening), kept it running for 657 performances, the longest original run for a musical in the century and the longest for any musical until *Irene* in 1919–1920. "After the Ball" would be interpolated in still another show thirty-five years later, in the second act of *Show Boat*—as both an homage to American musical tradition and a nostalgic evocation of the bygone 1890s.

Beneath many shows in contemporary urban American settings was a tension and uncertainty about the relationship of ethnic immigrant peoples to one another—and about their relationship to one other ethnic minority: the growing number of blacks moving from the rural South into the Northern industrial cities. Many Harrigan and Hart shows build to a comic riot between the white Irish Mulligan Guards and the black Skidmore Guards (impersonated by white players in blackface), both of which groups have been mistakenly booked into the same meeting hall or dining room at the same time. The intermingling of American black and white culture, black and white music, began its evolution in this earliest period of the American musical. The conflict and reconcilation of American white and black life would prove to be an important issue in the history of the American musical, both on stage and on film: from the Harrigan and Hart shows, through blackface stars like Al Jolson and Eddie Cantor, through *Show Boat*, to *Hallelujah* and *Stormy Weather*, to *Dreamgirls* and *The Cotton Club*.

Even before 1866, the year of *The Black Crook* and the year after the Civil War, the American minstrel show had fallen upon hard times. The classic minstrel show had three traditional parts. The first part, the minstrel line itself, originally played by white actors in blackface, later played by black actors also in blackface, is the section remembered today—misremembered, actually, as the entire minstrel show. After Mr. Interlocutor, the man

A classic minstrel line, all composed of Buster Keaton—from *The Playhouse*

standing dead center, issued the ritual command, "Gentlemen, be seated!" the line featured the songs, dances, and jokes of the two stars, the end men—always called Mr. Tambo (named for the tambourine, his rhythm instrument) and Mr. Bones (named for the "bones," or spoons, his rhythm instrument). The interlocutor was the rational "straight man," psychologically as well as physically in the center; the end men were extremes of comic behavior at the extreme ends of the line; between them for support were the singing, dancing, and ho-ho-hoing of at least six others.

The second part of the minstrel show was called the olio—meaning mixture, *potpourri*, hodgepodge—performed in front of the painted back-drop or curtain, which also came to be called an olio ("in one"—as later theater slang would call numbers performed in front of a curtain or drop). The olio featured a program of miscellaneous songs and specialty acts, performed without blackface. Buster Keaton's 1921 short comedy, *The Playhouse*, affectionately recreates these two parts of the classic minstrel show, as might be seen in any small American town (such as the one in Kansas where Keaton was born) at the turn of the century.

The third part of the minstrel show was a half-hour musical comedy sketch, often a burlesque of a major hit of the day—a little one-act musical in itself. The full-length American musical evolved from this final sketch. As the nineteenth century moved toward the twentieth, the three parts of the minstrel show went their separate ways. The olio expanded into the full

Two olio acts: Buster Keaton as his own partner in *The Playhouse;* (*right*) Gene Kelly and Donald O'Connor in *Singin' in the Rain*

evening of variety or vaudeville, the sketch into the full musical comedy or burlesque (like those at the Weber and Fields Music Hall), and the minstrel line into the all-black musical comedy or revue known, by the turn of the century, as a "coon show."

In the final third of the nineteenth century, particularly after 1865 and the movement of freed slaves into American social life, American musicals were all white or all black. Recall that in the first act of *Show Boat* the complication arises from laws that prohibit integrated casts. Although D. W. Griffith's casting of white actors in blackface to portray black characters in *The Birth of a Nation* (1915) strikes viewers today as one more sign of his racism, Griffith was following established theatrical custom. And theatrical custom—whether in 1915 or today—generally condones social practices and personal lifestyles that challenge the accepted custom of the nation as a whole. This era of racially segregated casts in the history of musical theater parallels a much later era of segregated casts in musical films—from 1929 (*Hallelujah*) to 1943 (*Stormy Weather, Cabin in the Sky*), when black American life could only be depicted (and exaggerated) in all-black musical films. Vincente Minnelli claims that the only way he could get a directorial assignment at MGM was to accept *Cabin in the Sky*, the all-black musical that nobody else on the lot wanted.

Although black musicals began to play theaters in black neighborhoods just after the Civil War, the first black musical to play a white theater for white audiences was *The Origin of the Cakewalk, or Clorindy* in 1898. Though unsuccessful, this revue introduced white Broadway audiences to the musical power of black rhythms and melodies—especially the songs of Ben Harney, a black singer-composer who had previously passed for white. Harney's music, according to the New York *Times*, initiated "a rage for coon

THEATRE COLLECTION, MUSEUM OF THE CITY OF NEW YORK

Bert Williams in a
publicity pose

songs"—the rage that would carry the American musical theater in an
irreversible direction. *In Dahomey* (1903) was the first full-length black book
musical to play a major Broadway house; it too was a failure. *The Southerners*
(1904), another failure, was the first integrated musical on Broadway,
although black cast members were relegated to very specific musical duties,
described by the *Times* as a "chorus of real live coons." The first successful
black musical would not open on Broadway until 1921, *Shuffle Along*, which
ran 504 performances, largely on the energetic score and hit song by Eubie
Blake and Noble Sissle, "I'm Just Wild About Harry."

This was a period when no less a personage than Al Jolson made his
1910 Broadway debut in blackface, singing a song by no less a composer
than Jerome Kern, called "Paris Is a Paradise for Coons."[7] The most
successful black performer of the period was Bert Williams, who, like
Jolson, performed in blackface—a theatrical convention that bothered him
but that he necessarily accepted. Williams reached Broadway stardom in
The Ziegfeld Follies of 1910, the same edition in which Fanny Brice made her
debut and the same year as Jolson's debut in the competing Shubert show at
the new Winter Garden. Williams's ethnic songs and jokes were black
mirrors of Brice's Jewish songs and jokes. For the next decade, Williams was
one of Ziegfeld's biggest stars, alongside Brice, Ed Wynn, W. C. Fields,
Will Rogers, and Eddie Cantor. By 1910, a single black headliner could

perform in an otherwise all-white musical if set apart in some specialty context. Williams could never appear on stage with Ziegfeld's white nudes, and a clause prohibiting that possibility had even been written into his contract. Although Williams himself claimed responsibility for the clause, that claim may simply have been a public relations maneuver by the Ziegfeld office. The tradition did not die quickly. As late as the 1940s Lena Horne could perform specialty numbers in otherwise all-white MGM musicals like *The Ziegfeld Follies* or *Till the Clouds Roll By*, only if she never sang or danced in the same frame with a white male. Black performers entered American musicals the same way they entered American life—one toe at a time.

What seems most interesting about Bert Williams today is that his name, not to mention his face, is far less familiar to Americans, both black and white, than that of those other stars who shared the Ziegfeld bill with him. His deadpan, poker-faced delivery and his underlying poise, strength, and wisdom (Williams usually made a monkey of his co-star straight man, often the fuming Leon Errol) were in sharp contrast to the slow-witted shuffling darkies of American films, theater, radio, and television over the next four decades. Williams's trademark song, "Nobody," was a comic existential assertion of self-sufficiency; he'd be able to take care of himself because there just wasn't nobody else to do it. Williams didn't sing about "Ol' Man River," as white creators later envisioned black endurance. He *was* Ol' Man River who kept rolling along because he didn't have much choice. Perhaps Williams's early death—in 1921 at the age of forty nine—accounts for his dim recollection today. Unlike Brice, Wynn, Cantor, Rogers, and Fields, he never lived long enough to carry his performances to younger generations of American audiences on film, radio, records, or television. Like so many names from America's distant theater past, the name survives but the vitality of his performances does not.

At the beginning of the twentieth century, when black music and the urban-ethnic American experience were silently and subtly pushing the American musical in a decisive direction, the big news in American musical theater seemed to be Viennese operetta and Victor Herbert. Unquestionably America's most gifted composer of theater music in this early period, Herbert enjoyed his greatest popularity with a string of successful operettas that stretched from *The Fortune Teller* (1898), *Babes in Toyland* (1903), *Mlle. Modiste* (1905), *The Red Mill* (1906), and *Naughty Marietta* (1910), through *Sweethearts* (1913). It was Herbert who united two nineteenth-century European traditions and brought the marriage to the American stage—the Irish parlor song to be sung and played at home and the German art song to be sung and heard in the the concert hall. Herbert's work summed up an entire era of American theater music with its inevitable leaning toward the forms, styles, sounds, and tastes of Europe. Born in Ireland, trained as a cellist in the conservatories of Germany and Vienna,

Herbert came to America with his wife, who was to sing at the Metropolitan Opera. In addition to composing theater music, Herbert (like André Previn, a later theater composer) became conductor of the Pittsburgh Symphony.

Herbert's training and background mirror those of the most distinguished composers of American theater music before him—Ludwig Englander, Gustav Luders, Gustave Kerker—and the operetta composers who followed him—Rudolf Friml and Sigmund Romberg. Just the names indicate the heritage.[8] Herbert is the only Euro-American composer before 1910 whose songs are remembered today, and his "best loved melodies," as they are called on record jackets, are inevitably of two types: the waltz and the march. Waltzes and marches, the soul and backbone of European operetta, served similar purposes for American residents of Operettaland. The waltz was the medium of love, either a solo for the leading lady, longingly dreaming of finding it, or a duet for the leading he and she after they've found it together. "Oh, I'm Falling in Love with Someone," from Herbert's *Naughty Marietta*, pretty much sums up the occupation of every operetta heroine on either side of the Atlantic. The march was the medium of manly courage and strength, either a solo for the martial leading he or an ensemble number for him and his merry band of gallant fighting men (like "Tramp, Tramp, Tramp," also from *Naughty Marietta*). Occasionally an operetta would play a little gender joke by letting the leading lady or the women's chorus sing a march, decked out in military uniforms (as in Sigmund Romberg's *The Desert Song* or Ernst Lubitsch's film *The Love Parade*). But the musical forms of these operettas, like the multistrand structures of their plots, were determined by gender: the march for the men and the waltz for the ladies. One of Herbert's most familiar marches, "I Want What I Want When I Want It," from *Mlle. Modiste*, pretty much summarizes the Operettaland male's vision of the world.

Given the musical styles of these scores, American musical shows built upon them were inevitably banished to Operettaland. Neither the sounds nor the sentiments made much sense in contemporary urban America. True enough, Herbert, like every other operetta composer, wrote hundreds of obligatory comic songs for the more modern and more typically American comic and soubrette—bouncily upbeat numbers, influenced by popular contemporary dance rhythms like the two-step and cakewalk. Herbert must not have cared much for this sort of music (or must not have felt very comfortable with it), for not one of his rhythm songs has been remembered, recorded, or numbered among his "best loved melodies." This musical void is in sharp contrast to the comic dialogue scenes of these operettas, which are still surprisingly funny and delightfully inventive. Bobby Clark demonstrated that comic inventiveness by clowning through a 1947 revival of *Sweethearts*, and the symmetrically named comics, Kid Conner and Con Kidder (originated by the comic duo of Fred Stone and Dave Montgomery), are a comic revelation in every revival of *The Red Mill*. In operettas the comics get the funny scenes and the romantic leads get the pretty songs. The comics come from the spirit of everyday America and the leads from an American fantasy of someplace that rhymes with Slobovia.

If Herbert's beautiful melodies never created an authentic American character or milieu, the American musical would be indebted to him for what he did accomplish: he proved that musical theater, a unified script and score, could arise from a single creative conception. And he proved that for the theater to be musical and the music to be theatrical, the show needed a whole score rather a random harvest of miscellaneous tunes. More then anyone before him, Victor Herbert demonstrated that the making of musicals could be careful, conscientious, conceptual, and craftsmanlike. Although he continued to write scores until his death in 1924, American taste in theater music had deserted him for a more informal, colloquial American sound a decade earlier.

That American sound could only declare its independence from nineteenth-century European dialects by declaring war on Herbert's two meal tickets—the march and, especially, the waltz. These musical forms didn't sound, think, or talk like modern Americans. Among the next generation of major American theater composers who were to create this new sound and style, only Richard Rodgers felt thoroughly comfortable with the waltz (and even the march). George Gershwin's occasional waltzes and marches were deliberate parodies, a few of Irving Berlin's standards were waltzes (while he reserved his marches for wartime), and not one of the most memorable Jerome Kern or Cole Porter songs is a waltz or a march. To musicalize the American spirit in an American setting meant bringing down the 3/4 and 4/4 signatures and running up the 2/4.

A truly American theater music meant more colloquial, more informal love ballads that were not waltzes and casually upbeat rhythm songs that were not the offal of European conservatory musicians who resented such tinkly trash. It meant singing that mirrored the ways American talk—and, by implication, feel and think: music that could capture the rhythms, moods, and nuances of contemporary American life in the theater. This music would begin to be written in the early 1910s by a surprising and unpredictable musical fusion of white ethnic urban American life and black ragtime and blues.

3

The Tin-Pan-Tithesis of Melody

A M E R I C A N   S O N G ,
A M E R I C A N   S O U N D

One of the favorite similes of American social history is to liken turn-of-the-century American urban society to a melting pot; the large industrial cities, New York, Boston, and Chicago, became kettles packed with ethnic European ingredients, simmering into a single American stew. Though the simile seems overdone as social history, it seems surprisingly relevant to American musical theater of the same period. From Vienna came the operetta; from France the *opéra-bouffe* and the type of vaudeville called madness (*folies* in French); from England satiric opera and the music hall; from Ireland sentimental ballads; from Eastern and Central Europe the minor harmonies of Jewish and gypsy violins; from Africa, by way of the American South, black upbeat rhythms and the spiritual lament; from the American hinterlands such hybrids as the medicine and minstrel show; while the circus extravaganza came from all over Europe and P. T. Barnum's New England showmanship. The kettle really started to boil in the first decade of the new century.

In 1901 the first movie was projected within a theater musical. In 1902 the tap dance joined the act: Ned Wayburn replaced his heavy wooden clogs with a lighter pair of leather shoes to which metal taps had been attached. As if in answer to this summons, Fred Astaire made his stage debut in 1905 as a child of six. Jerome Kern published his first song in 1902, Irving Berlin in 1907. George M. Cohan's first major musical came in 1903, Florenz Ziegfeld's first *Follies* in 1907. From the seasons of 1902 through 1904 poured a stream of American songs that are still sung today: "In the Good Old Summertime," "Listen to the Mockingbird," "Meet Me in St. Louis, Louie" "Toyland," "Yankee Doodle Boy," and that indestructible metaphor, "Give My Regards to Broadway."

The American popular song, which created the musical dialect of the American musical, also found its voice in the same decade, when the American popular music industry standardized the ideal of a singable song. It would contain two clearly demarcated sections: an informal verse and a more formal refrain (or chorus) of precisely thirty-two bars of music.[1] For fifty years this new type of song would be the basis not only of virtually every musical number in every musical but the essential musical base of American popular recorded music, dance music, and jazz.

The verse was an expository, introductory section, which led into the most familiar and memorable melodic section of the song, its refrain, the melody by which the song was recognized. With no set musical length—often sixteen or twenty-four bars of music but from as few as eight to as many as sixty-four—the verse was a more prosaic, recitative musical passage, freer in form, rhythm, and melody than the refrain. The verse of Cole Porter's "It's De-lovely" (*Red, Hot, and Blue*, 1935) provides a de-lovely illustration of its own introductory function:

> I feel a sudden urge to sing
> The kind of ditty that invokes the spring.
> So control your desire to curse
> While I crucify the verse.
> This verse I've started seems to be
> The tin-pan-tithesis of melody.
> So to spare you all the pain
> I'll skip the darn thing and sing the refrain.

Verses were useful tools in musical storytelling since they represented a middle ground between casual speech and the passion of song, between chatty dialogue in the book sections and rhapsodic song in the musical sections of a play or film. The verse moves from the specific to the general, the conversational to the emotional, the prosaic to the poetic. A verse was a kind of talking song and singing talk, more tightly structured musically and lyrically than the opera recitative, with clearly demarcated musical phrases and precisely rhyming patterns, but more wry, ironic, paradoxical, less assured, and less committed than the refrain.

The refrains of nineteenth-century American songs were very brief—a catchy eight-bar phrase or longer one of sixteen bars. The familiar Civil War songs, "Our Boys Will Shine Tonight" (1861) and "When Johnny Comes Marching Home" (1863) have simple sixteen-bar refrains. So do some of the most familiar hymns, like "Abide with Me" and "Nearer My God to Thee," which were very much popular parlor songs of the nineteenth century. Many hymnlike turn-of-the-century secular songs—like Monroe H. Rosenfeld's "Those Wedding Bells Shall Not Ring Out!" (1906)—told complicated stories of the fatal moral slip, the ruined marriage, and the anticipated reconciliation in heaven. In these maudlin songs of woe, long sixty-four-bar verses chronicled the dismal events, punctuated by a brief eight- or sixteen-bar refrain of eternal lament. Another nineteenth-century song form combined an eight-bar verse so snugly with its catchy eight-bar refrain that the two seemed an inseparable whole with an AB musical structure of sixteen bars ("Go Down, Moses" and many other spirituals or Stephen Foster's "Oh! Susannah" and "Camptown Races"). While Foster wrote songs for minstrel shows on black spiritual models, with simple but haunting eight-bar refrains ("Old Black Joe"), he wrote songs for the proper parlor on Scottish and Irish models ("Beautiful Dreamer," "Jeannie with the Light Brown Hair"). Their more complicated sixteen-bar refrains, in four-bar AABA sections, were already twentieth-century American popular songs in miniature.

The thirty-two-bar refrain of the twentieth-century American popular song expanded the simpler melodic idea of earlier songs into a more complicated musical structure, supporting more complicated verbal patterns of rhyme and turns of thought. The single most important figure at popularizing the thirty-two-bar form was Irving Berlin, and the single most important song his 1911 hit, "Alexander's Ragtime Band." Berlin's highly respected contemporary, Jerome Kern, was slow to abandon the sixteen-bar refrain—not until about 1914—and never distinguished himself as a composer until he did. By the late teens and early twenties, George Gershwin's songs assured the absolute dominion of the thirty-two-bar refrain. But by 1935 and *Porgy and Bess*, Gershwin could himself abandon the thirty-two-bar pattern to recapture the unsophisticated sincerity of earlier song forms in "Summertime"—a retreat to the sixteen-bar form of Stephen Foster and nineteenth-century spirituals. After World War II rock and country-western songs deliberately reverted to archaic eight- and sixteen-bar forms, suggesting the aspiration to sincerity, purity, and "naturalness" by rejecting the urban and urbane song structure of white European immigrants.

The thirty-two-bar refrains of twentieth-century popular songs are compact exercises in musical logic. The most common musical structure of the thirty-two-bar syllogism is AABA. The first eight-bar A section states the song's primary musical theme. In "Blue Skies," to take a familiar and hummable example, Irving Berlin's first film hit from the first filmusical, *The Jazz Singer*, this A section opens with the two words of the title and concludes with the ascending musical phrase for "do I see."[2] The first eight-bar section always states a song's most distinctive melody, the one that even the musically untrained can remember, the one that makes it a hit. For this reason, the A section is itself called the refrain, since it capsulizes the entire thirty-two-bar refrain in miniature. The second eight-bar section either repeats the opening refrain exactly (aiding the memorability that makes hits) or with a slight variation. In "Blue Skies," Berlin's second A section varies the phrase's words—blue birds sing their song—but repeats the opening melodic theme identically. This second section is often not

identical to the first A section but a slight variation on it (and notated as A')
so the melody can modulate logically into the B section.[3]

That eight-bar B section, called either the release or the bridge, sounds
like an absolutely new theme, although it is often a subtle variation on the
primary melody in the refrain or a return to a musical motif initially stated
in the verse. In "Blue Skies" the release begins with an ascent up the minor
scale on the words, "Never saw the sun," and ends on an unresolved
musical phrase under the words, "My how they fly." The two descriptive
metaphors suggest the function of this B section in the logical progression of
a song: it provides a release from the familiar melody of the refrain and it
provides a bridge to cross from the beginning of the song to its end. In
"Blue Skies," the modulation chord at the end of the bridge provides the
transportation back to the initial melody. The AABA song then ends with
an eight-bar return to its A section refrain, either identically or with a slight
variation (notated A' or A") to resolve its concluding statement with greater
finality. In "Blue Skies," the final A section introduces another verbal
variation—this time the days are blue—but repeats the opening refrain
musically. Although "Blue Skies" is a perfect AABA song, many songs of
this type are actually AA'BA", with no two A sections precisely identical.

Thousands of familiar American songs, sweet or hot, up tempo or
down, have been built on this basic musical structure: Berlin's "Remember"
and "Top Hat, White Tie, and Tails," Gershwin's "Liza," Rodgers's
"Manhattan," Porter's "I Get a Kick Out of You," Kern's "The Way You
Look Tonight," Leonard Bernstein's "Some Other Time," Harold Arlen's
"Stormy Weather," Hoagy Carmichael's "Two Sleepy People," Harry Warren's "42nd Street." Every composer for American musicals has built the
vast majority of songs on this pattern that emerged early in the century.

A second pattern of thirty-two-bar musical logic emerged at the same
time. Although less common, this Type II song is quite interesting.[4] Its
thirty-two-bar structure might be described as four eight-bar sections,
ABAC, which then break further into four-bar phrases of AA' BB' AA'
CA (or CA'). The first eight-bar section again states the main refrain—
often twice, with a variation for the second. In "Alexander's Ragtime
Band," to take another familiar and hummable Berlin example, the opening
A section breaks into two parts, each beginning with the invitation to
"Come on an' hear." The second eight-bar section (in "Alexander" it echoes
a bugle call) introduces a musical development immediately. The third
eight-bar section repeats (or slightly varies) the opening refrain ("Alexander"
invites us to "Come on an' hear" again). The fourth eight-bar section begins
with another absolutely new variation (in "Alexander" an echo of "Swanee
River"). For its conclusion, however, the final four bars return, literally or
suggestively, musically and/or lyrically, to the song's opening theme (in
"Alexander" we get the invitation to come an' hear yet again). This type of
song has, in effect, two bridges, one to connect the song's first and second

halves, and the other, a much shorter one, to connect the song's middle and end (which is also a return to the beginning).

While the Type I song assures memorability by repeating the melodic refrain twice at its inception and once at the end, the Type II song seeks familiarity by returning to the refrain in the precise middle of the song, diminishing the power of the release, then returning to it again for its conclusion. Extending the popular song to a thirty-two-bar musical progression posed a challenge to memorability, and the more complex thematic variation of a Type II song posed an even greater challenge. Though less common than the AABA type, some of the most memorable American popular songs met this challenge. Among them are Berlin's "A Pretty Girl Is Like a Melody," Kern's "They Didn't Believe Me," Porter's "You're the Top," Gershwin's "Swanee," Rodgers's "Falling in Love with Love," Warren's "Shadow Waltz," Arlen's "The Man That Got Away," and Vincent Youmans's "Tea for Two." Because the AABA song is more common and repetitive, the Type II seems more intriguing for its symmetry (two equal halves) and circularity (its end is its beginning). But the Type I has its own subtle complexities. Jerome Kern's "All the Things You Are," for example, never literally repeats itself in any of its A sections, and its second A section is not merely a variation on its opening but its melodic extension.

This kind of discussion raises a question about the art and value of such rigidly logical compact structures. As in any rigidly compact structure—the sonnet in Western poetry, the Haiku in Eastern—formal excellence arises from the interplay between the necessity of preserving the structure and the possibility of subtle surprise. The sonnet (the English term is derived from the Italian *sonetto*, or "little song") is, by definition, a fourteen-line poem, with each line (in the English tradition) based on five iambs. These fourteen lines can be divided as three groups of four, followed by a couplet (Shakespearean) or one group of eight lines and another of six (Petrarchan). Two equal groups of seven lines is possible but uncommon. The groupings of lines determine both the sonnet's rhyme structure and intellectual structure, for its development and resolution of ideas will be dictated by its linear groupings. Within each line, unexpected shifts in the pattern of iambic stresses emphasize points of intensity and turns of thought. Caesuras within lines and enjambments between lines allow similar interplay between expectations of structure and twists of thought.

The refrain of the American popular song allows a similar choice between two broad types (Type I is Shakespearean and Type II Petrarchan). The entire song, verse and chorus, allows interplay between music and lyric, between the verse and the refrain, between the refrain and the release. Like the sonnet, the structures of musical lines can play either with or against the structures of verbal sentences. Unlike the sonnet, a musical tag or coda allows the American popular song an extension beyond its own thirty-two-bar limit. Irving Berlin's seventy-two-bar "Cheek to Cheek" and

Cole Porter's 108-bar "Begin the Beguine" both accept the thirty-two-bar idea and destroy it. Over the last four decades, this paradoxical escape from the inescapable thirty-two-bar limit has increasingly dominated the most complex American theater music.

The formal interplay in the musical structures of songs actually determines the way musical numbers are planned and performed in musicals. Consider, for example, three hat-and-cane numbers written by Irving Berlin for Fred Astaire films: "Top Hat, White Tie, and Tails" for *Top Hat* (1935); "Puttin' On the Ritz," popularized by Harry Richman but recorded by Astaire in 1929 and danced in the 1946 *Blue Skies*; and "Steppin' Out with My Baby" for *Easter Parade* (1948). All three are Type I, AABA songs. All three are similar in subject (dressing up in fancy clothes). And all three are built on rhythmic and harmonic permutations of four identical variables: legato as opposed to staccato passages (flowing phrases with sustained notes in contrast to syncopated phrases with percussive notes), major and minor progressions. For example, while the refrain is major and legato but the release minor and staccato in "Top Hat," the refrain is staccato and minor and the release legato and major in "Steppin' Out with My Baby."

Astaire was certainly aware that these three Berlin musical structures were careful variations on one another (even the contractions, "Puttin' on" and "Steppin' Out," echo one another). So the choreography Astaire devised for "Puttin' on the Ritz" was a deliberate visual variation on that in the original "Top Hat." In the earlier film, Astaire danced with a chorus line of men who looked identical to him because they were dressed identically; in the later film, with the aid of trick photography, he danced with identical images of his own multiplied self. The choreography of "Steppin' Out" is a conscious third-generation variant on the visual theme of sameness and difference. Again with the aid of trick photography, Astaire dances in slow motion while everyone else around him moves at the normal speed. All three hat-and-cane numbers about "dressin' up" define Astaire's uniqueness, his difference from everyone else around him, even when dressed in the same clothes.

The way Astaire heard the musical and rhythmic patterns of each musical section—rising or falling, major or minor, fewer sustained notes or many brief notes, falling squarely on the beat or hitting the off-beat syncopations—also determined the way he danced to each section. He translated the musical characteristics of each passsage into visual terms: circular movement (generally associated with flowing musical passages) in contrast to linear movement (generally associated with syncopated phrases); the percussive tapping of feet and rapping of cane (in syncopated sections) in contrast to silently gliding steps and turns (in flowing ones). What Berlin wrote into the songs Astaire translated into his dancing body.

The structure of a song also controls important technical matters in its staging or shooting. In musical films, a song's structure usually dictates the relation between camera position and cutting; the best musical films rarely cut to a new camera position except precisely at the end of a musical phrase or directly on the downbeat of a new musical phrase or section. Moving camera shots frequently mirror shifts in the song's musical structure, not merely changes in the performer's physical position. On the stage, it is very rare to introduce new characters, new dancers, a new choreographic idea, or a new visual effect (even a light cue) except as dictated by phrases in the musical structure. The best musical numbers are musical-verbal-vocal-visual syntheses, and a song's musical structure provides the skeleton for that organic whole.

Finally, these musical numbers are built from variations generated by the proliferation of thirty-two-bar choruses. Just as the jazz musician states the melody in the first chorus, then goes about improvising variations on it in succeeding choruses, the musical number states its lyrical, musical, and choreographic themes in its first chorus, then goes on to permutations and variations in succeeding choruses. The most complicated musical numbers in American filmusicals (perhaps as many as a dozen choruses in a Busby Berkeley number) are a sort of visual jazz, anchored by the thirty-two bars of a song's structure. In musical plays, the proliferation of choruses is based less on visual or choreographic variation than on variations of verbal wit. The reason many theater songs can proliferate over so many choruses, particularly catalog songs like Porter's "You're the Top," Rodgers and Hart's "Bewitched," or Sondheim's "I'm Still Here," is because of the interplay of formal expectation and verbal surprise. While the formal structure of the song indicates precisely where the verbal surprise will come, and precisely what sort of surprise it will be, the specific verbal barb, twist, or jest, injected into that rigid pattern, is absolutely unexpected. The novelty of the verbal wit seems even more brilliant because it has invaded a pattern that seemed to deny the possibility of novelty.

These songs are extremely flexible, permitting widely variant renditions and interpretations, allowing the same song to convey different nuances of character. When Ethel Merman sang "I Got Rhythm" in the 1930 stage production of *Girl Crazy*, she defined the brassy urbanity of Kate Fothergill. When Gene Kelly sang the same song in the 1951 film, *An American in Paris*, he defined the exuberant ex-GI, Jerry Mulligan. The quality that linked these two different characters was their dynamic energy—which the song both captured and conveyed. If a sour and dour character were to sing "I Got Rhythm" (imagine a parodic vocal version by Oscar Levant, Kelly's friend in *An American in Paris*), the result would proclaim his lack of the very rhythm that the song claims he's got. These songs are flexible enough to permit different interpretative shadings but particular enough to suggest a view of life. This paradox is closely related to their longevity. "I Got Rhythm" is approaching sixty; Jerome Kern's first hit, "They Didn't

Believe Me," is over seventy; Berlin's "Alexander's Ragtime Band," the first
of these American-sounding hits, is over seventy-five. These ephemeral
trifles have lived a long time—both as songs and as numbers in different
musicals over their lifetimes.

Even while developing the American sound and style of its songs, the
American musical never cut its ties to Europe. The first decade of the
century was Victor Herbert's greatest period of popularity and influence;
1907, the year of Berlin's first published song, was also the year when the
most popular of all operettas, Franz Lehár's *The Merry Widow*, opened in
New York. The Golden Age of American operetta followed *The Merry
Widow*—from Rudolf Friml's *The Firefly* (1912), *Rose-Marie* (1924), and *The
Vagabond King* (1925) through Sigmund Romberg's *The Student Prince* (1924),
The Desert Song (1926), and *The New Moon* (1928). The operetta simply
refused to die—and isn't dead yet. The Golden Age of American operetta
coincided with the Golden Age of the American revue. The years between
1907 and 1928 saw regular editions of Ziegfeld's *Follies*, Shubert's *Passing
Shows*, George White's *Scandals*, Earl Carroll's *Vanities*, and Irving Berlin's
Music Box Revues. In these same years the native American book musical
also grew up.

Central to that growth was George M. Cohan—although there is
considerable disagreement about his contribution. Cohan is probably more
familiar today than any other turn-of-the-century musical figure. Although
largely a result of the indelible James Cagney performance in *Yankee Doodle
Dandy*, that 1942 outburst of Warner Bros. wartime enthusiasm, Cohan's
familiarity also arises from at least a half-dozen songs that remain close
cultural friends. What American can't sing at least some phrase from some
Cohan song? What American hasn't heard one or sung one around a piano
or campfire? There is an obvious consistency in the energy of those songs
and the energy of Cagney's dynamic portrait of Cohan.

Yet critics and historians of American musical theater don't much care
for Cohan in comparison to his contemporary, Victor Herbert. Later
composers and creators of musical theater have never acknowledged a debt
to Cohan, unlike their consistent admiration for Kern and Berlin. For
Richard Rodgers, who worked with him both in Hollywood (*The Phantom
President*, 1932) and on Broadway (*I'd Rather Be Right*, 1937), Cohan was a
has been (and perhaps never was) no-talent monster. Cohan's work receives
only cursory attention in most histories of the American stage musical, and
Cohan's name is not even mentioned in Alec Wilder's authoritative survey
of American popular song from 1900 to 1950.

We can pick through the Cohan controversy to find two facts. First, in
the decade of operetta's greatest dominance over American theater tastes,
Cohan's shows resolutely refused to skip off to Operettaland. His three
best, the 1904 *Little Johnny Jones* and two shows of 1906, *George Washington,*

George M. Cohan with the chorus of *Little Johnny Jones*

Jr. and *Forty-five Minutes from Broadway*, were firmly and proudly—sometimes too proudly—rooted in native American society, reflecting American patterns of speech, saturated with contemporary American humor, expressions of American cultural energy. Second, Cohan's songs, very much expressions of the same style and energy, remain the most memorable of that decade. The best of them remain as fresh and spirited as on the day they were written: "Yankee Doodle Boy" (commonly referred to as "I'm a Yankee Doodle Dandy"); "Give My Regards to Broadway"; "Mary's a Grand Old Name" (the lilting ballad that begins, "But it was Mary . . ."); "Grand Old Flag" (originally titled "Grand Old Rag"; public pressure forced a change of title, although Cohan's original implied his colloquial Irish affection for a friendly rather than sacred object); and "Over There," Cohan's last big hit, which in itself provides a capsule history of a war and an era. How could critics fail to acknowledge such powerful musical intuition that could produce so many songs—both words and music—that not only have become a part of American cultural history but seem to *be* American cultural history?

True, many Cohan songs are more like nineteenth-century parlor songs than twentieth-century theater songs: a summing up of the past—with heavy doses of Irish sentimentality—rather than a movement toward the future. The Cohan sweet songs evoke the sentimental story songs of the 1880s and 1890s. Many Cohan refrains accept the shorter structure of older songs; his best were waltzes or marches or yearned to be. But many lesser known Cohan rhythm songs, the rags and pseudo-rags he began to write early in the century, are decidedly modern. "Twentieth Century Love" is a bouncy 1903 two-step about the speed of modern life and courtship; the title alone reveals Cohan's consciousness of new musical forms. The new love requires a new sound, a new dance. No other American composer, with the exception of Irving Berlin, wrote so many good rhythm songs before World War I. Cohan's rhythm alone takes the national pulse of that period.

True, Cohan's musical shows were not truly integrated pieces of musical theater but melodramatic plays with vaudeville songs and jokes stitched in. Cohan, after all, began his theatrical career as a family act in vaudeville—one of the Four Cohans. He never quite left vaudeville behind—but neither have the very best American musical shows in some way or other. Some of the Cohan shows were curiously slotted: all the musical numbers in the first and third acts, the dialogue and melodrama in the middle act. In recognition of this oddity, Cohan sometimes called his shows musical plays. This disunity affected critical judgment in Cohan's day—and still does today. But the problem of unity in this inherently disunified form is more paradoxical than later historians of the musical have been willing to admit.

The real problem in assessing George M. Cohan as a historical figure seems to be that everyone—except his audiences—hated him. His exuberant flag waving seemed less than charming to most critics, even in the era of Teddy Roosevelt's Big Stick. That was a softly walking stick and Cohan never did anything softly. His music and his stage persona were inseparable from his producer-director-author-composer-lyricist-star egotism, which, for many at the time, seemed an especially vivid portrait of naked jingoism in this era of American imperialism.

Sustaining his reputation as a monster, in 1919 he came down violently on the wrong side of the Actors Equity strike. Who needed a union? He didn't. Eddie Cantor came down just as forcefully on the right side and may have owed the final three decades of his career to that moment—two months, actually—of courage. Not one of your good losers, Cohan remained in character and refused to join after the Equity victory. He vowed, with the stamp of his tap shoe, never to work on a stage with any member of the cursed union. Of course, he returned from this self-exile just often enough to make other writers, like Lorenz Hart and Richard Rodgers (whom he sneeringly christened "Gilbert and Sullivan"), quake at their staff sheets as inferiors to his own powers of songwriting. Cohan could never understand why it took two people to write one song.

There is another subtle problem—perhaps not so subtle—that separated Cohan from the direction of American theater music and muddied his place in its history. Simply put, Cohan was not Jewish—even if his last name was properly pronounced Cohen not CoHANN. Although he came from an urban, working-class, immigrant background, he was an urban Irish-

American, whose music seemed closer to the nineteenth-century Herberts and Harrigans than the twentieth-century Berlins and Gershwins. Despite its freshness and memorability, Cohan's music had little relationship to the future sound of American theater music, a blend of middle-European and Afro-American styles that would be mixed almost exclusively by American-Jewish composers. Not only was he not Jewish; like many of his generation, he was antisemitic and, feeling himself shoved aside by newcomers, reacted against the new generation of immigrants like any established member of society. He was also, to use an unlovely but functional term of a much later generation, homophobic. He openly despised that new breed of showfolk who were seeping into the profession through the union that protected all actors equally. No wonder Cohan's historical reputation is muddy; those who would create the twentieth-century American musical and shape the histories based on it were Jewish or gay or both.

We might ask why.

One reason that Jews became so important to Tin Pan Alley was that the infant music business, like the infant movie business, had inherited no prejudices against hiring Jews and no hierarchical structures to impede the progress of talented immigrants or the sons of immigrants. Both the music business and the movie business were, after all, showbiz—the risky crapshoot shunned by both the moral and fiscal establishment. The field lay wide open for brash young men with little to lose. In the early decades of this century, show business, whether music, movie, or stage, was the quickest route out of the ghetto for the young Jew—as it remains today for young blacks and hispanics. Not the safe, slow, dirt road of a traditional mercantile business, showbiz was the fast lane, straight up and out to the glitter—or down and out to the gutter.

The music business was not merely a branch of show business, a very young branch, but, like the movie business, its twin, born at the same time. In the final decade of the nineteenth century, the increasing number of parlor pianos and harmoniums guaranteed the sales of multiple copies of sheet music. Neither the music business nor the movie business had evolved its familial and corporate structures—often inseparable—of dominance and control. The stage had recently solidified those structures in the National League of Theater Owners, the so-called Circuit, forged in 1893. By operating every major theater from coast to coast, the Circuit controlled the bookings of every act and show in America. It guaranteed that theater production would henceforth be dominated by family names like Erlanger, Keith, Albee, Shubert, Frohman, Dillingham, Hammerstein, Ziegfeld. The music and movie businesses opened up to a young generation of immigrant Jews just as the stage business closed down to them.

Early in the century, the music publishing houses on West 28th Street in

New York City—Harms, Witmark, Remick—were, like the movie business with its tiny nickelodeons, beginning to realize enormous profits. It was far more likely for a song to sell a million copies of sheet music in 1905 than it was for a record to sell a million copies in 1985. Like the movie nickelodeons, the music business built its profits on very tall piles of nickels and dimes. Like the largest chains of nickelodeons, the music publishing houses were owned or run by Jews, like the powerful Max Dreyfus at Harms, who eagerly hired Jews. But just because Jews were welcome in the music business could not guarantee their success as composers. Except for screenwriters, the most admired artists in the movie business—directors, stars, cameramen, and designers—have seldom been Jewish.

One could point to the Jewish tradition of musical training and musicianship, a tradition which accounts for the high percentage of Jewish composers, soloists, and conductors in the twentieth-century concert world. But there is an important tradition of Jewish popular or folk music as well. In Chekhov's *The Cherry Orchard*, one of Ranevskaya's nostalgic recollections is of the local Jewish band. The metaphoric fiddler on Tevye's roof derives from this same folk-music tradition, called Klezmer—although the fiddler's tones were dubbed by the classical virtuoso Isaac Stern for the movie soundtrack. The most striking characteristics of this centuries-old Klezmer music, enjoying a major revival in American folk circles, are those it shares with American jazz. It relies heavily on improvisation, on minor chromatics (particularly the flatting of the third, sixth, and seventh of the diatonic scale), and on rhythmic syncopation (shifting the rhythmic accent from the measure's downbeat to its up or offbeats). The kinship of Klezmer and jazz is especially striking in certain American popular songs; the Andrews Sisters' recording of "Bei Mir Bist du Schön," Ziggy Elman's trumpet solo on the Benny Goodman recording of "And the Angels Sing," or Goodman's own clarinet solo in the famous Carnegie Hall concert of "Sing Sing Sing." The wailing clarinet and soaring cornet were as essential to a Jewish folk band as to a Dixieland jazz band. Among the most important musicians at Harlem's Cotton Club in the late 1920s were the black descendant of slaves, Duke Ellington, and the Jewish son of a cantor, Harold Arlen. And downtown on Second Avenue, the Yiddish Theater had been using songs for black characters (sung by Jews in blackface, of course) as metaphors for social oppression—whether of Jews or blacks—since the turn of the century.

Why are these two styles of music that should be worlds distant—certainly continents and ages distant—so close? The simplest answer is that they just coincidentally are. Jewish Central European musical traditions "just happened" to run comfortably parallel with the harmonies and rhythms of black rag, blues, and jazz. As oppressed peoples, both Jews and blacks found musical solace in the minor chords. Jews could easily assimilate black elements to polite white European musical fashions to create a palatable sound for cultured American tastes. While a Stephen Foster wrote black minstrel songs and white parlor songs, Jews put the two together. Jewish harmonies and rhythms proved a serviceable if accidental cultural bridge—between white and black sounds, Eastern and Western European styles, Europe and Africa, Old World and New. Jewish composers had the economic opportunity, the musical tradition, and the cultural smarts to mix the potion that would become American popular music.

A more speculative answer would be based on the ethnographic suspicion that cultural kinships are never accidental but based on centuries of uncharted cultural interaction and population migration. Patterns of musical similarity can be studied, like the patterns of linguistic shifts or the spread of folk tales, to trace the broader historical outlines of cultural exchange. Is the similarity of jazz and Klezmer a sign of some broader historical and cultural pattern that, like the common Indo-European linguistic root, links so many of the world's civilizations? Might Jewish migration have carried musical patterns northward from the Eastern Mediterranean circle that embraces North Africa and Asia Minor into Central Europe, only to reconnect with its African roots in America, through the music transported westward by slaves? This question is as interesting as it is unanswerable.

Just as speculative must be any search for reasons that musical theater and film should be so congenial to gay people and so receptive to the gay sensibility. One of the broadest possibilities is that the social opportunities of Jewish and gay people, both minorities in Western Christian culture, run surprisingly parallel—that the social tolerance of Jews and gay people (and, therefore, the patronage for their commercial products) has been inseparably linked throughout the Christian Era.[5] Show business has always existed on the fringes of social respectability—at least until tap dancers began to be elected senators and B-movie heroes presidents. The need for perpetually fresh talent never permitted show business the luxury of mainstream social discrimination. Social oddity seems inseparable from theatrical creation.

Perhaps there is something in two cultural clichés that make musicals and gay people especially suited to one another: musicals represent an extravagant and excessive frippery and gay people possess some special sensibility that finds an outlet in extravagance, excess, and frippery. For gay people to channel their creative energies into designing lavish costumes or spectacular sets, into dazzling directorial or choreographic conceits, into writing luxuriant tunes or witty lyrics, is to accomplish many useful social ends. For one, gay people can find gainful employment in a congenial vocation that benefits the culture as a whole, gay and nongay, producing "that sort of amusement which makes a sleep easier and the next day's work less like work after all."[6] Like musicals themselves, gay people can translate their alternative vision of human and social relationships into forms that both disguise it as societal critique and allow its implications to be clearly read. Michelangelo's "David," "Sagrada Familia," and Sistine Chapel "Creation," for example, channeled his homosexual desire into representations that were both abstract idealizations of cultural aspirations and extravagant proclamations of alternative taste.

The extravagant costume or witty phrase may please by its superficial brilliance, but beneath the conceit lies a question about making such conceits. That musicals seem both excessive and frivolous masks the same question. Why should a culture so devoted to productive, economical human activity care so much about and spend so much on excessive fripperies? Both witty musicals and gay wit adopt a deliberate pose of frivolousness, covertly engaging our culture in a debate about "earnestness," the very term underlying Oscar Wilde's comic monument, which rejects the importance of being earnest and can't avoid being earnest at the same time. For what such cross-cultural comparisons are worth, Wilde's classic play was contemporaneous with the birth of the movies, of Tin Pan Alley, and the rise of the American musical—the American home for the Wildean sensibility. The extravagant excess of musicals is simultaneously an act of rebellion, a burst of joy, and a cry of desperation—quite the opposite of a uselessly quiet desperation.

This masquerade of extravagant excess and outrageous frippery may blunt the force of a more open critique of earnest bourgeois society, which gay people (and Jewish people) might have made. But such a cavil is itself only possible in a period that permits (indeed encourages) gay writers to "come out" in their memoirs, which patronizes musicals about openly gay characters written by openly gay composers and lyricists, which bestows prestigious awards on openly gay playwrights and even allows a male director to acknowledge the contribution of his choreographer lover on a nationally televised award ceremony. Without any such public display, audiences for generations have known that the creators of their favorite musicals were often gay (even if that knowledge were never publicly acknowledged), just as they knew that the creators of their favorite musicals were Jewish.

This tacit knowledge allowed the musical to become a celebration of both social coherence and diversity. The unified diversity of the excessive entertainment onstage mirrored the unified diversity of the audience responding to it. As the mirror of *A Chorus Line* makes explicit, there are two chorus lines at every musical—the one onstage and the one in the audience. The American musical could touch this socially diverse audience and convert it into a chorus with one voice, in common enjoyment of a show that channeled minority sensibilities, whether gay or Jewish, into a communal celebration of its own American diversity.

4

Say it With Music

IRVING BERLIN

Where else but in America could a Russian Jew write the most successful popular songs for the two holiest Christian holidays?

Irving Berlin, born May 11, 1888, as Israel Baline in Temun, Russia, had to support himself from a very young age on New York's Lower East Side. With no formal education of any kind, Berlin taught himself everything from the language he would use to write his lyrics to the scales he would use to write his tunes. That education was good enough to make him the most successful songwriter in American history. "White Christmas" is the most successful popular song ever written. Since it was introduced in 1942 by Bing Crosby in Paramount's *Holiday Inn*, it has sold more copies of sheet music and records combined (in whatever vocal and instrumental version in whatever language) than any other musical composition ever. Berlin's royalties from this one song alone have been estimated in the millions of dollars. But he published (in his own music publishing house) nearly a thousand others, of which at least one hundred were as successful as any popular song has even been—with the exception of some of his own. Almost incomprehensibly, Berlin is the one patriarch who is still alive to collect his royalties. Though he no longer publishes new songs, old ones keep returning in new clothes. One of 1983's disco hits was a thump-thump version of "Puttin' on the Ritz." Irving Berlin is a songwriting institution.

Because he is such an institution, some have suspected that there is no Irving Berlin—that no single human being could have written all those hits in all those styles. Some staff of talented young composers must have been imprisoned somewhere, scribbling notes on music sheets to which Berlin merely signed his name (assuming he knew how to write). Several details of Berlin's personal life season these suspicions. First, there is the length of his career, from his first published song in 1907, "Marie from Sunny Italy" (for

Irving Berlin in 1911,
the year of "Alexander's
Ragtime Band"

THEATRE COLLECTION, MUSEUM OF THE CITY OF NEW YORK

which he wrote only the lyric), to "Old Fashioned Wedding" for the 1966 revival of *Annie Get Your Gun*. Then there is the difficulty of identifying a clear and single Irving Berlin style.[1] From sentimental waltzes like "Always," to bouncy rhythm songs like "Alexander's Ragtime Band," to the bluesy "Supper Time," to the sophisticated swing of "Cheek to Cheek," to the comedic "Doin' What Comes Natur'lly," Berlin demonstrates that he can do just about anything natur'lly. His songs, though influenced by other songwriters, sound like all of them and none of them. His personal motto could be another song from *Annie Get Your Gun*: "Anything you can do, I can do better."

Berlin's lack of musical training, his inability to read (much less write down) music, became as famous as his melodies. His personal piano (currently in the Smithsonian Institution) was noted for its mechanical lever that allowed him to transpose songs for different singers without encountering the treacherous mixture of white and black keys. Berlin composed every song in the key of F$^{\#}$, and if you fit your fingers on the five black keys you can randomly pick out many Berlin hit tunes.

Despite the cynical murmurs, there is not a single major American composer who has any doubts about Berlin as the genuine author of every Berlin song, nor a single major American composer who does not echo Jerome Kern's testament to Berlin's talent: "Irving Berlin has no place in American music. He *is* American music."

Berlin's most obvious talent was an uncanny ability to make song sound like speech—in a period when American musicals sought a musical dialect for the American idiom. Contractions, those most casual and familiar constructions of American speech, are important to many Berlin lyrics: the "Come on 'n' hear" that opens "Alexander's Ragtime Band," "What'll I Do?" "Say It Isn't So," "Everybody's Doin' It Now," "You'd Be Surprised," "Puttin' on the Ritz," "Let's Face the Music and Dance," "Doin' What Comes Natur'lly." Because he also writes the music, he writes those casual contractions into the notes to go with the words. When Berlin wrote "Say It with Music," he described his own method—to make singing a kind of saying. His songs reflect the colloquial, everyday speech patterns of casual American conversation.

Gone are the perfectly shaped vowels and crisply clipped consonants of the Continent and its operettas. English is a far more colloquial and conversational language than, say, French, with its grammatical differences between written and conversational usage, between the *passé simple* and *passé composé*. The American variant of English is even more committed to breaking down the barriers between writing and speech, matter and manner. Berlin's songs are more comfortably, casually, and convincingly American than anyone's before him—translating the American vernacular into singing talk and talking song. They also translated American talk into American dance: the Berlin sound of the early 1910s was both a cause and an effect of the new (and newly respectable) craze of social dancing in public places.[2]

Another source of Berlin's art is his chameleon musicianship; he is capable of turning any musical color to suit the story, situation, character, performer, style, and period for any particular song. He began his musical career as a song plugger on Tin Pan Alley (like Kern, Gershwin, Harry Ruby, and Harry Warren). The song plugger's job was to play new songs for stars, managers, producers, agents, anyone who came to West 28th Street shopping for new musical material. When they heard a tune they liked, they would buy the rights to sing it in some new show or act; only with this kind of public exposure could a song sell those thousands or millions of copies of sheet music for the parlor piano. The cunning song plugger not only had to know how to play the tune but how to plug it in the style of the singer, act, or show that was shopping for it. An Al Jolson would never buy a song without hearing it instantly as a Jolson number. Berlin learned very early to match the song to the singer.

Berlin's association with the revue also furthered his chameleonship. He did not write a book show until he was over fifty (*Louisiana Purchase*, 1940). And his second book show, *Annie Get Your Gun* (1946), contained more individual hit songs than any musical ever, before or since. Berlin's revue music made its Broadway debut with Fanny Brice—her comedic "Sadie Salome" in the 1910 edition of the *Ziegfeld Follies*. Certainly this Yiddish parody of an exotic cooch dancer must have been closer to Berlin's actual acquaintance than that Marie from sunny Italy. For two decades Berlin wrote for revues: whether for Ziegfeld or for Berlin's own productions, beginning with *Watch Your Step!* in 1914 and culminating in the annual editions of his *Music Box Revues* through the 1920s. Named for Berlin's own Music Box Theater on West 45th Street, he is still half owner of this busy Broadway house. For the two decades between *The Jazz Singer* and *Annie Get Your Gun*, Berlin alternated between Broadway revues (*Face the Music*, 1932; *As Thousands Cheer*, 1933) and Hollywood movies: *Top Hat*, *Follow the Fleet*, and *Carefree* for Astaire and Rogers at RKO; *Holiday Inn* and *Blue Skies* for Astaire and Crosby at Paramount; *Alexander's Ragtime Band* in 1938 at Fox, in which the history of Berlin's music becomes a history of twentieth-century America as well. Whether for films or revues, Berlin wrote sensitively and primarily to fit the personality of the performer and the temper of the times.

One of the reasons that Berlin could write a "Supper Time" (*As Thousands Cheer*), is that he was writing an Ethel Waters song—and he had heard her sing the blues. He could write a "Cheek to Cheek" (*Top Hat*) because he was writing an Astaire song—and he had heard Astaire make completely fluid sense of the complicated rhythmic and harmonic changes of Porter's "Night and Day." He could write a "Better Luck Next Time" (*Easter Parade*, 1948) because he was writing a Garland song—and he had heard Garland's tremulous sadness and loss in such songs as "Over the Rainbow" and "Have Yourself a Merry Little Christmas." And he could write "They Say It's Wonderful" (*Annie Get Your Gun*) because he was writing a Merman song—and he had heard her sustain those big notes for Gershwin and Porter. (Who else but Merman has ever made the open "won" of this song's "wonderful" sound so hugely wonderful?) Many composers of American film and theater music wrote less for the story, situation, or character of the show than for the star performer. Berlin and Cole Porter actually preferred to write for a star than a show. This performer-based writing was certainly not new in theater history: Shakespeare wrote very different clown roles for the buffoonish William Kemp than for the wittier Robert Armin. But writing for performers defies the neoclassical assumptions of unity that underly our dramatic criticism and our writing of theater history.

If Berlin could imagine songs for specific performers, he could also imagine them for specific emotional situations. Berlin could write a Christmas song because he imagined not a religious holiday but a social celebration of family and close friends within a picture postcard visual setting. Berlin wrote a singing Christmas card: the lyric of "White Christmas" refers explicitly to such cards, which implicitly control the song's imagery as well. The underlying melancholy of the song arises from the singer's separation from the setting (he can only dream about it) and, consequently, from the feelings within that setting. So too, "Easter Parade" (*As Thousands Cheer*) has nothing to do with Crucifixion or Resurrection but with the brightest feelings Berlin can imagine about the natural and visual setting of Easter—putting on smart new clothes and strolling down a wide avenue with others, communally enjoying a lovely day in early spring. With "Oh, How I Hate to Get Up in the Morning" (*Yip Yip Yaphank*, 1918) Berlin could imagine the way that the day-to-day drudgery of soldiering must have felt to the boys over there, not the triumphant expectations of Cohan's Yanks a-coming but (like Chaplin's satiric *Shoulder Arms* of the same year) enduring the boring, everyday routine once they arrive.

Berlin could write these songs not because of his musical technique but because of his imagination. He could invent little stories based on the strongest single feeling he could imagine about an event, and then imagine himself musically into that story. He could imagine these feelings because he could hear them musically and verbally as one. His imagination was his ear (which listened attentively to both the musical and conversational sounds around him).

This imagination, his knowledge of performers, and his ear made Berlin the best chameleon songwriter American popular music ever produced. Because he wrote both words and music, Berlin's songs reveal a tight weave of the two; Berlin hears his words as notes and his notes as words. Berlin's music always seemed more memorable than his lyrics. While the lyrics of a Cole Porter or Stephen Sondheim are so overtly clever and wittily brilliant that they overwhelm the music on first hearing, Berlin's musical tone and feeling are so strong that the individual words evaporate into the notes. Unlike Porter and Sondheim, Berlin doesn't want you to hear his words; he wants you to hear what his imagination hears—the total picture-feeling of a setting and event. The words do not call attention to themselves, largely because they are as important for their sounds as their sense.

There are hundreds of examples of Berlin's careful play with word sounds, including that extended and soaring first syllable of "wonderful" for Ethel Merman. In "White Christmas," Berlin weaves the mood of dreaming in the first line, not by putting the musical stress on the word, "dreaming," but on the two open diphthongs, "I'm" and "white," which become subtle internal rhymes, with a secondary emphasis on the soft "a" vowel of "Christmas." The stresses on the open vowel sounds draw out the line's length, giving it a sense of thoughtful revery to accompany the dreaminess of the wandering melodic line.

Berlin makes an exactly opposite choice in "There's No Business like Show Business' (*Annie Get Your Gun*); the punch of the song's opening line comes from the emphatic anapest linked to the downbeat of a measure, begun by every repetition of the "oh" diphthong:

> There's NO business
> like SHOW business,
> like NO business
> I KNOW.

And the clever alternation of the initial consonants that precede the repeating diphthong culminates in the final "know," unexpected because it is not part of the song's title, which is simultaneously a repetition and a rhyme (an "eye-rhyme," heard as a repetition of "no" but seen imaginatively as a rhyme with "show").

"I Love a Piano" (*Stop! Look! Listen!*, 1915) captures the tinkly sounds of the piano—particularly a ragtime upright of the tinny type Americans were hearing in saloons and nickelodeons (the song's lyric explicitly refers to an upright). As with "Alexander's" trumpet, Berlin achieves this instrumental sound in the song's opening line, also its title—breaking the word, "piano," into three distinct syllables (pee-ANN-oh), accented on the middle syllable.

"Say It with Music" (*The Music Box Revue* of 1921 and 1922) sounds unmistakably written for the cello, as if its sliding, liquid melody could only be expressed by a string instrument with the liquidity of a violin but in a deeper, darker, warmer register. The song makes conscious reference to a "melody mellow, played on a cello," and Berlin's musical emphases fall on the combined soft "e" vowel and liquid "l" consonant of "mel" and "cel" ("melody" and "mellow" become another repetition that is also a rhyme), a mellow blending of sounds that is precisely opposite the harsh sound of the "oh" diphthong in "There's No Business like Show Business." Given his conscious comparisons of vocal sounds to musical instruments, it should come as no surprise that Berlin wrote so many songs that depict human emotions as sayings with music: "A Pretty Girl Is like a Melody" (*Ziegfeld Follies* of 1919), "The Song Is Ended (but the Melody Lingers On)" (1927), "You Keep Coming Back like a Song" (*Blue Skies*), "Soft Lights and Sweet Music" (*Face the Music*), "Let's Face the Music and Dance" (*Follow the Fleet*).

Among the many shrewd sounds in Berlin songs are the aspirated sigh that opens "Cheek to Cheek" with the word "Heaven" or the childishly barking and bickering repetitions of "Anything You Can Do":

> No you can't. Yes I can.
> No you can't. Yes I can.
> No you can't. Yes I can, Yes I can.

The "yes" phrase is a singsong repetition, one step down, of the preceding "no" phrase, and the final three assertions climb the musical scale, as the musical elevation mirrors the argument's mounting agitation, intensity, and childishness.

When Berlin does execute a cute or tricky verbal twist, few of his listeners realize it. Two clearly paired Berlin songs, "All Alone" (1924) and "Always" (1925), conclude with triple endings that are conscious variations on one another.[3] The final lines of the two songs are syntactically so similar that they hide their subtle difference. The verbal phrases that conclude "Always" are precisely repetitive:

> Not for just an hour,
> Not for just a day,
> Not for just a year,
> But always.

As these lines build verbally toward longer periods of time (hour, day, year, always), Berlin's melody moves oppositely in counterpoint, pulling each of the temporally expanding phrases down a descending musical scale.

The concluding verbal phrases of "All Alone," however, are not perfectly parallel but contain a syntactic surprise:

> Wondering where you are,
> And how you are,
> And if you are
> All alone too.

While the first two interrogative phrases are independent clauses, the third is dependent on the verbal extension (and surprise) of the song's returning title to complete its meaning. Berlin does not build the musical pattern of this triple ending on a descending musical phrase but on identically repeated musical phrases. When its final question cannot be completed with those identical notes, the concluding need for the final three words comes as an even more interesting surprise. The differences in these two endings suggest a very careful and clever demonstration of subtle variation within apparently identical verbal and musical patterns. So often Berlin returns to a device he used earlier, only to show he can construct something just as interesting but just a little bit different.

Berlin's sensitivity to words as sounds controls another favorite device: his variations of tempi within the same song. His ability to shift rhythmic gears in midsong, as in the three hat-and-cane songs for Astaire, depends on his sustaining the vowel sounds of some phrases and clicking the crisp consonants of others. Berlin's great "double songs" (two different songs that fit over one another to become a single contrapuntal melody) are completely dependent on these internal variations of musical tempi and verbal sound. The verse of "Play a Simple Melody" (*Watch Your Step!*), the earliest of the double songs, asserts that modern music is too fast, rough, and raggy; the singer longs for the good old days, which were symbolized by the good old songs that mother used to sing. (The idea that old songs represent a time when life itself was simpler and sweeter can be traced back at least as far as Shakespeare.) The initial refrain of "Play a Simple Melody" follows the yearning of the verse by becoming an example of one of those old songs: a melodically simple but flowing sixteen-bar, AA structure typical of forty years earlier. This "old fashioned" refrain has very few notes (exactly thirty-two), lengthily sustained on their open vowel sounds.

The second refrain is a response by a different singer of an opposite temperament; he prefers the modern bounce and jangle of ragtime. His syncopated refrain contains almost twice as many notes as the sentimental singer's, and they snap with sharp consonantal jabs to emphasize the rhythmic syncopation: "If you will play from a copy of a tune that is choppy." The song's final section delivers the two refrains simultaneously; in effect, "Play a Simple Melody" is a forty-eight-bar song, structured AA BB A/B A/B. The result, given Berlin's clever control of varying tempi and verbal sounds, is that you can distinctly hear every word and every note of each refrain when both are sung simultaneously, as well as the contrapuntal interplay of their combination. The counterpoint of the two refrains represents both a conflict of opposing characters and a capsule history of the evolution of American popular music.

Berlin would use the technique for later double songs, among them "You're Just in Love" (*Call Me Madam*, 1950) and "An Old-Fashioned Wedding." "Play a Simple Melody," though less familiar, seems the most interesting—not only because it came first but because its conscious allusion to the history of American popular music plays a role in its conflict of characters. The song is both a story and a history—a little drama in itself, as so many of the best Berlin songs are. The uneducated Berlin had somehow got an education about American popular songs and styles that preceded even his arrival in America (for example, the reference to "Swanee River" in "Alexander's Ragtime Band").

Another example of historical awareness that serves a dramatic function is "The Girl That I Marry" from *Annie Get Your Gun*. Berlin deliberately wrote a sweet, old-fashioned waltz in the popular style of the 1880s and 1890s. The old-fashioned style conveys Frank Butler's outdated (and sexist) ideal of a perfect mate. The plot of the show turns on his sexist rejection of Annie as a superior marks*man*, implying Berlin's critique of the outdated ideals that the song's musical style suggests. Because *Annie Get Your Gun* was set in the 1890s, Berlin's historical waltz simultaneously evokes the period in which the action takes place and comments, some fifty years later, on the parallel progress of American musical taste and social values.

Another of Berlin's distinctive musical traits, suggested by Astaire's three hat-and-cane numbers, is the effortless shifting between major and minor harmonies in the middle of musical lines. Alec Wilder describes a moment in "Let's Face the Music and Dance," which Berlin also wrote for Astaire, as a "magical" shift from minor to major precisely on the word, "dance."[4] But Berlin works similar magic in any number of songs, usually by dispelling an overhanging mood of sadness or doubt (like "facing the music" of separation) at the very end of a phrase by an affirmative shift to a major chord (like the joy of "dance"). Although Berlin may have needed a secretary to notate his harmonies, he must have heard them in his head when he thought up the melodies, since a great many Berlin songs depend on these identical harmonic shifts.

A song that plays interesting games with variations of major and minor harmonies is "Blue Skies," that very familiar Berlin song (more familiar from *The Jazz Singer* than the 1926 show, *Betsy*, where it was first interpolated).[5] From its title one expects the song to be thoroughly sunny. In fact, the song is built primarily on minor chords which shift to the major in affirmation for the final three notes of every A section. The story that the chords suggest is that the singer has been through some troubled times, and some doubts linger about the future, but his or her feeling (something between a hope and a determination) is that the skies are clearing for good. While the text of the song, its explicit title and lyric, is filled with sunshine, the subtext of the song, its harmonic pattern, suggests plenty of dark clouds.

These harmonic patterns had acquired a name by the 1920s, when the flatted notes of jazz, the black keys of the C-major scale, became known as "blue notes." Berlin's song plays with this other meaning of "blue" in the lyric of its final A section, when the word describes not a literal color but a figurative emotion: "Blue days, all of them gone." When the blue days go away, the blue notes go with them and the song's conclusion resolves firmly and forever in the major. As if to demonstrate his playful knowledge of these musical patterns, Berlin wrote the obverse of "Blue Skies" less than a year later, "Shaking the Blues Away," for the *Ziegfeld Follies* of 1927. Despite its title, this song remains entirely in the major except for the final four notes of its first A section and much of its release, when the blue notes return to stick like burrs—so they require more shaking.

A summation song that displays virtually every distinctive Berlin technique is "Cheek to Cheek." Clearly written for the talents and style of a star performer, it is instantly identifiable as an Astaire song. Among the many things Astaire could do for a song was to make an extremely complicated musical composition hang together as if it were a very simple tune. And "Cheek to Cheek" is as complicated a song as Berlin ever wrote. A very long song of seventy-two bars, its refrains, each of sixteen bars rather than eight, use a familiar Berlin pattern of lengthily sustained, unsyncopated notes accompanying open vowel sounds. In these A sections, Berlin plays two opposing "e" sounds against one another—the soft "eh" of "Heaven," contributing to its aspirated sigh, and the long "ee" of "cheek" and its various rhymes.

Then the song constructs not one but two releases. The first of them is major (for the words beginning, "Oh, I'd love to climb a mountain"); the second is minor (beginning, "Dance with me"). The first of them uses many notes (sixty), syncopatedly and percussively, the second very few notes (twenty), many of them sustained. If Berlin were the kind of artist who ever wanted to show off, he could point to these two releases as equally interesting ways to develop the main theme: "You want a release that's major and rhythmic? I can do that. You want one minor and more passionate? I can do that, too. What the hell! I'll do 'em both. Freddy can bring it off." He brings it off all right. The song's complex structure— AABCA, each of sixteen bars, except for the disproportionate C section of eight bars—rolls off Astaire's tongue as if it were as simple as "I'll be loving you always."

Irving Berlin was the most successful American composer at making his musical art sound artless. He didn't care much about whole shows, "theatah," and "cinemah"; and he wouldn't see much use for this chapter. What he cared about was hit songs: take care of the hits and the musicals will take care of themselves. While Berlin's "theory" of the musical has been eclipsed by fancier ones, there are no hit musicals without hit songs. No American composer rivaled Berlin's instinct for hits—the right song, for the right performer, in the right style, at the right time, for the right audience.

The one consistent quality that defines a Berlin song is that it is simply right.

5

When E'er a Cloud
Appears in the Blue

JEROME KERN

At the opposite pole of American theater music from Irving Berlin stands Jerome Kern. He made sure his music sounded very much like art. He wrote scores, not hits—although he wanted hits to jump out of the scores. While Berlin seems the prototype of the self-taught, enterprising immigrant, hustling his way through a musical marketplace where songs were bought and sold by the gross, like woolens only a few blocks uptown, Jerome Kern was a more genteel figure with a genteel background and reputation to match. Born in 1885 in New York, where the Kern family had resided for forty years, his father could afford to give him piano lessons, send him to high school, and enroll him in musical conservatories both here and abroad. Growing up in a proper bourgeois home of the late-nineteenth century, Kern inherited the reigning tastes of his class. In theater music, those tastes meant a preference for the cultured art songs of England and the Continent. Though he was the first great American-born composer of theater music, many of Kern's sensibilities were formed in and by Europe, and he never abandoned them for a totally vernacular American sound. Kern straddled the Atlantic throughout his career—in style and in fact.[1] He did not abandon his regular trips to London—where he learned to write shows, where he continued to write them even after his American success, and where he met his wife—until his musicals moved in the opposite direction, to Hollywood.

Kern's rigorous musicianship, his commitment to the musical integrity of a song, can be understood by his unique method of composing. Kern wrote the music first, then handed the manuscript to the lyricist, whose job was to hang words on that musical structure. According to his biographers, Kern never would change a single note to suit the sense of a lyric.[2] Although this musical integrity may seem admirable, particularly in a

Jerome Kern at the piano, working with Ira Gershwin on *Cover Girl* in 1944

culture that believes words irrelevant to songs, it is also a bit maniacal (and the claim may well be apocryphal). Collaborative theater songs do not usually evolve in this way. Nor in its opposite—of a complete poem to be adorned with notes (although both Hart and Hammerstein sometimes worked this way with Richard Rodgers). Kern himself was moved to write "The Last Time I Saw Paris" after reading a nostalgic Hammerstein lyric to the occupied city.[3] It is more common and pragmatic for composer and lyricist to work together in a dynamic interchange, hammering out the musical and verbal structure together—particularly fitting the opening line of music to the opening line of the lyric, from which the rest of the song follows as a logical consequence. Not Kern.

Nor did he write for performers as Berlin did. Even Kern's songs for Astaire—"The Way You Look Tonight," "Pick Yourself Up," "A Fine Romance" (*Swing Time*, 1936) or "Dearly Beloved" (*You Were Never Lovelier*, 1942)—seem less distinctively Astaire songs than Astaire songs by Berlin, Gershwin, or Porter. Kern expected performers to sing his material as he had written it, to adopt its style rather than for him to adopt theirs. Kern's favorite singer was Irene Dunne, because of both the delicacy and the accuracy of her singing style, singing his tunes the way he imagined them, submitting her interpretation to the authority of his composition. The preference explains Dunne's presence in so many films with Kern scores (*Roberta, Sweet Adeline*, the 1936 *Show Boat, High, Wide, and Handsome* and *Joy of Living*).

This was no genial "Papa" Kern but a musical monster who may well have killed himself by flying into the rages that caused strokes. He was famous for screaming at performers who took liberties with a melody or arrangers who took liberties with harmonies. He fought these liberties through the legal arm of ASCAP: The American Society of Composers, Authors, and Publishers, which Kern (along with Herbert, Berlin, and others) founded in 1913 to guarantee the payment of royalty on any song played in public. Kern, outraged by the licentious looseness of jazz musicians with the tunes, styles, and rhythms of his songs, sought to prohibit jazz bands from playing any ASCAP song. Even after his death, Kern's estate carried on the composer's war with jazz, successfully prohibiting the sale or broadcast of Maynard Ferguson's wildly screaming trumpet version of "All the Things You Are." Kern himself exercised this integrity exactly once during his lifetime when he refused to allow any songs from *Sitting Pretty* (1924) to be performed in public or on radio. A lack of public exposure contributed to the show's early demise. Although Kern was a man of musical principle, he also wanted hit shows and hit songs. When shows flop, their songs usually go down with them.

For all his pure musicianship, Kern wrote his very best songs with his very best lyricists—P. G. Wodehouse, Oscar Hammerstein II, Dorothy Fields, and Ira Gershwin. Kern's weaker songs were written with lyricists whose names are understandably forgotten today—Harry B. Smith, Herbert Reynolds, Anne Caldwell, Graham John. A frequent Kern collaborator, Otto Harbach, falls somewhere between. Kern was very comfortable with Harbach (born Hauerbach a decade earlier than Kern), a product of that taste and time toward which Kern's own music leaned. Kern and Harbach even appear on screen together in *Men Against the Sky* (1930). However, Harbach provided the weakest sets of lyrics ever attached to a great score (*Roberta*, 1933). Take "Yesterdays":

> Youth was mine,
> Truth was mine,
> Flaming fire and strong desire,
> Forsooth, was mine.

Although the song conveys a nostalgic longing for the past, and its lyrics deliberately tend toward the archaic, which era of English speech is "forsooth" thought to represent?

Why is the musical quality of a Kern song so dependent on his lyricist? Perhaps an innovative collaborator stimulated Kern's imagination more than an indifferent one. Because the lyricist is also the first critic to hear a melody, he or she might very tactfully suggest that Kern discard or rework a weaker tune. Only a lyricist with the stature of a Hammerstein, Wodehouse, or Ira Gershwin would have the temerity to suggest that a new Kern song might be inferior to his highest standard. Or perhaps the simple fact is that Kern's best songs tend to be his most mature songs and the older Kern didn't work with inferior lyricists. The craft of writing lyrics had itself matured over the decades of Kern's career, for Kern's standards of musicianship set the demanding standards for lyric craftsmanship as well.

Even Harbach's excessive lyric to "Yesterdays" suggests an important quality of a Kern song. The sweet sadness of a Kern ballad demands a highly imagistic, poetically heightened lyric. The brilliantly slangy and vernacular Ira Gershwin aspired to the dreamily poetic when working with Kern on "Long Ago and Far Away" (*Cover Girl*, 1944). The witty P. G. Wodehouse would suppress his irony for the sweet melancholy of "Till the Clouds Roll By" (*Oh, Boy!*, 1919) or the contrast between poetic expectation and prosaic reality of "Bill" (from the 1927 *Show Boat* but written a decade earlier). Even a solid citizen of Tin Pan Alley like B. G. (Buddy) De Sylva, who specialized in 1920s bounce, could produce poetry for Kern—"Look for the silver lining when e'er a cloud appears in the blue." Perhaps "e'er" leads inevitably to "forsooth" under the spell of a Kern melody. Not surprisingly, Kern's most sympathetic collaborator, though over a decade his junior, was Oscar Hammerstein II, America's most consciously poetical lyricist.

Kern songs reveal a high degree of musical complexity that is also effortless, lyrical, fluid, and coherent. His combination of complexity and comprehensibility surpasses that of any other American theater composer. Every American composer of musicals, from Gershwin to Rodgers to Sondheim, acknowledges Kern as the greatest "pure composer" ever to write for musical theater and film. Kern's spell of poetic melancholy was best described by a lyricist who never worked with him—Lorenz Hart. The lyric to "My Romance," a Rodgers and Hart song of 1935, contains a general reference to popular music that is also a specific homage to Kern:

> My romance
> Doesn't need a castle rising in Spain,
> Or a dance
> To a constantly surprising refrain.

Kern is the composer of those constantly surprising refrains. What made them surprising was their length, or, rather, the extreme length of their musical phrases that turned, twisted, ascended, descended, continuing for a full eight measures, or sixteen, or longer, prolonging the wait for the inevitable resolution, the return to the anticipated root and key, for an unimaginably long musical time, until the final surprise of reaching it. Kern could prolong and sustain individual musical ideas longer than anyone who wrote American songs, but these ideas, despite their length, were surprisingly memorable, singable, hummable, and haunting. Kern simultaneously defied the basic thirty-two-bar song structure and used the logical outline of that structure to make a song comprehensible, even while he was obliterating it.

"They Didn't Believe Me": measures nine through eighteen

The technique can be heard in "They Didn't Believe Me," Kern's first international hit, the second American popular song to sweep the Western world. The Kern kernel, pointing the way toward his mature work, occupies measures nine through sixteen—a single uninterrupted phrase, eight bars long, that wanders surprisingly and complexly up the diatonic scale, then descends to a resolution that is not quite a resolution but a transition to the next section. The complicated song is anchored by two double statements of the title words (by Herbert Reynolds), which cleverly fall on the only musical repetition in the entire refrain. That refrain, a Type II variant, can only be diagrammed by breaking its eight-bar units into four-bar sections:

A (a-b)
B
A′ (a′-c)
C (b-d)

The second section, eight bars long, is the single undivided phrase of measures nine through sixteen. The opening musical phrase returns with a variation (a′) to begin the second symmetrical half of the song in the seventeenth measure, and the twelve notes of the repeated title phrase, stated initially in bars five through eight at the end of the first section (b), return in measures twenty-five through twenty-eight to begin the song's final section. The final four bars of the song (d) refer to the opening two bars of the ascending B section. Despite this complex musical shape, the song was an immediate hit and remains as fresh today as it was over seventy years ago. For all the modernity of its refrain, the song's verse is never sung, primarily because its bouncy two-step rhythm and squirrelly tune seem not only inconsistent with the relaxed refrain but sound very much like 1914 (or even earlier).

Many memorable Kern songs adopt the idea of "They Didn't Believe Me"—extremely long and complicated musical lines anchored by some recurring repetition of notes, perhaps emphasized by accompanying the words of the title. In "Till the Clouds Roll By," measures nine through sixteen reveal a similar wandering complexity to those same measures of "They Didn't Believe Me." So do measures nine through sixteen of "Look for the Silver Lining" (*Sally*, 1920), "Bill," and "Make Believe" (*Show Boat*). Kern obviously liked to establish the main theme clearly in the first eight bars, execute a very tricky variation in the next eight bars, then devote the rest of the refrain to explicating the odd shift. Kern's very last song, "Nobody Else But Me" (for the 1946 revival of *Show Boat*) plays such bizarre melodic and harmonic games in measures nine through sixteen that only Mabel Mercer and Bobby Short have been able to make singable sense of them. Or Kern might reserve his tricky surprises for the release. Because "Can't Help Lovin' Dat Man" was written as a parody of a torchy "coon song" in *Show Boat*, Kern preserved a more conventional AABA structure, reserving his tricky melodic leaps for the release in measures seventeen through twenty-four. He makes a similar choice in "I'm Old Fashioned" (*You Were Never Lovelier*, 1942) when the bizarre melodic climbing and harmonic twisting of measures seventeen through twenty-four make modernist mockery of the song's old-fashioned idea of life and love.

Other Kern songs do not bracket their melodic and harmonic surprises within specific passages but weave an entire composition of unexpected developments and changes. Both the A and B sections of "Smoke Gets in Your Eyes" (*Roberta*) are composed of a single, unbreakable eight-bar phrase, difficult to fathom (and to sing), but Kern helps the listener with the song's firm AABA structure, whose repetitions make a strange tune an old friend by song's end. A similar choice accounts for the popularity of "The Way You Look Tonight" (*Swing Time*), whose striking loveliness earned Kern the first of his two Academy Awards. The song was virtually thrown away in the film: Astaire sings a lone, unembroidered chorus, seated at the piano, while Rogers, washing her hair, looks a comic fright, undercutting the song's romantic claim about the way she looks. Still, listeners had little difficulty responding to the complicated, continuously climbing eight-bar phrases of its refrains and the bizarre melodic leaps and harmonic shifts of its release.

If there is an essential Kern song it is "All the Things You Are," from his last Broadway show, *Very Warm for May* (1939), which he wrote with Oscar Hammerstein. Kern himself believed this song so complicated that no ordinary theatergoer could possibly remember it. He was amazed—and delighted—when he heard people whistling it on the street. Despite its outlines of an AABA structure, the song is more accurately described as AA'BA": it never precisely repeats any musical phrase. The second eight-bar section is not only a variation on the opening A section but an extension of it. The first sixteen bars of the song form a single descending line, among the very longest of Kern's long lines. After the song leaps upward for a release that is somewhat simpler than the refrain (except for an unexpected key change in the twentieth measure), it executes its greatest surprise in its return to the refrain. The final A section begins on the identical tone with which the release ends, but it modulates to a new key, converting the G-sharp to an A-flat (an enharmonic change, in the musical jargon). The result feels as if the singer has soared to a new height of power and passion for the final statement of the refrain (no wonder singers love this song), rising to a new pitch both literally and figuratively. The sense of soaring climaxes with the song's first exploding top note, an E-flat in the thirtieth measure, accompanying the word, "day," then soars beyond that with its final three notes in a climactic coda that propels the song four bars past the thirty-two-bar expectation.

Kern had executed a similar surprise in "The Song Is You" seven years earlier (*Music in the Air,* 1932); its release also ends with the tone that becomes the first note of the returning refrain, accompanied by a key change. But in "All the Things You Are," Kern prepares for this surprise with a parallel one earlier, as the song moves out of the verse and into the refrain. The verse, written in the key of G, ends with the root (the G), that slides up a half tone to become the new root of the song's refrain, in the key of A-flat. This slide from G to A-flat at the beginning of the refrain prepares for the later transition from G-sharp to A-flat at the return to the refrain from the release, giving the entire song a powerful sense of symmetry. Hammerstein's lyric emphasizes this symmetry by using the identical word, "You," to end the verse and begin the refrain. While the relationship

"All the Things You Are": modulation from verse to refrain.

from release to final refrain

of verse to refrain gives us parallel notes (both roots), same word, but different keys, the relationship of release to returning refrain gives us different word, different keys, but same note. Hammerstein's lyric throughout is a perfect example of the poetic sensibility that the Kern sound demands: "the promised kiss of springtime," "the breathless hush of evening that trembles on the brink of a lovely song," "the angel glow that lights a star." "All the Things You Are" is all the things Kern is.

Kern always seemed more a theater composer than Irving Berlin, both because Kern wrote for book shows rather than for revues and because Kern, unlike Berlin, never wrote popular songs independent of film and theater scores. After an apprentice decade of delivering interpolated songs for shows written by or credited to others, Kern got the chance to write his own scores after the success of an interpolation—"They Didn't Believe Me" in the 1914 *The Girl from Utah*. The result was the first series of modern musical comedies—with an emphasis on the play rather than the production, with a carefully matched script and score, and without the line of ladies' legs. The Princess Theater shows, as the series came to be called, was named for the tiny Princess Theater on West 39th Street. Its 299 seats guaranteed both that the production would be more modest and that the audience would be more elite—not quite as elite as at the Metropolitan Opera House down the street, but as close to it as the Princess was to the Met. These were smart "little shows" for an emerging American smart set. Their entertainment burden fell on the book, the lyrics, the tunes, and the performers rather than on the designer, the chorines, and the budget. Wit, style, grace, and charm replaced the size, splash, and splendor of its Broadway contemporaries—whether at the Hippodrome, in the *Ziegfeld Follies*, or in Operettaland. Not all half-dozen shows played the Princess (some were too costly or too successful for the little house), but they all shared the Princess spirit.

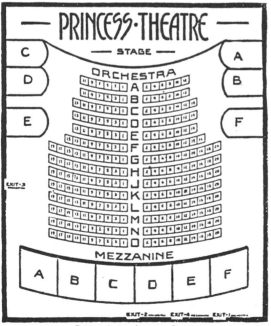

A seating diagram of the tiny Princess Theater

The first series of truly modern American musicals was not quite so truly American but, like Kern himself, straddled the Atlantic. While Kern spent much of his apprenticeship in London, his librettist, Guy Bolton, was born in England to American parents; his lyricist, P. G. Wodehouse, was a thoroughly British humorist, as his later series of Jeeves novels proved. The Princess Theater shows (among them, *Very Good Eddie*, 1915; *Oh, Boy!*, 1917; and *Oh, Lady! Lady!!*, 1918) as well as *Leave It to Jane* (1917) attached the satiric British spirit of Gilbert and Sullivan spoof to the mores, speech, styles, and dances of American youth. The action was inevitably confined to highly contemporary settings (exactly one per act, given the tiny Princess stage) where American youth was thought to congregate: the college campus; the Greenwich Village apartment; the Long Island mansion; the transatlantic ocean liner; the Honeymoon Inn in the country.

Although few of Kern's loveliest melodies come from these shows ("Till the Clouds Roll By" from *Oh, Boy!* and "Go Little Boat" from *Miss 1917* are clear exceptions), the series sharpened his writing of catchy, comic upbeat songs. "Cleopatterer," in *Leave It to Jane*, turns the Great Egyptian into a Little Egypt, a cooch dancer who "gave those sly Egyptian ginks something else to watch except the Sphinx." While one doesn't think of Kern as a writer of rhythm songs, these comic numbers were miracles compared to those of contemporary operettas. Later comic numbers reveal the result of Kern's lessons at the Princess. In "Life Upon the Wicked Stage" from *Show Boat*, Oscar Hammerstein's lyrics draw a comic contrast between the alleged wickedness of show business life and the mundane reality of everyday survival:

> When you let a fellow hold your hand, which
> Means an extra beer or sandwich.

> or

> Wild old men who bring you jewels and sables
> Only live in Aesop's Fables.

Kern supports the contrast with a tune that might be described as an American gavotte, a cross between a bouncy two-step and a stately minuet, a thoroughly catchy and engaging blend with Hammerstein's lyric. Kern's ability with comic upbeat numbers would serve him well in the rhythm songs he would write for films with Dorothy Fields. Their Kern element is the surprising musical complexity of certain phrases: the picking-up leaps of "Pick Yourself Up" (*Swing Time*), the bouncing-up jumps of "You Couldn't Be Cuter" (*Joy of Living*, 1938), and the bizarrely meandering release of "I Won't Dance" (*Roberta*), perhaps the most difficult release Kern ever wrote.[4] In the Princess Theater shows Kern first learned to have musical fun.

As a theater composer, Kern's career leads up to and away from *Show Boat* in 1927. While perhaps not Kern's best show melodically,[5] *Show Boat* is by far his most important historically and his most ambitious theatrically. It was the first American musical to tackle an explicitly serious social subject without reducing it to embarrassing claptrap. That subject was race—the legal separation and subjugation of the black race in the post-Civil War South. *Show Boat* became the first American musical to translate the operetta's romantic attachment to historical settings into a moral question about history and to translate the operetta's romantic attraction to the class structure into a moral concern with American class distinctions that history had not eradicated. The other theme of *Show Boat* is show business. Not coincidentally, the separation of the races haunted the history of the musical itself—both in the pseudo-black music that white Jewish composers were writing for musicals (like Kern for this very musical) and in the rigid separation of white and black casts.

This racial problem within show business occupies the subplot: Julie LaVerne, the mulatto actress who passes for white, is exiled from Cap'n Andy's riverboat the *Cotton Blossom*, when her mixed parentage becomes public knowledge. Hammerstein twisted the conventional multistrand plot of operettas by making his subplot a tragic one—an impossible love between Julie and Steve, her white lover, that cannot (and does not) end happily. The tragic subplot, based on racial conflict and social inequality, would become a Hammerstein trademark—from *Show Boat* to *South Pacific*, *The King and I*, and *The Sound of Music*. Hammerstein also emphasizes a purely metaphoric character, the black stevedore, Joe, who serves no function in the show except as choric commentator and patient seer, all knowing and all enduring. If Joe wandered to Broadway from Edna Ferber's Mississippi, he also wandered uptown from the Yiddish Theater's depiction of oppressed blacks. Joe transcends his close kinship to Uncle Tom on the strength of one Kern and Hammerstein song. Like the spirituals of black slaves, Joe's singing of "Ol' Man River" is both a comfort and a philosophy, a statement of belief in life's continuity and of resignation to his place in it.[6] A song had become a philosophy. There had never before been any song like it in an American musical.

Both "Ol' Man River" and Julie's "Can't Help Lovin' Dat Man" translate the racial question into musical terms. Their titles alone indicate a device Hammerstein borrowed from the "coon songs" so popular two decades earlier—the white singer's exaggeration of black speech patterns to ridicule the mentality of the "coon." Kern's dignified and soulful melodies allow Hammerstein's dialect not to burlesque the singer but to maintain a dramatic continuity between speech and song, as Hammerstein would with other dialects in later scores with Richard Rodgers. For Hammerstein, there was to be no difference between a speaking character and a singing character. Paul Robeson's definitive rendition of "Ol' Man River," magnificently

Paul Robeson's "Ol' Man River" (from the 1936 film)

captured in the 1936 film directed by James Whale, even emphasizes the black dialect when Robeson makes the title sound more like "Ol' Man Reeburr." The defiant dialect contrasts the black man's confidence in *what* he is saying (Joe doesn't care about grammar or pronunciation but ideas) with his limited means of *how* to say it, imprisoned in a foreign language only partially taught him by whites. While the dialect of Hammerstein's lyric emphasizes the confinement of the character within his culture, the power of the flowing Kern melody expands his vision to almost infinite comprehension.

In contrast, Julie's dialect song, "Can't Help Lovin' Dat Man," is a deliberate and exuberant pastiche of a "coon song." Irene Dunne's outrageous (and funny) impersonation of "coon shuffling" in the 1936 film reveals the song's subtle burlesquing of white attitudes and assumptions about the lives of blacks. As in "Ol' Man River," Hammerstein relies on natural imagery ("fish gotta swim, birds gotta fly") to suggest that, despite her lover's shiftlessness, the black woman remains faithful to him. The black woman has become Ol' Man River, enduring her "lazy," "slow" mate cause she just can't help it. Is this more black stoicism, the female equivalent of Joe's, or a parody of black stoicism, or both simultaneously?

For all its thematic innovation, *Show Boat* drags along plenty of conventional Operettaland baggage: the dashing riverboat gambler with the operetta name, Gaylord Ravenal; the *Cotton Blossom*'s leading lady with a matching operetta name, Magnolia Hawkes; the obligatory soubrette and comic, Ellie and Frank, who work aboard the boat; the clownishly paternal Cap'n Andy and his comically acerbic wife, Parthy. The sprawling narrative, riding the endless chronological river of Edna Ferber's novel, meanders fitfully through countless decades in the second act. It finally docks at the obligatory happy reunion: the aged Gaylord returns to Magnolia, their daughter, Kim, and the *Cotton Blossom;* even Cap'n Andy, who died mid-journey in the novel, makes it to the finale. *Show Boat* stops just one mortal step short of Hammerstein's ending for *Carousel*, with the return of Billy's ghost from heaven for his daughter's graduation.

There was no vast, unbridgeable gulf separating *Show Boat* from its operetta contemporaries; after all, the show was produced by Florenz Ziegfeld, who was happy to make theater history if he could make money at it. There are striking similarities between *Show Boat* and Sigmund Romberg's operetta of the preceding year, *The Desert Song*, to which Oscar Hammerstein also contributed book and lyrics. Like *Show Boat*, the narrative of *The Desert Song* is based on the legal separation of two races—the ruling white French and subservient Arab Riffs in North Africa. While Magnolia of *Show Boat* longs for the "Make Believe" of romance, Margot of *The Desert Song* sings just as longingly of "Romance." While Gaylord, a gambler in gentleman's disguise, answers Magnolia's dreams, Pierre, a rebel leader in weakling's disguise, answers Margot's. As in *Show Boat*, sexual dalliance between the races produces the most serious social consequences in *The Desert Song*. Like Julie LaVerne, the woman of "exotic race" is more openly lustful in *The Desert Song*. Azuri, the Arab dancing girl, is a cross between Mata Hari and Little Egypt, the sexual tigress that no reticent white Magnolia or Margot could ever be in an American musical. This open sexuality, violating the bourgeois prohibition of sex outside marriage, leads inevitably to death or banishment for the offending lovers—whether in *Show Boat* and *The Desert Song* or *South Pacific* and *The King and I*. Hammerstein's conscious commitment to racial equality runs headlong into the unconscious sexism of lingering nineteenth-century theater convention, in which female chastity is the only antidote for tragedy. The woman (especially the nonwhite woman, as in *Madame Butterfly*) who enjoys sex before marriage (especially with a white man) must always lose the man she truly loves, then die (like Cho Cho San) or drink herself into the gutter (like Julie LaVerne).

Kern, like Puccini, elevates conventional material beyond the conventional by conceiving *Show Boat* as a whole score rather than a scattering of songs. First, the score is full of incidental music—leitmotifs for individual characters, tonal underscoring for certain scenes—that exists independently of any musical number. As in Puccini, music in *Show Boat* weaves through the narrative and around the dialogue—rather than being relegated to separate song slots. Second, Kern builds a history of American theater music into his own historical saga of American musical theater. The "coon song" ("Can't Help Lovin' Dat Man" and "Gallivantin' Aroun'"), the jaunty two-step ("I Might Fall Back on You"), the cakewalk ("In Dahomey"—a quotation from the first black musical), the sentimental waltz ("After the Ball," interpolated from *A Trip to Chinatown*) are performed on the stage of the *Cotton Blossom* or on some other in the show, just as they were performed on stages over the years that the show chronicles. Kern's division of the score between onstage production numbers and offstage character numbers makes *Show Boat* the first musical to include a conscious history of the form within a new example of the form.

Finally, Kern designed songs as musical anagrams of one another. "Cotton Blossom" and "Ol' Man River" are such close musical kin they suggest an organic relation between the boat and the river on which it travels. As in the Ferber novel, the *Cotton Blossom* is more than a mere water craft and more than a mere floating theater. Like Huck Finn's raft in Twain's novel of the river as a road through life, the *Cotton Blossom* is a time machine. It is a center of human society and civilization, traveling the river much as its human occupants travel through life. The boat is more than the center of human life in the story: it is human life itself. Kern's musical anagrams of "Cotton Blossom" and "Ol' Man River" translate Ferber's literary metaphor into musical terms.

Though very similar musically, the differing tones and rhythms of the

"Cotton Blossom" (from the 1946 Broadway revival)

two songs emphasize a key distinction: for whites the river provides a place
of play, to watch a show, while for blacks the same river is a place of hard
and servile work. The whites who work aboard the boat have the glamorous
jobs, the blacks who work aboard the menial jobs. It is a workplace and a
home for both whites and blacks, but it is not an equal place for both. It is,
however, considerably more equal than those segregated places of home and
work off the boat, away from the river, just as Huck's raft provides the only
refuge where a white boy and black man can become friends. Kern's songs
imply that show business itself, like the *Cotton Blossom*, is not a perfect place
of social justice, but it is a lot more just than any other place of business in
American society.

The verse of "Cotton Blossom" is of twenty-four bars, with an ABA
structure. The eight-bar A section of the verse is identical to the brief
eight-bar verse of "Ol' Man River." These identical notes, however, are sung
in a rhythmic, energetic cadence rather than with the somber intonation of
"Ol' Man River," which evokes the weary sadness of the spiritual.
Hammerstein's lyric uses the same strange word, "Mississippi," to emphasize the musical identity of the two passages: "Dere's an ol' man called the
Mississippi" for "Ol' Man River," "Niggers all work on the Mississippi" for
"Cotton Blossom." This original 1927 lyric, euphemized to "Darkies all
work on the Mississippi" for the 1936 Universal film, lost all its racial
suggestions with "Here we all work on the Mississippi" for the 1951 MGM
film. The evolving history of this single line is itself a history of American
linguistic propriety. The 1936 film, which also uttered "coon," faced
American racial inequality far more fearlessly than the glossier but lifeless
1951 film, which placidly consigned this injustice to the distant, departed
past.

The B section of the verse of "Cotton Blossom" becomes the B section
of the refrain of "Ol' Man River," the same melody as "Tote that barge, lift
that bail," but in a much sprightlier rhythm. The A section of the refrain of
"Cotton Blossom" uses the same four notes as the familiar A section of the
refrain of "Ol' Man River," but as opposed to the ascending notes that
accompany the title words, "Ol' Man River," the same four notes descend
to accompany the title words of "Cotton Blossom." The soft vowels and
consonants of Hammerstein's title words to "Ol' Man River" contribute to
the eternal, endlessly rolling sound of that musical phrase, while the sharp
"t" and "b" consonants of "Cotton Blossom" contribute to the more playful
and punctuated sound of those notes. To preserve the musical parallel with
"Ol' Man River," the refrain of "Cotton Blossom" has no release; it has
already sung its release, the same as "Ol' Man River," in its verse. "Cotton
Blossom" is a simple sixteen-bar refrain of the AA type, popular in the
1880s when the narrative is set. "Ol' Man River," however, is a modern
thirty-two-bar popular song, uniting the apparent timelessness of spirituals
with modern musical form.

A diagram may make the interlocking structures of these two songs clearer:

COTTON BLOSSOM		OL' MAN RIVER	
Verse:	A	Verse:	A
	B		
	A	Refrain:	C'
			C''
Refrain:	C		B
	C		C'''

As if in conscious demonstration of their musical thinking, Kern and Hammerstein wrote a new song for the 1936 film to extend their musical anagrams. "I Still Suits Me" was a new duet for Joe and Queenie, the stevedore and his wife who works in the kitchen, tailored to the powerful Robeson presence and the comic muttering of Hattie McDaniel. The song is a careful musical anagram of the verse of "Can't Help Lovin' Dat Man," which also inverts the idea of that song. While "Can't Help Lovin' Dat Man" was a comic lament by the black women (Julie and Queenie) about male shiftlessness, "I Still Suits Me" provides the male response—no matter how lazy or slow I seem, my life makes sense to me. The song is as right for Joe, the comfortable pal of "Ol' Man River," as it is in response, musically and lyrically, to "Can't Help Lovin' Dat Man." Ironically (and Kern must have realized this little joke), "I Still Suits Me" is also a musical variation of Fats Waller's 1929 hit, "Ain't Misbehavin'," which Hammerstein's lyrics also echo. Such complexly playful word-music constructions reveal careful thinking about the way to translate social statements and character values into purely musical terms.

This tight weave between musical idea and narrative idea is Kern's contribution to the form of musical theater. Although later Kern work deepened the texture and complicated the structure of individual songs, he never surpassed the conceptual wholeness of *Show Boat*. His shows became increasingly retrospective, withdrawing from contemporary America to a conscious Operettaland. *Sweet Adeline* (1929) followed *Show Boat* back to the musical stage of nineteenth-century America but left its social and moral baggage behind. Both *The Cat and the Fiddle* (1931) and *Music in the Air* (1932) crossed the Atlantic to explore the making of operettas themselves. Kern had become nostalgic about the fading form and sound to which he had dedicated his life, now disappearing beneath the cacophonous waves of hot jazz and talking pictures.

Roberta, Kern's last major show, also traveled abroad—to a Paris fashion salon. It was consciously built on a cultural clash between graceful, Old World, classbound Europe and contemporary democratic America (personified by the jaunty Bob Hope in his first major role as bandleader Huckleberry Haines). Ladislas, a former prince, now fallen to mere doorman (or doormat) of the fashion emporium, was a virtual refugee from postrevolutionary Operettaland; Kern wrote several songs for Ladislas that yearned to return there. As in *Show Boat*, Kern weaves musical history into the musical itself, for Ladislas suggests a spent European tradition that can only be revivified by the energetic American pop music of a Huckleberry Haines. Kern also built musical history into *Roberta* with the casting of Fay Templeton, a star of American musicals since the 1880s of Kern's birth. Templeton became a virtual incarnation of nineteenth-century operetta on the twentieth-century musical stage. Known publicly and grandly as Madame Roberta, Templeton is actually plain Aunt Minnie from the U S of A, not so unlike Kern's own masquerade as an uppity English composer in his apprenticeship. Kern had become very self-conscious about building his musical bridges between Europe and America, old forms and new.

Like his theater scores from *Show Boat* to *Roberta*, Kern's many film scores, which occupied him in a decade of failing health, retreated to the long ago and far away. Very few were set in the here and now of contemporary America (*Swing Time* was a rare exception), preferring either the there of Europe and South America (*Roberta, Music in the Air, The Cat and the Fiddle, You Were Never Lovelier, One Night in the Tropics*) or the then of nineteenth-century America (*High, Wide and Handsome, Can't Help Singin', Centennial Summer*).[7] Even the contemporary *Cover Girl* flashed back to the nineteenty-century musical stage. Kern seemingly wrote more waltzes in Hollywood between 1935 and 1945 than in his entire career on Broadway. With "I'm Old Fashioned," Kern not only stated the sentiments of a film heroine but his own commitments as well.

Kern's genius was to be both old fashioned and new sounding at the same time. When he died in 1945, he, more than any other American composer, had built the bridge between American music and musicals of the nineteenth and twentieth centuries—between *Adonis*, the musical hit of 1884, one year before his birth, and *Swing Time* of 1935. Kern translated a tradition of musical narrative into a medium that could not even have been imagined in 1885. If one of Kern's most stirring songs asks "Why Was I Born?" in both the show and film of *Sweet Adeline*, one answer must be that Kern was born to write songs like that for shows and films like those. More than any other single figure, Kern brought nineteenth-century European musical grace, complexity, construction, and taste to twentieth-century American song, musical theater, and musical films.

George and Ira Gershwin in 1935

6

Pounding on Tin

GEORGE AND IRA GERSHWIN

If Irving Berlin suggests the composer as songwriting institution and Jerome Kern the composer as peerless craftsman, George Gershwin suggests the composer as archetypal myth. Combining Berlin's Jewish Lower East Side immigrant instincts with Kern's ambitious musical complexity, Gershwin's music seems a metaphor for democratic American creativity itself—the self-taught and self-made man not just as Commercial Success but as Revolutionary Artist. Alongside his success in the musical marketplaces of Broadway, Hollywood, and Tin Pan Alley are his achievements in those loftier realms of concert hall and opera house. No concert or operatic music by any other American composer is programmed, played, and sung so often by the world's most accomplished orchestras and soloists in its most respected opera houses and concert halls.

Born Jacob Gershvin in Brooklyn on September 26, 1898, George was two years younger than his brother Ira, born Israel Gershvin in lower Manhattan. The Gershvins had only recently shortened the family name from Gershovitz, and they would all adopt George's w two decades later. Because Ira seemed the serious student and George the hellion, the upwardly aspiring Gershvins bought a parlor piano to cultivate their older and apparently more friable son. Ira would never go near the thing (just as he would later drop out of the City College of New York). At the age of ten George amazed the entire clan when, without a lesson, he sat down one day to play sensational sounds. He had picked up the notes and fingering on the streets, watching street and saloon musicians, both white and black, pounding out tunes for fun and profit. George began his serious study of the piano in 1910 with Charles Hambitzer, his most influential teacher. Even after making the acquaintance of classical music and theory, he maintained his friendship with the sounds and rhythms of the new popular music he heard everywhere around him—published songs by Berlin and, his favorite, Kern; unpublished songs by still anonymous black ragtime pianists.

In 1914, not yet sixteen, Gershwin went to work at Remick's, the youngest song plugger ever to work on Tin Pan Alley. Gershwin's dexterity at the keyboard, his ability to augment tinkly tunes with driving syncopations, dazzling harmonic variations, and contrapuntal bass lines quickly became a legend on "the street." Young George knew he wanted out of song plugging and into songwriting (and show writing). He published his first song in 1916, memorable for the length of its title, if nothing else: "When You Want 'Em, You Can't Get 'Em; When You've Got 'Em, You Don't Want 'Em." The first Gershwin song gave its regards to a Broadway show the same year when "The Making of a Girl" was interpolated in an otherwise Sigmund Romberg score for *The Passing Show of 1916*.

Gershwin's influence on American music began with his first big hit, "Swanee," sung in a 1919 Broadway flop, *The Capitol Revue*, then carried by Al Jolson, who heard it and loved it, into *Sinbad* later that year. The driving energy and rhythms that young Gershwin used to plug the songs of others now plugged one of his own. "Swanee" hammered its way to popularity on the restless, churning drive of its verse, the similarly churning drive of measures three-four and nineteen-twenty (accompanying Irving Caesar's words, "How I love ya, how I love ya," and "Waitin' for ya, prayin' for ya") and the dazzling rhythmic surprise as this Type II song comes out of its B section and returns to the A motif (accompanying the surprising words, "D-I-X I Even"). This first Gershwin hit set the pattern for many that would follow: a clear, fixed musical pattern suddenly shattered by a startling surprise; words that rap the notes into the ears in the same way that hammers rap the piano's strings; and the underlying sense of perpetually seething, driving, restless energy—moving, moving, moving.

One adjective to describe Gershwin's spirit, music, and career is restless. His songs and orchestral scores alike suggest a restlessness in their driving rhythm. For Gershwin the piano was a percussion instrument before it was a keyboard instrument, and its insistent drive hammered out its resolve to get moving and keep moving, somewhere, anywhere. But there was a similar restlessness in his approach to life and art. He could never sit still, personally and professionally; even at the famed parties of the "Gershwin Circle," he spent the evening at the keyboard, plugging his own tunes incessantly and inexhaustibly the long night and morning through. This habit led to any number of barbs and stories. When he asked a friend if his music would be played a hundred years hence, the friend answered: "It will—if you're there to play it, George." And in 1933 Cole Porter's *Nymph Errant* promised a very special party: George Gershwin would *not* play the piano.

In the same way that he pushed his restless energy into a piano's keys, he pushed his artistic aspirations toward ever-increasing challenges of form and complexity, both musical and theatrical. At the time of his death, Gershwin was pushing himself toward an entirely new artistic challenge, devoting more time to painting canvases than composing scores. No sooner had he hurdled one obstacle than he searched for another.

His brother Ira, in addition to providing the perfect word sounds to punctuate and accentuate George's music sounds, also provided some emotional ballast to anchor George's compulsive restlessness. George's driving piano may have kept the "Gershwin Circle" spinning, but Ira was the affable social force at its center—a genial, casual elf who would rather play cards, play the horses, play word games, play with his cigars, play anything to avoid work. He was able to write only by turning his work into play, and no other American lyricist was ever so insistently and consistently playful as Ira Gershwin—toying with the sounds of slang, fracturing spellings and pronunciations, punning with off-rhymes and eye-rhymes, banging on words as percussive sounds just as George banged on the piano's keys as percussive hammers.

For a sample, here are two juicy Iraisms: a single line from the parodic "Song of the Supreme Court Judges" (*Of Thee I Sing*, 1931) and a single line from the equally delicious parody, "By Strauss" (originally from the 1936 *The Show Is On*, but most familiar from the 1951 *An American in Paris*). As the Supreme Court justices introduce themselves and their official functions to the audience, they inform us:

We're the AKs who give the OKs.

The punch of the line comes from the rhyming and rhythmic interplay of the slangy abbreviations, AK and OK, but there aren't many people (at least outside New York) who could tell you the meaning of the initials, AK. Although the precise etymology of the initials OK is still a mystery, the sense of their combination is perfectly comprehensible. The initials AK, however, are Yiddish slang, a colloquial abbreviation of *alter kocker,* meaning "old shit." It is as amusing a way for Supreme Court justices to describe themselves as it is unlikely that they would even know such a term. Ira's manipulation of this outrageous pun, based on parallel slang initials from two different languages, not only reveals his own vocabulary as a linguistic melting pot but American slang itself (especially in show business, where Yiddish is argot for Jews and non-Jews alike) as a flavorful linguistic stew.

Equally playful is "By Strauss," its very title a punning reference both to a composer and to a euphemistic expletive, like "by golly." In this deliberate parody of a Strauss waltz, the singer disparages the dissonant noise of modern popular music—including Gershwin's, whose sound Ira describes as "pounding on tin." He longs for the sweet strains of the Viennese master and exhorts the modern noise to disappear in another linking of apparently unlinkable linguistic categories:

So I say to ha-cha-cha, *heraus!*

How can you possibly construct a coherent clause by joining a term of onomatopoetic American slang (ha-cha-cha) to a German command that rhymes with Strauss? Ira Gershwin not only yokes them into a coherent statement, consistent with the song's preference for old German culture to contemporary American argot, but even makes the incompatible words alliterate, their commonly aspirated "h" aiding the conversion of linguistic absurdity into thematic consistency.

This playfulness made the Gershwins the first great American writers of song parodies, songs that, like "By Strauss," parodied another type or style of song but demonstrated a musical integrity in their own right. "Just Another Rhumba" (1937) parodied the plague of Latin-American dances; one of Ira's rhymes for "rhumba," not the easiest of words to rhyme, is the singer's confession that the exotic rhythm has been a torment since "last Septumbah." The lovely ballad, "Isn't It a Pity?" from *Pardon My English* (1932) evokes the genteel sophistication of the Noël Coward sort of English love song. What kind of title is "Isn't It a Pity?" for a love song? And what other ballad includes references to Heine (rhymed with China) and Schopenhauer (rhymed appropriately with sour). "Sam and Delilah," from *Girl Crazy* (1930) parodies the he-done-her-wrong frontier song (like "Frankie and Johnny"), turning biblical legend into a frontier folktale of a floozie who fell fer a swell buckeroo by the same of Sam. "Blah Blah Blah," from the film *Delicious* (1931), parodies the clichés of sappy love songs with George's treacly tune and Ira's refusal to write any coherent words, except the hackneyed rhymes to conclude every line—"blah blah blah blah moon, blah blah blah blah June." The Gershwin flair for parody would culminate in *Of Thee I Sing*, whose entire score is an unbroken succession of musical parodies.

One of Ira's great contributions to George's music was this sense of play, the ability to juggle word sounds as energetically and innovatively as his brother juggled music sounds, to create what Alec Wilder called the thoroughly "cheery" ambience of a Gershwin song. Another was his sympathetic hearing and understanding of precisely what brother George was doing in a particular song. Ira would design a lyric to showcase that musical structure and idea. The Gershwin songs were generally quite simple, far simpler than the lengthy lines of a Kern song. But George used this simplicity as a familiar ground to set off some surprising, unexpected figure. The kick of many Gershwin songs can be traced to the one tiny twist that violates and vivifies the entire musical pattern. Brother Ira's lyric made sure that the little surprise would be both heard and felt as a wonderful surprise.

This Gershwin style—the simple song ruptured by the odd surprise—can be attributed not only to the teamwork of the two brothers but also to their decisive early collaboration with Fred Astaire. George and Fred met when both were still in their teens. George substituted for the regular pianist during rehearsals for Astaire's first Broadway show, *The Passing Show of 1919*. Astaire remembers them sitting side by side, amusing each other at the keyboard. The two teenagers on the brink of stardom vowed they would one day do a show together. They actually did two shows and two films together, Astaire's biggest early hits among them. Although Astaire's singing range was narrow, little more than an octave, he was able to execute complicated melodic and rhythmic changes with great precision, rapping the word notes percussively into the ear just as he rapped those rhythm sounds into the floor with his taps. Kern, Porter, Berlin, and Gershwin all agreed that Astaire was America's greatest male singer of theater music. Astaire would introduce, popularize, and make his own more of their songs than any other singer in the history of American musical theater and film. Only Ethel Merman comes close.

A clear example of the Gershwin-Astaire collaboration is "My One and Only," from the 1927 *Funny Face*. The refrains of this AABA song are very simple, except for a massive intrusion in measures three and four of every A section. While the first two measures of each A section sustain just five notes (to state the title or some rhyme for it), and the final four measures of each A section just eight notes, measures three-four pack in as many as twelve, a rattling, percussive barrage of rushing sounds. Ira's lyric is almost impossible to sing at this tempo ("What 'm I gonna do if you turn me down?" "There isn't a reason why you should turn me down"), turning articulate words into noisy clattering. Astaire makes perfect percussive sense of these word notes by converting them into something less like singing than tapping; the onomatopeia of the two measures transmutes words into taps. Astaire's London cast recording of *Funny Face*, with Gershwin himself at the piano, shows how conscious they were of this percussive game.[1] Astaire literally converts those measures into tap dancing in the second chorus, not singing measures three-four but tapping them on the studio floor. He sings the first five notes, taps the next twelve, then sings the final eight of every A section. Word notes and tap sounds are interchangeable.

A favorite Gershwin technique was the insistently repeated note, hammering the urgency and energy of a song at the listener. The "taps" in measure three of "My One and Only" begin with six identical notes. In "Embraceable You" (*Girl Crazy*) ten identical notes near the end of the verse drive the lyric, "listen to the music of my heartbeat," with the urgent rush of the singer's appeal. Eight repeated notes at the end of the release, accompanying, "Come to papa, come to papa," parallel the urgent appeal that concludes the verse. Ira ends this appeal with "do," a broad, open sound on a sustained whole note, a third higher than the repeated note, as if the singer has breathlessly rushed over his appeal, then caught his breath to underline it emphatically. The lovely verse of "But Not for Me" (*Girl Crazy*) begins with five repeated notes. So does the familiar refrain of "They Can't Take That Away from Me" (from the 1937 film, *Shall We Dance?*).

Many Gershwin surprises are rhythmic, springing some unexpected syncopation on a firmly established pattern. Like Irving Berlin, Gershwin varied sustained and syncopated phrases; while Berlin built rhythmic shifts into complete four- and eight-measure phrases, Gershwin springs surprises in one- and two-measure jabs. Take the Gershwins' first (and best) song about rhythm itself, "Fascinating Rhythm," from *Lady, Be Good!* (1924). In the verse of the song, the singers (originally Fred and Adele Astaire) confess to being possessed by a persistent rhythm that "pit-a-pats in my brain." The verse lays down a strict metronomic beat to mirror this persistence: for the first sixteen measures, the initial note falls squarely on the downbeat. But the final four bars of the verse, its "vest," reverses the rhythmic pattern (Ira called it the vest because its four scanty measures enclose the verse's sixteen-bar body). The first note misses the downbeat and catches the upbeat in measures seventeen, eighteen, and nineteen.

The refrain permutes this pattern of rhythmic expectation. In the first two measures, the opening of each musical and verbal phrase falls squarely on the downbeat. But something odd happens at the end of the second measure: the third musical-verbal phrase, a return to the title, begins on the upbeat of the second measure and sustains through the upbeat of the third measure.

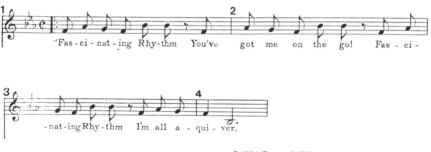

Ira's alliterative "g" ("Got me on the go") emphasizes the regular downbeat immediately preceding the rhythmic surprise, when the single "Fascinating" sustains itself over the boundary between measures two and three. The downbeat falls in the third measure without any new word to announce it—a downbeat both felt and missed. This tiny trick provides the fascination of this fascinating rhythm, both for the singer, possessed by it, and the listener, who soon will be.

Then this Type II song's B section executes yet another rhythmic variation on the pattern.

Each morn-ing I get up — with the sun, (Start a hop-ping nev-er stop-ping) To find at night, no work— has been done. I know that

The ninth and thirteenth measures begin not on the downbeat but on the upbeat after a quarter rest; the eleventh and fifteenth measures contain a single sustained note, which sets off two different surprises in the twelfth and sixteenth measures. The twelfth contains eight notes, a musical hopping that parallels the hopping in its never stopping statement and clattering consonants. The surprise of the sixteenth measure is its beginning with a quarter rest, followed by three pickup notes that allow the song to return to its main statement in the seventeenth measure directly on the downbeat. The result of this playful trickery is a rhythmically complex song about rhythmic complexity, a song about rhythmic fascination that is fascinating because its rhythms can never be predicted or taken for granted.[2]

An even more familiar Gershwin rhythm song about rhythm is "I Got Rhythm" from *Girl Crazy*. In this song, rhythm becomes not a torment but a philosophy of meaningful existence: if you got rhythm, you don't need anything more (including grammar). The rhythm secret of the song is that measures one, three, and five of every refrain begin on the upbeat, distributing just four notes over each of the two-measure phrases. But the seventh measure leaps at us ferociously on the downbeat with an aggressive aspiration, "Who," followed by seven rushing word notes, "could ask for anything more?" rattling along speedily behind it. Another clever strategy of this ungrammatical rhythm song is that it is unrhymed: its words become pure jabs of rhythmic punctuation. The only suggestion of rhyme is that all three A sections of the refrain end with the identical "more;" the real rhymes sneak into the release: "mind him" with "find him" and "door" to rhyme with all those repetitions of "more." Many songs for *Porgy and Bess* would similarly shun rhymes to depict the sincere feelings of simpler folk.

A sure sign of Gershwin consciousness is the use of the identical question, "Who could ask for anything more?" in two later songs: the parodic waltz, "I'm About to Be a Mother" from *Of Thee I Sing*, and "Nice Work If You Can Get It" from the 1937 film of *A Damsel in Distress*. Like "I Got Rhythm," "Nice Work" defines a simple but meaningful life. The rhetorical question, "Who could ask for anything more?" closes the release, the obverse of "I Got Rhythm," in which it closes every refrain. As if to emphasize the companionship of the two songs, Ira uses the same rhyme of "more" with "door." These two songs are so similar in structure (AABA), theme (the simple life), and rhyme that their two releases are literally interchangeable. (Try a little experiment: hum or whistle the refrain of "I Got Rhythm" and then insert the release of "Nice Work;" then hum or whistle the refrain of "Nice Work" and insert the release of "Rhythm"; both results are perfectly coherent.)

For just one more example of the clever variation the Gershwin brothers construct on their own material consider "I Got Plenty of Nothin'" from *Porgy and Bess*, yet another song about the simple but meaningful life. Its ungrammatical title phrase recalls "I Got Rhythm" as does its spare rhyme scheme. Although the song avoids the "Who could ask" question, it does sneak the most memorable rhyme of its companion songs into the refrain—"door" and "more." Ira coins a wry aesthetic law: in a song about having a lot because you got a little, you gotta rhyme more and door.

The partiality to blue notes is another familiar Gershwin trademark. The blue note arrives unexpectedly in a Gershwin song, rupturing a simple melodic pattern, usually at the very end of a musical phrase. It owes its power to this climactic strength. After wandering either up or down the scale in fairly predictable steps, the Gershwin phrase comes to a halt on an unexpected flatted note that, paradoxically, cannot resolve that phrase but does by switching the key signature from major to minor. The opening phrase of "I'll Build a Stairway to Paradise," from *George White's Scandals of 1922*, climbs into the ear with its blue note on the word "day," after both the music and the lyric (by Ira and B. G. DeSylva) have dutifully climbed a series of steps to pause for breath on a "blue" landing. The opening refrain of "Somebody Loves Me" (for the *Scandals* of 1924) leaps at the listener by returning to an identical blue note for every repetition of "who?"

The longing and loneliness of "The Man I Love" (1924)[3] float on its blue notes at the ends of musical phrases. Written at the same time as the "Rhapsody in Blue," the song translates orchestral blueness into vocal ballad. But it balances the singer's blues with the rhythmic variations that propel the jollier Gershwin rhythm songs. The first six measures of every refrain begin on the upbeat after a quarter rest, but the seventh begins assertively on the downbeat with the singer's vow to "make him stay." The rhythmic pattern of the refrain mirrors its psychological structure: the singer is searching for something she lacks (the six measures beginning with the rest) but when she finds it she'll certainly know what to do about it (the seventh and eighth measures of three emphatically sustained half notes). This rhythmic play keeps a Gershwin love song from ever becoming very sad or sticky: never as melancholy as a Kern ballad, never approaching the desolation of a Rodgers and Hart ballad. Even after falling out of love forever, as in "But Not for Me" (*Girl Crazy*), the singer can draw an ironic comparison between her skies of gray and a Russian play, she can rhyme "dismiss" with "his kiss," and (in the second chorus) offer an outrageous pun (for a sorrowful love ballad):

> When every happy plot
> Ends with a marriage knot—
> But there's no knot for me.

Some Gershwin songs seem so simple that they evoke the style of nursery songs. Many of them were written for Adele Astaire—with her reedy babyish voice and her impishly babyish persona. The best of her "baby songs" is "'S Wonderful" (*Funny Face*). This song's most obvious melodic trait is its descending three-note phrases, DUM-dum-dum (accent on the first note), both in its refrain and its release. Rather than pin proper three-syllable words on these three dums, or compound three-syllable assemblages of shorter words, Ira contracted five syllable phrases into a three-syllable nonsense word by eliding the initial "s" into the syllable that followed it. The delight of the lyric comes from contracting grammatical English, "It is wonderful," into jazz-baby slang, "swonderful." The contraction begins even in the song's verse. Ira begins his linguistic assault by chopping a syllable off the ends of words: fashion becomes "fash," passion become "pash," emotion becomes "emosh," devotion becomes "devosh." Its vest ends the verse with a terrific bit of word play: Ira's rhyme for "blah," the slangy description of the way all other boys make her feel, becomes "Just you alone fill me with Ah!" The final syllable is a sigh of emotion, an expressive sound rather than the anticipated noun.

Then the refrain sets about its business of contracting the beginnings of words and phrases, not their endings as the verse did: 'Swonderful, 'Sawful nice, 'Swhat I long to see. The most playful contractions produce the most cacophonous clash of consonants—'Smarvelous, 'Sparadise. For a reprise of the song, in reference to a doctor's fee, Ira concocts 'Sniquitous (It's iniquitous), and for *An American in Paris* he could extend the pun into French: 'Sexecptionelle (rhymed both with 'Swhy I fell and 'Sno bagatelle). The "S" stands as easily for the French "c'est" as the English "it's," which are both contractions in the first place. The three-syllable word game gets a twist in the release when George's music swells more feelingly and Ira opens up to full-throated, broad-voweled three-syllable words—glamorous and amorous.

A slightly earlier baby-talk song was built on the word, baby—"Do Do Do" for *Oh, Kay!*. Although not written for Adele Astaire, it sounds as if it might have been. Built on three-note phrases like "'S Wonderful," those ever popular dum-dum-dums, "Do Do Do" stresses them equally.

> Do do do
> What you done done done
> Before, baby.

Rather than creating a whimsical slang, Ira emphasizes the thumping childishness of George's tune and rhythm with heavy alliteration of the hard sounds, "d" and "b," and repetitive monosyllables (do do do, done done done, don't don't don't, won't won't won't). Ira tips his hand in the release:

> Baby, see,
> It's A B C
> That I love you and you love me.

It would be perfectly infantile were it not for the spectacular triple-rhyming of two English words with the first three letters of the alphabet—driven by George's follow-the-bouncing-ball tune, five-finger exercising up and down the scales, as if it too were practicing its ABCs or do re mis.

A final baby song, based on children's lessons and written for the voice of Adele Astaire, is "He Loves and She Loves" (*Funny Face*). More complicated than the dum dum dums of "'S Wonderful" or "Do Do Do," this song plays two musical patterns against one another. Built on steadily descending phrases (a favorite Gershwin progression), the melody leaps up repeatedly to a recurrent top note, even as its progressions descend. The general effect suggests the child's game of descending a flight of steps but hopping back to the top step, only to continue the descent again. Ira's lyric emphasizes this musical pattern by returning to the identical word, "love" (or some declension of it), every time George's musical line returns to its identical top note. But Ira's lyric makes the song especially schoolkiddish by basing its repetitions on the conjugation of the verb, "to love"—he loves, she loves, they love, you love, and I love too—an English version of the most basic Latin textbook exercise: *amo, amas, amat*.

Most of the memorable Gershwin songs were written for a series of book musicals, from *Lady, Be Good!* in 1924 to *Girl Crazy* in 1930. The early Gershwin musicals cheerily adopted the conventions and assumptions of contemporary "smart shows," spiritual, even literal, descendants of the Princess Theater. Guy Bolton and P. G. Wodehouse, who wrote the Princess shows with Kern, wrote the books for the Gershwins. The Gershwins also echoed the Princess in their titles—*Lady, Be Good!* borrowed an exclamation point from *Oh, Lady! Lady!!*; *Oh, Kay!* the slang of *Oh, Boy!* These were bright, breezy modern shows with topical themes (like bootlegging) and topical settings (from a Long Island mansion to the Wild West), small casts, amiable jokes, flippant themes, Astaire dancing, and songs songs songs.

But the same restless energy that led Gershwin to Aeolian Hall and his attack on the boundary between serious concert music and popular jazz, led him to push against the presumed limits of musical theater. In 1922 Gershwin wrote "Blue Monday," a one-act folk opera (with B. G. De Sylva) based on black American life. Too demanding a piece for the frivolous *Scandals*, it was performed only once (but later revived as *135th Street*). Late in the decade, the Gershwins collaborated on several versions of *Strike Up the Band*, their first wedding of political satire to musical comedy. The middle period of Gershwin work, from 1931 to 1935, grew from these two radical conceptions of musical-theater possibility: the parodic pseudo-operetta, *Of Thee I Sing*, and the "folk opera," *Porgy and Bess*.

However different in musical color, the later opera grows directly from the earlier mock-operetta. Neither could be described as a series of dialogue scenes punctuated by individual songs. Songs overflow their thirty-two-bar banks on a flood of codas, recurring leitmotifs, recitatives, and interwoven reprises. There is no sense that songs have been slotted into scenes: whole scenes are built of complexly interwoven musical passages. Although *Show Boat* committed itself to thematic seriousness before these Gershwin shows, it did so within the familiar conventions of the ruling operetta. *Of Thee I Sing* and *Porgy and Bess* reveal more thoroughly systematic thinking about the conventions and form of musical theater than any previous American musical.

Of Thee I sing (1931) was the first American musical to win the Pulitzer Prize for drama (*South Pacific* came next). A surprising and controversial choice in the same year as O'Neill's *Strange Interlude*, the only creative collaborator not cited by the Pulitzer Committee was merely George Gershwin himself. It was apparently unclear whether a composer contributed to a "drama." *Of Thee I Sing* was also the first American musical to be published as a book, as dramatic literature, with an explanatory preface by that intellectual ogre, the critic George Jean Nathan. These two facts alone indicate both its extraordinary departure as a conception for musical theater and its extraordinary success.

Of Thee I Sing is a *reductio ad absurdum*, the reduction of American politics and government to the absolutely trivial and hopelessly absurd. In spirit it resembles the burlesque and trivialization of government and diplomacy in the 1933 Marx Brothers movie, *Duck Soup*, which was very much fashioned in the image of *Of Thee I Sing* (especially its final twenty musicalized minutes). *Of Thee I Sing* also sang of the customary intellectual level of musical shows by trivializing weighty matters of state into the frothy stuff of musical comedy. It translated the self-conscious theatrical parody of Gilbert and Sullivan operettas into the native terms of American culture, American vernacular speech, American popular music, and American musical comedy.

For those unfamiliar with this infrequently revived show, a plot summary will indicate its clever and conscious self-parody. An American political party (name unspecified but Democratic implied) searches for some slogan to sell its presidential candidate, John P. Wintergreen (originally played by William Gaxton), to the American public. They conduct an informal political poll, asking the cleaning lady, tidying up their smoke-filled room, what is most important to her in all the world. Her immediate answer is money. Only after some prodding does she confess that the second most important thing in the world is love. Adopting "Love" as their campaign slogan, the pols stage a beauty contest in Atlantic City; its winner will become First Lady of the Land by wedding Wintergreen on Inauguration Day—*if* he wins the election. But Wintergreen himself falls in love, not with the winner of the pageant—Miss Diana Devereaux, the loveliest flower of all the Southland—but with Mary Turner, a mere official at the pageant, who bakes the most delicious corn muffins Wintergreen has ever tasted. The presidential campaign becomes a national soap opera, "John Loves Mary," in which Wintergreen proposes to Mary at every campaign rally and Mary agrees to accept him if the voters make John their presidential choice. Only by electing him president can true love be served. The election is a landslide victory for "Love," and the first act ends on the steps of the Capitol where John is simultaneously sworn in as president and married to Mary.

The Romantic Road gets rocky in the second act when Diana Devereaux, enraged because she has been jilted, provokes an international crisis. Diana, it turns out, is the illegitimate daughter of an illegitimate son of an illegitimate nephew of Napoleon. Just as the Senate is about to impeach Wintergreen for insulting France by dumping Diana, Mary bursts into the Senate chamber to announce she is pregnant. The Senate cannot impeach a presidential papa, for "Posterity is Just Around the Corner," a delicious musical mockery of Hoover's own political slogan. The international incident is resolved by marrying Diana off to Vice-President Alexander Throttlebottom (originally played by Victor Moore), the first practical use ever discovered for a vice-president. The triumph of the Wintergreen presidency is celebrated in the show's finale with the birth of twins—after the Supreme Court has duly decided on the constitutional gender of each infant.

Virtually every song in the show is a parody of some kind of song from some other kind of show. The title song is a clear indication. Although its music (a march) and title phrase (a quotation from "America") suggest the martial anthem and patriotic hymn, it is really a love song. In Ira's initial line of lyrics, "Of thee I sing, baby," the final word of colloquial affection undercuts the archaic patriotic diction of the preceding phrase. The remaining words of the song connect a string of banal platitudes lifted from other love songs: "You're my silver lining" (a reference to Kern's "Look for the Silver

Lining"), "You're my sky of blue" (a reference to Berlin's "Blue Skies"), and so forth.

One musical parody bounces gleefully after another in this score conceived as total parody. "Wintergreen for President," the campaign marching song (almost every march Gershwin ever wrote is in this score), has no lyrics at all except for the endless repetitions of the title and a few rag-tags and bob-ends of political clichés:

> He's the man the people choose.
> Loves the Irish and the Jews.

Ira has translated the romantic clichés of "Blah Blah Blah" into their political kindred. George weaves references to the musical clichés of political rallies into the song as well, including "Hail, Hail, the Gang's All Here" and "There'll Be a Hot Time in the Old Town Tonight." Wintergreen's ballad, "Some Girls Can Bake a Pie," defending his love for Mary and her muffins, is a sappy and lyrical love tune adorned with deliberately unlovely and unromantic references to foods—quinces, blintzes, turkey stuffin's (gotta find a rhyme for muffins). Diana Devereaux, angrily interjects, in vocal recitative, "Who cares about corn muffins? All I demand is justice." Forced to rule on Diana's question, the AKs of the Supreme Court decide for corn muffins rather than justice.

Diana Devereaux's song of sorrow is a parodic waltz, "Jilted," (almost every Gershwin waltz is in this score too); it refers to other torchy songs of the same type:

> Just like in the "Frankie and Johnny" song,
> He done me wrong, he done me wrong.

The French diplomatic corps sing a jaunty parody of a French music hall strut, accompanied by nonsense jumbles of French and pseudo-French words:

> Garçon, s'il vous plait,
> Encore Chevrolet coupé.

The French Ambassador's song, asserting Diana's relationship to Napoleon, is yet another march, this time a deliberate parody of "La Marseillaise." What rhyme could Ira possibly find for "Napoleon?" The Frenchman declares that America is a land "where nought is sacred but the old simoleon." The finale of jubilation, "Oh, Trumpeter Blow Your Golden Horn," is a parody of both martial music and the heavenly trumpet of Gabriel, braided with parodies-within-the-parody: "The Farmer in the Dell" (for the secretary of agriculture), a sea chanty (for the secretary of the navy), and a way-out-on-the-lone-prairie ballad (for the secretary of the interior). The score and show conclude with a rousing but irrelevant reprise of the title song, which exuberantly confirms the evening's absolute nonsense.

Very few of the show's songs could ever be or have ever been removed from their theatrical context to become popular hits. The title song is an exception, always performed rhythmically as a swing song rather than a march, diverting the listener's attention from its nonsense lyrics. The parodic love song, "Who Cares?" is another, despite its unromantic topical references to such subjects as bank failure in Yonkers (to rhyme with "kiss that conquers"). Most of the show's "songs" are lengthy musical passages, woven from several song structures. The final scenes of both acts one and two are totally musicalized, over ten minutes of dramatic action either fully sung or rhythmically recited to musical underscoring.

Another of the show's delights was its joyfully iconoclastic and jocularly cynical book by George S. Kaufman and Morrie Ryskind, the pair who would write *A Night at the Opera* for the Marx Brothers. Imbued with the same hard-bitten, witty energy that marks nonmusical plays of the same period by Ben Hecht and Charles MacArthur or by George S. Kaufman and whomever, the characters in this world are tough-talking, hard-drinking conmen of sharp head and tongue but no heart, scruple, or sentiment whatever. If they have any virtue, it is a refusal to lie to themselves about their patently selfish motives. Typical of these cynical Prohibition-era plays, absolutely everyone in public positions of power and responsibility drinks openly and frequently—including Wintergreen, the president of the Republic.

Like so many of the best musicals, *Of Thee I Sing* also displays dazzling innovations in staging and stagecraft. At a political rally in Madison Square Garden, political speeches share the arena with a scheduled wrestling match. As the orator soars on the wings of purple prose—"not for us the entangling alliances of Europe, not for us the allying entanglances of Asia"—the two wrestlers become entangled and allied in grotesquely contorted positions that comment on the turns and twists of rhetorical flight. The show also projects the longest and funniest piece of film footage ever seen in a stage work—a brilliant parody of a movie newsreel to chronicle Wintergreen's landslide victory. The theater audience reads such election returns on the screen as:

New York, N.Y.
    126 election districts report:
        WINTERGREEN 72,639
        BRYAN.. 128
        Absent 4
        Late.. 2
                and

Of Thee I Sing: the parodic yoking of opposites: A combination wrestling match and political rally at Madison Square Garden; the combined president's desk and first lady's vanity table. (June O'Dea, Lois Moran, William Gaxton, and George Murphy)

Hollywood, Cal.
     WINTERGREEN 160,000
     MICKEY MOUSE... 159,000
     GLORIA SWANSON'S FIRST HUSBAND............ 84,638

There are newsreel shots of Wintergreen, casting at least a half-dozen votes
for himself, and of the vice-presidential candidate, Throttlebottom, identi-
fied as "an unidentified man." At the newsreel's conclusion, there is a "flash
of the Metro-Goldwyn-Mayer lion. It opens its mouth. It crows."[4] The
whole show crows and cooks from start to finish.

How did this playful trivialization of serious issues please audiences in
the darkest early years of the Great Depression? The play's parodic premise
is pointedly political: the economy, the government, the political system,
and the whole wide world are one big mess. The script refers explicitly to
Mussolini, European war debts, governmental corruption, political patronage, and economic mismanagement—not to mention Prohibition as the
ultimate metaphor for governmental folly. In the face of such pervasive and
seemingly ineradicable social ills, the act of laughter seemed a mark of
sanity. *Of Thee I Sing* is a clear indication that a certain broad segment of the
American population viewed the political chicanery and moral hypocrisy
around them with hard heads rather than soft hearts, with sly suspicion
rather than uplifting commitment. The election of Franklin D. Roosevelt
and the end of Prohibition, hopeful signs for many of these cynical wits,
was a year away; and the election of Adolf Hitler, just as terrifying a sign
for these same wits, many of them Jewish, was a year beyond that.

These changes in political climate partially explain the failure of the
Gershwin-Kaufman-Ryskind sequel, *Let 'Em Eat Cake* (1933), in which John
and Mary are deposed by a Fascist revolution. Totalitarian movements were
not a very risible subject in the same year as Hitler's rise in Germany. Like
most sequels, *Let 'Em Eat Cake* lacked the original's energetic joy—merrily
baking a whole new theatrical pie while mixing the musical and parodic
condiments to fill it. The real formal evolution for the Gershwins would
not be yet another political parody but *Porgy and Bess*, not so much a new
form as a new tone—a shift from musical and political pastiche to the
musical depiction of personal and social morality. *Porgy and Bess* laid serious
dramatic and musical material over the formal blueprint of *Of Thee I Sing*.
As in *Of Thee I Sing*, whole scenes and dramatic segments were constructed
entirely from interwoven musical motifs and structures—scenes of daily life
in the black tenement of Catfish Row, of sorrow in the house of mourning,
of sexual ecstasy on Kittiwah Island.

Porgy and Bess straddles "musical" and "opera" in important and healthy
ways. Originally produced as a musical show in a Broadway house, not an
opera house, it was staged by Rouben Mamoulian, noted for directing both
stage and film musicals (from Paramount's *Applause* in 1929 to the original

Broadway production of *Oklahoma!* in 1943). Its cast shunned trained opera singers for a mix of talented black amateurs (like Todd Duncan as Porgy) and skilled black showmen (like the Harlem hoofer, John W. Bubbles, as Sportin' Life). The Gershwins paid for their daring to create a 1935 piece of musical theater, neither Broadway fish nor opera fowl; to its first audiences *Porgy and Bess* seemed too heavy for one and too raw for the other. But its eventual popularity and esteem also arise from the theatrical and musical fact that *Porgy* is neither an opera nor a musical but a vital meeting of both, rising to the emotional heights of operatic power with its feet firmly planted in the rich soil of American music and musicals.

Some social objection might be heard today to the show as one more chapter in a long racist tradition of American minstrel shows and "coon songs": the manipulation of stereotypic black characters and stereotyped depictions of black life by white artists for the profit of white producers and the amusement of white audiences. The roots of *Porgy and Bess* can indeed be traced from minstrels to "coon shows" to *Show Boat*. It plays on white audience beliefs that, generally speaking, blacks are more shiftless, less educated, more sexual, less dependable, more primitive, less sober than whites. But then "grand" opera has always relied on characters, of whatever race or clime, who were more passionate and less reasonable, more extreme and less temperate in their behavior than the average lot of ordinary citizens.

If *Porgy and Bess* is a late chapter in a racist theatrical tradition it is also an early chapter in something else. The affection and admiration of its white composer for the black musical sound and style in which he was working (and in which he had always worked) were undeniable. The Gershwins called the piece a "folk opera," not in reference to folk music (of which it has none) but to folk art—an art "of the people," as Gershwin believed his own art to be. He acknowledges his personal debt to the art of the streets, to the black rags and jazz that he heard as a boy on the sidewalks of New York. He spent months of research on the islands off the Carolina coast, steeping himself in the traditional black rhythms, harmonies, and vocal sounds around him. The play's black point-of-view is evident in the treatment of its few white characters, the policemen and other white figures of authority, whose laws, values, and activities are not only unsympathetic to the black world of Catfish Row but irrelevant to it. The white characters in this "folk opera" speak but do not sing; they are not the opera's "folk."

Another fact of black social history must be acknowledged about *Porgy and Bess*. When it appeared in 1935, there was no such thing as a black opera singer or serious vocalist (with the unique exception of Paul Robeson). Black opera was an oxymoron: there were no blacks in the world of Mozart, Wagner, Rossini, and Verdi (*Otello* excepted, always sung by a white in blackface). Gershwin explicitly restricted performance of *Porgy and Bess* to black singers, a condition the Gershwin estate has respected since his death.

The first black American woman to sing at La Scala, Leontyne Price, traveled there on the 1952 world tour of *Porgy and Bess*. Since then, the road for blacks to the international opera stage and concert hall has traveled through *Porgy and Bess*. For George Gershwin that would have been reason and satisfaction enough to have written it.

Most of the musical numbers in *Porgy and Bess*, are, like those in *Of Thee I Sing*, thirty-two-bar American popular songs that have been so complexly interwoven, padded with codas, preceded by recitatives, linked by musical bridges, that the boundaries of the thirty-two-bar song fade and blur. A clear example is one of *Porgy's* most haunting melodies, "My Man's Gone Now," Serena's lament for her slain husband. This is an eighty-bar musical structure (including rests and repeats) that might be diagrammed: AXAXBB'YX'AB"X". It would be a perfect thirty-two-bar AABA song were it not for the interspersed interruptions, X and Y, of five to eight bars each, and the doubling of the release. The interruptions are without articulate lyrics, except for the Y section, which repeats the final words of the B section as a litany. They represent passages of unverbalized wailing, of keening, for the mate who is gone forever. Emotionally, the song suggests that the woman's articulate ability to verbalize her grief (in the A and B sections) breaks down altogether (in the X and Y sections), giving way to groans of inarticulate mourning. Musically, the sections of chanting permit the song (and the singer) to rise to heights of emotion and demonstrations of virtuosity that would be impossible within the confines of the thirty-two-bar song, anchored to the process of reason by articulate words and to the rule of logic by the AABA structure. This is a song that overflows its banks, and the result is a flood of intense musical emotion that no other Gershwin piece ever attained.

The rhyming pattern of this song, and every other in *Porgy and Bess*, also contributes to its emotional power. Co-lyricists Ira Gershwin and DuBose Heyward (who wrote the novel and play on which the opera is based) suppress any tendencies toward clever, catchy rhymes. The only rhymes in "My Man's Gone Now" accompany the final word of each A section (even more distanced by the chanted X sections). The occasional rhyme fixes the song's structure for the listener without sacrificing Serena's spontaneous expression of grief. A character who feels such grief totally lacks the self-conscious intellection implied by tricky rhymes. "I Loves You Porgy" also confines its rhyming to the ends of refrains ("mad" with "glad"), with no rhymes at all in the release. Only "It Ain't Necessarily So" concocts clever rhymes for its mock sermon—"liable" with "Bible," "gospel" with "poss'ble," "home in" with "abdomen." Sung by the self-consciously manipulative Sportin' Life, he spins his sophistical web with sophisticated rhymes. Even patterns of rhyme define character.

So do the structures of songs. "Summertime" adopts a radically simplified and shortened song structure: two sixteen-bar refrains, AA', similar to songs written generations earlier, just before the Civil War, in the era of slavery and the spiritual. Its only rhymes close each eight-bar section— "high," "cry," "sky," and "cry" again—a simple, repetitive pattern that suggests the spontaneity of the singer's lullaby, singing her child to sleep, making up the words as she goes along, more like humming than the singing of premeditated lyrics. And "Summertime" has no verse. The Gershwins, who had denied their obligation to obligatory verses in *Of Thee I Sing*, banished them almost entirely from *Porgy and Bess*. The exceptions are songs in which verse joins refrain in an inseparable musical compound (for example, "A Woman is a Sometime Thing"), another common form in the Stephen Foster era of American song. By 1935 the verse of the American popular song, heavily influenced by these same Gershwins, had evolved into a complexly detached musical and verbal commentary—far too self-consciously bemused for the citizens of Catfish Row. For the sake of dramatic unity and character consistency, the Gershwins renounce their dexterity with both rhymes and verses. Although less consciously a self-contained history of the musical than *Show Boat*, *Porgy and Bess* contains its own history of American song forms.

Both the musical and theatrical inventions of *Porgy and Bess* would fix the future of American musical theater and film. Musically, the two major trends in theater songs after *Porgy* were toward elimination of the verse (not all verses to be sure, but the verse was no longer obligatory) and toward writing longer and more complicated refrains that broke the basic thirty-two-bar law of song structure. Dramatically, *Porgy and Bess*, following the lead of *Show Boat* but building with absolute consistency on its example, defined a song or musical passage as a highly particularized expression of just that character just then just there. No American piece of musical theater had adhered so ruthlessly to this principle before *Porgy and Bess;* no major piece of American musical theater would retreat from it after *Porgy and Bess*. Because some of its characters, like Sportin' Life, were more comical than others, and some of its moments, like Porgy's "I Got Plenty of Nothin'," sunnier than others, *Porgy and Bess* was able to inject comedic variety into its otherwise serious drama, maintaining the entertainment diversity of a musical within the dramatic unity of a play. American musicals after *Porgy* would also use comic characters and moments to flavor serious scripts with the spice of musical diversity.

The final period of the Gershwin's career seemed a retreat to a safer artistic haven: to Hollywood for the scores of *Shall We Dance?*, *A Damsel in Distress* (both for Astaire), and *The Goldwyn Follies*. Many see these scores as a regrettable if inevitable decline from a previous peak of innovative achievement and commercial disappointment. But of the twenty songs they wrote for the three films, a dozen are among their most memorable gems: "They All Laughed," "Let's Call the Whole Thing Off," "Slap That Bass," "I've Got Beginner's Luck," "They Can't Take That Away from Me," "A

Foggy Day," "Things Are Looking Up," "I Can't Be Bothered Now," "Our Love Is Here to Stay," "I Was Doing All Right," "Love Walked In," and "Nice Work If You Can Get It." Nice work indeed. More relaxed and polished than their 1920s ancestors, these late Gershwin songs were more assured if less driving, warmer if less mischievous.

The relaxed pressure of a Hollywood schedule gave Ira plenty of free time for card playing, horse playing, pool playing, and pool lounging. The relaxation agreed with him—for the next fifty years. George did not slow down at all: he painted, planned his weekly radio show, made frequent concert appearances, and studied musical theory with an emigré from Hitler's Germany named Arnold Schönberg. Gershwin's fatal brain tumor came upon him so quickly that he barely took the time to notice it and never had the time to fight it. In February of 1937, unable to remember one of his own piano passages during a concert, he submitted himself to a series of tests. When they revealed nothing, his doctor diagnosed simple exhaustion. By May he was simply too exhausted to work. In late June he entered the hospital. He was dead on July 11 at the age of thirty-eight.

His full life and quick death seem the stuff of myth, not mortal experience. His thirteen mature creative years were so brief and so intense that he seems to have martyred himself for his art. Brother Ira was no martyr; he would continue to work occasionally and amiably, if neither so devotedly nor conscientiously, with other composers for two more decades—most ambitiously with Kurt Weill on *Lady in the Dark* (1941), most electrically with Harold Arlen on *A Star Is Born* (1954). There would be a Gershwin resurrection on the MGM lot a dozen years after George's death. *An American in Paris* would gather many of those who had either worked with the Gershwins or sat in their Circle—a filmusical séance that invoked Gershwin's music as a materialization of his unseen spiritual presence, guiding the mortal labors of those who continued to toil in the musical vineyards below. The Gershwin ghost has continued to materialize—from *Funny Face* in 1957, to the background score of Woody Allen's *Manhattan* in 1979, to the Broadway pastiche, *My One and Only*, in 1983. While so many American popular artists feel an irresolvable conflict between the broadest cultural contact and the highest artistic integrity, George Gershwin's career still serves as inspirational proof that it ain't necessarily so.

7

Only Possible with Music

MOVIE MUSICALS
1927–1932

On August 6, 1926, fourteen months before *The Jazz Singer* opened on Broadway, Warner Bros. released its first Vitaphone film program: a sonorized silent film, *Don Juan*, with a recorded orchestral track, preceded by a canned program of musical acts that married the image to the soundtrack and the vaudeville show to the concert hall. After a Will Hays welcome from the cinema screen, the New York Philharmonic played the overture to *Tannhaüser*, Mischa Elman played Dvorak's *Humoresque*, Marion Talley sang "Care Nomo" from *Rigoletto*, a Russian chorus evoked "An Evening on the Don" with "a wealth of charm,"[1] Roy Smeck twanged seductively on the guitar, Efrem Zimbalist fiddled variations on Beethoven's *Kreutzer Sonata*, and Giovanni Martinelli boomed "Vesta la giubba" from *Pagliacci*.

This first soundfilm buffet dipped golden nuggets of kultchah in the sockola sauce of Hollywood and Broadway, like the future stage shows at the Radio City Music Hall, with its *corps de ballets* and its Rockettes, its symphony orchestra and its pit band, its opera singers and its dog acts. If the first Vitaphone program overdressed in concert hall respectability, the second Vitaphone program of October 1926, kicked off its shoes with more popular entertainers: The Four Aristocrats, George Jessel, Elsie Janis, Eugene and Willie Howard, and Al Jolson. Jolson's dynamic performance on this second Vitaphone bill led Warner Bros. to a different idea for the third: not a filmed series of vaudeville and concert acts followed by a sonorized feature, but a sonorized feature that would itself contain the vaudeville show.[2] The plot could stop for a song, but since Jolson, rebelling against the strictures of his religious father, played a popular entertainer, the plot didn't stop at all but showed the man at the work he loved.

Then the unexpected happened on the set of *The Jazz Singer*, during Jolson's filming of Berlin's "Blue Skies." The unexpected was always expected with Jolson, who made taking his audience by startling surprise a regular routine. *The Jolson Story* (1946) recounts the magic moment when Jolson stopped the dreary action of an overlong show to address his audience directly: "Look folks, this is pretty rotten, so I'll tell you how it all comes out; he marries her and she marries him, and now that that's settled let me sing you a few tunes." "Blue Skies" had been planned in two choruses: Jolson would sing the first chorus of the song straight, as Berlin wrote it, and the second chorus "jazzy," the typical Jolson pattern for rhythm songs (first chorus sweet and second chorus hot). The unexpected happened between the two choruses.

Jolson started to talk, seated at the piano, vamping with his left hand, vamping with his mouth: telling his Jewish mama, Eugenie Besserer, about a trip to Coney Island, where she'll meet the Ginsbergs and the Goldbergs and a whole lot of bergs, where they'll ride the shoot-the-chutes and through the tunnel of love so he can kiss her and hug her and squeeze her (Freudian enough?), and where she'll wear pink—or else. And after a pause and a laugh, "Or else you'll wear pink." Mama sits motionlessly on the piano bench (mustn't interfere with the star), making squeaky little laughs ("You're gettin' kittenish," Jolson warns her), trying not to look too stupid or too scared (what's he going to do next?) and not to crack up and not to move and not to spoil the take. She almost succeeds. The moment was (and still is) a sensation.

Why? The word "novelty" leaps immediately from most historians, but novelty hardly explains the enduring charm and energy of the moment six decades after it is no longer novel. More likely is its sudden and spectacular demonstration of the wholeness of face and speech, song and talk; the energy and imagination of the rambling, improvised lines come from the same source as the spirited rendition of the Berlin song. Jolson acted through his singing and sang as he acted—moving from song to talk and back to song again without breaking the mental thread of a whole performance. For the first time, a film audience witnessed the performance power a Jolson represented—not of gesture alone, nor facial reaction, nor charmingly articulate speech, nor enthusiastic musical delivery, but the whole package together, of a single piece. When Jolson prophesied, "You ain't heard nothin' yet," Jolson's trademark line even before he went to Hollywood, he turned out to be talking about more than just his next number. Out of *The Jazz Singer* sprang the Hollywood musical.

The narrative sections of *The Jazz Singer* were talkless and songless—not silent to be sure, since the film's sonorized score, a melange of Tchaikovsky hits, screeched incessantly. Only the musical numbers of the film were synchronized, as they had been in the previous Vitaphone programs. The means of moving from one order of reality or style to another, generated by technology in *The Jazz Singer,* became a conceptual problem for every musical film to follow: What conventions would lead from the ordinary prose of conversation to the poeticized expansiveness of song and dance? The problem was no different for films than for stage musicals. Both had to combine an entertainment diversity of individual numbers within a dramatic unity that contains and explains the means of transportation from everyday prose to stylized song.

The conceptual problem evaporates if the musical film's narrative just happens to be about a musical performer like Jolson. Musical performers perform as a matter of course—on a stage, to be sure, but they might even perform in some spontaneous and improvised way within everyday settings, since performers are likely to do just about anything. Performance is a way of life. Jolson's *Jazz Singer* initiated the Star Performer Musical, in which both the film and the show-within-the-film are built around a star—as they would be for Fred Astaire, Judy Garland, and Liza Minnelli. The alternative Group Performance Musical would be initiated by MGM's first musical (also its first sound film), *Broadway Melody*, and Warners' *On with the Show* (both 1929), in which all the "kids" invest their energy in the musical numbers and the show built around them. In Hollywood musicals, performers perform.

Out of *The Jazz Singer* also came the tension between white and black musical performance—so important to the stage musical from minstrels through Harrigan and Hart to *Show Boat*. The final number of *The Jazz Singer* features Jolson in blackface and white gloves, on bended left knee, banging his chest, pounding his gloves, warbling to "Mammy"—addressing both some traditional blackfaced idea and his Jewish mother in the audience. He would black up to pine for many dear departed at Warner Bros.—most wrenchingly for "Sonny Boy" in *The Singing Fool* (1928), most uncomfortably with "Goin' to Heaven on a Mule" in *Wonder Bar* (1934). The blackface tradition then passed to the Goldwyn lot and Eddie Cantor, who, like Jolson, had been blacking up for decades. Fred Astaire blacked up once, for "Bojangles of Harlem" (*Swing Time*, 1935), his homage to a dancer (Bill "Bojangles" Robinson) and a tradition that had powerfully shaped his own. In the 1930s, even women (Irene Dunne in *Show Boat*), children (Shirley Temple in *The Littlest Rebel*), and boys (Mickey Rooney in *Babes in Arms*) blacked up. So did Marion Davies, Winifred Shaw, and Shirley Ross. If movie blackface began with Jolson, it also ended with him. In a neat historical irony, the last blackface performance in a Hollywood musical was Larry Parks's impersonation of Jolson at Columbia, in *The Jolson Story* (1946) and *Jolson Sings Again* (1949).

Warner Bros. musicals of 1929 also filmed genuine black performance. *On with the Show* featured two songs by Ethel Waters, one of which was "Am I Blue?" *The Show of Shows* featured black solo dancers and chorines in the grandiose "Lady Luck" production number. In both films, black performance and white performance remained strictly segregated. While MGM's 1929 *Hallelujah* similarly exploited black performance for white enjoyment, its all-black cast portrayed scenes and songs of the American black experience more sympathetically than any Warner film. *Hallelujah* could be made and released by a prestige studio like MGM because it isolated black life from any contact with white life, like all-black musicals on Broadway. But a *Hallelujah* leads directly to a *Porgy and Bess* and may well have influenced its conception.

Hallelujah (directed by the white King Vidor) enjoyed clear advantages over white filmusicals of 1929. It never suffered the stylistic embarrassment of moving from prosaic dialogue to heightened song because song was an intrinsic part of everyday black experience in the film. Songs flowed in, through, and around daily life—whether at work in the fields or at dinner in the home. Singing was intrinsic to social life, not an isolated exception to it. The independent black filmusical of the same year, *Hearts in Dixie* (its director, Paul Sloane, was black), also made singing and dancing intrinsic to the social functions and foundations of black life. Its lack of budget contributed to a lack of self-consciousness, allowing spontaneous black performance to demonstrate itself without excuses and decoration.

Hallelujah and *Hearts in Dixie* also took advantage of performances by exceptionally talented singer-actors, like Daniel L. Haynes and Nina Mae McKinney, previously unknown to white audiences. The freshness and energy of the black performers, their exuberance, spontaneity, and charm, make a striking contrast to the wooden line readings and stilted song renditions in most white musical films of 1929. *Hearts in Dixie* recorded the delightful musical antics of black children, who act, sing, and dance with an energetic vitality and unselfconscious sincerity. The black kids of *Hearts in Dixie* contrast strikingly with *Sunny Side Up* of the same year, in which a chorus of white kiddies has been instructed to march, sing, and smile like a band of dwarf zombies, enacting the most slavishly terrible children's parody of an adult wedding ceremony. The difference between the children (and most of the adults) in the two films is the difference between white puppets and black people.

The black talent in *Hallelujah* and *Hearts in Dixie* implied a vast network of accomplished black performers, excluded from the mainstream outlets of white entertainment, who performed within exclusively black circuits of stage and film musicals for exclusively black audiences. For every *Hallelujah* or *Hearts in Dixie* produced for a white audience—and the latter begins with a dour white man asking white indulgence for the black revels they are about to see—there were dozens of black filmusicals produced for some twelve hundred black movie houses. A white filmusical occasionally tapped that rich vein of talent—particularly in 1929 when the studios were willing to try any entertainment concoction that might work.

Hallelujah was also far superior technically to most musical films of 1929. The technological problems of Hollywood's conversion to synchronized sound are well known, both from histories of film and from fanciful

Black song and blackface imitation: Daniel W. Haynes in *Hallelujah*; Irene Dunne in *Show Boat*; (*below*) Al Jolson in *The Jazz Singer*.

retelling in *Singin' in the Rain* (1952). The general problem was to obtain a satisfactory simultaneous direct recording of image and sound on the set. Early microphones were large and insensitive (so speakers sat or stood very close to the bush or canister where it had been buried). There were no sound mixers to permit the use of two recording microphones (so actors huddled together to speak into the same bush or canister). There was no boom (so actors could not simultaneously walk and talk). And the noisy camera had to be encased in a soundproof booth with a single glass window to view the set (restricting both camera movement and character movement). Oddly imbalanced and meaningless compositions, based on the maximum number of persons who would eventually enter the frame, were very common in early sound films (*Broadway Melody* provides numerous examples). An even subtler visual restriction infected film decor. In a mature silent film, decor became a virtual character itself; specific objects or the visual interplay of objects and humans deepened the meaning and commentary of every film image. The demands of sound recording overrode the precise use of such objects, converting decor into a mere visual backdrop rather than an integral unit of meaning in visual narrative. These technical difficulties, which cramped every sound film in 1928, had been largely solved by 1930. The year between, 1929, was the one of desperate innovation.

Musicals were even more cramped by these restrictions than other films. To record a musical number, the entire orchestra trekked to the sound stage, where performers sang directly into the recording microphone during filming, backed by the musicians in their off-frame "pit." There is a little joke (or lie) in MGM's *Till the Clouds Roll By* when Jerome Kern strolls onto an MGM sound stage to see an entire symphony orchestra (in white satin tails, no less) assembled to accompany the movie singers of his music. This 1945 joke was no joke on the set of *Broadway Melody* in 1929.

By early 1930 every musical number would be prerecorded in a sound studio, then postsynched on the set (matching lip movements to the singing sounds). One number from *Broadway Melody*, "The Wedding of the Painted Doll," in two-strip Technicolor, was recorded first and filmed afterward, as were two numbers for Ernst Lubitsch's 1929 *The Love Parade*. The method has obvious advantages of both sound and sight. The quality of the sound recording and the vocal performance can be controlled and assured in advance. Filming on the set can then be much freer, concentrating exclusively on a visual interpretation of the number and a projection of its musical energy into visual space. The film director enjoyed considerable freedom to play with visual imagery, divorcing its strict synchronization to vocalized lyrics, which could carry on without visual aid. A film could juxtapose any arresting, ironic, evocative, or clever visual image with the continuity of prerecorded music. *Hallelujah* adopted precisely this strategy, allowing separately recorded song to seep into its independently photographed visual images, many of them shot outdoors. The singing of Irving Berlin's "Waiting at the End of the Road" in *Hallelujah* (even in an all-black musical there was Irving Berlin) could be attached to almost documentary images of the cleaning, ginning, and baling of cotton.

The most influential demonstrations of the independent play of music and images were the early films of Walt Disney, beginning with *Steamboat Willie* (1928), his first sound cartoon. The movements and noises of cartoon goats, pigs, cows, and cats were imaginatively synchronized to the precise sounds, tones, and beats of "Turkey in the Straw." Disney's cartoons were wonderful musical films, even if they weren't exactly musicals. While early filmusicals followed Disney's lead by realizing that living people could sing like cartoon cats, he followed their lead in 1937 by drawing cartoons that sang like people. When Snow White sang "One Love" or "Someday My Prince Will Come," she became a female impersonator, moving her lips in synchrony with sounds she never made; she achieved credibility, however, as a living presence simply because those lip movements defined her as the author of those sounds. Female impersonators in cabarets, exaggerating the twitches of, say, Judy Garland while they twist their lips to her recordings, draw upon the same source of conviction in the wholeness of lip movement and voice. Snow White was a female impersonator in several senses of the term. But then so was Judy Garland herself on a set, miming and lip-synching to her own voice.

Almost every musical number in an American film since 1929 has been dubbed; very few songs have been recorded on a movie set, right then, right there, while the camera was turning. A powerful exception was Paul Robeson's "Ol' Man River" for the 1936 *Show Boat*, which sought to capture the spontaneity and power of a whole performance—like Jolson's first song in *The Jazz Singer*. A question inevitably arises: if you don't have a Robeson or Garland, why not prerecord some other, "better" voice to issue from the lips of your star, as if she or he were Snow White? The answer is the technique known commonly as "dubbing" or "lip-synching"—synchronizing the lip movements of a movie face with a voice other than his or her own. Despite the demonstration to the contrary in *Singin' in the Rain*, the technique of grafting one voice onto another face in filmusicals was uncommon until the 1950s, when it became either artistically or commercially necessary to feature nonmusical performers in filmusical adaptations of Broadway hits.[3]

Despite the practical ease of dubbing, and the simple fact that dubbing is no different from the usual technique of filming musical numbers, its results have consistently ranged from the barely acceptable to the absolutely disastrous. Audrey Hepburn sings more expressively in *Funny Face*, with her own little scratchy, breathless, untrained voice than she pretends to do in *My Fair Lady* with Marni Nixon's lovely soprano. How can that be? *The Jazz Singer* answered this question in "Blue Skies" when Jolson ambled effortlessly between singing and talking. Jolson poured his performance alternately and identically into his talk and his song, poured his ideas, energy, feelings into that speaking or singing voice—its sounds, colors, volumes, nuances, timbres. The nonsinger has been robbed of an expressive acting instrument. Although Audrey Hepburn can telescope her ideas and feelings into Eliza's spoken dialogue—and into Eliza's gazes, gestures, movements, poses, paces—when it comes time for Eliza to sing, which is the most powerful action a character can perform in a musical, Audrey Hepburn can only play Snow White to Marni Nixon's idea of the way Eliza *thinks* through singing.

A performer like Fred Astaire talks, taps, sings, walks, flicks a cigarette, examines his nails, even stands still in harmonious rhythmic cadences. The performer in a musical does not merely make singing sounds but external-izes inner states through the sounds and phrases of a singing instrument. Among the few and striking exceptions are the two Jolson biopics at Columbia, in which Larry Parks sang with Jolson's dubbed voice. Aided by the extreme stylization of his blackface makeup and the extreme stylization of imitating Jolson's delivery and gestures (acquired by a careful study of Jolson's films), Parks built an extraordinary impersonation of the wholeness of Jolson's performance. In musicals, to repeat an axiom, musical performers perform—and a nonmusical performer is an oxymoron. Hollywood adapta-tions of Broadway musicals in the 1950s and 1960s drained themselves of a powerful resource without this kind of performance.

Film adaptations of musical stage successes did not wait until the 1950s. Among the film musicals of 1929 were Warner Bros.' *The Desert Song* and RKO's two-strip Technicolor version of *Rio Rita*, featuring the comic duo of Bert Wheeler and Robert Woolsey. Far more interesting, however, was Hollywood's groping toward a musical form somehow indigenous to film. The most common solution until 1930 was the starstudded revue with its origins in that alternative stage tradition—the minstrel show, vaudeville, and burlesque. Most of these revues were pure compilations of musical numbers and comic sketches, feature-length extensions of the first Vitaphone programs, unsullied by any pretense of narrative paste between numbers. Universal's *King of Jazz* (1930) packaged Paul Whiteman's orchestra, John Boles's voice, huge production numbers staged by John Murray Anderson, and a hit song, "It Happened in Monterey." *Paramount on Parade* (1930) was a pure parade of Paramount contract talent in musical sketches—Maurice Chevalier, Clara Bow, Lillian Roth, Nancy Carroll. MGM's *Hollywood Revue of 1929* shipped the parade to Culver City, where Cliff Edwards ("Ukulele Ike"), Jack Benny, Conrad Nagel, Charlie King, Joan Crawford, even Buster Keaton and Laurel and Hardy sing, dance, and joke in an intermina-ble succession of vaudeville turns. Warner Bros.' *The Show of Shows* was just as interminable with Beatrice Lillie, Irene Bordoni, Frank Fay, Winnie Lightner, assorted dog acts and assorted others, mostly dogs of one kind or another.

Bessie Love and Charles King in *Broadway Melody*, the original backstager

Other early filmusicals linked the numbers of the onstage revue to a backstage story with two inevitable complications: difficulties of putting on the show (either financial or personal problems); and difficulties in sorting out the romantic couples (which could, in turn, produce those difficulties of putting on the show). The backer of the show, whose usual interest in show business was monkey business with the star, the chorus girls, or an assortment of both, could jump ship and take his bundle with him (*On with the Show*). The male star might not be able to decide between two sisters in the cast (*Broadway Melody*). The backstage world was a place of sex, power, and money, more seamy and sordid than the world at large (especially in the burlesque world of Rouben Mamoulian's 1929 *Applause*). This backstage world of 1929 would lead directly to *42nd Street*, four years later.

Still other early filmusicals fell somewhere between, suggesting some kind of narrative in the early reels, then abandoning it altogether for the onstage show. Like every major studio, Fox offered filmusical revues, and its *Happy Days* (1930) is very instructive about the difficulties of this early form. The excuse for this musical revue is that Colonel Billy, proprietor of a showboat, spiritual cousin to Cap'n Andy, has fallen upon hard times. The showboat's entertainment is outdated; its audiences have deserted it for more modern shows—like talking pictures. To fish Colonel Billy out of the financial soup, the loyal trouper, Marge (played by Marjorie White, Fox's spunky soubrette of the period), troops to New York, hoping to convince some big-name talent who got their start on Billy's boat to come to Memphis for a gala benefit show.

Marge invades the all-male precincts of an actor's club (modeled on the Lamb's or Friar's), in the disguise of a male page. We witness Warner Baxter performing magic tricks; he observes to his cronies, "I've had a lot of complaints about my tricks lately," a sexual *double entendre* implying the reason Hollywood would need a moral code to control such talk. Several stars sit around playing cards—George Jessel, Walter Catlett, Will Rogers. When Marge makes her appeal for help, the stars are more than willing: "We can give the same show in Memphis that we gave at our last revels." To which another responds, "Well, we'd have to clean it up." Sure enough, the stars all troop to Memphis. After thirty plodding minutes of preparation, the film can finally get down to business and on with the show, which includes: a minstrel act (perhaps one hundred men in blackface); George McFarlane (a whiskey tenor); El Brendel (a dialect comedian inexplicably esteemed by Fox);[4] George Olson and his orchestra; Charles Farrell and Janet Gaynor in a domestic love song, followed by a parody of this domestic bliss (with Walter Catlett in drag); and the finale, "Crazy Feet," a hot jazz dance that wishes it had been written by Gershwin.

During these interminable festivities, lasting over an hour, there is one—exactly one—cutaway reaction shot of Colonel Billy, enjoying the show from his box. There is never any further reference to the solving of Billy's financial problems (not even a shot of someone, say Marge, handing Billy a check or wad of greenbacks). When the show ends, the film stops; Billy and his showboat drop out of the glass bottom of the film's "plot" to disappear beneath the murky entertainment waters. Despite the narrative holes in this ill-made cloth, the film points toward important future concerns of musical films.

First, the film is conscious of its historical roots and traditions; it knows that the origins of this film go back a century. Not only is it aware of its roots in the minstrel show (with a long minstrel sequence, followed by an olio), but it feels a responsibility to sustain and revivify that tradition. For the next two decades, Fox musicals would proclaim their conscious connection to the vaudeville tradition.

But if *Happy Days* leans backward toward the minstrel show, it leaps forward into film. Several of the numbers display uniquely cinematic tricks: split-screen effects, impossible telescopings of time and space within individual numbers on stage, dissolvings of objects into apparently identical ones of surprisingly different sizes, dissolvings of spaces into apparently identical but surprisingly different ones. Many of the kaleidoscopic visual devices associated with Busby Berkeley make their first appearance here—not so much Berkeley's bizarre camera angles as the feeling of entering a visual labyrinth where spaces are inexplicably locked one inside the other.

Happy Days: stage-bound production numbers with cinematic gimmicks (Janet Gaynor and Charles Farrell in an enormous nursery)

We enter a completely imaginative space only possible in a film, not in the real world or on any real stage. *Happy Days* articulates an aesthetic law of the filmusical: visual tricks, produced by uniquely cinematic devices, are as essential to movie musicals as music itself. The visual tricks and the musical score are partners in the fanciful stylization of human experience.

The best of the early Fox musicals, *Sunny Side Up* (1929), was also its first all-talking film. Neither a star performer musical nor a revue musical, it weaves narrative musical entertainment from ordinary domestic threads: Janet Gaynor and Charles Farrell, Fox's romantic duo from the silent period, star in a light romantic comedy with interwoven musical numbers. Neither Gaynor nor Farrell typically played show folk: she was the sweet, wholesome girl next door (just one irony of her 1937 *A Star Is Born*); he the suave, debonair playboy who longs to settle down. The Gaynor-Farrell films dressed a familiar American democratic myth in cotton and calico: love triumphs over class differences and kindred souls triumph over external obstacles. This was a very serviceable motif for filmusicals since stage musicals had always been built around the same conflicts of love and social class.

In *Sunny Side Up*, Janet plays Molly, a sweet, ordinary resident of a lively New York City lower-middle-class ethnic (unspecified but very white) neighborhood; Charles Farrell plays Jack, a Long Island millionaire, who cracks up his car in Molly's neighborhood on (when else?) the Fourth of July. We know that Jack is no drunken playboy since the accident results from his swerving the car to avoid hitting a child in the ethnic street. Molly has been dreaming of love by looking at Jack's picture for quite some time (she's seen it in the society pages), but she has justifiable concerns about his moral sincerity when she sees him in the flesh. A suitable plot device brings Molly (and her gang of neighborhood friends) to Southampton, where the true-blooded Americans can experience the blue-blooded high life. As opposed to the sincere ethnic street, everyone on Long Island has stepped from the pages of *The Great Gatsby*. The three essential activities are drinking cocktails (during Prohibition), keeping women, and gossiping about those who keep and those who are kept. Molly herself is thought to be one of the kept because (thanks to that same suitable plot device) Jack is paying her bills. But Jack has let us know he is a different sort of guy. His romantic urges are thoroughly middle class: he wants a wife not a mistress. Sure enough, the two young, charming, pretty people get together at film's end when Molly prefers Jack to the alleged comedian El Brendel.

How do they get the big musical numbers into this little domestic romance? The answer takes us to that suitable plot device, which we might call the "amateur show" convention, the revue masquerading as amateur entertainment. Molly is no professional entertainer to be sure, but she is a lively amateur who participates in her neighborhood's Fourth of July show. One lengthy sequence of musical numbers is devoted to this show, includ-

The frigid Eskimo beginning of "Turn on the Heat" from *Sunny Side Up*

ing the film's lively title song, which begins as Molly's solo but ends as a very communal group sing. Molly, amateur though she be, performs so spiritedly that Jack invites her (and her friends—including the spunky soubrette, Marjorie White) to Southampton for their amateur charity show. This charity show produces yet another string of musical numbers. It concludes with the very first delightfully outlandish production number in filmusical history, "Turn on the Heat," in which the chorines and the decor evolve incomprehensibly from Eskimo Iceland to tropical Tahiti.

The only other musical numbers in the film are intimate, private ones, moments of reverie rather than extroverted performance. The first of these, "I'm a Dreamer (Aren't We All)," establishes what we might call the "zither convention." Molly sits in her own apartment and dreams longingly of love (as every proper operetta heroine is wont to do), dream-singing while she accompanies herself informally on some handy stringed instrument previously sitting on a shelf or hanging on the wall (zither, Autoharp, guitar, and ukulele are all acceptable). This reflective (rather than performed) kind of number contains no orchestration other than the strings she apparently strokes by herself, a clear attempt to achieve a muted stylization, midway between conversation and song, that is radically different from the highly stylized numbers performed at the two shows. Other musical numbers also begin informally and spontaneously, perhaps when Jack accompanies himself on the piano as he wishes, "If I Had a Talking Picture of You."

That the titles and tunes of these songs remain familiar should be no surprise. The Broadway trio of B. G. DeSylva, Lew Brown, and Ray Henderson who wrote them was perhaps the most successful songwriting team of the twenties.[5] They had written the hit 1927 musical show *Good News* and such hit songs of the Jazz Age as "You're the Cream in My Coffee," "Black Bottom," "The Varsity Drag," and "The Best Things in Life Are Free." Their songs, which captured the spirit and energy of the decade's dancing youth, really made it possible for flappers to flap. Fox brought them to Hollywood for filmusical flapping, the very first important Broadway team to be royally imported. Unfortunately, their creative collaboration was as close to its end as the decade. The team was breaking up, and its catalyst, DeSylva, would soon change jobs at Fox—from songwriting to film producing—as both Arthur Freed and Howard Dietz would at MGM.

Sunny Side Up set a pattern at the Fox studio for over two decades. Fox musicals would always be more domestic than musicals at MGM, Paramount, RKO, or Warner Bros.—devoted to neighbors, home, and family. And for a very good reason. Fox musicals were woman-centered, and Fox's musical stars were always women—Janet Gaynor, Alice Faye, Sonja Henie, Betty Grable, Marilyn Monroe, even Shirley Temple, as opposed to the male musical centers of the other studios. Fox musicals began with a woman's urge not merely to achieve professional success and capture a lover (the two goals of male-centered musicals) but to weave success and love into a permanent, stable domestic relationship. Because show business is a notoriously impermanent and unstable business, the conflict in many Fox musicals was between the woman performer's career and her desire for a meaningful domestic life of home, husband, and children.

The most inventive early thinking about marrying a musical to film took place at Paramount. Between 1929 and 1932, three Paramount musicals— *The Love Parade, Monte Carlo* (both directed by Ernst Lubitsch), and *Love Me Tonight* (directed by Rouben Mamoulian)—brought this first period of filmusical history to its climax. The three films have much in common and, despite their distinct personalities, suggest a cycle. All are set in Europe rather than in America; none is about professional entertainers. All exhibit a high degree of fanciful stylization, descending from the stage operetta's conflict of romantic love and social class; none is constrained by this stage heritage but seeks cinematic extensions of stage conventions. And all three are very conscious that they are musicals. Despite their different directors, Lubitsch clearly guides the Mamoulian film as its spiritual father.

Ernst Lubitsch was one of the most respected directors of the silent era, both for the historical films he made in Germany and the comedies of manners he made in Hollywood. Among the trademarks of his silent films were his visual sense of decor, his ironic wit, his observant awareness of internal psychology, his refusal to underestimate the power of sexual desire in human experience, and his interplay between the apparent and the actual, the visible and the hidden. They hardly seemed suitable for musicals. He had far more in common with the dry irony of Wilde and Coward (whose plays he adapted into films) than the sticky sugar of Lehár and Strauss. After four musicals between 1929 and 1932, Lubitsch would return to his droll comedies of manners—completing only one more musical in the final fifteen years of his career. But in 1929, when talkies meant singies, it seemed perfectly sensible for a clever Hollywood director imported from Germany to transport a German genre to Hollywood. Despite his operetta name, the short, stout Lubitsch had little in common with these idealized princes, dukes, countesses, and their consorts. As a lyric in *Love Me Tonight* would almost put it, the son of a gun was nothing but the son of a Jewish tailor.

The Love Parade is such an impressively fluid sound film for 1929, packed with stunningly clever visual and sound surprises, that it is easy to pardon its faults.[6] It is also very much a Hollywood sound film of 1929, with all its attendant clumsiness and insecurity. The patterns of cutting and movement in the film are more static and less fluid than in any Lubitsch film, before or after. The camera was painfully imprisoned within its glass booth, even for musical numbers, most of them recorded directly on the set. The decor is generally less subtle and less detailed than in any other Lubitsch film, particularly for Maurice Chevalier's song of sexual exasperation, "Nobody's Using Them Now," and the first duet for the soubrette and comic, "Let's Be Common." Both look like nothing so much as olio numbers from vaudeville shows, shot in front of a flat painted olio drop impersonating the great soundstage outdoors, the floor covered by the mats of an indoor lawn, solely for the convenience of sound recording and filming. The film also seems bound by its operetta score (Victor Schertzinger and Clifford Grey) and conventions. The inevitable "tomboy" soubrette (Lillian Roth) and "pixieish" comic (Lupino Lane), the leading lady's maid and leading man's valet, have descended so literally from stage ancestors that their two irrelevant numbers exist solely because two duets are obligatory for such characters in operettas.

If the film contains sequences that are visually weaker than anything Lubitsch ever did, silent or sound, singing or talking, it also contains sequences that are as dexterous and inventive as anything Lubitsch ever did. Two musical numbers strategically divorce the singing soundtrack from the visual images that accompany them. "Paris Stay the Same" is the raffish Chevalier's farewell to the ladies of Paris. Lubitsch intercuts static shots of Chevalier's singing with shots of many ladies, sitting on balconies in front of French windows, sipping champagne and smoking—the scenic attractions of Paris that Maurice must leave behind. In the song's second chorus, Chevalier's valet bids a parallel farewell to Paris, and Lubitsch intercuts shots of this second singer with shots of the French maids and

serving girls whom the servant leaves behind. This progression reveals a
more skillful weaving of the operetta multiplot (first the master sings, then
the servant echoes) than the film's obligatory comic duets. In the final
sixteen bars of the second chorus, Lubitsch executes a stunning surprise:
the progression continues from master to servant to dog. Maurice's hound
contributes his own farewell to Paris. It is easy enough to synchronize
modulated dog yapping, perfectly on pitch and in tempo, to filmed mouth
movements. Then Lubitsch cuts away from the canine Caruso to show the
many Parisian poodles to whom the singing dog yowls his farewell. Never
before had a living dog been able to yap a solo in a musical, and Lubitsch's
delightful realization of this sound-film possibility may well have descended
from Walt Disney's singing cartoon animals.

A second musical number to divorce visual image from musical track is
"Stand and Cheer," Queen Louise's (Jeannette MacDonald) rousing military
march at the head of her country's troops. Lubitsch juxtaposes the recorded
song with close-ups—marching men, military drum rolls, sounding trumpets—
and far shots of Queen Louise on horseback, much too distant from any
camera or microphone to have been recorded directly during the take. Early
in the film, Louise acted very much the operetta heroine when she sang
"Dream Lover," the prototypical operetta waltz of romantic yearning. But
"Stand and Cheer" is a deliberate reversal of the operetta assumption that
operetta women think only of love in waltztime and operetta men of

Jeannette MacDonald in cross-gender regalia for "Stand and Cheer" in *The Love
Parade*

military glory in marchtime. Louise's march reveals the film's conscious awareness of the operetta conventions it is scrambling. Co-scenarist Guy Bolton, veteran writer for the Princess Theater and Gershwin's Astaire shows, builds *The Love Parade* on a surprising reversal of sexual roles and gender expectations.

Count Alfred (Chevalier) is a very unfettered man about Paris, like Danilo in the 1907 *Merry Widow* (and like the 1934 Danilo Chevalier would play for Lubitsch). Lubitsch brilliantly depicts Alfred's sexual power over his prey in the film's opening sequence. A distraught, jilted lover shoots him point-blank, accompanied by the convincingly sharp crack of a shot on the synchronized soundtrack. Inexplicably, Alfred continues to smile; he has not been hit. Only later do we discover that the pistol was loaded with noisy blanks. Lubitsch's viewers have been as stunningly surprised as Alfred, for the pistol we could see and the shot we could hear did not produce the synchronized result we expected.

Such scandals lead to Alfred's recall from Paris to his Operettaland home, Sylvania, which asks him to make a political marriage—just as Marshovia asks the supreme sacrifice of Danilo. Count Alfred marries Queen Louise, who, according to Sylvanian law, retains all political, economic, military, and social power, regardless of marriage. Queen Louise goes off to work (the marching song), while Alfred suffers the indignity of being a mere househusband—in effect, a gigolo, a decorative sexual accessory kept by a dominant woman. Alfred's eventual revolution is an act of sexual politics. He simply announces his intention to defect to Paris, where he can regain his male position of power.

Alfred and Louise attend the ballet, their last public display of affection. While they watch the show on stage, they perform a show in their box, playing Loving Queen and Prince Consort. It is theater within the theater, and Alfred even plays director, the Lubitsch within the film, when he instructs Louise on how to play her scenes: to smile, to applaud, to appear in "the very best of humor." Of course, the clash of romantic and political, private and public obligations resolves operettically—when Louise pronounces him, "My king!"

Many of the reversals and ironies of this first Lubitsch musical were familiar from his silent films—particularly debunking the American myth that the male was always wiser and always the aggressor in sexual affairs, the woman only the innocent and passive recipient of male advances. Lubitsch's females are often much more shrewd about sexual drives than their idealizing mates. Lubitsch also played frequently and suggestively with the connection of love and money. In the American mythology, true love could never be bought: the one human aspiration that could never be commercialized or commoditized was love. When its crass imitation was bought, however, it was exclusively purchased by men from women. The European Lubitsch, who knew otherwise, enjoys ironic circumstances in which women (like Louise) seem to buy the affection of male admirers (like Alfred).

Lubitsch's first musical seems less committed to sexual equality than to a theory of sexual natural selection. Beneath the film's debunking of operetta conventions lies a familiar (and sexist) operetta premise: men are inherently superior to women in certain sexual matters, and nature itself demands that the woman serve the man in those matters.[7] Even the film's comic Freudian symbols (like the tiny versions of Alfred's props in comparison to the queen's enormous ones) suggest the operation of nature in the human subconscious. According to the class system of this operetta film, although queens may be more privileged by law than prince consorts, men are more sexually privileged by nature than women. Louise's calling Alfred her king at film's end marks her recognition and acceptance of this law of nature. Given the power and charm of Chevalier and MacDonald (both individually and together), Louise understandably feels the power of Alfred's presence, just as MacDonald feels Chevalier's.

Paramount had scored a terrific casting *coup* when they imported the exuberant Maurice Chevalier from the Paris music hall to sing alongside the lovely but spunky Philadelphia soprano, Jeannette MacDonald. Chevalier's ebullient charm, his combination of stylization and spontaneity, his Frenchness of speech, style, and outlook (as a Frenchman it was both more probable and more acceptable that his sexual appetites would overstep the boundaries of conventional American monogamy) all made him one of the great stars of early American musical films. Even with that sexual energy, *The Love Parade* seems burdened by its residue of stage-operetta conventions and its constriction by uncooperative sound-film machines.

These same burdens do not weigh upon *Monte Carlo* (1930), Lubitsch's next musical, a leap in both technological mastery and conceptual fancy. Lubitsch is no longer the servant of his machines or his conventions but completely their master, no longer tentative or hobbled in his approach to a musical film. The result is the first truly whole American filmusical—technically, stylistically, and thematically—not part stage operetta and part filmusical, but a unique and whole conception of an operetta in film for film. Unfortunately, the film lacks MacDonald's Chevalier. After Paramount's rich strike in the music halls of Paris, the studio tried prospecting in the music halls of London. The result was Jack Buchanan, star of British musical comedy and light dialogue comedy, an intimate member of the set that included Beatrice Lillie, Noël Coward, and Gertrude Lawrence. In the intimacy of a Hollywood movie set, Buchanan seemed "a smarmy British wimp" with "a voice like tapioca pudding on a high speed and the most irritating laugh a leading man ever tried to get away with."[8] Buchanan would redeem himself two decades later with a role much better suited to his fussy style—the pretentious Jeffrey Cordova in *The Band Wagon* (1953). It is impossible to admire and enjoy the conceptual cleverness of *Monte Carlo* without excusing Jack Buchanan.

Monte Carlo is the first American filmusical that is fully conscious of its origins as an entertainment, situating itself within a tradition, aware of its history and of its place in that history. The film explicitly acknowledges its ancestry at its climax, which, like the final scene of *The Love Parade*, takes place inside a theater. Rather than attending a ballet, the squabbling romantic couple of *Monte Carlo* attends the performance of an operetta, whose plot turns out to be identical to that of the film itself. In *Monsieur Beaucaire*, the operetta-within-the-operetta, a prince of France, disguised as a barber, has been rejected by an aristocratic lady because of his apparently lowly origins. In the plot of *Monte Carlo*, Count Rudolph Farrière (Buchanan), disguised as a barber, has been rejected by Countess Helene Mara (MacDonald) because of his apparently lowly origins. Rudolph uses the plot of *Beaucaire* to inform the countess that he is really no barber but, as the onstage operetta chorus eternally sings, "The barber is a nobleman." Rudolph can inform the countess of his noble birth in a song that he himself is not required to sing. But while the prince in *Beaucaire* casts aside his faithless lover, leading to Helene's expectation that Rudolph will do likewise, Rudolph reverses the ending of his own life's operetta when he declares, "I like happy endings."

While watching *Monsieur Beaucaire*, Duke Liebenheim, the rich rodent who is Rudolph's rival, derides the show with an aesthetic sneer applicable to *Monte Carlo* itself: "A silly story, only possible with music." Lubitsch knows that to tell a story with music, as both *Monsieur Beaucaire* and *Monte Carlo* do, defines the kind of telling it will and can be, transforming the silly into the sensible. When the countess tells Otto that the story isn't so silly, that a lady can fall in love with her hairdresser even without music, she has seemingly forgotten all her own numbers. But Lubitsch hasn't forgotten. He knows that singing calls a particular fictional world into being—a separate, distant, and ideal realm of luxury, idleness, romance, and fancy, in which the final pairing of the romantic couple, often by means of surprising or outlandish but delightful contrivances, is the single rule of the game.

To tell a story in a world of music means the wearing of opulently rich costumes within elegantly attractive settings. In *Monsieur Beaucaire*, the immense powdered wigs (in an operetta about a barber), flowing hoop skirts, gleaming silk breeches, and Louis XVI salons are the exact eighteenth-century antecedents of *Monte Carlo*'s coiffured hair styles (in a film operetta about a barber), high-fashion French gowns, elegant formal evening wear, and Art Deco salons. *Monte Carlo* is among the very first and remains among the very loveliest of Art Deco designs (Hans Dreier) in film history. *Monte Carlo* suggests that in so far as a stylized, centuries-old tradition of musical narrative (like *Monsieur Beaucaire*) can still be told in the twentieth century, it will be told in exactly this style, in this medium, called the Hollywood movie musical, with exactly these counts and countesses, as distant from their contemporary audiences as were the princes and ladies of *Monsieur Beaucaire* from their bourgeois audiences. Perhaps *Monte Carlo* rewrites the ending because Hollywood's more democratic operetta conventions forbid the unhappy variant.

But if *Monte Carlo* demonstrates that eighteenth-century entertainments can be brought to the twentieth, it also shows that they cannot arrive without wearing the cultural clothes of this century. One element in the world of *Monte Carlo* is absolutely different from the "silly" world of *Monsieur Beaucaire*: a psychological theorist named Freud. Although set in the fanciful operetta world of rich dukes, disguised counts, Art Deco casinos, and the fabled resort that gives the film its title, that world is suffused with contemporary sexual psychology. This intimate psychology makes *Monte Carlo* quite unlike any other operetta, just as it typically makes Lubitsch films quite unlike anyone else's.

The film's first shot frames an ornate jewelry box, which opens to reveal two wedding rings—for the countess, Helene Mara, and her intended, Duke Otto Liebenheim, who offers her money without sexual joy. This is the first of the film's many images of boxes, of opening boxes up and locking boxes shut. They imply Helene's central emotional problem—opening herself sexually to another. She perpetually runs away from marriage to Otto, who only offers to buy her, to keep her in a legalized box of prostitution. The opening or closing of a box translates the countess's emotions into explicitly sexual terms, suggested by the usual kind of comic Freudian objects with which Lubitsch films abound. If Lubitsch was the countryman of Lehár and Strauss, he was also the countryman of Freud and Schnitzler. When the countess sings, "Beyond the Blue Horizon," she delivers the song's first chorus enclosed in her train compartment, a locked box. For the second chorus, she opens the window to thrust her head out of the box, into the air. The shots of the train's locomotive, a thrusting phallus toward the right edge of the frame, accompanied by the surging rhythm of the train's wheels, turn this typical operetta song of longing into the most sexually explicit of any operetta daydream.

Later in the film, just when the countess seems ready to open the box of her emotions completely, Lubitsch executes a stunning scene of premeditated sexual repression. The countess has been out on the town with Rudolph—dining, dancing, drinking. She is so carried beyond the blue horizon by his first kiss that she lets fall the handful of banknotes he has given her, letting them scatter over the floor—the material embodiment of her scattered resolve. She has abandoned her grasping for money, her explicit concern throughout the film and the single attraction of Duke Otto. As she surrenders the money, it seems certain that she is about to surrender everything else—particularly given the explicit connection of sex and money in the Freudian dream symbolism.

Suddenly, the countess bolts, moves across frame quickly to the left into her bedroom, where she locks the door behind her, leaving Rudolph alone on the other side of the door. Then she takes the key to that door and locks it in her dresser drawer. Then she takes the key to the dresser and locks it inside her jewelry case. Then she stows the key to the case under her pillow. She is not locking Rudolph *out* of her bedroom but locking herself *in* a box, refusing the temptation to open herself to Rudolph's "key." This slyly psychological and sexual implication is not the stuff of operettas. Lubitsch returns coyly to her late-night repression in an ironic morning-after awakening. The bleary-eyed countess is incapable of admitting her maid (the dry ZaSu Pitts) to her bedroom the next morning without retracing the entire locking process, reversing the journey of the keys from pillow to box to dresser to door.

In the film's final sequence, a reprise of "Beyond the Blue Horizon," the countess and Rudolph share the box of her train compartment, both of their heads thrust out the window and into the open air. The thrusting phallus of the train's locomotive is the film's final image. The countess has opened herself up to let someone else in. The film that began with the opening of a box closes with the surging of a locomotive.

Soloist MacDonald and her orchestral train accompaniment in *Monte Carlo*

No wonder the most memorable number of the score (Richard Whiting and Leo Robin) is "Beyond the Blue Horizon." Upon it Lubitsch constructs the first sensational Big Number in an American filmusical, the first extended musical sequence in which song, story, style, and meaning combine with a pyrotechnical display of cinema's visual devices. To put it simply, these Big Numbers are justification enough for the entire genre. "Beyond the Blue Horizon," an odd duet for soprano and train obligato, begins even before the vocal passage with a twelve-measure musical introduction, scored for orchestral strings and percussive train sounds. The first dazzling picture-sound montage in film history, rapidly intercut pictures of the train's surging motion accompany the pulsing rhythms of its rolling wheels, the percussive toots of its whistle, and the huffing puffs of its smokestack. Not merely a brilliant technical demonstration, the musical-visual synthesis introduces the mood of both singer and song—the surge of forward movement, the expectation of adventure ahead. MacDonald sings the verse and first refrain of the song inside her train compartment, supported by off-frame sounds—the rhythm of the train's wheels, punctuated by the shrieks of the train's whistle or the clangs of its bell—a synæsthesic weave of irresistible expectation.

For its second refrain, Lubitsch executes a subtle surprise that parallels the singing dog of *The Love Parade*. When Countess Mara opens the window to feel the air and sun outdoors, she views vineyards strewn with tiny dots of distant people, waving to her passing train. The prerecorded soundtrack gives these sixteen bars to a chorus of voices, which, juxtaposed with the shots of these dots in the fields, demands an inference—those waving workers are the chorus for this section of the song. But it would be impossible for such faraway folks to make such full singing sounds; only the juxtaposition of seeing them and hearing voices leads us to interpret them as the literal source of the sound. Lubitsch once again demonstrates the imaginative reconstructions an audience performs when watching cinema images juxtaposed with asynchronous musical recordings.

None of the other numbers in the film has the same visual and musical force as "Blue Horizon," but Lubitsch manages to inject some clever twist or subtle comment into every one of them. The opening, "Day of Days," is a chorus welcome to Operettaland (both the costumes and the castle are quaintly Tyrolean). It informs us of the impending wedding, introduces the smugly satisfied bridegroom, and forecasts trouble when a sudden rainstorm sends the feet of the wedding party scurrying for shelter. We have obviously entered a unique world where only stories with music are possible and all is possible with music. Duke Liebenheim's "She'll Love Me and Like It" lets us know he is a comically repellent fool (she won't ever love him because she could never like him); his listeners second our suspicions in repetitive responses to his claims, "He's a simp, he's a simp, he's a simp-le hearted soul"; "He's an ass, he's an ass, he's a nasty tempered brute." "Give Me a Moment Please," Rudolph's song of love to Helene, is an ironic duet transmitted by telephone, reducing Rudy's voice to the pinched nasality of telephone sound in contrast to Helene's full-throated replies to her receiver. Lubitsch was dreaming up as many clever games to play with his musical soundtrack as he could.

"Trimmin' the Women" also plays clever games—the male trio manages to drink tea and munch cake while singing, producing a comic musical mush. The number also introduces a surprising dissolve between its first and second choruses. While the music plays continuously, dissolving images denote a spatial and temporal break as the trio moves instantaneously from park bench to tea table. The device would become an essential tool of filmusical technique: laying a continuous musical passage over a discontinuous series of visual images, a paradoxically continuous discontinuity. Lubitsch demonstrates the method once again in the love song, "Always in All Ways," a jaunty rhythm tune that Buchanan sings to MacDonald before their night on the town. After two choruses in her apartment, they stroll rhythmically out the door, into her automobile, and off to the casino. A continuous orchestral passage sustains a sequence of disconnected cuts that implies a single process—the beginning of the night that will end with the unlocking of her emotional box (but the locking of her bedroom door). Although there is no actual dancing in this film, these cuts serve as the song's dance chorus: space itself dances to continuous orchestral music.

Love Me Tonight, the film that brought the Paramount cycle to its culmination, enlarged this choreography of space. While the Robin-Whiting score for *Monte Carlo* was serviceable enough to keep space hopping, the score for *Love Me Tonight* made space a ballerina. The distinguished Broadway songwriting team, Richard Rodgers and Lorenz Hart, produced three of their most memorable songs for *Love Me Tonight*—"Isn't It Romantic?" (the film's leitmotif), "Lover" (one of Rodgers's loveliest waltzes, virtually thrown away in the film), and "Mimi" (ever afterward associated with Maurice Chevalier). Even the score's highly integrated comic numbers are musical-visual gems.

Love Me Tonight also brought a change of directors from Lubitsch, the Paramount master, to Rouben Mamoulian. Like an army of others from Broadway, Mamoulian marched into movies in 1929 when they began singing and talking. Lubitsch was the deeper and more complex man of the cinema, Mamoulian the brilliant but shallow trickster. Lubitsch camera positions, showing either much more or much less than any character could perceive, were based on a belief that human perception, human vision, was itself limited and fallible—an interesting premise for the cinema, so dependent on visual perception. Mamoulian enjoyed camera tricks and bizarre camera angles for their own visual sake. Athletic juggling dominated his first sound film, *Applause* (1929), a melodramatic backstage story of life in the burlesque world sprinkled with a few musical numbers.[9] Mamoulian's bizarre camera angles and editing tricks added whatever life they could to an otherwise static film with dreadful performances (except for Helen Morgan), dead decor, and a dreary script. In *Love Me Tonight* Mamoulian's athletic camera found a more amenable subject for its stunts. This was a thoroughly playful, "silly" world, only possible with music, and camera stunts are stylistic kin of musical turns. If Mamoulian's camera work is more decorative than Lubitsch's, it is also more gymnastic. What *Love Me Tonight* loses of *Monte Carlo*'s psychological observation it gains in exuberant agility.

Love Me Tonight retrieves Maurice Chevalier for Jeannette MacDonald. Though she may not personally have cared much for him, the film is delighted to have them back together. It pays homage to their descent from Lubitsch, for the characters they play are merely named Jeannette and Maurice, an acknowledgement of who they are and that they are the star team of *The Love Parade*. To call characters by the names of their stars is another little game only possible with music. While Lubitsch's references to musical tradition were necessarily confined to stage operetta in *Monte Carlo*, by 1932 Lubitsch films themselves serve as Mamoulian's tradition for conscious self-reference.

Love Me Tonight begins with three successive musical numbers, over fourteen nearly consecutive minutes of musicalized narrative that very clearly define it as an artistic world where things only possible with music will certainly be possible. The performer of the first musical number is the city of Paris itself, the sights of the city's morning waking, carefully synchronized with rhythmically percussive musical sounds. The opening of windows, the rising smoke from chimneys, the sweeping of streets, beating of carpets, shaking of towels, pounding of shoemakers—all are carefully choreographed to a specific rhythmic sound. Although the idea grows from the musicalized train of *Monte Carlo*, Mamoulian's technique owes other obvious debts: to Disney's musicalizations of social life; to René Clair's musicalization of Paris life in *Sous les toits de Paris* (1930); to a genre of silent films, called "City Symphonies" (like Walter Ruttmann's 1927 *Berlin: die Symphonie einer Grosstadt*), which edited the shots of everyday city life according to musical rhythms and patterns. *Love Me Tonight* gives us a city not as symphony but as song and dance, the first American filmusical to musicalize Paris.

Also to magicalize it. The musical and the magical are cinematic allies. For Paris to sing and dance requires the modern act of movie magic—the synchrony of separately recorded sounds and filmed images. *Love Me Tonight* is a modern movie fairy tale, complete with a princess emprisoned in a castle and a prince charming who frees her from an evil spell. The film makes visual or narrative references to "Sleeping Beauty," "Rapunzel," "The Princess and the Frog," "Rumpelstiltskin," and "The Little Tailor" (for this prince charming will turn out to be nothing but a charming tailor).

Inside the enchanted castle, characters fall inexplicably into deep sleep (especially Jeannette's sister, played by Myrna Loy), as if under the spell of some witch. Three strange crones (presumably Jeannette's aunts) spend the entire film in toiling and troubling and odd incantation. These three fates, or three witches, or three stepsisters turn out to be beneficent spirits in this fairy tale, for at the end of the film they reveal the tapestry they have been weaving. It depicts a knight on horseback in shining armor, jousting with a castle to rescue a captive princess on her balcony. What they have been weaving, it turns out, is the film itself, woven from threads of celluloid images.

From a musical performance by the city itself, the camera swoops into the window of a city room to seek a human protagonist, Maurice, just as, twenty years later in a conscious homage, Vincente Minnelli's camera swoops into Gene Kelly's Paris bedroom in *An American in Paris*. Maurice, arising that morning (as Kelly does), sings the verse and refrain of the opening song, "That's the Song of Paris," after the city (like the train of *Monte Carlo*) has played the orchestral introduction. His refrain reveals Maurice as a human extension of the city's musical-magical spirit. That spirit makes him the film's prince charming, not his social class nor his knight's costume in the tapestry. Ironically, Maurice finds the city's song more noise than music. That is another reason he is this modern film's prince charming: he is a cynical pragmatist, not a romantic idealist.

The film's second number evolves directly from the "Song of Paris" when Maurice takes his musical spirit out of his room and into the streets; his greeting, "How're You?" touches the lives of his fellow citizens with the energy of song. The bouncy Rodgers tune is vibrantly infectious, and the surprising Hart lyrics keep us listening for every unexpected rhyme:

> Hello Missus Bendix,
> How's your appendix?

> or

> Bonjour Mister Cohen,
> How're things goin'?

Maurice's vital energy, mirrored by his rhythmic song, his brisk walk, and dynamic Mamoulian tracking shots, pulls his listeners (both the citizens of the movie's Paris and the citizens of the movie audience) into his charmed circle of magical-musical power.

The third musical number continues after a brief dialogue interlude inside Maurice's tailor shop. The crowning jewel of this opening musical trilogy, it is also the Big Number of this musical film—"Isn't It Romantic?" Despite its title, the song begins very unromantically with Maurice's pragmatic address to a customer during a fitting, dressing the tune, like the man, with his personal set of workaday lyrics. They refer not to a woman as a vision of romance but to a wife's cooking, scrubbing, and sewing. After all, the tailor Maurice's material is not shining armor but plain old cloth. For Maurice, the title of the song is a rhetorical question with a negative answer.

The customer takes the jaunty tune out of Maurice's shop and into the streets where he hums it happily to himself, without lyrics. A taxi driver and his musician fare hear the tune and hum its infectious melody; the musician takes the tune up to write it down, translating its notes into "words" like C, C, A, B-flat. The musician fits a proper lyric to this notation aboard a train, overheard by a platoon of soldiers, who take the song with them into the countryside, where they sing it rousingly in march tempo, accompanying their maneuvers. A gypsy on the road hears the march and transforms it, lyrically and vigorously, into the strains of a gypsy violin at night around a campfire. The sounds of the romantic violin rise to the ears of Jeannette MacDonald as she stands on her balcony in the romantic moonlight. She sings a final, full chorus of the song adorned with her own romanticized lyric, envisioning a prince in shining armor, describing the harmony between her operetta longings and the magic of the night. The song that began as a cynical rhetorical question ends as an affirmative romantic sigh.

The surprising odyssey of this song literally connects the laborer Maurice (who begins it) to the princess Jeannette (who concludes it) in a single musical process. It also connects his metaphoric spirit to hers, the spirit of the magical but practical Paris (with which the film began) to the pining princess in her castle fortress. Maurice's vigorous spirit will free the princess from her prison, merely by her realizing that to join her spirit to his, she need only sing with him. The song's journey connects the city with the country (where fanciful events always occur in fairy tales), transforms day into night (when fanciful events always occur), and links the magic of a musicalized modern city to the magic of a musicalized fairy-tale castle. The Big Number, "Isn't It Romantic?," is merely the entire film of *Love Me Tonight* in miniature.

The song ends with the irritating thump of a ladder against the princess's balcony, the intrusion of reality upon the romantic dream. This comic reality is the very unprincelike, uncharming, unromantic but aristocratically eligible suitor (Charles Butterworth) who climbs the ladder to seek Jeannette's affections. Vapid, lifeless, and unattractive (like Duke Otto in *Monte Carlo*), he can provide no answer to this maiden's prayer. When her real prince does come for her, he will not arrive by romantic ladder in the moonlight but by modern automobile in the full light of day. Her prince will be a modern, common man of the movies, not an aristocrat from ancient tales and tradition.

The journey of a song: "Isn't It Romantic?"—from tailor shop to city street to taxicab to military unit aboard a train to gypsy camp to the princess on her balcony

The prince first encounters the chilling power of the dragon he faces in an odd musical number, which might be called "Maurice Enters the Castle." The number is a wordless spatial dance, set to the tune of "How're You?"—contrasting the energy and vitality of Maurice with the dead rigidity of the castle's architecture. Maurice says, "How're you?" to the castle by striding through the vast spaces of its empty rooms, accompanied by assertive musical phrases, traversing its tiled floors, opening its glassed doors, surveying its endless corridors, ascending its marble staircases, and striding to its very top. No other figures participate but the two combatants: the vital, modern, common man and the ancient, dead architecture whose classbound values have been translated into lifeless stone. Maurice has no difficulty taking the castle's measure, scaling its ramparts, conquering it from bottom to top, an "entry" to the princess within it—prisoner of the castle by choice because she carries its social weight, its spell, within her.

Getting the princess out of the castle is the business of the film's final number, another cinematic dance without dancing, in which Jeannette finally comes after her prince. She realizes she loves him during an enchanted love duet, the title song, "Love Me Tonight," sung while both are asleep. With the magic of voice-over and split screen, the two visually share the same bed in their spell-laden dreams. Despite the dreams, Jeannette has discovered that Maurice is not the baron her brother (Charles Ruggles) introduced but a Paris tailor, come to the castle not to collect her but to collect her brother's unpaid bills. When Maurice rejects the stone castle to return to Paris (as Chevalier threatened in *The Love Parade*) by train (another modern machine), Jeannette must go after her prince if she wants him. She must overcome his cynicism with her own romance.

She chases after his train on horseback—on which the urban Maurice demonstrated his woeful inadequacy during an aristocratic hunt. Aided by a racing orchestral reprise of "Love Me Tonight" and modern cinematic montage, Jeannette has become the knight on horseback, a reversal of sexual roles typical of this ironic operetta cycle. Magically enough, her old-fashioned mount overtakes the new-fashioned machine. The lady knight confronts the smoke-puffing iron dragon head on (in an awesome Mamoulian low-angle shot). She stops the locomotive dead in (and on) its tracks. Only after she conquers this dragon—and the blindness of her own class prejudices—can the prince conquer his cynicism and accept the possiblity that princesses exist.

Beneath this operetta, like every other, lie certain views of social class. *Love Me Tonight* spins a modern American fairy tale. In the contemporary American world of automobiles, trains, cities, the urban bourgeoisie—and movies—class differences no longer exist, or are no longer important, dead and rigid encrustations of worn and spent belief. If *Monte Carlo* became modern by injecting contemporary psychology and sexual energy into the operetta world, it never surrendered the idea that distinctions between social classes define all other human relationships: the count must be a count and not really a barber if he is to win the countess. As the son of a tailor, Lubitsch knew very well that tailors didn't win countesses (or anything else) in Monte Carlo. But in *Love Me Tonight* the prince must really be a tailor if he is to waken the sleeping princess: no aristocrat could do the job. The sanctuaries of the upper classes must be crashed if their occupants are to be reawakened as people rather than frozen statues and romantic poses. *Love Me Tonight* is more aggressively a modern American movie musical by equating movie musicals with modernity and mythic American classlessness in the first place.

It took Hollywood less than four years to learn the real secret of Jolson's first song in *The Jazz Singer.* Filmusicals were not operettas or variety shows on film. They were American Magic—transcending space, time, and social rigidities on a magic carpet of American song. It was only possible with music.

The Kaleidoscope Waltz

BUSBY BERKELEY

If Ernst Lubitsch brought one stage musical tradition to Hollywood, Busby Berkeley brought another: the opulent vaudeville revue, symbolized by the *Folies Bergère* in Paris and the annual editions of Florenz Ziegfeld's *Follies* at the New Amsterdam Theater on West 42nd Street. After youthful experience as a choreographer of military drills during World War I, Berkeley became assistant to Sammy Lee, choreographer of the Ziegfeld *Follies*. Berkeley's first personal Broadway success was as choreographer of the 1927 *A Connecticut Yankee*. After two seasons of staging the annual Shubert shows, Ziegfeld's bargain basement competition, Berkeley returned to Ziegfeld in 1929 to direct Eddie Cantor in *Whoopee!*. He traveled with the star to Hollywood to direct the musical numbers for what would be his first film and Ziegfeld's last.[1] Ziegfeld was nearing the bankruptcy and ill health that would kill him in 1932. Berkeley was just beginning a career that would conjure the spirit of Ziegfeld's stage in uniquely cinematic terms.

Berkeley's film career splits into three unequal parts: an apprenticeship with Samuel Goldwyn and Eddie Cantor (1930–1933);[2] his most influential period at Warner Bros. (1933–1937); and a woeful servitude to MGM and Twentieth Century-Fox (1938–1953). At the center of Berkeley's work in all three periods was the heart of Ziegfeld—the showgirl and the staircase. Title it "Seminude Descending a Staircase." Of course, Berkeley quickly learned that the seminude need not descend very much in the movies. The staircase could descend—or twirl, rise, and slide—and the camera could descend—or rise, twirl, and glide—while the girls smiled and stood stock still. But to understand Berkeley, both his charm and his excesses, means to understand Ziegfeld as well.

Ziegfeld wove several aesthetic traditions, both low and high, into a single theatrical garment. From the lowliest regions of show business—the burlesque house with its "art models," the nineteenth-century museum with its "art-study" *tableaux vivants*—came the taste for "artful" display of suggestively nude female forms. Female nudity was legally permitted on the New York stage if it were properly decorated. Such "art" bore a close relationship to the more culturally sanctioned sort, without the quotation marks, of female nudity—from Praxiteles to Picasso—as a metaphor for some generalized idea and ideal of beauty. The Ziegfeld Girl was the trashy sister of the Rembrandt, Rubens, or Renoir nude; and Berkeley, like Ziegfeld, saw his adorned female models as one more instance in an ancient tradition, seasoned by contemporary entertainment tastes. To see these walking nudes on a Ziegfeld stage, dripping with beads and drowning in feathers, was suggestive enough to keep the tired businessman awake and respectable enough to keep his wife impressed (or, perhaps, instructed).

In the eyes of Hollywood, particularly after MGM signed Billie Burke, his second wife, Ziegfeld came as close as any showman ever did to God Almighty. In *The Great Ziegfeld* (1936) and *The Ziegfeld Follies* (1946), MGM translated Ziegfeld's famous habit of calling down from his balcony office to performers onstage, uttering his opinions or instructions as a disembodied voice from the heavens, into William Powell, speaking to us from some angelic executive office that God had apparently rented him. Or Ziegfeld might never appear in the film at all, remaining a mere off-frame spirit, like God himself, represented in mortal affairs by his pope, Noble Sage (Edward Everett Horton in the 1941 *Ziegfeld Girl*). Busby Berkeley, who directed the musical numbers for this film, was Ziegfeld's cinematic Noble Sage.

If the union of Ziegfeld, Berkeley, and Goldwyn (who saw himself as a second-generation Ziegfeld) made sense enough, the union of Berkeley and Eddie Cantor was something else again. Berkeley's lavish musical numbers seemed irrelevantly dumped into stories built around Cantor's comic clumsiness, cowardice, and prissiness. The Berkeley numbers with the Goldwyn Girls have little to do with the Cantor parts of the picture, except at an occasional intersection for a chorus or two. But even Cantor's numbers have little to do with the plot and more to do with their simply being expected of him.

He was one of the strangest of movie stars, an acquired taste that you had to be living in about 1930 to acquire. Unlike Jolson, Mae West, W. C. Fields, or the Marx Brothers, his equals and contemporaries, Cantor has never inspired later generations of idolators, imitators, and commentators. His films are as rarely revived as remembered. It is not difficult to see why. Cantor played one of the least physically attractive, least emotionally appealing, least strong, least pleasant, least mature, least smart, and least adept comic characters in American film history. He was a very odd duck, reminiscent of some loony refugee from the deranged world of silent film comedy. And that was exactly what he wanted to be.

Eddie Cantor's banjo eyes with Ruth Hall and Lyda Roberti in *The Kid from Spain*

In *Whoopee!* Cantor's horn-rimmed glasses suggest Harold Lloyd. In *The Kid from Spain* (1932), directed by Leo McCarey, Cantor's fluttering hand gestures recall Oliver Hardy (whom McCarey directed at the Hal Roach studio in the twenties). In *Whoopee!*, *The Kid from Spain*, *Roman Scandals* (1933), and *Kid Millions* (1934), Eddie plays the innocent in a love scene, vamped by an aggressive soubrette—either comical or maniacal—who tries to rape him, just as Harry Langdon endured female attack in parodic love scenes. "Have you ever been fired by passion?" growls one tigress in *Roman Scandals*. "No, but I've been fired by everyone else," Eddie purrs. In every film, Cantor faces mortal danger—from American gangsters, Mexican desperadoes, Roman tyrants, Egyptian sultans, and wild animals on the rampage—just as Lloyd, Langdon, and Keaton faced mortal dangers in silent comedies. Even Cantor's most famous feature—those banjo eyes— recall the tools of a Ben Turpin. Cantor played those eyes like a virtuoso. They roll rapidly in synchrony; they rise in innocence, then fall straight down in condemnation; or one eye disappears behind a dropping eyelid while the other dances a solo.

Like the silent clowns, Cantor was a tiny man facing murderous foes—bigger, stronger, smarter, meaner, and tougher. Unlike Lloyd or Keaton, Eddie survives not because of physical dexterity (a virtue of physical comedians) or ingenuity (he has none), but because luck and the plot would have it so. Like Harry Langdon, his greatest strength is his innocence. If the Cantor comedies look back to the silents, they also look forward to Danny Kaye, Goldwyn's next Jewish musical-comedy star, plucked from Broadway to face mortal dangers in Hollywood musicals. In comparison to Kaye, Cantor was a tinier, frailer creature, historically and spiritually closer to the silent clowns before him.

Cantor also packed his films with anomolous references to his own Jewish heritage. In *Whoopee!* Eddie's friend, a half-breed Indian in love with a white girl, demands to be treated as an equal. He protests to Eddie: "I went to your schools." Eddie wonders: "An Indian in a Hebrew School?" Later in the film, Eddie adopts the alias of Big Chief Indie Horowitz to haggle over the prices of Indian artifacts and blankets. In *Roman Scandals*, on the block at the slave auction, Eddie (here Eddiepuss), advertises his own value: "Look at these skins," slapping his arm and leg, "imported from Russia." This form of self-reference came directly to movies from audience asides on the vaudeville circuit and at the *Follies*.

So did Cantor's defining himself as a woman among men. In several films Cantor frequently kisses men (for whatever plot reason). In *Whoopee!*, seeing his half-breed Indian friend without a shirt, he observes, "He's cute, isn't he?" In *The Kid from Spain*, caught in the girl's dormitory at college, Eddie confesses: "I'm a naughty girl." If the plot of *Kid Millions* resembles Harold Lloyd's *The Kid Brother* (Eddie is the effeminate runt in a family of male brutes), Eddie also plays Cinderella, the harried housekeeper whose fairy godmother (a lawyer) brings him a dowry that frees him from his evil stepfather and three male stepsisters. The Cantor films save their ultimate weapons for attacks on Eddie's butt—not Chaplin's kicks or Keaton's pratfalls, but phallic thrusts by Roman swords, the horns of bulls, and even the biting beak of a goose.

Berkeley's musical numbers in these Cantor films had very little to do with any of this. Cantor's famous song, "Makin' Whoopee" (*Whoopee!*), delivered with a delightfully droll, understated intimacy directly to the camera's lens, was irrelevant to anything else in the film. He delivers the film's other hit, "My Baby Just Cares for Me," to a hostile sheriff to prove that he is a singing black cook. Now, he got to be black by hiding in a gas stove that just happened to explode when someone struck a match. And he pretends to be a singing black cook so the sheriff won't believe he is the white man on a wanted poster. The only purpose of this logical whirligig is to supply his excuse to perform the digressive blackface hit that everyone expects him to sing, reason or no.

Such digressions, however, permitted Busby Berkeley's visual exercises in white and black, the primary visual pallette of monochrome. In *Roman Scandals*, Berkeley sets "Keep Young and Beautiful" at the mud baths, where a chorus line of lovely white blondes is attended by a chorus line of jazzy black maids. The women's dresses evolve from white to black, their skin evolves from white to black, the set evolves from white to black, the music and dance evolve from white lilt to black tap. By reducing racial blackness and whiteness to polar opposites of visual decor, Berkeley strips them of their social and historical significance, converting them into mere elements of design. Cantor, after falling into a mud vat as the excuse for blackface song, becomes a decorative racial composite—blackface above white legs. With lyrics by Al Dubin and music by Harry Warren, and with the spunky child-midget Billy Barty, in blackface, running around to peek at the ladies, the number seems a dress rehearsal for Warner Bros.

There is something outrageous about making an agonizing American social issue—slavery and its consequences—a mere pretext for pretty patterns. Part of the charm of this outrage is that it seems so naive, so unaware that it is performing what might be considered a social atrocity. The most outrageous of these Berkeley concoctions—Jolson's "Goin' to Heaven on a Mule" in the 1934 *Wonder Bar*—is so insensitive and insulting in its black stereotypes that the film is rarely shown today in theaters (and the number is cut for showings on television). There is yet another atrocity in *Roman Scandals*—a Berkeley number in which women slaves cavort in writhing patterns of sadomasochistic belly dancing, whipped while chained to what appears to be a gigantic marble wedding cake. The Ziegfeld staircase has been transformed into a spiraling mountain of ramps for perfectly arranged circular formations of choreographed agony. This aestheticizing of slavery and death (a rebellious slave dives off the cake to her destruction) produces the paradoxical effect today of many Berkeley numbers—laughter at the monstrous audacity of his not seeing anything about a social situation except an opportunity for decorative design; wonder at his energetic execution of that design and absolute commitment to its visual evolution.

One type of Busby Berkeley number transforms the social into the geometrical (as these two numbers from *Roman Scandals* do). Another transforms the sexual into the geometrical. Although there are strong whiffs of sexual smoke in these Roman numbers, a more typical example of an early Berkeley sexual exercise is the opening of *The Kid from Spain*. Set in the women's dormitory of a college campus, this Berkeley number provides a peek at a location, rife with sexual suggestion, from which the male is forbidden entrance. Girls arise from seemingly hundreds of beds, wearing attractively inviting white negligees. They dive into a swimming pool for a morning dip (doesn't every college dorm room have a pool?). Still wearing their high-heeled pumps, they swim into a series of patterns that incorporate the pumps as a conscious element of visual design. The female bodies, viewed from a crane high above, congeal into kaleidoscopic fragments, using the water as the visual ground for geometric human configuration.

After departing the pool, the girls retreat behind screens to change clothes. Their suggestive striptease becomes decorative silhouette, two-dimensional shadows on the cloth barriers that separate their bodies from the camera's gaze. The cloth screens become metaphors and surrogates for the cinema's silver screen, a projection of light and shadow that coalesces into suggestive forms, reducing three-dimensional bodies to two-dimensional shapes, removing the male viewer from the potential objects of desire by converting them into flat, immaterial images. When the camera threatens their safety, by beginning to travel around the cloth barrier to the other side of the shelter, the girls let out a scream that summons the hag who attends them and whose grim presence ends the musical revel. The number is a sketch for the fuller water ballet, "By a Waterfall," from the 1933 *Footlight Parade*, and striptease silhouette, "Pettin' in the Park," from *Gold Diggers of 1933*.

The third type of Berkeley musical number was not the social situation or sexual location converted into kaleidoscopic geometry but an abstract evolution of geometric design built around a visual object. Berkeley objects descend directly from Ziegfeld's famous gimmicks—balloons, fans, feathers—that teasingly both covered and displayed the female form. Berkeley's first film sketch of this kind is "Stetson Hat" in *Whoopee!*, built around the huge ten-gallon hats worn by the ladies of the Ziegfeld line. The objects allowed kaleidoscopic shots from above, converting circular brims into evolving patterns of bouncing balls, and shots from the floor, allowing the emergence of pretty faces from beneath those large brims. Later Berkeley objects—violins, pianos, waterfalls—would permit his lengthiest, most dazzling displays of visual virtuosity, unfettered by any constrictions of narrative, social, or spatial logic.

"Stetson Hat" from *Whoopee!*: Berkeley's first overhead shots

Even Berkeley's very first film established the basic steps or "moves" on which he would build his visual configurations: the shot from directly above, reducing the individual human figures below to mosaic tiles, removing them from any concrete spatial referents; a line maneuver, the wave, modulating a ribbon of female bodies into the rise and fall of a wave as it rolls toward the shore; a moving-camera strategy, the inverted V, pushing the lens through the isosceles triangle created by a row of female dancers' legs, crotches at the apex; another moving-camera strategy, the massive pull-back, beginning with a confined space and pulling back to reveal a vast setting of unimaginable size and infinite space. Berkeley married the camera crane, which D. W. Griffith first used in 1916 to traverse the epic Babylon of *Intolerance*, to the Ziegfeld showgirl. As early as *Whoopee!* the showgirls execute the only step a "dancer" ever needed for a Berkeley film, that old standby, the time-step. Berkeley choreographed space, not people.

In three years at Goldwyn, Berkeley explored the visual dynamics of black and white—the contrast of white dresses surrounded by gleaming black sets or reflected by a shiny black floor; black dresses surrounded by gleaming white sets or reflected by a shiny white floor; blond hair opposed to black hair and white skin opposed to black skin. If Berkeley was insensitive to racial and social implication, he was extremely sensitive to chiaroscura. He was also sensitive to the visual contrast beween the circle and the line. Circular forms of dancers contrasted with the linear angles of the sets; circular movement evolved into linear patterns, which then resolved to circular ones. The two visual systems of Berkeley's canvas were the opposition of black to white and circle to line, which could then be mixed, contrasted, evolved, and synthesized in the course of any musical number.

He took these graphic elements to Warner Bros. early in 1933. For three years he drew them with abandon on celluloid canvas, unfettered by the script, the budget, the shooting schedule, or common sense. Though he worked with different Warner Bros. designers (Anton Grot, Jack Okey, Robert Hass, Willie Pogany), Berkeley's numbers always displayed the same kaleidoscopic chiaroscura. Because he remained, as on Broadway and at Goldwyn, choreographer, not director, his sole responsibility was to the musical sequences of films. Of fifteen films at Warner Bros., he directed the dialogue sections of only two (*Gold Diggers of 1935* and the 1937 *Hollywood Hotel*). This practice freed Berkeley to concentrate exclusively on musical sequences. It also allowed Warner Bros. to invest far more time in Berkeley's musical gems while any staff director shot the dialogue paste on some other soundstage. Berkeley could extend his numbers to conceptual infinity because he could shoot them over extended periods of weeks, rather than rammed into the hours or days that shooting schedules allotted musical numbers in program pictures.

Berkeley also benefited from a historical coincidence. He inaugurated his cycle at Warner Bros., the most Democratic and pro-Roosevelt studio, in the same year as the inauguration of FDR and his NRA. Though the Berkeley numbers were excessive—and excess is their most striking characteristic—they also put an excessive number of people to work. In all three 1933 Berkeley films—*42nd Street*, *Footlight Parade*, and *Gold Diggers of 1933*—a temperamental character learns his or her responsibility to the entire group. Putting on a show represented jobs for two hundred people. The same could be said about Berkeley production numbers. The despotic director in these Berkeley films, Julian Marsh (Warner Baxter) of *42nd Street* or Chester Kent (James Cagney) of *Footlight Parade*, can be seen as little FDRs, the strong leader putting a large community of productive working people back to work.[3] Berkeley's excesses were socially useful in 1933.

The three 1933 films are the purest examples of Berkeley's style—the first three in the Warner Bros. cycle, probably the best three, and the three most obviously conceived as a unit. There are three Big Musical Numbers in each film, and the numbers occur in precisely the same order. The first is always built on a sexually suggestive location—a honeymoon train to Niagara Falls ("Shuffle Off to Buffalo" of *42nd Street*), a park teeming with amorous couples ("Pettin' in the Park" of *Gold Diggers of 1933*), and a "Honeymoon Hotel" teeming with wedded couples (*Footlight Parade*), some of whom may not be so wedded.

Next comes the abstract-geometric number, based on a visual object or idea. "Young and Healthy" (*42nd Street*) is based on the pure contrast of black-white and circle-line, "The Shadow Waltz" (*Gold Diggers*) on the circular hoop skirt and the violin (itself a composite of linear bow and neck joined to circular body). "By a Waterfall" (*Footlight Parade*) is based on streams, sprays, and pools of water: "A modern waterfall splashing on beautiful white bodies," in Chester Kent's description. He somehow gets this inspiration by seeing black slum boys at play in a streaming fire hydrant.

"I'm Young and Healthy": Berkeley's inverted V

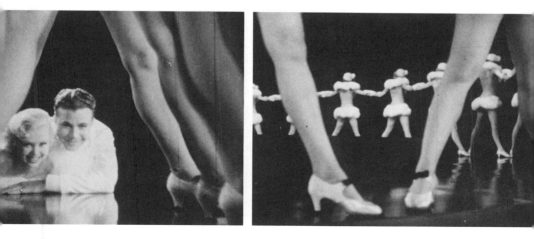

Finally, comes the number of social commentary: a survey of high and low life on "42nd Street"; a plea to "Remember My Forgotten Man" (*Gold Diggers*), the generation that once marched off to war but now marches on the bread lines; and "Shanghai Lil" (*Footlight Parade*). This number begins by surveying a sleazy saloon on some sinister waterfront, full of drugged Oriental hookers and the international gallery of men who exploit them, only to end as a literal cartoon.

The music for these numbers (lyrics by Al Dubin and music by Harry Warren) is as similar as their visual plan and sequential order. Tin Pan Alley tunesmiths rather than Broadway composers, Dubin and Warren captured the energy of an era—its rhythms and dances—just as De Sylva, Brown, and Henderson did a decade before. Both their lilting ballads and up-tempo tunes became, and remain, familiar standards. If Warren's music kept American couples dancing in public, it kept Busby Berkeley's images dancing on film. Warren's simple eight-bar phrases build a thirty-two-bar refrain in sharp, bold outlines, a firm musical container for the liquid of Berkeley's ever dissolving visual figures.

Warren's scores for the 1933 Berkeley films are built on exactly three musical themes, one for each type of number. The sexual location number is always constructed as a bouncy AABA fox-trot, with musical phrases so similar that the refrains and releases of the three songs can be used interchangeably. (Try whistling the refrain of "Pettin' in the Park" with the release of "Shuffle Off to Buffalo"; or the refrain of "Honeymoon Hotel" with the release of "Pettin' in the Park." These new songs make perfect sense.) The abstract geometric number attracts a more lilting tune, an actual waltz for one of the three films ("Shadow Waltz"), a more fluid Type II ballad for another ("By a Waterfall"). The social commentary number for all three films gets an AABA song in a minor key, with a tempo that either is or suggests a march. Their refrains are so similar musically that the first four bars of "Forgotten Man" can be combined with the final four bars of

"The Shadow Waltz": A free-form Ziegfeld staircase in monochrome kaleidoscopy

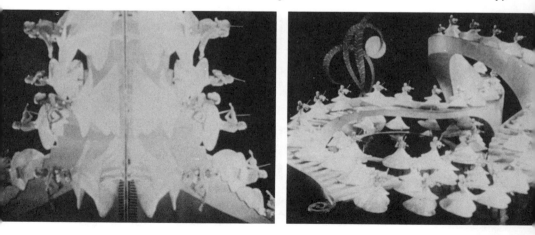

"Shanghai Lil" to produce a completely logical new refrain. Warren was permuting identical musical themes just as obviously as Berkeley was permuting identical visual themes in the three films.

They knew they were playing these visual-musical games. The confession comes in *Footlight Parade*, the most reflexive film of the cycle. Chester Kent's "prologues," live musical entertainments to precede the movie, are themselves Busby Berkeley musical numbers: figuratively, because the prologues resemble musical numbers in their purpose to balance a movie narrative with musical entertainment; literally, because the prologues *are* the Big Musical Numbers of *Footlight Parade*. In a confessional moment, Kent despairs of getting a new idea for a prologue: "We've had flowers, pictures, tables, radios, statues, more tables, sofas, pianos." (The pianos would come in *Gold Diggers of 1935*.) The line might have come from Berkeley himself, in conference with Dubin and Warren, racking their brains to come up with yet another new and clever visual gimmick to generate yet another number based on yet another waltz or march or fox-trot. Facing Berkeley, Dubin, and Warren was the perpetual pressure to do the same thing somehow different, better, or bigger than before.

There are only two other types of musical numbers in the three films: the informal rehearsal number and the formal rehearsal number. The informal number, always performed in rehearsal clothes, mere fragments sung at the piano or danced in formation, implies the rigors of rehearsal and backstage life. The formal number was always performed in full costume for a dress rehearsal ("You're Gettin' to Be a Habit with Me" for *42nd Street*, "Sittin' on a Backyard Fence" for *Footlight Parade*, "We're in the Money" for *Gold Diggers of 1933*). It would evolve over three or four choruses, less than half the length of a Big Number. Unlike the Big Numbers, it represented movements and activities that could actually occur on a theater stage, viewed from low frontal angles, as if the camera were seated in the front row alongside the show's director. It might, however, inject one impossible spatial surprise—like Ginger Rogers appearing on both the far left and far right ends of the same chorus line during a single tracking shot in "We're in the Money."

The split between Big Numbers and rehearsal numbers in the Warner cycle indicated the curious way musical sequences were slotted into the stories. While most musicals seek some stylistic convention for weaving numbers through an entire narrative, the Berkeley musicals save their Big Numbers for the big bang at the very end, after the narrative complications have been tied into marriage knots or swept under societal rugs. The Berkeley musicals are so end-heavy that many of them conclude with the three Big Musical Numbers in a row, one after the other. The rehearsal numbers are appetizers to take the edge off our visual hunger until the Big Numbers finally serve the orgasmic musical feast. What this construction lacks in balance it gains in sock. The Big Numbers are the headliners that always top the bill of vaudeville entertainments.

The Busby Berkeley musicals are odd mixtures of ordinary program pictures in the economical Warner Bros. style, shot by Warner program directors, with spectacular musical sequences for their climaxes. Rather than Chester Kent prologues, these films add Busby Berkeley epilogues. The first film of the cycle, *42nd Street*, is the most honest and the most sleazy in its peek behind the footlights. Its narrative sections take their texture from a convincing inside view of the battles, rigors, jealousies, gossip, bitchiness, chaos, and sexuality of backstage life. "Pretty Lady," the show-within-the-film, is bankrolled by "daddy" Abner Dillon (Guy Kibbee), with a thirst for bare leg. Between sips, he also keeps the show's star, Dorothy Brock (Bebe Daniels). Both chorus boys and stage-door Johnnies put the make on the girls, and many of them, like Anytime Annie (Ginger Rogers wearing a monocle and carrying a Pekingese), rise to Park Avenue luxury on the anytime trading of sexual favors for material tokens. In a telling little scene, a stern landlady lectures Peggy Sawyer (Ruby Keeler) that men are absolutely not permitted in women's rooms; at the same time, behind her back, a girl in the hallway kisses the man who has just left her room.

If the narrative sections of *42nd Street* are the spiciest of the cycle, there is also the most at stake in "Pretty Lady": Everyone, from its director to the kids in the chorus to the kid from the chorus who becomes a star, really *needs* that hit. There is less at stake as the cycle progresses. In *Gold Diggers of 1935*, the show is merely a charity benefit at a resort hotel for the very rich. No one needs the show to succeed and only the bunco Russian (Adolphe Menjou), swindling the millionaires, even cares if it is produced. Backstage life after *42nd Street* also gets progressively cleaner, rife with suggestions of male inclination staunchly repulsed by showgirls, blameless and stainless. The girls are unjustly suspected of sexual intentions by blue-nosed outsiders who consider themselves morally superior to showfolk.

The enemies of shows and show people in these films are the rich, sophisticated elite who despise the entertainments of the common people— the popular, democratic, mass-entertainment arts, of which movies consider themselves a prime example. The two Boston Brahmins of *Gold Diggers of 1933*, J. Lawrence Bradford (Warren William) and Faneuil H. Peabody (Guy Kibbee again), are certain that showgirls are "cheap and vulgar" gold diggers, swindling upstanding men of their upright cash. Gold diggers are glorified prostitutes. Ezra Ounce (F. Hugh Herbert), the eccentric millionaire of *Dames*, establishes the Ounce Foundation for the Elevation of American Morals to eradicate shows and show folks. He has sawed off the twisted branch of the family tree (Dick Powell) who committed the cardinal sin of producing a show ("Sweet and Hot"). But Ounce has his own weakness—an unquenchable thirst for Dr. Silver's Golden Elixir, a patent medicine, both sweet and hot, which floats him into a show on a humanely drunken cloud. These films embarrass their upper-class persecutors by manipulating the same self-righteous moral clichés.

The struggle between showfolk and moralistic rich folk in the films is an explicit metaphor for Hollywood's battle with the new Production Code, the industry's own Ounce of prevention. The Warner Bros. cycle acknowledges the coming of the Code.[4] In *Footlight Parade*, the Chester Kent studio hires a moral adviser (F. Hugh Herbert again), as every Hollywood studio did, to make sure its productions can play in Peoria. The censor's power evaporates when he is discovered in the arms of Miss Vivian Rich, a gold digger in sophisticate's clothing who heads the studio's Department of Style and Taste. Miss Rich (the initial consonant of her name once slips to a "B") is dismissed from the Kent studio with Joan Blondell's blessing: "As long as there're sidewalks, you've got a job." Although the films attribute the pressure for censorship to the cultural elite, the Eastern upper classes, the actual pressure for control of film content came from middle-class and working-class organizations (like the Catholic Legion of Decency), who represented the faithful audiences of movies, not their enemies. The conflict between blue bloods and showfolk in Warner Bros. musicals was another formulation of that battle in filmusicals between high and low entertainments.

Once the obstacles to mounting the show-within-the-film have been overcome—the money has been secured, the romantic couples have been sorted out, the moralists have been silenced, the grueling weeks of rehearsal have finally ended and it is opening night at last—the film audience can sit back to receive its musical-visual reward for sticking it out (like the cast of the show) to the end. Berkeley's building of these musical rewards shows an increasing consciousness and complexity as the cycle progresses from 1933 to 1935. Their formulas cannot be so easily categorized as the 1933 trio. Though both *Dames* and *Gold Diggers of 1935* offer informal rehearsal glimpses of the cast at work, both drop the formal rehearsal number. Instead, Dick Powell croons a love ballad in some natural location (a park, on a lake, on the Staten Island ferry) to "naturalize" the singing of songs, make them part of life, not just theater. None of the three Big Numbers of *Dames* conforms precisely to the basic Berkeley types. "The Girl at the Ironing Board," a nostalgic waltz, combines the social (a proletarian work place) and the sexual. Joan Blondell, backed by a chorus of singing and dancing BVD's on a clothesline, finds herself buried beneath the male underwear when the number climaxes with a BVD gang bang. The lilting "I Only Have Eyes for You" combines the social (the subway and the theater district) with a geometric idea and object (based on the human eye). The bouncy "Dames" combines the sexual (watching show girls awaken and prepare for rehearsal) and the geometric (based on evolving trapezoidal and semicircular shapes). By 1934 Berkeley was seeking hybrid variations of his three pure types as another way to do the same thing but different.

The numbers also grow as the cycle progresses. The numbers of *42nd Street* are the briefest ("Shuffle Off to Buffalo" evolves over five choruses, "Young and Healthy" over six, and the title song eight). The three numbers of *Gold Diggers of 1933* are consistently longer (seven, five, and ten choruses respectively). The three numbers of *Footlight Parade* longer yet (eight, twelve, and nine choruses respectively). Those lengths become standard for such later numbers as "I Only Have Eyes for You" (eleven choruses), "Dames" (also eleven), and "The Words Are in My Heart" (nine). Yet another way to do the same thing differently was to do the same thing longer. In extending their lengths, Berkeley also invested more in their shapes. The fully developed Berkeley number is a perfect circle. It begins with a clear visual statement, evolves to another in the second chorus, then to yet another in the third. It enters the free-form center of the number (the fourth through, say, eighth choruses) and then, in its final chorus, returns, step by step, to the exact visual imagery, camera position, and musical phrases of the opening for its conclusion.

"The Words Are in My Heart" from *Gold Diggers of 1935* provides a clear example of Berkeley's careful construction. Both musically and visually a variation on the abstract geometric "Shadow Waltz" two years earlier, "The Words Are in My Heart" is another flowing waltz in which gliding pianos replace the former fiddles.

"The Words Are in My Heart." First and second chorus: Dick Powell's serenade sits atop the piano of a singing trio.

First Chorus: Dick Powell sings the verse and chorus to a blond listener in a setting that suggests the lawn of some antebellum plantation; her blond hair drips downward in spiraling ringlets while his velvet-lapeled jacket suggests the same period. Berkeley always states the main theme of a Big Number with the solo singing of a verse and initial chorus (often by Dick Powell to Ruby Keeler, later by Winifred Shaw or Tony Martin).

Second Chorus: A Berkeley pull-back reveals that this antebellum pastoral idyll has inexplicably (that is, magically) frozen into a ceramic *objet d'art*, perched atop a white spinet. This chorus is apparently sung (but obviously lip-synched) by three ladies, dressed in white gowns, beside the spinet (three witches? fairies? muses? graces?) But exactly how were Powell and lady fair frozen into figurines? Exactly how could this process have been witnessed by the supposed audience in the resort hotel? And exactly what spatial relationship might this spinet have to the supposed stage? Does the stage itself sit atop the spinet, like the world on the shoulders of Atlas? It would be a mistake to believe that Berkeley was not aware of these questions. Movies, like ceramic *objets d'art*, freeze people and places into permanent objects of contemplation.

Third Chorus: This chorus, purely instrumental, begins with a close-up of a pair of hands on piano keys—belonging, we presume, to one of those ladies at the white spinet. Another Berkeley pull-back, however, reveals these keys to be played by a total newcomer, one of at least sixty fair ladies in white dresses, all of them playing white baby-grand pianos (no spinets

"The Words Are in My Heart." Third chorus: from a pair of hands to an infinite Ziegfeld staircase of pianos

for this crowd), artfully arranged on an immense circular structure, one of Berkeley's circular evolutions of a Ziegfeld staircase. The white baby grands turn in waltztime while the smiling ladies sway in rhythm, pretending to play them. The musical instruments have become their dancing partners.

Fourth Chorus: The camera catches the turning pianos from various extreme angles, high above and obliquely from the side, during another instrumental chorus. The circular structure mysteriously disappears to allow the white pianos themselves to dance into geometric formations on the flat black floor. The white baby grands, controlled by faceless men hidden beneath them, wearing black trousers that make them virtually invisible against the black floor, have become genderless dancing partners of the women who play them.

Fifth Chorus: Also instrumental, the camera from high above views geometric formations of the white baby grands as dancing white lines upon a shiny black sea. The grand pianos, like the earlier violins, synthesize the circle and the line—linear keyboards and keys (themselves black and white) with circular bodies.

Sixth Chorus: The lines of pianos continue to weave in rhythm as unseen female singing voices return. The women leave the pianos to their own devices and the pianos oblige by leaving the frame at the end of the chorus.

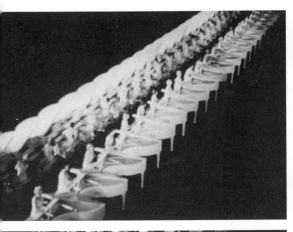

"The Words Are in My Heart." Fourth through sixth choruses: geometric patterns of faces and pianos

Seventh Chorus: The white-dressed women sway, wave their hands, and dance, standing on the black floor for the first half of the chorus. Then they return to their piano benches, which have come back to fetch them. Berkeley gives us close-ups of their smiling faces floating through the frame, unattached to any clear spatial coordinates.

Eighth Chorus: The women now dance atop their pianos, swaying to the instrumental waltz. As seen from high above, the pianos converge into an immense, perfectly rectangular white dancing surface, fitting together precisely like the pieces of a jigsaw puzzle. A lone white-dressed dancer waltzes atop the rectangular white floor, engulfed by the surrounding blackness of the floor and walls, suspending her white dance in a vast black void.

Ninth Chorus: Riding another Berkeley pull-back, the camera leaves the white-dressed lady to her swaying and returns to a close-up of a keyboard, precisely duplicating the shot that began the third chorus. This time, however, the pull-back returns us to the three ladies at the white spinet who "sang" the second chorus. The camera seems to have traveled backward through a latticed mirror just above the spinet's keyboard, suggesting that

"The Words Are in My Heart." Seventh chorus: the women sway, then turn to their piano partners

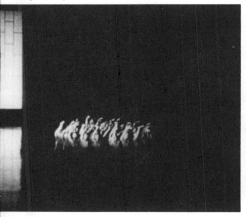

"The Words Are in My Heart." Eighth chorus: lone dancer atop a piano platform

choruses three through eight have somehow taken place "through the looking glass," in a magical region "inside" the white spinet. The three ladies blow out some candles and ascend a staircase (presumably to sleep, but who knows where), as a clock strikes midnight. This device seems to explain the number's spatial mysteries as myth and magic at the witching hour. But it no more "explains" or "motivates" the spatial incongruities than Dick Powell's supposed dreaming in "By a Waterfall" and "I Only Have Eyes for You." Neither magic nor dream can explain the ability of a theater audience to see these images in precisely this way.

The camera returns to the ceramic figurines atop the spinet (remember them?). It tracks forward so Dick Powell can come to full-sized life again to warble the final eight bars of the refrain. If Powell begins a Berkeley number, he always ends it with eight concluding bars. The perfect circle closes when Powell kisses the lady with the blond ringlets, their embrace reflected in a pool of water. The reflecting pool is a final metaphoric comment on the cinema and the entire number: a mirage of reflected light that presents apparently substantial bodies in apparently real spaces that are merely projected images, which exist nowhere at all.

The most interesting idea in this number is Berkeley's deliberate divorce of concrete images and objects from clear referents in physical space. It is an attempt to convert the visual into the musical. There are two obvious differences between musical sounds and cinema images. First, a musical sound (B-flat, for example, on an oboe) does not necessarily refer to anything in reality or resemble anything we can recognize (by whatever principle of resemblance) other than itself; musical sounds are pieces of sense data without meanings. Although entire musical phrases can be said to resemble natural sounds (the roll of waves, the twitter of birds) or emotional states (an ode to joy), they do so according to principles of simile and conventions of correlation. Second, sounds float free in space, not embedded in a specific context as sights always are. While a sight is either to the right or left, placing the precise location of a sound is often impossible. Characters on a movie screen appear to be speaking even if the character is a pair of BVDs and the sound comes from behind the viewer.

Berkeley composes a visual-musical symphony in which images float as free as music in the air, in which the organization of images is controlled, like music, by an internal principle of logic—of statement, development, and variation. In Berkeley's numbers, the screen dissolves the spaces of the physical world into a purified visual medium of air and light (and sometimes water). "The Words Are in My Heart" does not take place "inside" a spinet so much as "inside" its music, which has no inside (or outside) because it has no spatial dimension or extension. No other commercial Hollywood filmmaker who began by photographing physical bodies was so thoroughly committed to transforming physical entities into abstract units of retinal music.[5]

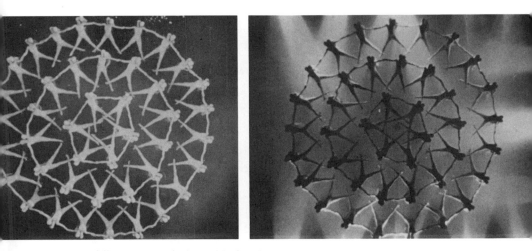

"By a Waterfall": abstract design with female units

But for all the interest of this abstraction, Berkeley's goal of stripping visual images of their social and natural referents is doomed to failure. Visual images may be thought of as potentially *like* musical notes, and a system of their elaboration can be based on internal logical principles of visual design—black and white, light and shadow, circle and line. In the end, however, the visual images continue to resemble what they are images of. Smiling women's faces remain smiling *women's* faces; female legs remain legs, not diagonal lines and inverted V's. At the very least, the Berkeley numbers cleverly play the conscious game of dissolving the recognizable into musical abstraction and resolving the abstraction into the recognizable again.

White pianos may contain no moral or social implications in themselves, but what happens when the pianos shelter "invisible" male partners (just as the amoral water of "By a Waterfall" hides "invisible" males who partner the visible women)? What are we to think of a number that contains only one visible man, Dick Powell, and multitudes of women? By removing male competitors, the number encourages the direct voyeuristic attachment of the male spectator to all these women as candidates for his private fantasy harem. "By a Waterfall" hangs suspended between classical myth and literal wet dream. Though the women's headgear suggests the mermaids and Nereids who inhabit the rocks and pools of siren myth, Powell awakens from his dream with wet trousers.[6]

What Berkeley gives in pornographic interest with one hand, however, he takes away with the other. If he encourages the male pleasure of looking at the female form (as Ziegfeld did), he so geometricizes and abstracts the female body as an element of visual design that the women, in kaleidoscopic far shot, are no longer always recognizable as women. Berkeley aestheticizes his women far more than Ziegfeld, whose showgirls necessarily remained walking female bodies, not petals of plastic design. Even the smiling faces and shapely legs of Berkeley's women reduce them to mannequins of abstract geometry. Those many decapitated faces and disembodied limbs of

"By a Waterfall": visual references to classical nymphs

Berkeley's women are so identical—and so removed from each other—that two potential sources of desire have been amputated: the mystery of individuality and the harmony of a whole body.

Not surprisingly, "By a Waterfall" was a great favorite of Adolf Hitler, whose own visual propaganda reduced human beings to visual fragments of awesome architecture and mythical abstraction. The Berkeley aesthetic is not far removed from the Nazi cult of beauty. In the end, it is difficult to determine if Berkeley's abstract-geometric visual conceptions are more intriguing because of the way they decorate women as male fantasies or the way they so overdecorate the human form that the human disappears altogether into patterns of pure form.

Even more odd than Berkeley's abstractions are the smarmy leers of his sexual-location numbers, usually personified by Billy Barty, posing as a precociously horny baby. Although opposite in age to the dignified elders and moralistic censors impersonated by the Kibbees and Herberts, Barty displays the same ogling spirit. He voraciously stares at the female shadows in "Pettin' in the Park" while the girls change their rainsoaked clothing behind protective screens. He then intrudes upon their shadowy pseudo-privacy by mischievously raising the screens, exposing the girls to audience view. Here Billy becomes both the accomplice and the antagonist of the director. While Berkeley arouses desire with artistic silhouettes, projecting light upon screens, analogous to the movie screen illuminated by its projector, Billy wants to destroy the artistic projection to see the naked bodies themselves. At the conclusion of "Pettin' in the Park," Billy hands Dick Powell a can opener to remove Ruby Keeler's metal blouse when the girls emerge from behind their screens with sexual protection—form-fitting iron maidens that encase their torsos in metal plates. Billy's strategy once again attacks the director's decorous disguise with a basely practical and phallic tool. While Berkeley searches for metaphors—silhouettes, projections, screens, metal covers (like the cans of film)—Barty wants the thing itself.

Barty always messes things up in these numbers. He might be thought of as comical: the impish spirit of Puck, playing tricks on the fools that mortal lovers be. Or he might be thought of as maniacal: the pure and

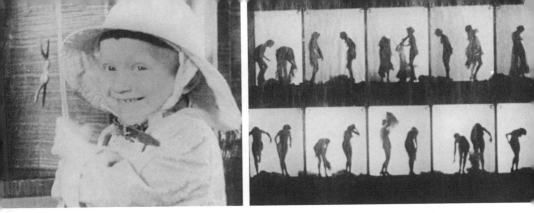

Art and pornography in "Pettin' in the Park": strip-tease silhouettes and Billy Barty's leer

unfettered id, refusing to sublimate its absolute lust and transmute it into the acceptable and civilized forms of artistic design. In Freudian terms, Billy is the infant who wants to crash the primal party and, amazingly enough, almost gets in. In "Honeymoon Hotel" Billy marches down the corridor in his pajamas, accompanying other bridegrooms on their smiling way to their supposedly first we-know-what. He follows negligeed women into their rooms, crawls under their beds, and finally winds up under the covers—with Dick Powell (until Ruby Keeler duly replaces Billy for the final eight bars). Nor does the number keep it a secret that the main event is the act that produces more Billies. "Honeymoon Hotel" ends with a closeup of a magazine, whose pages riffle to the portrait of an infant (just as "By a Waterfall" ends with three baby birdies in a nest). No wonder these sexual numbers were the first to go when the Code came to Hollywood.

Equally bizarre, though in a different way, are Berkeley's numbers of social commentary and criticism, in which the moral implications of the images as representations of human and social misery conflict with the purely formal conception of Berkeley's kaleidoscopic design. How seriously can we take the plight of America's "forgotten men," who now march in breadlines, when Berkeley aestheticizes their misery into pleasantly evolving patterns? How seriously can we take the plight of Shanghai's whores, drunks, and junkies when their down-and-out lives in sleazy saloons merely provide a backdrop for Ruby Keeler's tap-dancing? Do Shanghai women tap dance? Why is she wearing those braids? Why has her "r" become an "l" (as in "velly good")? Why, other than for Berkeley's expertise with military drill patterns, does Shanghai become a backdrop for American military marching that evolves into representations of the American flag, FDR's face, and the NRA eagle? At least Berkeley found something for men to do while visible: what they always do in operettas march. Berkeley's flag waving seems no less imperialistic than George M. Cohan's.

The impulse for these numbers is obvious—to do something relevant, meaningful, and serious in a musical number (especially at socially conscious Warner Bros.) other than weaving purely visual or sexually suggestive tapestries. Berkeley's "Forgotten Man" genuinely wants to capture the urgency of "Brother, Can You Spare a Dime?," which the Warren tune

Fitting Ruby Keeler into the visual design: with blond curls (and Dick Powell) for "The Shadow Waltz"; with dark braids (and James Cagney) for "Shanghai Lil"; with sequined swimcap for "By a Waterfall"

evokes. But the hooker leaning on the lamppost (Joan Blondell), and the wailing black woman in her slum room, and the drunk sleeping on the pavement all seem refugees from some other movie, only to become parenthetic irrelevancies to Berkeley's rap-tap-tapping and marching marching marching.

Precisely these tensions make Berkeley so intriguing, so outrageous, so vigorous, so endearing, and so enduring. There is a terrific energy in the inherent contradiction between his film images as purely "musical" design and the sexual, social, and moral implications of the images, which refuse to shed their signification. Berkeley's studio bosses must have sensed the tensions and suggestions too. Not only were Berkeley's sexual numbers expunged by 1935 but so was the inverted-V camera maneuver through the legs of show girls. Even his attack on logically contiguous space was rejected as excessive and impossible. The new fashion in Hollywood musicals, influenced by the competing Astaire-Rogers filmusicals at RKO, was to maintain the stability of real space. Berkeley numbers after Warner Bros., whether at Fox or MGM, maintain the integrity of contiguous spatial relationships: no matter how lavish, most could conceivably have been mounted on a real stage in a real theater. The musical climax of *Ziegfeld Girl* goes to great pains to show that the huge, revolving circular structure fits snugly beneath the proscenium arch of a theater stage. That proscenium arch was a metaphoric shadow of his studio bosses, confining Berkeley's visual flights within the boundaries of spatial possibility.

Many of Berkeley's assignments at MGM take him back to the turn of the century. Berkeley had become an antiquated relic with no purpose in the present except to evoke nostalgia for a thankfully dead past. Many numbers in *For Me and My Gal* (1942) or *Take Me out to the Ball Game* (1949) were recreations of old-time vaudeville turns on theater states—visually inert, filmed in a single take and set in very shallow space against a painted olio drop. These numbers are unrecognizable as uniquely Berkeley pieces. So were most of the numbers in the three Mickey and Judy "barnyard" musicals ("Let's put on a show in the old barn, kids"), his other assignment at MGM. If Berkeley was the Dead Past for MGM, he was also Childhood Innocence. Only at the barnyard climax of *Babes in Arms* (1939) or *Strike Up the Band* (1940) could Berkeley smash the proscenium arch into fragments of musical mosaic.

If MGM saw Berkeley as the past, Fox saw him as a bizarre and exotic fruit, just right for the bizarre and exotic lady with the fruit, Carmen Miranda. Berkeley's most famous Technicolor number suggests his usual outrageous contradiction between formal pattern and sexual allusion: Miranda's "The Girl in the Tutti-Frutti Hat" for *The Gang's All Here* (1943), a Berkeley abstract based on the banana. The dance of show girls with bananas as male partners (it was wartime) was the most suggestively lewd number of Berkeley's entire career. His formal tools are again the circle and the line (synthesized by the banana's shape) and a contrast of shades (emerald green in opposition to banana yellow). The abstract evolution of these shapes (the bananas rise and fall in the ladies' hands, the ladies wear them as erect headgear, the bananas slide and ride between their legs) produces the fully paradoxical Berkeley effect of wonder at its visual kaleidoscopy and howling at the conscious or unconscious outrageousness of the sexual suggestion. That the number was produced and released in 1943 indicates that many folks inside and outside Hollywood either did not know what images implied or did not much care. After all, it was wartime.

Although less familiar today, Berkeley's most exhilarating late pieces were for MGM's *Million Dollar Mermaid* (1952), a fanciful biography of Annette Kellerman, the swimmer who became a star of both early twentieth-century vaudeville and silent films. Berkeley spun variations of his old "By a Waterfall," this time in color, for Esther Williams (whose swimming, like Kellerman's, combined the sports business with show business). Although Berkeley never destroys possible stage space as thoroughly as he did at Warner Bros., *Million Dollar Mermaid* grants him the freedom to evoke the legend of the immense Hippodrome with physical activities and visual transitions that could never have occurred there, no matter how vast the theater nor unlimited its resources. Once again, Berkeley concentrated on the Big Numbers while another director (Mervyn LeRoy, his old partner

Return to "By a Waterfall" with Esther Williams in *Million Dollar Mermaid*

from *Gold Diggers of 1933*) worried about the dreary dialogue. Once again, Berkeley uses his old tools: an object (water itself—not only a physical and visual medium as a deep pool but as dynamic geysers, fountains, sheets, and curtains); formal variations on visual patterns (the line and circle); and the conflict of opposing shades (fiery red with golden yellow, themselves in visual conflict with bright blue water). Berkeley adds another formal contrast to his pallette by intermixing the four elements—water, fire (smoke and flames spurt from the water itself), air (diving or sliding from high above into the water below); and earth (the power of gravity keeps these visual motifs together).

As in the Warner Bros. cycle, *Million Dollar Mermaid* is conscious of itself as a conflict and synthesis of high and low entertainment forms. The swimmer Annette Kellerman shares the Hippodrome bill with the famous ballerina Anna Pavlova; Kellerman's father, a classically trained musician, conducts the Hippodrome orchestra to accompany the acts. As in the Warner Bros. cycle, a woman is falsely accused by Boston blue bloods of immorality and indecency when Kellerman's one-piece bathing suits, which she defends for their practicality, are banned in Boston. As in the Warner Bros. cycle, Berkeley makes a reflexive visual connection between his musical numbers and the process of cinema. The glass frame of Annette Kellerman's swimming tank, which permits her audience at the Hippodrome to view her ballet, is figuratively and literally a cinema frame, which also permits the film audience to view the ballet. The rectangular glass frame of a water tank has evolved into the glass lens of the camera and the projected rectangle of the cinema frame. Screen rectangles are much safer than glass ones; Kellerman's career ends tragically when the glass frame of her swimming tank breaks while shooting a movie.

Berkeley and Le Roy Prinz would together stage the Indian ceremonial dances of MGM's *Rose Marie* (1954), another nostalgic reunion and revival. Both Berkeley and Prinz descended from Ziegfeld's Sammy Lee,[7] and the dynamic, diminutive Prinz, who staged prologues for Sid Grauman in the 1920s and 1930s, was the explicit model for Cagney's Chester Kent in *Footlight Parade*. Berkeley returned to Broadway in 1970 to stage another nostalgic revival—the 1926 hit, *No, No Nanette*, complete with Ruby Keeler. This final show was distinguished by the usual Berkeley virtues—a vigorously "young and healthy" corps of time-stepping tappers, their costumes fashioned as part of the musical design, cavorting with physical objects like beachballs, woven into the choreographic conception.

Like one of his formally perfect numbers, Berkeley's career was a complete circle, ending, as it began, with Broadway success. He died in 1976 after his final lullaby on Broadway.

An Astaire scrapbook: performing with Adele in 1906; a dapper twelve-year-old in 1911; with Adele in *The Band Wagon* in 1931

9

Gonna Write My Footsteps on the Sands of Time

FRED ASTAIRE IN BLACK AND WHITE

Fred Astaire is the single most remarkable figure in the American film musical. He is also among the most remarkable figures in the American stage musical. His first stage appearance in 1905 at age six was contemporaneous with Victor Herbert and George M. Cohan shows. His first major Broadway role in 1918 was contemporaneous with George Gershwin's Broadway debut. His film debut in early 1933 was contemporaneous with both the Paramount operettas and the Warner Bros. Busby Berkeley musicals. Fred Astaire's career merely *is* the history of the American musical. Astaire is to the twentieth-century musical what Chaplin is to its comedy—not its only master, to be sure, but its most glorious and enduring presence.

The parallels between Astaire, Chaplin, and another master of silent film comedy, Buster Keaton, are striking. Astaire was born in Omaha in 1899, just four years after and one state north of Keaton. All three were child performers, and all three began in family acts—Astaire with sister Adele, Keaton with his mother and father, Chaplin with an adopted family, the "Eight Lancashire Lads." All three performed novelty acts in vaudeville, the music hall, and the medicine show—that lower branch of show business. Astaire's original act, "Juvenile Artists Presenting an Electric Musical Toe-Dancing Novelty," was a stair dance, tapping with his sister up and down a flight of steps, which just happened to light up like Christmas for the finale.

Both the steps and the lights forecast future Astaire routines. The routine up and down a flight of stairs would return in "Cheek to Cheek" (*Top Hat*, 1935), with a twirl over a Venetian bridge, and "Never Gonna Dance" (*Swing Time*, 1936), with a dance below and above a gleaming black Bakelite staircase. Astaire's MGM ascensions would dispense with the material stairs altogether: he climbs a coatrack to dance on the ceiling in *Royal Wedding* (1951) and climbs nothing at all to dance on air in *The Belle of New York* (1952). The cinematic tricks derive from the other motif of Astaire's kiddie act—new-fangled gadgets like the electric lightbulb. While the electrical climax of "A Shine on Your Shoes" (*The Band Wagon*, 1953) recreates Astaire's kiddie climax on a grand scale, other Astaire routines make the cinema itself their most miraculous gadget: his dances with his own elongated shadows in "Bojangles of Harlem" (*Swing Time*) and with his own multiplied self in "Puttin' on the Ritz" (*Blue Skies*, 1946). Astaire's cinema tricks that multiply the physical self literally duplicate those in Keaton's 1921 short, *The Playhouse*.

Coming from that turn-of-the-century playhouse, like Chaplin and Keaton, Astaire knew that a headliner needed a trademark, a prop or costume that said, simply and immediately, "This is me." Astaire's trademark, his top hat and cane, is probably the second most familiar in American cultural history—after Chaplin's bowler, reedy cane, and floppy shoes. Unlike Chaplin's shoes, memorable for their look, Astaire's shoes are distinguished only by their sound (which is the reason Astaire's shoes never became a part of his icon). Simply to see a top hat and cane announces Astaire's appearance—as it does at both the beginning of *Top Hat* and *The Band Wagon*.

The trademarks not only identify a performer; they also symbolize a view of human experience, a way of life, a mediation between the way a character sees the world and the way the world sees the character. The costume both conceals and reveals. For the first third of *Swing Time*, Astaire, who is broke, is taken for a rich and proper swell simply because he wears a top hat and tails (his wedding outfit, the only clothes he owns). It is not just that he wears the clothes but that he knows how to wear them; they fit him—both physically and spiritually. This fit is exactly the opposite of Chaplin. The Tramp pieced together an outfit from the ill-fitting scraps of society's uniforms, implying that he does not belong in any of them but knows they exist. He is aware of the social roles they demand and he has the creative ability to put his outer costume, as well as his inner commitments, together for himself. Astaire accepts the social uniform of formal wear with such consummate ease that he does not so much borrow society's idea of formal grace as define the connection between grace and formal wear in the first place. The grace does not move from the costume to confer style on its wearer but from Astaire to confer grace on the costume.

These visible trademarks always suggest a paradoxical relationship between what the character seems and what the figure is. The Astaire paradox is suggested by a trivial piece of business, easily overlooked but pointedly inserted in almost every Astaire film: Astaire smokes cigarettes. He is a dancer who smokes. He smokes exactly one cigarette in exactly one scene of *Top Hat*, *Swing Time*, and *Shall We Dance?* He puffs on a pipe in one scene of *Swing Time* and *Carefree* (1938). These moments of smoking are so irrelevant to anything in the films that one wonders why they are so pointedly there. Astaire doesn't waste motions or gestures. Smoking becomes central to Astaire's films with Vincente Minnelli. In *Yolanda and the Thief* (1945) Astaire's smoke provides the transition into the dream ballet and identifies it as a dream; in *The Band Wagon*, Astaire's smoke identifies him as a casual hoofer rather than a fancy dancer.

Smoking reveals a trait of Astaire's internal being, disguised and covered by the elegant formal clothes. He is capable of the casual, spontaneous, and unpredictable, of doing something he isn't supposed to do. Dancers *don't* smoke (as Cyd Charisse reminds him in *The Band Wagon*). His smoking was a deliberate, if casual, flaunting of the rules of the game, providing a glimpse of the private self beneath those formal and exquisite wraps—if you paid careful attention. The removal of clothing is an invitation to intimacy that is never extended by public persons in public. Astaire's cigarette is the peccadillo that makes him accessible to mere mortals. While Chaplin's bizarre assemblage of sartorial segments demands speculation about the kind of spiritual unity that could have produced this chaos, Astaire's costume fits him so well, at rest or in motion, that it easily suggests that's all there is. Like Keaton's "Great Stone Face," Astaire's costume is so coldly and icily elegant that it refuses to give more than a hint about what lies inside.

The interplay of outer appearance and inner feeling reveals Astaire's unique blend of form and spontaneity. Its essential demonstration is "Top Hat, White Tie, and Tails" of *Top Hat*. Astaire is dressed exactly like every other male in the line (twenty to twenty-four of them, the exact number varies from shot to shot). All wear top hats, black tails, and white shirts; all grasp identical black canes with white tips; circular white carnations dot every lapel. Astaire has not been distinguished from the members of this chorus line by any detail of dress. The traditional method of costuming gives the soloist a more colorful, more elaborate variation of the chorus costume. What distinguishes Astaire from this mass, which he eventually "shoots" with his cane, like ducks in a shooting gallery, is not the way he looks but the way he thinks. Astaire conceived the trope that a chorus line of identically dressed men resemble identical, soulless targets in a shooting gallery. He also conceived the trope that a cane could be a rifle, a machine gun, or a bow and arrow—just as Chaplin conceived a myriad of uses and impersonations for his cane—and that taps could make a declaration of war or love (Astaire's taps do both in this film). For Astaire, a person, like a dancer, was not defined by external physical appearance but mental agility; dancing was a mental activity, not a physical one. The dancer is a maker of tropes.[1]

Astaire adopted this tension between imagination and appearance for the same reason Chaplin and Keaton did. In the photogenic myths of

Hollywood, Chaplin and Keaton were deficient as physical human beings: too small to compete in either the world of men (in battle) or women (in love). If their little figures are outmatched they are not outsmarted. Chaplin and Keaton translate their imaginative agility into miracles of physical exertion and determination. Fred Astaire was in the same physical boat— not tiny, but thin, too old (even in 1933), balding, not at all lovely to look at. But beneath this physical surface is Astaire's wisdom. He is the most knowing of screen figures, usually incapable of error. As Jerome Kern put it, "Fred Astaire *can't* do anything bad." Astaire knows something at the beginning that it takes everyone else the entire film to discover. He always knows that Ginger is going to marry him (whatever she thinks of him upon their first encounter); he also knows how to put on a show (whatever everybody else claims to know in *The Band Wagon*). Those few films in which Astaire plays a con man or minor sinner, only to reform in the end, are among his least characteristic and least effective (*Yolanda and the Thief*, *The Belle of New York*).[2] In most films Astaire is so perfectly omniscient as to be scarcely mortal. He'd better smoke, if only to show he *can* do something bad, even if he does it as beautifully as he does everything else.

In Astaire, as in Chaplin and Keaton, we see versions of the myth of singularity, exactly opposite the myth of communality and commonality in Busby Berkeley's interchangeable chorines. There is something not of this world about these supermen. Astaire's solo dances, whether at RKO, Paramount or MGM, address a single question: What makes Astaire different from *everybody* else? The answer is that he is not quite mortal, not subject to mortal and physical law. In his very first film, MGM's *Dancing Lady* (1933), Astaire and Joan Crawford float off together on a magic carpet; fifteen years later, in MGM's *Easter Parade*, Astaire dances in slow motion while everyone else moves at the usual mortal speed. Astaire doesn't inhabit the same physical universe as anyone else. This suggestion becomes explicit in *Royal Wedding* and *The Belle of New York* with his ability to walk on walls or on air, a freedom from gravity not accorded ordinary mortals. Not for nothing does Yolanda mistake Astaire for an angel in *Yolanda and the Thief*.

Astaire is a creature of air, not flesh; he is as much the musical's Ariel as Gene Kelly is its Caliban, anchored to the earth. One can't imagine flesh, bone, and muscle beneath Astaire's elegant outfits; they seem filled by air itself, no more solid than the smoke of his cigarettes. Like Chaplin and Keaton, Astaire is a material body aspiring to become pure idea. The idea is visible in the smallest gestures: the way his body becomes a perfect diagonal line that bisects the frame when he collapses in a chair at the end of "No Strings" (*Top Hat*); the way his talking alchemically evaporates into singing at the beginning of the same number; the way that even the clink of ice cubes or the squirt of seltzer become accompanying percussion instruments, punctuating the offbeats of musical measures. No wonder composers loved to write for him. He *can't* do anything bad.

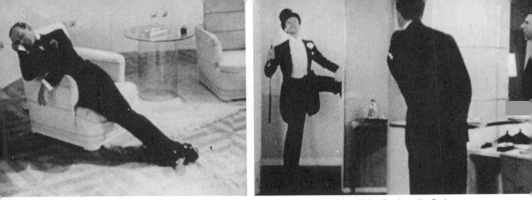

Dancing while not dancing in *Top Hat*: bisecting the frame after "No Strings"; flying from his dressing room (and Edward Everett Horton) for "Top Hat, White Tie, and Tails"

The universe this perfection inhabits is a pretty lonely place, no less for Astaire than for Chaplin and Keaton. The search for someone to share that world, that dance floor, is as central to the Astaire films as it was for Chaplin's from *The Kid* to *Modern Times*. Astaire's search for a perfect dancing partner was a search for the special being who might tap off (and tap with) his own singularity.[3] He only found her once: Ginger Rogers, in a remarkable series of black-and-white films at RKO between 1933 and 1938. When the series began Astaire was dangling dangerously between the end of one career and the beginning of another.

With the close of *The Band Wagon* early in 1932, the curtain fell on his twenty-five-year partnership with Adele, who left the stage to marry a British aristocrat. Although Fred was the brains behind the act, Adele was more fetching onstage. Most figured he was finished without her. His first solo stage musical, Cole Porter's *The Gay Divorce* (1932), was only a moderate success. Astaire had personally commissioned the show—less as a farewell to Broadway than as transportation to Hollywood. The move didn't promise success. Astaire didn't look like a Hollywood leading man. His photogenic allure was summed up by that anonymous (and perhaps apocryphal) studio executive who assessed a 1928 Astaire screen test: "Can't act. Can't sing. Balding. Can dance a little." Musicals had become unfashionable in 1932 Hollywood—not the star vehicles for a Chevalier or a Cantor but those interminable musical revues that flooded the first two years of synchronized sound. And *The Gay Divorce* was fraught with production peril—a racy book, racy songs, even a racy title (how could divorce be merry in the American mass morality?).

RKO, who bought Astaire and *Gay Divorce* in 1932, didn't know what to do with either. They loaned him to MGM for *Dancing Lady*: let another studio take the first chance. Then RKO dumped him into a piece of Dolores del Rio exotica called *Flying Down to Rio*. During the climactic dance number, "The Carioca," Astaire just happened to dance a few of its endless choruses with one Ginger Rogers, imported from Berkeley musicals at Warner Bros. RKO figured that a film featuring the dance duo might be possible with a title change: *The Gay Divorcée*. While divorces can't be happy, divorcées can be as merry as widows.

The birth of Fred&Ginger, two as one and one as two, came midway through *The Gay Divorcée*.[4] Fred sings the only Porter song to reach the film, "Night and Day," then invites her to dance with him. She resists his invitation repeatedly, moves away, tries to leave the room, but he cuts off her paths of escape, forces her to join him in stylized motion, and leaves her (and us), two choruses later, mute, motionless, transfixed. It was the first Fred&Ginger duet—even if the miming of Fred's invitation, Ginger's rejection, and the total seduction is more explicit in "Night and Day" than it would be in later duets. The difference between the first and second halves of this movie is the difference between "Night and Day." Early in the film there are numbers for miscellaneous members of the cast—even a comic duet ("Let's K-nock K-neez") for an anonymous chorine (the young Betty Grable) and, of all people, Edward Everett Horton. This obligatory vestige of musical convention evaporates in the film's final half into the only issue that matters—the emotional progress of Fred&Ginger charted in their songs and dances.

From this point the essential Fred&Gingers became less clear. Joan Fontaine, who can't hold her half of the floor or frame in a dance duet, is Ginger's pale replacement in *A Damsel in Distress* (1937). In *The Story of Vernon and Irene Castle* (1939), the final film of the cycle, Fred&Ginger dance less as themselves than as retrospective recreations of an earlier dance team, to which their own performance style is powerfully indebted.[5] In *Roberta* (1935) and *Follow the Fleet* (1936), Fred&Ginger share both the billing and the plot with another couple (Randolph Scott and Irene Dunne). Because the two films descend from the familiar double plot of stage musicals (not surprisingly since *Roberta* was itself a stage musical), Fred& Ginger have been demoted from romantic leads to comic and soubrette. *Carefree*, with far less song and dance than other films in the cycle, is as much a screwball comedy about psychiatry as a musical—so self-conscious about Fred&Ginger expectations that it inverts or avoids most of them. *Top Hat, Swing Time*, and *Shall We Dance?* are the three purest Fred&Gingers— the most popular, most frequently revived, most representative of the cycle at its best.

Consider the three scores: one by Irving Berlin, one by Jerome Kern (with Dorothy Fields), one by the Gershwins—premier composers of American theater music of their generation. Berlin wrote two other scores for the cycle (*Carefree, Follow the Fleet*), both Kern (*Roberta*) and the Gershwins (*Damsel in Distress*) one other. Somebody connected with the cycle—probably Astaire—must have said something like, "Let's get the best guys we can to write our songs." And somebody else connected with the cycle—probably its producer and RKO's studio head, Pandro S. Berman—must have said, "Sure." Berman, a very unflamboyant, quiet figure has almost no reputation whatever in the annals of Hollywood legend. His strength as a producer seems to have been to know what he didn't know and to allow those who did to do it. Like Arthur Freed at MGM, Berman had the taste to recognize quality and the sense to keep quiet in its presence. The good sense and good taste of the Fred&Ginger cycle begins with Astaire and Berman at the top.

Around their solid scores the three essential Fred&Gingers built books that were closer to their contemporary movie cousins of screwball comedy than to their theater ancestors of musical comedy. Like Katharine Hepburn and Cary Grant in *Bringing Up Baby* or Irene Dunne and Cary Grant in *The Awful Truth*, Fred&Ginger discover (or rediscover) their feelings for one another by experiencing together joyful, playful, wonderful adventures. While for Grant and Hepburn or Dunne, the adventures are childlike games of "fun,"[6] for Fred&Ginger the adventures are singing and dancing. Typical of this style of comedy, two potential obstacles lie between the union of the central couple: internal matters of spirit (Ginger finds Fred insufferable upon first meeting in *Gay Divorcée, Top Hat, Swing Time,* and *Shall We Dance?*) or external matters of social form or propriety (Fred or Ginger is already engaged to someone else, or believes the other is already married to someone else). This kind of comedy is always based on mistaken identity. Ginger mistakes either Fred's social identity (as a marriageable partner) or spiritual identity (as a gigolo in *The Gay Divorcée,* a noisemaker in *Top Hat,* a thief in *Swing Time,* a foreign hand-kisser and heel-clicker in *Shall We Dance?*). Her most important mistake in identity is not to "know" him as a dancer, a mistake he clears up in their first dance together—leaving only the external obstacle (who's really married to whom) to overcome.

Like all descendants of Roman New Comedy (Shakespeare and stage musicals among them), the Fred&Gingers turn on structural symmetries. In *Top Hat* there are two hotels (in London and in Venice), and two rooms in each (one above and one below), and two times that Astaire's tapping on the floor of his room announces his presence to Ginger below, and two others times when Fred taps on a wooden platform (at the Thackeray Club and as a cabbie), and two times that Ginger slaps Fred's face, and two times that the servant Bates (Eric Blore) concerns himself about a collar (with Edward Everett Horton's necktie at the beginning and his own clerical disguise at the end). In *Swing Time* there are two weddings that don't take place (at the beginning and the end), and two times that the drawing of cuffs on a pair of pants delays those weddings, and two presumed fiancés, Margaret (Betty Furness) for Fred and Ricardo (George Metaxa) for Ginger, and two older but wiser sidekicks (Victor Moore for Fred and Helen Broderick for Ginger), and two nightclub owners competing for Ricardo's orchestra, and two cuttings of the cards for the services of that orchestra. In *Shall We Dance?*, there are two dog-walking sequences aboard ship, two ships (a transatlantic liner and a transhudson ferry), two artistic managers, Jeffrey Baird (Horton again) and Arthur Miller (Jerome Cowan), two photographs in newspapers (a stork flying above an ocean liner and the apparent representation of Linda Keene lying in bed with Petrov), and two uses of masks to represent the face of Ginger Rogers (once on the photographed dummy and once on all the chorines in the film's finale).

This symmetry traditionally serves as a source of both pleasure (the elegance of shape) and credibility (in inherently improbable narratives like musicals and screwball comedies). These are always comedies of errors; while one error may be a misfortune and two a sign of carelessness, an entire comic universe of errors defines error as life itself. Symmetrical coincidence becomes probable in a universe ruled more by mathematical logic than everyday sense. Fred&Ginger symmetries provide one more example of the way all musicals combine the logical and the impossible. Most responsible for both the flavor and artful construction of their scripts was Allan Scott, not always listed in the credits as sole (or even primary) contributor but an important member of the creative team for every film from *Roberta* to *Carefree*.

Typical of New Comedy, *Top Hat, Swing Time,* and *Shall We Dance?* surround the two lovers with a gallery of stock comic types, characters of "humors," as Ben Jonson called them. The types as well as the players recur from film to film. The lumpishly dense Edward Everett Horton pays attention to little, notices less, and puts his foot in his mouth (if he knew either that he had a foot or a mouth) by making two reactions to every event—an immediately sincere and libidinous one, followed quickly by the socially corrected and constricted one. Eric Blore, floridly mannered, fuming, flustered, and fussy, is capable of more harumphs followed by more single-, double-, and triple-takes than previously imagined by any comedian, ancient or modern. Helen Broderick is worldly wise and casually cynical—the perceptive observer and knowing deflater of male vanities and female clichés. Erik Rhodes impersonates the typical European gigolo in the American mind—sleazy, oily, effete, overly concerned with his clothes, his style, and his honor, probably as willing with men as women. The number of gay aspersions these films manage to cast on Rhodes reveals the way wise creators could slip anything past the literal-minded keepers of the Code. Rhodes suggestively proclaims, "I am no man; I am Beddini." And when Beddini kisses her husband in an act of reconciliation, Helen Broderick wryly observes: "Go right ahead, boys. Don't mind me." In the world of Fred&Ginger, Erik Rhodes is Mrs. Malaprop.

There is a reason for this gallery of not very young, not very attractive, and not very sensual comic types in these films around Astaire. They make him look younger, more attractive, more right as Ginger's partner. Fred's rivals for Ginger's affections in the films are either the ludicrous Rhodes, the slimy George Metaxa (whose speech, looks, and manner suggest Bela Lugosi's Dracula), or the wimpy William Brisbane. These rivals make even that perennial cluck of screwball comedy, Ralph Bellamy, look like a sexual powerhouse. As proof, Bellamy plays Astaire's rival in *Carefree* with more genuine threat than any previous rival.

There is also a traditional reason for the gallery of comically unappealing types in this kind of comedy: the paradoxical relationship of the romantic couple to the expectations of ordinary society. On the one hand, the romantic couple is unique, separate, distant from this society. Fred& Ginger enter an absolutely private physical space when they dance—no other dancers to be seen. By implication, they enter a private spiritual space as well. But marriage means accepting the same moral constrictions as those that make the comics grotesque parodies of withered and infertile normality. In *Shall We Dance?*, Jeffrey Baird (Horton) is the custodian of the culture's aesthetic values ("I forbid that. That's not art.") and Cecil Flintridge (Blore) is the custodian of its moral values, the keeper of the keys who only unlocks adjoining hotel rooms when their occupants are legally married. Unlike Lubitsch's countess in *Monte Carlo*, these American adults cannot be trusted to keep their own Freudian keys. Like F. Hugh Herbert in the Berkeley musicals, Flintridge impersonates some presumed commissar from the Hays Office.

The way for the romantic couple to marry, to join the conventional society of their comic elders without losing the vitality that makes them more attractive and less withered is to preserve the unique spirit of their affection. For Fred and Ginger this means to continue dancing together as Fred&Ginger. This kind of comedy always suggests metaphoric and mythic unities: the union of the two lovers represents the triumph of nature and the return of spring, the renewal of life in the coupling of the young and healthy who promise the creation of new life.[7] The metaphor gets a surprising twist since the natural union they represent is a union of mind, spirit, and body through art, not nature. Fred offers Ginger a space in his private world of pure idea, where they withdraw from the world to an imaginative place of performance (every duet takes place on a literal or figurative stage). The dance establishes, celebrates, and confirms their spiritual union, not as a metaphor for sex but for something better than sex.[8] Better because their dance enacts the idea behind sex—the absolute union of mind and feeling through bodily contact and activity, the coming together of male and female who are two but one, physical but mental, rehearsed but spontaneous. They never end their films with a kiss (until *Carefree*) because the physical dance with which the films end is a more powerful projection of feeling into physicality than the mere touching of lips. Their dances mime the myth of modern marriage—too perfect ever to be achieved by mere mortals but a representation of the idea beneath our imperfect mortal strivings.[9]

The numbers in these films are metaphors. They are not decorative epilogues to the narratives, as the Berkeley numbers are. Nor do they sing of plot and character overtly, as numbers in dramatic musicals do. In *Top*

Framed symmetries: "Isn't It a Lovely Day"

Hat, Swing Time, and *Shall We Dance?* there are three Fred&Ginger duets. The first ("Isn't It a Lovely Day," "Pick Yourself Up," and "They All Laughed," respectively), is always Fred's invitation and Ginger's initiation, when she learns that dancing with Fred is like nothing else in the world. She tries to resist his invitation, then either joins because she must (on a nightclub stage or in a dance school) or because it might be fun (in a park during a rainstorm). Their dance begins tentatively, after either he or she sings the song's verse and chorus. She seems to try to copy his gestures and steps at first. Then, in the second chorus of the dance, the music and movement shift into double time and she can anticipate his steps even before he does them; she no longer needs to watch him to do exactly as he does.

How is it that they can dance together so perfectly without rehearsal? Astaire and Rogers have rehearsed, of course. Astaire planned the dances with Hermes Pan, who then taught the steps to Rogers (a procedure she came to resent mightily as the cycle spun forward). But there is a difference between the rehearsed Astaire and Rogers and Fred&Ginger (or Pete Peters and Linda Keene, or whatever they call themselves in the film). Fred&Ginger dance perfectly together because they belong together. They already know the steps because they already intuitively know each other.

This metaphor is mirrored by Astaire's shooting style, which refused to chop a dance into pieces but sustained it in lengthy takes. Astaire controlled the shooting and cutting of his musical sequences, just as Berkeley did at Warner Bros.; Mark Sandrich was a particularly self-effacing partner in deference to Astaire's performance wisdom. But whether directed by Sandrich, George Stevens, William A. Seiter, or Henry C. Potter, the shooting styles of the dances are identical. The camera does not merely provide a clear and intimate view of the dance; as in Chaplin films, it emphasizes the wonder of movement in space by maintaining the stability of space—exactly opposite to the Berkeley premise. When space is busy moving, movement within space loses its power. Within that continuous space and time, the camera frames the couple as perpetually symmetrical figures in a perfectly balanced frame. The implication is that their attuned spirits are as harmonious as the frame's fearful symmetry. These duets are really trios—for two dancers and dancing camera. It even had a name—the "Astaire dolly," specially constructed by Sandrich (trained as a physicist and engineer) so it could track, glide, and turn with them perfectly. In their dances, movement, feeling, space, and music are one.

The second duet confirms this initial experience, reminding the couple (especially Ginger) of what is at stake in their union, often when the external obstacles that the narrative throws in their path threaten to block their union forever ("Cheek to Cheek," "Waltz in Swingtime," and "Let's Call the Whole Thing Off," in chronological order). As in the Berkeley films, these numbers feel the pressure of novelty, of coming up with some new variation on a pattern, expected both from the initial duet and the previous films in the cycle. "Cheek to Cheek" is more highly charged than the saunteringly playful "Isn't It a Lovely Day" earlier in the film; "Waltz in Swingtime" is a paradox (a jazz waltz); and "Let's Call the Whole Thing Off" is the most novel of all: a dance duet on roller skates. While Chaplin had skated ecstatically in *Modern Times* a year earlier, Astaire translated Chaplin's singular exhilaration into the unified ecstasy of Fred&Ginger.[10]

The third dance duet differs in the three films. Only in *Swing Time* is it a full and private duet, "Never Gonna Dance," an agonized mime of parting and separation. "Never Gonna Dance" is the opposite of "Night and Day," which initiated these duets—the late-night suspicion that they may never dance again together, the necessity of her leaving him, his hopeless appeal that she stay, her inability to tear herself away, their prolonging the dance as long as they can until she twirls hysterically out of his life, seemingly forever. Then the plot itself twirls one more time to whirl them back together again when the sun shines.

The other two final dances are embedded in larger production numbers ("The Piccolino" and "Shall We Dance"). The production numbers indicate a clear expectation of the mid-1930s filmusical. Both derive from "The Continental," the Academy Award winning song of *The Gay Divorcée*, an attempt to out-Berkeley Berkeley with seventeen minutes and eleven choruses of visual variation. Fred&Ginger merely drop into these fancy doings for an occasional chorus. Though the number is a Berkeley imitation in its visual variations, it maintains the spatial integrity of the Astair-RKO style by refusing to dissolve a clearly defined dance floor into infinite spacelessness (although the dancers' costumes magically change without temporal explanation).

By the time of *Top Hat*, "The Piccolino" both does and does not take this kind of obligatory production number seriously. The choreography for the anonymous chorus exudes the Berkeley aroma (whites and blacks, circles and lines, long cloth cummerbunds woven into the choreographic conception). But the song itself is an ironic comment on choreographic exotica. Its lyric informs us that the tune was written by a Latin who lived in a flat in Brooklyn—probably an ironic Irving Berlin reference to himself, the Russian born, New York bred author of "The Piccolino."

There are two other types of musical numbers. One is the vocal solo for Astaire, sung not danced in a single chorus ("The Way You Look Tonight" in *Swing Time*, both "I've Got Beginner's Luck" and "They Can't Take That Away from Me" in *Shall We Dance?*). A variation is the three-chorus vocal duet, "A Fine Romance," from *Swing Time*, sung but not danced. The surprise of these numbers is that we expect them to be. Instead, they suggest Astaire's casual appeal, the way he can move easily and gracefully from talk to singing that feels like talk. They also demonstrate Astaire's brilliant phrasing of a song verbally and rhythmically, the reason composers liked to write for him. He never fudges a note or a beat, explicating a song's musical structure through his "readings" of its word-notes and note-words. For Astaire singing was as much an act of thought and style as dancing—not physical vocalization but spiritual emanation, his answer to those who said he can't sing. Although composers worried that potential hits were thrown away by this simple treatment (George Gershwin was especially upset by the lack of dancing to "They Can't Take That Away"), even a single Astaire chorus was enough to turn a wonderful song into a memorable hit.

The final type of number in these three films was Astaire's dance solo. Astaire was the prime mover (in both senses) of these numbers, which became extended metaphors for the films as a whole. These metaphoric solos derive from "I Won't Dance" of *Roberta*: it begins with

"The Way You Look Tonight": simple serenade from a "feelthy piano"

Astaire's playing what he calls "feelthy piano," moves from his playing a musical instrument to playing his vocal instrument to playing his physical instrument, and concluding with the most spectacular unadorned solo dancing in cinema (by Astaire or anyone else).[11] For Astaire to declare "I Won't Dance" is a contradiction in terms; he could no more not dance than not breathe—and he proves it before the number ends.

Top Hat defines Astaire as a modern American dancer: "Every once in a while I find myself dancing." As an American he is not British (in a film set in London); as a modern he is not a man of the nineteenth century (in a film that begins in the Thackeray Club, founded in 1864, named for a Victorian novelist). As a dancer, Astaire is very much not silent: his taps rebel against the rule of *SILENCE!* at the Thackeray Club. Musical entertainers can't be silent, just as musical films can't be silent films. The opening sequence in the Thackeray Club is a deadly parody of silent film. As a modern American dancer, Astaire talks with his feet. His talkies are feeties.

In the "Top Hat, White Tie, and Tails" solo, the Thackeray Club has been translated into the chorus line of dress-alike, move-alike (and, by implication, think-alike) robots, whom Astaire shoots by pointing his cane and rapping his taps (as a single rifle shot or, in parodies of the St. Valentine's Day Massacre and William Tell, as a volley of machine-gun fire or a flying arrow). The link between the robots of the chorus and the robots of the Thackeray Club becomes explicit when, for his curtain call, he aims his cane at the members of the Club seated in a nearby box and taps them dead too (as he tapped his assault in the film's opening scene). Astaire can do any number of things with his taps and cane. He converts it into a percussion instrument in the song's verse when he just happens to rap his cane against the telegram in his hand precisely on the syncopated off-beats of Berlin's tune, then just happens to rap it against the floor on some precisely coordinated off-beat in Berlin's highly syncopated release.

Astaire also translates the sounds, rhythms, and musical patterns of the song into visual correlatives. Astaire equates the flowing, unsyncopated phrases of Berlin's refrains with circular choreographic movements and with languid strolling or standing; he equates the syncopated, percussive musical phrases of Berlin's release with linear movements and pervasive rapping of taps and cane on the floor. Circle and line, the two familiar visual vectors of choreographic cinema design, have been attached to the musical phrases of Berlin's composition, either flowing or syncopated. Astaire then varies the visual opposites in ensuing choruses, just as he varies the accents of Berlin's musical phrases. Using both taps and cane, he raps Berlin's syncopation in double time. His figure combines circle and line when his tapping motion describes a perfect circle around the axis of his linearly rapping cane.

Even the decor participates in this visual-musical synthesis. Scenic designer Carroll Clark has created a backdrop from three primary elements. Circularly scalloped clouds in the middle grays of the monochromatic scale accent the number's linear forms and its extremes of black and white. Slender lampposts topped by glowing white circular globes parallel Astaire's linear cane and costume, dotted with a white circular carnation. And behind him stands, of all things, the Eiffel Tower. Why the Eiffel Tower in a number on a London stage, in a film which makes no reference to Paris? Perhaps that tower, like Astaire, represents a synthesis of linearity and circularity. The Clark design emphasizes this suggestion with curving lines, rising to its pinnacle, trimmed with fancifully semicircular scalloped lattice-work instead of the rectangular grillwork the tower actually displays. Or perhaps the tower, like Astaire, represents a synthesis of old and new. This late nineteenth-century structure consciously rejected the ponderous solidi-ty of earlier architectural design. Or perhaps the tower, like Astaire, is an edifice of air, anchored below but soaring above, solid yet ethereal. Or perhaps the Eiffel Tower is ultimately a monument to itself, one of a kind, nothing else like it—exactly like Astaire himself.[12]

There is a political suggestion in this singularity, a contrast of his American independence with European conformity. The chorus line of identically uniformed dancers, like the regimented members of the Thackeray Club, suggests the social rigidity of European life—of its class and value systems. There may be a specific allusion to the goose-stepping Nazis in Germany and Brown Shirts in Italy (the film will travel to an Italian city that looks nothing at all like Italy). This political suggestion arises from the ominously low and threatening camera angles that accompany the marching return of this army in evening clothes for the number's final chorus—the most idiosyncratic camera angles in the entire Fred&Ginger cycle. Astaire is forced to shoot them before they engulf him. As political metaphor, Astaire's dancing suggests that the uniformed and uniform must be re-pulsed by free and spontaneous invention. But the contrary is equally important. Any human construction (whether the Eiffel tower or an Astaire dance) is based on formal principles of design without which spontaneous invention cannot exist. Astaire never destroys the balance between formal rigor and spontaneous invention, between the classical form of nineteenth-century Europe and the modern spontaneity of twentieth-century America. That balance is precisely who Astaire *is*, what the word "Astaire" means in our culture.

Swing Time changes the subject from Astaire to Fred&Ginger. The two meet by accident (just as Fred accidentally met Ginger at RKO), first on the street, then (after Fred's pursuit) in the studio where Ginger works. The two dance together clumsily at first because Fred doesn't let on that he already knows how to dance and Ginger doesn't know Fred's identity as a dancer. They eventually pick themselves up to perform so brilliantly that Eric Blore, the studio head (dance studio or movie studio), decides they should perform publicly together and arranges an audition (or screen test). Blore, with no other function in this film, plays both studio boss and agent,

"Top Hat, White Tie. and Tails": contrasting visual likeness and difference, one and many, circle and line

even devising appropriate costumes—black evening clothes for him, long white dress for her. Their dance combines "a little of each" type Blore's studio offers—aesthetic, ballroom, and tap. Although a self-conscious reference to the aesthetic ballroom tapping of Astaire's solo work, the "little of each" just as aptly describes Fred&Ginger. The result is a kind of marriage, produced by a studio gamble, and *Swing Time* is as full of gambling as it is of consummate dancing and unconsummated weddings.

Astaire's solo in *Swing Time*, "Bojangles of Harlem," honors the tradition that embraces both Fred and Fred&Ginger. The number is a deliberate variation on "Top Hat." No less than Berkeley, Astaire faced the routine pressure of doing the same thing but different. In "Bojangles of Harlem," Astaire dances with a chorus line of apparently identical women rather than men; blackened faces surmount light-colored outfits rather than the white faces that surmount the black suits of "Top Hat." The decor of "Bojangles" is based not on towering verticals with punctuating circles, but dominant circles (boutonnierres, derby hats, polka dots) sliced by sliding diagonals. Both the "curtains" that slide open to expose the stage and the floor of that stage are semidiamonds, rather than the semicircles of "Top Hat." These diagonal shapes are identical to those of the cuffs sketched twice on a pair of pants to postpone the film's weddings. Although much is purely decorative about the white-black racial contrast in "Bojangles of Harlem," it never becomes as insensitive as Berkeley's purely formal games in *Roman Scandals*. Astaire doesn't smear the color on a specifically lower social class as Berkeley does. Nor is the blackface the traditional ultrablack, with glaring white outlines around the mouth and eyes, but an evenly dark tan.

The choreography of the number is a careful contrapuntal interplay of rhythmic and visual elements. Instead of his rapping cane in "Top Hat," the extensions of Astaire's tapping feet in "Bojangles of Harlem" are his slapping palms, in which he carries slap-taps to snap their percussive claps in complex answers to his taps on the floor. Astaire traces a clear historical line—from the spoons rattled by Mr. Bones in minstrel shows to the rhythmic hand-slaps that were a trademark of Bill "Bojangles" Robinson to the slap-taps and cane-raps of Fred Astaire. Black dance and black music become the literal backdrop for Astaire's dancing; the three elongated shadows projected on a screen behind him are both literal shadows and historical shades.

Sometimes Astaire dances in perfect unison with those shadows, performing identical steps; when the four figures dance in unison, the three shadows seem believable projections of Astaire's dancing self. But the figures frequently go their own ways, either Astaire or his shadows performing a variation that excludes the other. Only when the shadows and Astaire part company do we realize that the shadows cannot literally be shadows, triple projections of Astaire's movement just then just there, but some cinematic device tricked up to resemble literal shadows. Astaire is not

"Bojangles of Harlem": projection on a screen

dancing alone, accompanied by three shadowy emanations of himself; he somehow has split himself into four parts, one of whom dances in the foreground and the other three in the rearground as shadows. Astaire dances as all three shadows. Who else but Astaire dances like Astaire?

He has consciously brought a performance tradition that began with the black minstrel show of the nineteenth century into the art and technology of the twentieth. Fred Astaire and *Swing Time* and Fred&Ginger and movie musicals are marriages of these historical shadows: of black and white music, black and white dance, black and white film, live stage shows and mechanical entertainments, electricity and light (without which you can neither project shadows nor movies). Astaire's dancing in the foreground is no more and no less a shadow on a screen than the shadows of Bojangles (who are also Astaire) behind him. Fred&Ginger are shadows—as all movies are mere shadow shows and as all musical movies are shadows of a long tradition of song-and-dance performance.

Shall We Dance? pursues the examination still further into the kinds of representations movies provide. Of all the Fred&Ginger films, it is most conscious of itself as a movie and most filled with references to filmic and photographic representation. Its cinematic self-references can be traced to the little deception Fred invents that allows him to dance "The Continental" with Ginger in *The Gay Divorcée*: he places a paper cutout of a dancing couple on a phonograph turntable and aims an electric light to project its revolving shadows on the wall. Fred&Ginger are no less dancing shadows projected on the wall of a movie screen. *Shall We Dance?* also builds a brief routine on a phonograph, a late-nineteenth century entertainment machine invented at about the same time and by the same Thomas Edison who invented both the movies and the electric lightbulb.[13]

The film introduces Ginger as a photograph, dancing a rhumba in the riffled pages of a "flip book"—what the nineteenth century called a flioscope (one of many movie ancestors based on persistence of vision, the optical illusion that makes movies possible). Of course, a 1937 French flip book was famous for providing not dancing entertainment but pictures of a more lurid sort. Movies themselves have been linked with representations of pornography and accused of their immoral influence from their first appearance in the 1890s. *Shall We Dance?* also exhibits still photographs—in which seeing is believing since photographs cannot lie. If Fred&Ginger share the same bed in a photograph, they must be married (certainly the Hays Code would not permit an alternative inference). The superficial appearances of photographs demand spiritual inferences about those who share their frames (for example, who loves whom or is married to whom). Movie frames provoke similar inferences and interpretations. Can it be possible that Fred&Ginger are merely movie actors and dancing partners, rather than the lovers their frame-sharing suggests? Are they any more than masks, dummies, and wax figures in such frames? What is the difference between Astaire and Rogers as people and Fred&Ginger as photographic representations? What is the difference between the wax figure of Ginger that sleeps beside Fred and the shadowy image of Ginger that dances beside him? This confusion between reality and appearance, human actor and character mask, has always been closely connected to the appeal of Hollywood.

If *Shall We Dance?* acknowledges that movies are photographic, mechanical, and electrical projections of appearances that seem like truths, it also acknowledges that Fred&Ginger movies are a uniquely American blend of high and low cultural forms. Astaire masquerades as the Russian Petrov since no audience would take an American ballet dancer named Pete Peters (or Fred Astaire) seriously. He attaches metal taps to his ballet slippers, combining "tap" with "aesthetic." To add "ballroom," he needs a dancing partner, a Linda Keene who knows popular dances like the rhumba, a hoofer from the vaudeville stage (just as Rogers hoofed from a Warner Bros. Gold Digger to Astaire at RKO). Like Geroge Gershwin who wrote the film's songs, Fred Astaire is the locus where "Broadway and Ballet Merge," as the film's newspaper headlines proclaim. The film is unthinkable without Gershwin. It is also unthinkable much earlier than 1937, one year after Rodgers and Hart's *On Your Toes*, a Broadway show choreographed by George Balanchine of the Ballet Russe (like Petrov), in which jazz and ballet merged (and which Astaire rejected as a film property). American dance was born in this same period as a merger of ballet, jazz, and Broadway. Martha Graham, Agnes de Mille, and Jerome Robbins followed Balanchine as choreographers of both Broadway shows and original ballets by such American composers as Copland, Rodgers, and Bernstein. Astaire and Gershwin (individually and together) personified this merger.

Shall We Dance? is so conscious of its many themes that it needs not one but two Astaire solo dance numbers, which both derive from their immediate ancestors. "Slap That Bass" is performed by Astaire in the midst of identically dressed men (as in "Top Hat") who are black (as in "Bojangles"); "Shall We Dance" is performed by Astaire backed by a chorus line of women (as in "Bojangles"), dressed (indeed masked) identically (as in "Top Hat"). The opposition between the two numbers—the jazz of "Slap That Bass" (even its title suggests black jazz musicians) and the artiness of the final ballet—demonstrate the two poles of Astaire's (and the film's) aspirations.

Astaire dances "Slap That Bass" with a chorus of shadows (as in "Bojangles") that have been frozen into mechanical rigidity (like the chorus line of "Top Hat"). His chorus members are the shadows of gears and pistons in an ocean liner's engine room. If Astaire can mime the movements of machines, he just as clearly demonstrates that he is no more a machine than a mechanical figure in top hat and tails. Astaire syncopates the rhythms and permutes the rigid movements of the machines—because he is a dancer, not a machine. But without their formal regularity and mechanical dependability, Astaire's stylish variations would have no ground, no setting, no rhythmic constant to show them off. As in "Top Hat," Astaire is the master of the tropes. And the trope of "Slap That Bass" is that the machines are Astaire's bass—providing the metronomic beat that walks up and down the basic chord progressions of the number, permitting both the melodic and rhythmic embroidery of the soloist.

The concluding ballet of *Shall We Dance?* gathers all the film's themes—indeed the central themes of the entire cycle—into an ultimate statement. A lone Astaire dances with a chorus line of identical figures, yearning, however, not to dance alone but with another who might complete and complement him—the Ginger he fears he has lost forever. Like "Never Gonna Dance," the ballet suggests the pain of loss and separation; as in "Bojangles of Harlem," Astaire converts a whole chorus line into a single partner, wearing two different white-black costumes for the two sides of his character—an arty Petrov outfit for the ballet section and his trademark tails for the song section. First, he "tweests" (as Petrov playfully pronounces the word for Linda's benefit) with the balletic contortionist, Harriet Hoctor (who, according to Arlene Croce, "can be taken for nothing human"). He then glides with the totally human Ginger (or her dancing effigies) in the usual combination of tap, aesthetic, and ballroom. He sings a bouncy Gershwin tune, which urges us to stop moping and start dancing, in the midst of a dance with alternating mope and bounce. The number celebrates the ultimate wedding of opposite needs that has driven the entire cycle—the way black needs white, circle needs line, jazz needs ballet, song needs dance, white music needs black music, male needs female, projection light needs moviehouse dark, shadows need bodies, masks need faces, and Fred needs Ginger.

The careers of Astaire and Rogers moved in different directions when

Fred&Ginger faced the music and stopped dancing together. Rogers had become increasingly irritated with Astaire's conceptual control and Astaire had become jealous of Rogers's growing stardom. Their final dance in *Carefree*, "Change Partners," suggested either a metaphor or a parody of her enslavement and his desperation: Astaire is her Svengali, hypnotizing his enchanted marionette into making the moves he directs. In the early films of the cycle, her tentativeness in the presence of a star like Astaire led to subtle comic nuances. The coy smirk on her face during Astaire's vocal chorus of "Isn't It a Lovely Day" clearly showed that she was enjoying the song and knew she would enjoy the dance, while keeping her amusement a sly secret between her and us. By the time of *Carefree* both Rogers and Astaire knew that she was a star herself. Although her comic trances under the hypnotic spell of psychiatric treament must have amused her 1938 audiences, her oh so cute Gingerisms seem overacted today. As a team they were the third most popular box-office stars in 1936 (behind Shirley Temple and Clark Gable), but Astaire's star fell steadily while Rogers's steadily rose over the next decade. Her one filmusical (*Lady in the Dark*, 1944) provided the opportunity for more hypnotic trances, but her nonmusical films (*Kitty Foyle*, 1940; *Roxie Hart*, 1942; *The Major and the Minor*, 1943) won her fame and an Academy Award.

Although Astaire did not desert the filmusical, the filmusical seemed to have deserted him. The next decade was the most distressing and demeaning of his long career. Rather than sought as a star performer in his own right, those studios that sought him at all only wanted him to partner a contract star who needed a little classing up. Only one was a real dancer—Eleanor Powell, whom Astaire partnered in *Broadway Melody of 1940*. This first film after Ginger is among the best of Astaire's black-and-white non-RKOs. With three wonderful Cole Porter songs ("I've Got My Eyes on You," "I Concentrate on You," and an interpolated "Begin the Beguine"), it is by far the most stylish, classy, and careful of MGM's entire *Brodway Melody* series. The 1938 *Melody*, in comparison, seems confused about whether Sophie Tucker is a former entertainer who runs a rooming house or is Sophie Tucker.

Broadway Melody of 1940 is also Eleanor Powell's best movie by far. Powell's problem as an MGM star was that she was a terrific dancer—the most pyrotechnically dazzling female dancer in film history. Unfortunately, her singing was dubbed and her acting stilted—limited to silent smiling while the camera shot around her. Unlike Astaire, she was not a total performer-stylist who danced but a dancer who was obliged to recite lines. Either she lacked a total performance style or MGM never helped her find one, sticking her with the dreariest imaginable assumptions of sweet ingenuehood that had nothing to do with her dazzling performances in musical numbers. In a twist of self-reference, *Broadway Melody of 1940* is built on Powell's desperate need for a style, which could only be found with a new dancing partner—certainly true for Powell but no less true for Astaire.

Astaire's solo in the film is a fetishistic dance with two surrogate props for Powell herself: her photograph on a piece of sheet music and her compact case. The props extend his fetishistic dancing with masked Ginger surrogates in *Shall We Dance?* Set to "I've Got My Eyes on You," Astaire not only has his eyes on Powell's image but she's got her eyes on him, watching him without his knowing it. He begins by deftly accompanying himself at the piano (as in "I Won't Dance"), using the sheet music, and he concludes with his deft juggling of the compact, timed perfectly to roll off an awning and into his hat while he dances (just as he perfectly times the hitting of golf balls to his dance steps in *Carefree*). Even with the change of partners and studios, Astaire met the challenge of doing the same thing but different.

This is just as true of the Astaire-Powell duets. Their first—in a park—evokes the familiar Fred&Ginger park duets: an isolated space for their private dance, three choruses shot in a single continuous take. Rather than the complementary harmony of Fred&Ginger's "Isn't It a Lovely Day," the duet adopts the tap-dance convention of the "challenge dance": "I challenge you to do this," one dancer seems to say, and "All right, can you top this?" the other dancer responds. Powell can keep up with Astaire all right, the way no other partner on film ever could, but the result is an entertaining battle of technical tools and choreographic wills. Their two climactic onstage duets also descend from *Shall We Dance?*. The first, "I Concentrate on You," is balletically aesthetic—a rare chance for Powell to show she can do something dignified, other than her spectacular splits, kicks, bends, and leaps. The second, "Begin the Beguine," is ballroom-tap, brilliant but bloodless, an exciting competition with no clear winner. Although the film draws on Astaire's class and style, neither the dancing nor the story has the same *meaning* as the harmony of Fred&Ginger. Astaire seems a guest who dropped into Powell's series for a visit, rather than her full and equal partner.

He was even less fortunate with other partners, who couldn't much dance or hadn't yet on film. Astaire was invited into these films to expand the star's range for her public, to show she was a real performer, not just another pretty face. The idea descended from Astaire's partnering Joan Fontaine in *A Damsel in Distress*, disguising the fact that she couldn't dance. In "Things Are Looking Up," he deposits her behind some convenient tree trunk (a real tree in a real park for this film, as opposed to those soundstage parks with Ginger), then comes back to fetch her after executing his brilliant moves. The single worst Astaire film by far is *Second Chorus* (1940) at Paramount—and not because Paulette Goddard couldn't dance with him. The idea of this film was for Astaire to support the Artie Shaw Orchestra; in the big-band swing era it made sense for a movie to feature seated musicians, with a dancing visual stylist at the edges. Although even the most uneven Astaire films of the 1940s can be counted on for several good numbers, only the final number of *Second Chorus*—of exactly three choruses—is even tolerable. Astaire again weds jazz and symphonic music, this time by means of the trope that an orchestra conductor is a kind of dancer and his baton a kind of cane.

Astaire did better with Xavier Cugat and Rita Hayworth in two films at Columbia. Cugat's puzzling popularity partially resulted from the battle between ASCAP and BMI in the early 1940s. ASCAP, representing the most prestigious American composers and lyricists, demanded high royalty fees and exclusive contracts from movie studios and radio stations. BMI (Broadcast Music Incorporated) represented lesser known composers who accepted lower royalties—swing hits of the dance bands, country-and-western songs, Latin-American rhumbas and tangos. When ASCAP pulled the compositions of its members off the radio, the networks rhumbaed south of the border for talent. This was a battle that ASCAP had to lose—the first massive invasion of an alternative American popular music that signaled the end of the thirty-two-bar song's hegemony. The Xavier Cugats of the world were the immediate beneficiaries of radio exposure.

ASCAP composers remained in Hollywood to write for them. Cole Porter wrote one score for Astaire-Cugie-Hayworth (*You'll Never Get Rich*, 1941) and Jerome Kern another (*You Were Never Lovelier*, 1942). Although Porter was the master of Latin exotica, only one beguine for the Cugat film was worth beginning, "So Near and Yet So Far." Hayworth and Astaire danced comfortably together, but the films were more than a little uncomfortable with Astaire's age. (A close friend of Hayworth's parents, the Cansinos, Astaire first met Rita as an infant in their arms). Both Columbia films dispense with the Astaire solo—too expensive and arty. Both convert the Fred&Ginger duets of internal spiritual communion into pleasant external displays of classy ballroom dancing. Though the scripts strew those perpetual external obstacles in the path of Fred and Rita's race to true love, as they did for Fred&Ginger, the internal spiritual obstacle is a mere convention that we simply must accept on faith.

If big-band swing pushed a solo stylist like Astaire into the background, World War II did very little for him either. He was no more a communal foot soldier than a communal jitterbugger. Both were restricted to America's youth and Astaire was too old to be drafted. How could he make musicals in wartime when there were more pressing social tasks than finding a dancing partner or embodying some idea of balance between form and spontaneity? Armies were teams; even those who stayed home had to join the American team in some way or other. How could Astaire join a team if he didn't even inhabit the same universe as anyone else?

One clumsy answer, in *You'll Never Get Rich*, was to show Astaire as a team player when he absolutely had to be: a Broadway choreographer who stages his show at the army barracks, the World War II equivalent of the charity show. One way that eccentric showfolks could contribute was to do shows for Uncle Sam. Even in the army Astaire resembles some kind of swell. Tossed in the guardhouse for impersonating an officer, Astaire's fellow prisoners are all black. The black prisoners and the white Astaire sing and dance together, demonstrating his familiar integration of white and black styles. It would be the strongest and sincerest propaganda statement Astaire could make. Large numbers of black Americans were first drafted in 1942, even if they remained in segregated regiments. Astaire's army was already integrated.

Astaire's uniform as an Air Force pilot fits him better in *The Sky's the Limit* (1943). Like Astaire, a pilot is a soloist whose skill is a combination of technique and imagination, daring and cool control. A pilot is a member of a team (as a dancer is a member of a production team) who works solo. Astaire partners Joan Leslie in this film; she was an able enough dancer from another family vaudeville act, but she rarely danced in movies. This return to RKO gave Astaire his best original score (Harold Arlen and Johnny Mercer) since he left, including "My Shining Hour" and "One for My Baby (and One More for the Road)." The film also contrasts Astaire's agile physicality with the wisecracking wit of Robert Benchley, the kind of foil that Edward Everett Horton had provided in the Fred&Gingers. Benchley, the wry but wordy editor of a fashionable magazine, is Fred's rival for Leslie's affections, the kind of rival who, for all his drollery, makes Fred look the better catch. The film is as entertaining as any Astaire movie between 1939 and 1946.

It contains one moment, however, that is deliberately and metaphorically excruciating. One of Astaire's Air Force buddies (played with chilling menace by Robert Ryan) loathes him and envies him: envies his stardom (Astaire is an ace pilot), his singularity (Astaire deserts his buddies for solo adventures), his style (he refuses to wear the same uniform as everyone else on leave). After a mournful night of more than just one too many for the road, Ryan forces Astaire to perform an embarrassingly awful snake dance in a public bar, the type of dance more appropriate to a female cooch dancer (if to anyone at all) than a male Astaire. He protests, shows his embarrassment, tries to get Ryan to change his mind, but Ryan remains adamant and Astaire reluctantly makes the dreadful snaky arm and ass motions for as brief a time as Ryan will permit.

The terrible moment suggests the revenge of the ordinary guys in uniforms—those identically dressed chorus members whom Astaire executes in *Top Hat*. In the team spirit of the war years, which coincide with Astaire's own fall from stardom, the anonymous chorus takes its revenge on the singular star. The dance, which Astaire improvised on the set, is also his personal metaphor for the stupidities of Hollywood producers, writers, and studio executives, who can force him to play a role or do a dance that is wrong for him, that makes him look bad, embarrassing for him to do and for us to watch, simply because they have the power to make him do it. This snake dance is as nasty, as bitter, and as uncomfortable a moment as in any Astaire film.

The snake dance suggests Astaire's new trouble with his sidekicks. Victor Moore and Edwart Everett Horton were old enough, dry enough, and dried up enough to make Astaire look physical, graceful, and vital. But the studios that Astaire visited between 1939 and 1946 were nervous about his lack of stereotypic sex appeal. In *Broadway Melody of 1940* he must share the plot, the frame, and even the dance numbers with the handsome George Murphy, an MGM contract player who was one of Eleanor Powell's regular fellas. Astaire doesn't make Murphy, the only hoofer to become a United States senator, look too bad in the dance sequences. Murphy, who plays a shiftless drunk, doesn't make Astaire look too bad in the dialogue sequences. But Astaire had never before faced a younger and better looking rival—in a story that spins from a mistake in telling the two male dancers apart, of separating the real Astaire from the imitation Murphy.

This same discomfort affects the pairing of Astaire and Bing Crosby at Paramount for *Holiday Inn* (1942) and *Blue Skies* (1946), in which Fred drops in on yet another studio's star. If Bob Hope showcased Crosby the singing comic, Astaire showcased Crosby the singing hoofer. At least Astaire shared the billing, the numbers, and the frame with an equally savvy stylist who acted through musical performance. The two stars share terrific Irving Berlin songs (with whom Astaire had been closely associated), and the films treat Astaire with both respect and admiration. His favorite and most admiring director at RKO, Mark Sandrich, directed both; but Sandrich's sudden death in the middle of shooting *Blue Skies* accounts for much of that film's gloom. His legacy is the brilliant "Puttin' on the Ritz," which Sandrich and Astaire planned together as a deliberate variation on the identical dancers of "Top Hat" and the split-screen shadows of "Bojangles of Harlem." Despite the musical pleasantries of the Bing&Freds, Astaire could not find a comfortable home in somebody else's films at somebody else's studio. He retired from the business in 1946.

Two Technicolor disappointments for MGM in 1945 and 1946, *The Ziegfeld Follies* and *Yolanda and the Thief*, sealed his decision. He had again been hired to make a lovely contract player, Lucille Bremer, look like a dancing actress. With a mediocre score (Arthur Freed and Harry Warren), the bland Bremer, yet another exotic South American setting, and a silly script (the religious Bremer mistakes conman Fred for an angel), *Yolanda* was Arthur Freed's first flop at MGM. It was also the first film in seven years that Astaire had been asked to carry by himself, and he couldn't. But it had a spectacular surrealistic dream ballet (Vincente Minnelli's first), as well as a director and producer on their way up. In 1948 Freed would bring Astaire out of retirement to join them.

10

It Feels Like Neuritis But Nevertheless It's Love

RICHARD RODGERS
AND LORENZ HART

The career of Richard Rodgers is a capsule history of the American stage musical from 1920 to 1970. With Lorenz Hart, his first collaborator, Rodgers's 1920s musicals were playfully inventive; their 1930s musicals more consciously tested the boundaries of musical-theater possibility. With Oscar Hammerstein II, his second collaborator, Rodgers's 1940s musicals moved toward a totally integrated American music drama, a native American opera; the 1950s brought a hardening of the creative arteries into rigid Rodgers and Hammerstein formulas and reverential film transcriptions of their stage works. Without either collaborator, Rodgers's 1960s musicals sank steadily with the genre as a whole. There almost seem to be two Richard Rodgerses—the clever tunesmith with Hart and the revered institution with Hammerstein. The two are more alike than they appear. The difference is Hart and Hammerstein.

Like George Gershwin and Irving Berlin, Richard Rodgers was a self-taught musician, observing his mother at the parlor piano, on which he first practiced his scales. Like Jerome Kern, Rodgers came from a respectable middle-class Jewish family; both his father and elder brother were physicians. Rodgers grew up on the Upper West Side, New York's affluent Jewish neighborhood. Lorenz Hart, from the same kind of family, grew up in the same neighborhood. So did Hammerstein, grandson of opera impressario, Oscar Hammerstein I, son of vaudeville producer Willie Hammerstein. Hammerstein and Hart were classmates at Columbia University. He introduced Rodgers to Hart in 1918. More experienced than either, Hammerstein was already working with veteran composers. Rodgers was only sixteen in 1918, seven years younger than Hart and Hammerstein, but he knew he wanted to write theater music like his idol, Jerome Kern. Hammerstein thought Hart might also have a future in theater music—if he lived long

Rodgers and Hart at the piano, as producer Dwight Wiman looks on

enough to have a future at all. For even at twenty-three Hart was an
alcoholic, unable to work before noon (when he shook his hangover from
the previous night) or after five (when he began drinking again).[1] Rodgers's
mother doubted that Hart would live past twenty-five.

Lorenz Hart was certainly the most tortured and probably the most
talented lyricist in the history of the American musical. If Kern was
America's greatest "pure composer" of theater music, Hart was its greatest
"pure lyricist." There is more going on inside a Hart lyric, and inside
Hart's head, than in anybody else's. Hart was the most confessional of
theater lyricists—the most able and willing to put his own feelings,
thoughts, pains, sorrows, fears, joys, misery into the words of songs for
specific characters in musical plays. What he could never say aloud, even to
his closest friends in private, he let characters sing in public. He was a gay
bachelor who wrote the best love lyrics for women and the most joyous
lyrics about falling in love and the most melancholy lyrics about falling out
of love.

To call him physically unattractive would be an understatement. Photographs reveal a darkly scowling face atop a body just an inch or two taller
than a midget or dwarf. Rodgers describes his first impression upon
meeting him:

His appearance was so incredible that I remember every single detail.... The total man was hardly more than five feet tall. He wore frayed carpet slippers, a pair of tuxedo trousers, an undershirt and a nondescript jacket. His hair was unbrushed, and he obviously hadn't had a shave for a couple of days. All he needed was a tin cup and some pencils.... Feature for feature he had a handsome face, but it was set in a head that was a bit too large for his body and gave him a slightly gnomelike appearance. (*Musical Stages*, p. 21)

Since so many Hart love lyrics, from "My Heart Stood Still' in 1927 to "Wait Till You See Her" in 1942, are based on physical appearance—on falling in love by looking and seeing—he must have been wretchedly self-conscious of his appearance in the eyes of others. He begins the verse of "Glad to Be Unhappy" (*On Your Toes*, 1936) with a glimpse in the mirror:

> Look at yourself!
> If you had a sense of humor
> You would laugh to beat the band.

What saved Hart from tears was his laugh to beat the band.

Rodgers summarized the result of that first meeting: "I left Hart's house having acquired in one afternoon a career, a partner, a best friend, and a source of permanent irritation." The irritation arose from fundamental differences between the two collaborators. Rodgers remained middle class

Lorenz Hart at work, standing at the mirror

in both his social and moral outlook. He would always be the business manager for the team, the one who managed contracts, fees, and royalties, who could be depended on to show up for appointments on time and to finish his work on schedule. He would settle down with one woman for the remainder of his life. Hart was both psychologically and morally incapable of middle-class respectability. He would finish his work fitfully but quickly—in short, brilliant bursts—after which he would disappear for days. Rodgers knew Hart went on binges, but not where and with whom. It may have been either an innocent or willful ignorance. He knew Hart frequented a theater bar, Ralph's (like all theater bars, "mixed" in its sexual orientation) and the Luxor Baths (not precisely a gay bathhouse in the 1920s and 1930s, but not precisely nongay either). He either did not know or pretended not to know that Hart spent time in the seamier waterfront saloons on both sides of the Hudson, in the company of aspiring chorus boys, sailors, hustlers, and other drifters, with whom he traded for sexual attentions and from whom he received bruising injuries.[2]

It was not easy for Hart to wander between the glittering world of Broadway and the sleazy world of hustlers—not only because of the way he looked but because of the way he had been brought up. He was a college-educated, middle-class, Jewish-American boy in a period when closet doors remained tightly shut. So it was liquor—more and more of it—that eased the transportation between his two worlds. As his life brought him more and more Broadway success, his periods of drinking became greater and greater, periods of working shorter and shorter—until his tiny body broke down altogether in 1943.

His refuge was the way he spied the world from inside his closet, a view he could simultaneously reveal and disguise with song lyrics. Many of his lyrics are very private, personal confessions hiding behind the conventions of the popular song and the dramatic requirements of particular situations in musical plays. He was writing private jokes and private observations for the most private audience of all—himself. No other theater lyricist wrote such frankly physical love songs. As he confessed in "Have You Met Miss Jones?" (*I'd Rather Be Right*, 1937), he believed in matter over mind. Love for Hart was a kick in the stomach, a bang on the head, or a blow to the chest. It entered through the eyes with a blast and flew to the other organs with a rush that made the singer inarticulate, not merely unable to speak but even to breathe, leaving him (or, more frequently, her) a total wreck (when Rodgers's music departs from its steady steps to jump wildly in surprising intervals). In "My Heart Stood Still" (*A Connecticut Yankee*, 1927), the singer has been reduced to physical reflexes after just one look at the beloved. Love is a physical illness in "It's Got To Be Love" (*On Your Toes*): it feels like neuritis, tonsilitis, sunstroke, and fallen arches so it *must* be love. Hart can parody the same metaphor in "This Can't Be Love" (*The Boys from Syracuse*, 1938): it *can't* be love just because the singer doesn't feel sick.

These descriptions of love as physical illness reveal that Hart, whatever his own physical appearance, felt the agonizing physical joy of astonishment by sighting a spectacular love object who takes away the breath and destroys his faculties. Because he knew these sensations so intimately, Hart could parody the sentimental clichés of idealized love in other love songs. In "Where's that Rainbow?" from *Peggy-Ann* (1926), the sad singer searches unsuccessfully for comfort from other love songs: "I'm Always Chasing Rainbows," "Till the Clouds Roll By," even Rodgers and Hart's own "The Blue Room." The loveliest of their songs that is both a sincere statement of emotion and an ironic comment on the literary clichés of other love songs is "My Romance" (*Jumbo*, 1935): the singer's romance doesn't need castles in Spain, soft guitars, blue lagoons or the month of May, doesn't need anything at all—but you.

If love for Hart can be a joyous agony, it can also be a pain in the neck. In "I Wish I Were in Love Again" (*Babes in Arms*, 1937), the singers are caught between the pain of being in love and the pain of not being in love. In love there are sleepless nights and daily fights. Out of love you miss the kisses and you miss the bites. You're sane, but you'd rather be gaga or punch drunk. In love, there are blackened eyes, furtive sighs and "conversations" with flying plates. There are hackneyed words—"I love you till the day I die"—and the self-deception that believes such lies. Only one thing is sure with a Hart love lyric: you can't win one way or the other.

In Hart love songs, life has stuck a pin in the balloon—as the verse to "Spring Is Here" puts it (*I Married an Angel*, 1938). Hart's lonely lovers surrender to self-pity, spiced with just enough ironic laughter to beat the band. Pouring his own feelings into female vessels who have lost their men, Hart understood what it meant to lose or never win the man of his dreams. The refrain of "Spring Is Here" depicts a season when everyone has fallen in love—except the singer, whom nobody loves or needs. In "Nobody's Heart Belongs to Me" (*By Jupiter*, 1942), the singer pretends not to care that no one wants her. In "It Never Entered My Mind" (*Higher and Higher*, 1940), the singer never imagined she'd awaken to order orange juice for one, playing solitaire, scratching her own back. In "Glad to Be Unhappy" (*On Your Toes*), the singer yearns for the pleasure of sadness, the gladness of unhappiness, that love always means. "With someone you adore," she sings, "it's a pleasure to be sad." Hart knew this pleasure well: might his deepest unrequited love have been for the sixteen-year-old Rodgers? Instead, the lovesongs became his beloved—his only requited love.

Rodgers's melodies play a contrapuntal game with all this melancholy. If the two men seemed complementary opposites socially and psychologically, the same can be heard in their theater songs. Rodgers set Hart's biting, cynical, brutal, and intellectual lyrics to lovely, lyrical, sweet, and simple melodies. His favorite musical device was that most elementary of musical maneuvers learned at the parlor piano: marching up or down the major scale. The verse of their first hit song, "Manhattan" (*The Garrick Gaieties*, 1925), simply climbs the major scale, while the refrain of their second hit, "Mountain Greenery" (from the second *Garrick Gaieties*, 1926), first climbs down then up the same scale. Snuggled comfortably within almost every Rodgers tune is a simple scale. The release of "The Blue Room" (*The Girl Friend*, 1926) climbs the scale, just as its lyric climbs to an inviting blue room upstairs. The third and fourth bars of "Have You Met Miss Jones?" and the poignant B section of "Spring Is Here" climb the scales as well. "Johnny One Note" (*Babes in Arms*) alternates the major scale with a repetitive single note to tell its musical story of a singer who rejects every note of the scale but one. Even with Oscar Hammerstein, Rodgers stuck to his scales. The verse for "It Might as Well Be Spring" (the movie, *State Fair*, 1945) ascends and descends the major scale in formless vocalizing to convey the singer's listlessness. The booming refrain of "Oklahoma!" (1943) begins with an indispensable orchestral run up the scale. Appropriately enough, Rodgers's last big hit was a hymn to the musical scale itself—"Do Re Mi" (*The Sound of Music*, 1959).

If simple variation on the musical scale was Rodgers's most familiar technical trick, Hart's technical signature was his playfully complicated rhyming enjambment, often attached to a surprising triple rhyme. Their first copyrighted song, "Any Old Place with You" (1919), saves a Hart surprise for its climax. The singer will go absolutely anywhere with or for the beloved:

> I'd go to hell for ya,
> Or Philadelphia.

Their first hit, "Manhattan," opens with one:

> Summer journey to Niag'ra
> And to other places aggra-
> Vate all our cares

And "Mountain Greenery," sprouts many more:

> Beans could get no keener re-
> Ception in a beanery.

> or

> While you love your lover, let
> Blue skies be your coverlet.

Although Hart tended to move away from his trademark device later in his career, one of his very last lyrics triple-rhymes with breathtaking brilliance. In "To Keep My Love Alive" (the 1943 revival of *A Connecticut Yankee*), Hart rhymes varied types of interfamilial murder—fratricide, patricide—with the singer's slaying one of her many husbands by her mattress side.

Rodgers's sweetly naive melodies balance Hart's oddball subjects (like murdering an infinite series of husbands) and verbally exhaustive catalogs (like "To Keep My Love Alive"). Hart wrote the complicated lyrics for these songs first, then Rodgers dressed them in inordinately lovely musical clothes. "To Keep My Love Alive" marches innocently up, down, and around the scales—like a child's five-finger exercise—while the singer details exactly how she bumped off every single one of her husbands. For the coda, which concludes each chorus with the word "alive," the bottom drops out of the Rodgers scale to sound the most comically funereal of notes, accompanying the most vital of words. In "Too Good for the Average Man" (*On Your Toes*), Rodgers's melody is a pastiche of a delicate minuet, something a nine-year-old Mozart might have tossed off, while the singer catalogs the ills of modern life: the stale smell of fancy nightclubs, waking in an alcoholic ward, birth control apparati, and a psychoanalyst who informs him that he's a girl. Rodgers's melody for the rarely heard verse of "My Funny Valentine" (*Babes in Arms*) is a lovely pastiche of an English madrigal (roving up and down the scale), to contrast with the minor harmonies of the song's passionate refrain. "I Like to Recognize the Tune" (*Too Many Girls*, 1939) disdains the noisy modern sounds of jazz and swing; Rodgers carves a childlike, bouncy tune from major chords that might have been written by some simple soul who never heard of jazz.

In their best songs, Hart's acid lyrics cut through Rodgers's sweet sounds like a knife. In "Falling in Love with Love" (*The Boys from Syracuse*), one of the most lyrical waltzes ever written by an American, the singer bitterly chides herself for the childish foolishness of believing in anyone. In "There's a Small Hotel" (*On Your Toes*), the sweet melody and sweet description of the countryside come to an abrupt halt in the release with a rhetorical question, "Who wants people?" Although Rodgers admired the way Hart was able to capture the feeling of two newlyweds who needed no one in the world except each other, nothing in the song (or show) indicates that these lovers are wed. Though they intend to use the bridal suite, this "small hotel" is one of those "honeymoon hotels" in the era before motels (and modeled on a rather notorious New Jersey inn that Hart apparently knew well). In "Dancing on the Ceiling" (*Simple Simon*, 1930), the Rodgers melody dutifully and innocently climbs up and down the scales while the Hart lyric describes the thoughts of a woman lying in bed alone at night, imagining her beloved dancing above her head, describing nothing so much as a masturbatory fantasy. With a Hart lyric, one always reads between the lines, and the sweet and sweeping Rodgers melodies make for very thick camouflage: the tunes so innocent, the words so wise.

Rodgers began writing shows with Hart in 1918 when both were counselors at Camp Paradox. Paradox alumni also included Hammerstein and Arthur Schwartz. No other summer camp ever produced so many masters of musical theater. Compared to Irving Berlin, Jerome Kern, even George Gershwin, Richard Rodgers was always less a songwriter than a man of the theater. He published comparatively few songs (less than half the number published by Kern, a quarter the number published by Berlin). He rarely wrote songs except for theater or film scores and he never worked in Tin Pan Alley. He was far less comfortable in Hollywood than Berlin, Kern, and the Gershwins, who had been trained to write songs to order and shared the Hollywood hunger for hit songs rather than whole scores.

How did you write Broadway musicals if you didn't rise from Tin Pan Alley? The alternative answer was amateur musical shows. From summer camp, Rodgers and Hart moved to college—the 1920 varsity show at Columbia University, *Fly with Me*. Although Hart had already been graduated and Rodgers had never enrolled at Columbia College (only briefly at the university's extension), they nonetheless succeeded Oscar Hammerstein as authors of the varsity show. For five years they remained discouraged authors of mere amateur shows. Rodgers even deserted popular music for serious study at the school that would become known as Juilliard. Their last act of charity led to their first professional break in 1925. The prestigious Theater Guild, raising money for more important productions, presented an informal musical revue on Sunday, May 17, at the Garrick Theater, where its production of Ferenc Molnar's *The Guardsman* (starring the Lunts) was dark. Propelled by its Rodgers and Hart score, the revue was such a success on its single Sunday that it reopened for a long run in the fall. It led to a second *Garrick Gaieties* the following season.

The big hits from the two *Gaieties*, "Manhattan" and "Mountain Greenery," proclaim Rodgers and Hart's knowledge of the relationship of song form to theater form. The songs are deliberate variations on one another: the first about the city, the second about the country. The songs were written as duets for the same pair—Sterling Holloway and June Cochrane—in the same slot in each show. The melodies of the two tunes are variations on one another. The clever triple-rhyme schemes of both tunes are variations on one another. The references and images of the two songs are variations on one another—Mott Street, pushcarts, Coney, the Bronx, and Staten of "Manhattan," blue skies, mosquitoes, wood, and scenery for "Mountain Greenery." These were not two random songs but carefully conceived numbers for symmetrical theatrical purposes.

The Rodgers and Hart shows that followed through the 1920s, most of them with books by their close friend, Herbert Fields, sought new and surprising landscapes for musical shows to inhabit. They avoided both the Operettaland of Romberg and the modern American opposite of the Gershwin and Princess Theater shows by walking between them—making musicals by combining topical contemporary issues, American history, and American literature. *Dearest Enemy* (1925), set during the American Revolution, was a sly piece of musical irony in which the act of sexual seduction becomes an act of patriotism, delaying the advance of the British troops and allowing the tattered American army to beat a successful retreat. *Peggy-Ann* was the first American musical based on the Freudian psychoanalysis of dreams and *A Connecticut Yankee* the first based on a story by Mark Twain, contrasting the values of modern America with the chivalric romance of an Arthurian Operettaland. No song better distills the show's historical juxtaposition than "Thou Swell," its very title an oxymoron of irreconcilable levels and periods of English language usage.

In 1931 Rodgers and Hart departed for Hollywood—for four unpleasant and, in their minds, unproductive years. That Hollywood unproductivity merely included *Love Me Tonight*, one of the best original scores ever written for a film; the complicated score for a political folk-fable, *Hallelujah! I'm a Bum*, starring Al Jolson; and three of Bing Crosby's biggest hits ("Soon," "It's Easy to Remember," and "You Are Too Beautiful"). Hart also wrote a snappy set of new lyrics for Ernst Lubitsch's 1934 film of *The Merry Widow*. The impression of Hollywood inactivity for Broadway composers was more a state of mind than a point of fact, arising from the limited responsibility of songwriters in Hollywood: they write the songs but are only occasionally invited to the set. On Broadway, songwriters are full members of the creative team: cutting, rewriting, reslotting, revising daily as a show races toward opening night.

They raced back to Broadway in 1935 breathing the fire of innovation. With George Abbott they created the first stage musical to make modern dance intrinsic to its choreographic (and narrative) conception—*On Your Toes*. For the next decade, Rodgers shows, with Hart or Hammerstein, would include a lengthy ballet by a major modern choreographer—George Balanchine (*On Your Toes, Babes in Arms, I Married an Angel*), Robert Alton (*Pal Joey*, 1940), Agnes DeMille (*Oklahoma!*, 1943; *Carousel*, 1945; *Allegro*, 1947). The ballets replaced dialogue scenes with lengthy dramatic passages of pure dance rather than the usual song and dance. Rodgers, Hart, and Abbott also wrote the first American show to musicalize Shakespeare, *The Boys from Syracuse*, based on *The Comedy of Errors*, and the first American musical of the century based on Greek myth, *By Jupiter*, adapted from Julian Thompson's *The Warrior's Husband*. Rodgers and Hart mixed the whole range of arts, from ballet to poetry, into the entertainment cake of musical theater.

Unlike the exotic escapes to Operettaland before them, Rodgers and Hart shows use the distant literary terrain to make pointed comments about contemporary American society. The song that introduces the modern American audience to the values of Greek culture, "Jupiter Forbid," includes references to other places in the world that are not at all like the setting of this musical—where there are signs, "Keep Off the Grass," in spring; where you could kiss only if you hid. The place with the signs where you had to hide (and Hart knew about hiding) was called America. The book, which Rodgers and Hart themselves wrote, turns on an ironic reversal of genders with its war between the patriarchal Greek army and the matriarchal Amazons. In Amazonian society, the women go off to war and the men stay home to stir the soup on the stove. Hart could make plenty of sly observations about American gender expectations and stereotypes. These Rodgers and Hart shows of 1935 to 1943 expanded the scope, style, and subject matter for American musical theater—crossing frontiers into territories which had never before admitted singing and dancing.

The show that went furthest and deepest into that territory was *Pal Joey*. John O'Hara had written a series of thirteen stories in the form of fictional letters that ran in the *New Yorker* in 1939, an epistolary novel of correspondence between a lowlife nightclub singer, Joey, in Ohio and Chicago and his musician friend Ted in New York, which he signed, "Pal Joey":

> DEAR PAL TED,
>   Well at last I am getting around to knocking off a line or two to let you know how much I apprisiate it you sending me that wire on opening nite. Dont think because I didnt answer before I didnt apprisiate it because that is far from the case. But I guess you know that because if you knew when I was opening you surely must be aware how busy Ive been ever since opening nite. I figure you read in *Variety* what date I was opening in which case I figure you have seen the write ups since then telling how busy Ive been and believe me its no exagerton. (p. 7)[3]

A key irony of O'Hara's epistolary choice is that Joey can barely write; his spelling, grammar, and syntax reveal more education on the streets than in any schoolroom. Rodgers and Hart translated this irony into the show's most familiar love song, "I Could Write a Book," the conning seduction of an innocent woman by a man who can't speak a proper sentence, much less write a book.

Even more ironic than Joey's misuse of the language in the O'Hara letters is his view of the world: other people only exist to advance his own sexual and vocational ends. All women are mice—little animals for his personal amusement. All nightclubs are cribs—tight places where he displays what he presumes to be his suave, sexy, debonair wares. If he had a sense of humor, he would laugh to beat the band. But Joey doesn't laugh. He is even too blind to see the laughter of others around him, unaware of the contempt with which everyone treats him. He is run out of an Ohio town when he starts mousing around with the banker's daughter. He drifts to the South Side of Chicago where he gets and loses jobs in various cribs, doesn't get or gets and loses various mice—some sweet, some smart, one rich socialite, mostly girls who work the cribs. By the end of his last letter

Joey is out of work again, but Ted's new band is on the way up. Why won't Ted hire him as the band's singer? Joey blames Ted for his rotten luck and breaks off the correspondence as Ted's "Ex Pal Joey (Hate yr guts)." The novel ends without concluding as Joey drifts off to who knows where, to write more letters to whoever.

O'Hara wrote another letter—suggesting to Rodgers that they make the letters musical.[4] The idea appealed to Larry Hart, who had hung out in plenty of cribs, standing at the bar with guys who had nothing but mouth—full of themselves and their ambitions—attached to the sexy body that was their meal ticket. Plenty of them probably had no more grammar, syntax, or pronunciation than O'Hara's Joey. But how do you set a musical in this seamy world? This was no Operettaland but fleabag, smoke-filled, South Side Chicago in the late years of the Depression. You couldn't weave Joey into some typical multiplot without killing the idea of who Joey is and what he represents. Imagine Joey's conversion, by the One True Mouse, to real love, while his comic roommate, Ted, finds same with the cigarette-girl soubrette in the crib. The smart decision was to build the musical, like the letters, as an unflinching study of Joey himself—his egoism, stupidity, sexiness, selfishness, blindness—surrounded by the sleazebag atmosphere and stale aroma of the world where he lived, worked, and conned. It was a musical with exactly one nice character—so irritatingly innocent that she made even Joey seem appealing.

Although O'Hara wrote the show's first draft and receives sole credit for the book, he took little interest in the production, forcing on Rodgers, Hart, and Abbott the inevitable rewriting that every musical gets in rehearsal. Drawn freely from incidents and characters sprinkled through the letters, the show's plot is worth recounting since fewer are familiar with it than with the 1957 film, a pleasant enough movie for Frank Sinatra (converted to love, as always, by the One True Mouse), but which isn't *Pal Joey*.

Joey gets a job in a cheap South Side Chicago nightclub after its owner, Mike, is satisfied that Joey has no exotic vices—"nose candy" or a taste for young boys. Joey's vice is plain and simple: women. He puts the make on a sweet mouse, Linda English, who will believe anything. Standing in front of a pet shop window, he recollects his pet terrier, Skippy, back in the days before the crash, when his wealthy family owned a huge estate.

JOEY: Well, one day I was coming home from the Academy. I was going to an Academy then, about ten miles from the estate. I didn't learn much there, except how to play polo and of course riding to hounds. So this particular day I have reference to, I was returning to our estate. They opened the gate for us and about a mile up the road I saw Skippy coming. Oh, he could always tell the sound of the

Rolls every afternoon. Of course, the poor old codger was half blind by that time, but we gave him a good home. So I was sitting up with the chauffeur and I saw Skippy coming. He was up near the main house, about a mile or so, and I instructed the chauffeur, I said— Chadwick—be careful of old Skippy, and he said—yes. But with Skippy you couldn't tell, because his eyesight was so bad. Well—do you want to hear the rest of it?

LINDA: Did you run over him?

JOEY: It wasn't the chauffeur's fault, really. Not actually. But daddy discharged him anyway. Mother erected a monument over his grave. (*She cries*) Skippy's, I mean. (p. 127)

A woman of a very opposite sort, Vera Simpson, a rich socialite, strolls into Joey's crib on a night of slumming, accompanied by her usual anonymous escort. Joey insults her—his way to handle a mouse of this species—assuring Mike that she'll come back. She does. Vera takes Joey as her lover (he thinks he's taking her). She buys him new clothes, rents an apartment for their "love nest," and bankrolls his dream—his own classy nightclub, Chez Joey. A blackmailer, Ludlow Lowell, the funniest and wittiest of blackmailers in American theater history, gets wind of who's paying whose bills.

LOWELL: Uh, dear Mrs. Simpson. I bet you're wondering to what you owe the honor of this visit—like in the old plays. Or maybe you're not wondering, but I will tell you. Seating myself on the chaise lounge—(*He does so*) and casually puffing my butt—my object is blackmail.

VERA: Well, I'll be damned.

JOEY: I'll be darned.

LOWELL: I have decided that you are an intelligent woman of the world, Mrs. Simpson. A woman that has been around— not too long, of course...

VERA: Thanks for that anyway.

LOWELL: Glad to. Now a woman of the world, charming, intelligent, fascinating—she knows that the time comes to pay the piper.

VERA: Did you say viper?

LOWELL: Haw, haw, haw. Not bad. Not bad. Viper. Vinshield Viper. Like that one? Well, to continue, you know that the day of reckoning must come, and here it is. I reckon that $20,000 is a good day's reckoning. (p. 213)

Vera gets rid of this vinshield viper by phoning Deputy Police Commis-

PHOTO: FRED FEHL

Pal Joey: Joey (Gene Kelly) with the mice and with Linda English (Leila Ernst), observed by a young Stanley Donen

THEATRE COLLECTION, MUSEUM OF THE CITY OF NEW YORK

sioner O'Brien, asking for a little favor in return for the large Christmas gifts she sends each year to the boys. Vera confesses she's been a "bad girl again—just about the same kind of thing that happened two years ago." O'Brien runs Ludlow out of town and Vera tosses Joey out of her life—to keep her wealthy husband from finding out about her "little fun." Joey stands alone in front of the pet shop window—out of work and broke. When an attractive mouse walks by, he follows her toward the wings—as the curtain falls.

How do you get this story with these kinds of characters to sing? Rodgers and Hart adopted the clear and clever plan of Kern and Hammerstein's *Show Boat*. There would be two kinds of numbers—plot numbers (sung by characters to one another) and nightclub numbers (sung by performers on stage). The plot numbers express character feelings and intentions (usually sly, selfish, or sexual) while the performance numbers create the seamy atmosphere and energetic rhythm of the nightclub world. If the score owed its division to *Show Boat*, it also owed it to the division in the Astaire films between performance numbers and plot numbers. For the nightclub numbers Rodgers and Hart wrote both affectionate reconstructions of a musical style very different from their own (as the Gershwins had done in *Porgy and Bess*) and outrageous parodies of that alternative style of music (as the Gershwins had done in *Of Thee I Sing*).

The two most outrageous parodies are least familiar since they never made it onto the 1951 Columbia recording.[5] One is the brassy opening of the show for Joey and the girls: "Chicago," an absolutely forgettable upbeat tune with unmemorable lyrics, a song that might be sung by any line of not very talented chorus girls in any tacky nightclub in any 1940 American city. A little joke with this number follows in the classy Chez Joey of the second act. While the setting and scanty costumes for the number change from cheap Chicagoan to exotic Moroccan, the girls sing the identical tune with the identical words—substituting only Morocco for Chicago. ("There's a great big town on a great big lake called Morocco!") Same song, same crib. Only the mattress is different. The second parody is very overdecorated, "In the Flower Garden of My Heart," a fancy production number at Chez Joey, warbled by a Ziegfeldian tenor, surrounded by the mice on dress (or undress) parade, disguised as flowers. Rodgers delights in the dumbest, least inventive tune he can imagine, which Hart adorns with the silliest rhymes ("whisk us" with "hibiscus," "holy" with "gladioli").

More affectionate and accurate at creating the brassy feel and sound of the swing era are the colloquial "You Mustn't Kick It Around" and "Plant You Now, Dig You Later" for Joey and Gladys Bumps, the lead singer at the crib. Even the titles reek of 1940 swing and slang. "That Terrific Rainbow" is a terrific "Red Hot Mama" homage to Sophie Tucker for Gladys Bumps and the girls; the bump-and-grind beat of a torchy tune accompanies a lyric based on colors, each of which cues a change of gel on the follow spot, from red hot to orange flame to green with envy to white with cold.

Of the plot numbers, even the unfamiliar songs are gems. In "What Is a Man?" Vera answers her rhetorical question with Hart's unqualified admiration for the entire male sex, "from Charlie Chaplin to Charlie Chan." For "Our Little Den of Iniquity," Rodgers writes a delicate minuet to accompany Joey and Vera's enumeration of the sexual activities that their apartment permits. The best (and best known) of the show's plot numbers is "Bewitched, Bothered, and Bewildered." Typical of Hart, it depicts love as a purely physical sensation that overwhelms all other human behavior. Typical of Rodgers, the tune is based on coyly simple steps, adding an innocent charm to its blatantly sexual confession. The essential trick of "Bewitched" is its contrasting long and short lines, anchored by Hart's patented triple-rhymes on the repetitive word, "again." The "againness" of this song, its delight in repetition, is its most striking musical, verbal, psychological, and comic trait. This is not a new sensation for Vera but one that she feels again and again and again:

> Vexed again,
> Perplexed again,
> Thank God I can be oversexed again:
> Bewitched, bothered, and bewildered am I.

For all the familiarity of the song, there is one lyric that was (and still is) regularly bowdlerized when popular singers record it. Instead of

> Couldn't sleep,
> And wouldn't sleep,
> Until I could sleep where I shouldn't sleep.

we get:

> Couldn't sleep,
> And wouldn't sleep,
> When love came and told me I shouldn't sleep.

I'm not sure how Hart would have felt about love's becoming so chatty.

The song was so popular in the show that it required encore after encore, again and again and again, as well as a second act reprise, when Vera decides she is "Bewitched, Bothered, and Bewildered No More." Many of these additional verses have never been recorded (some have even been lost), but one goes:

> Slipped again,
> Flipped again,
> My chastity belt is unzipped again.

This is as delightfully raunchy as theater songwriting had ever been. The song's verse, also very infrequently heard with its original lyrics, begins with another example of Hart's writing from painful and personal experience:

> After one whole quart of brandy,
> Like a daisy I awake.
> With no Bromo Seltzer handy
> I don't even shake.

Apparently, love is more physically powerful than the shakes.

Pal Joey's other showstopper is "Zip," a pure digression, one of those specialty numbers to blow the fresh air of diversity into a book-heavy second act. The idea for the number comes directly from the O'Hara letters when a newspaper columnist, Melba, interviews Joey upon the opening of his club. The apparent opposite of one of Joey's mice, he describes her in his letter to Ted as "Lesbo"; then he discovers she is terrific in bed. Joey, amazed that someone can look so bad and love so good, is usually the most naive resident of his own manipulative universe. The musical alters Joey's revelation (he never sleeps with Melba) but keeps his stereotyped view of female sexuality in contrast to Melba's combination of mind and body. The show's Melba is less "Lesbo" than intellectual in stereotypical glasses, who, despite her prim look, "can't drink Irish except straight."

Joey feeds Melba the usual line about his upbringing and background:

JOEY: Well, the kids were sitting around singing and playing the piano and there was this society singer from New York—I grew up with her—Consuelo Van Rensselaer, Connie. I grew up with her, but I didn't see her much after Daddy lost his fortune. (MELBA *chokes on her drink*). . . . We were sitting around singing all the old songs. Dardanella. Who. The oldies. Suddenly everybody stopped singing and I was the only one. It was a lovely old tune that Mother used to sing to me before going out to some big society ball. . . . So Connie was sitting in a corner, and she was crying softly to herself. It reminded her of something. It was just the mood it got her into. So when all the others applauded, she just sat there crying softly.

MELBA: Then did she say—you ought to be singing professionally, and introduce you to Pops Whiteman, and he gave you your first break, then you sort of sang with several other bands, and in night clubs, and that's how you happened to come to Chicago? Okay. I'll write it. (pp. 178–79)

As usual, Joey is three steps behind someone he thinks is three steps behind him.

Then Melba rips off her glasses to sing "Zip," recounting her interview with a Minsky stripper, modeled on Gypsy Rose Lee. This stripper, it turns out, is a sexy intellectual (like Melba) who ponders the great cultural issues of the day while she works—Stravinsky, Picasso, Schopenhauer, Dali, Saroyan's plays, Lippman's column, Stokowski's conducting, Jergens Lotion, misogyny, movies, Mickey Mouse and Rooney, heterosexuality, Whistler's mother, *Charley's Aunt*, Shubert's brother. Rodgers's melody is another parodic delight—of the stripper's bumps and grinds. The catalog of cultural references acquires an extra edge of irony in contrasting the stripper's external physical activity and internal mental activity.

The one romantic ballad of the show is also a parodic joke. "I Could Write a Book" begins with a deliberately idiotic verse—reciting the alphabet, from A to G, then counting, from one to seven, as Richard Rodgers repeats the same G twenty-six times.[6] Both the composer and lyricist announce that this is a really dumb song by a conman dope to a woman even more stupid than he is. The refrain is deliberately repetitive and drippy, driving its parallel between books and love into the ground. Yet the song became a hit outside the show, sung by very good singers without a trace of irony. Divorced from its ironic context, Hart's simple lyric is so sincere, Rodgers's simple music so charming, that the song can be sung and felt straight. Rodgers and Hart were masters of creating the song that suggested one idea in its dramatic context and another outside it—precisely the aim of this first generation of composer-lyricists.

There had never been a musical like *Pal Joey*; bitter, cynical, seamy, sordid, with no romantic resolution, no change of heart, no happy ending—no ending at all. Both Joey and Vera will continue to do exactly what they have done because there just isn't anything else they can do. Although no formal breakthrough—like *Show Boat*, *Of Thee I Sing*, or *Porgy and Bess*—*Pal Joey*, influenced by all three, was the first musical to explore its characters in depth. Despite the class differences of wealth and education, Joey and Vera were two of a kind, both hedonists commited to nothing except what they could touch, taste, and lie on, to, or with. Brooks Atkinson, theater critic of the New York *Times*, barometer of literate mainstream taste, was appalled: "Can one draw sweet water from a foul well?"

Despite Atkinson's doubts, and despite legend to the contrary, *Pal Joey* was a hit in its first 1940 run and an even bigger hit in its 1952 revival—when Atkinson recanted and pronounced the show a classic. Although both productions starred the same Vivienne Segal as Vera, the 1952 Joey was the dependable dancer Harold Lang, while the 1940 Joey was merely Gene Kelly. Kelly made the original Joey something special and Joey made Kelly a star. The ballet that closes Act I, when Joey's vision of the world becomes the nightclub of his imagination, was the first of Kelly's dream ballets. Even after the trip to MGM, Kelly never completely rinsed off the aroma of Joey. In comparison to the ethereal Astaire, Kelly would always seem more common, venal, vulgar, selfish—in short, mortal. He escaped into dream ballets because he was so solidly anchored to the earth below.

No previous American musical show depicted the underbelly of American lowlife as convincingly as *Pal Joey*. Lorenz Hart knew plenty about that underbelly. It finally finished him. Rodgers could not get Hart to work on *By Jupiter* without committing him to a hospital, installing himself next door with a typewriter and a rented upright piano. Rodgers exasperatedly left Hart for Hammerstein six months before Hart died. But Hart's spirit was already dead. After being banned from rehearsals of the 1943 revival of *A Connecticut Yankee* for his erratic behavior, he was thrown out of the Martin Beck Theater on opening night, screaming abuse at both performers and audience. He did not go gently into that goodnight. His monument remains not only some of the best American theater songs of the century but a series of shows that stood poised between two ideas of a musical: as an innovative theater conception and as an entertaining collection of inventive numbers. With Hammerstein, Rodgers abandoned the number for the concept.

The one master who continued to march against the movement of musical-theater history—writing shows for their songs rather than songs for a show—was Cole Porter.

11

Do Do That Voodoo That You Do So Well

COLE PORTER

Cole Porter was the only major American theater composer who was not Jewish. Nor was he born or raised in New York—even if his songs exude the essence and quintessence (to use his own phrase) of New York sophistication and chic. No other American's songs seemed to say, over and over again, "I Happen to Like New York"—either explicitly (like this 1930 song) or implicitly. But then no other American's songs said, over and over again, "I Love Paris," like that 1953 song. Porter's New York was worlds away from the teeming, ethnic, working-class city of Berlin, Gershwin, and Rodgers. His was the New York of Fifth Avenue, Cartier's, and the Plaza, the New York of "spiritual" New Yorkers, who, then as now, were born in places like Peru, Indiana, where Porter was born in 1891. He emigrated to New York not through Ellis Island but, like many Broadway shows, through New Haven, the high road to New York for wealthy midwestern WASPs at the turn of the century: Eastern prep school, Yale, and Harvard Law (which he left to study music).

Songwriting for Porter seemed more a diverting hobby than the business it was for Irving Berlin, whose songs were his trade; more an agreeable pastime for Porter than the passion it was for Gershwin, who rejected a dependable trade because he was possessed by music. The typical image of Porter plops him on a piano bench, icebucket of champagne at his side, amusing himself and a smiling circle of smart friends with a witty ditty tossed off between sips of the bubbly. This image of Porter as dilettante makes him seem both more and less attractive than his Jewish brethren: more because he didn't debase a delicate and ephemeral talent with business contracts, royalty fees, and production schedules; less because his icy detachment drains his songs of the energy that gives the others so much heart. There is something attractively aristocratic and engagingly elitist in

Cole Porter at the piano in 1938

this Porter portrait, an idea of talent and its display that can be traced back to the supremely talented amateur of the Renaissance who never debased his skill by becoming too proficient or professional at it. In a century of bourgeois professionalism, Porter's aristocratic amateurism is a model of both elegance and decadence.

It is also a completely false picture of Porter's relationship to his music. The Porter myth arose from many sources: his own impudent and imprudent youth; his lavish expatriate life between 1919 and 1928; the slants of newspaper reporters and columnists who (then as now) fulfilled the expectations of their middle-class and working-class readers; a ludicrous 1945 film "biography" at Warner Bros., *Night and Day*, in which Porter is impersonated by (who else?) Cary Grant; and Porter's own reticence, which eschewed any display of personal feeling in public (and even in private). It was neither proper nor polite to reveal very much about oneself; his inner life was simply not public business. That life suggests less the dilettante aesthete than the sly and shy little boy and man who never felt completely comfortable nor completely acceptable in public unless he was at the piano, singing one of his cleverly naughty songs. He was only amusing at the piano amusing to himself and, he suspected, to others. There may have been less voraciousness in Porter's need to entertain than in Gershwin's all-night sessions at the keyboard, but that didn't mean Porter was less needy: merely, given his upbringing and personality, less obvious.

Porter was the one *goy* in American popular and theater music. He was as conscious of it as everyone else in the business. Like most from his background in his era, he was antisemitic as a matter of course. Jews were those impolite, less educated, less polished new arrivals in America, pushing to get ahead. The patriarch of the Porter family, J. O. Cole, Porter's grandfather, had made his millions a generation earlier. Typical of American patterns of immigration and upward mobility, the social detritus of the previous generation, having achieved material comfort and social respectability, look down on the detritus of the new generation with understandable disdain and (of course) fear. The only Jews who were always welcome *chez* Porter—whether in Paris or Venice—were songwriters: George Gershwin, Richard Rodgers, and, Porter's favorite, Irving Berlin.

Porter jokingly said that to be successful in American theater music meant writing "Jewish music." Jewish composers made the same joke all the time. Oscar Hammerstein, working with Kern in 1928 on a musical version of Marco Polo's journey to the East, asked about the musical style for the show: Italian? Chinese? Kern answered quickly: "Same kind as always. Good Jewish music." Porter got into trouble with his Jewish brothers when he made an explicit musical Jewish joke in public. The release of "My Heart Belongs to Daddy" (*Leave It to Me*, 1938), is built not only on minor Jewish cadences but on an inarticulate musical wailing that sounds very much like Jewish cantorial prayer. The implication is that "daddy," the dirty old man with the dough, is Jewish. But Porter's songs are full of "Jewish music"—if Jewish means the tendency to slide into minor chords, the blue notes, or to slide back and forth between the major and minor scales. While George Gershwin or Irving Berlin leaped to a minor scale or pounced on a blue note, Porter glided between them. No other American theater composer slid as gracefully and subtly between major and minor than Porter. In "Every Time We Say Goodbye" (*The Seven Lively Arts*, 1944), Porter's lyric explicitly refers to the sorrow of parting as a change from major to minor, accompanied by a musical phrase that changes in precisely that "Jewish" way.

Porter is as remarkable in the American music business for being gay as *goy*. Not that there weren't (and aren't) many gay writers of American theater music. Porter, however, seemed a unique midpoint between a Lorenz Hart, with his personal public messages in almost indecipherable code, and a liberated contemporary composer more willing to proclaim openly, "I Am What I Am." Porter lived his gay life in the Edwardian, Wildean manner and manor. He was literally and figuratively a product of the age and style that produced an Oscar Wilde comedy of manners like *Lady Windermere's Fan*. And comedies of manners are always about matters of sexual propriety, not table manners. Openly scandalous or improper sexual behavior produce an inevitable result—ostracism from a surrounding society with particular views of proper sexual behavior. One might dally with a chauffeur or gardener, or with a gigolo (Porter sketched one in a song with "just a dash of lavender" in his nature), or even with the son, cousin, brother, or father of someone in one's own drawing room (the most dangerous of dalliances—as Wilde discovered), so long as the bedroom door never opened onto the drawing room. There was gossip and rumor, to be sure, but one concrete fact (like Lady Windermere's telltale fan) was worth ten-thousand whispers. Porter lived within a paradoxical society for whom gossip was a social necessity but an act that provoked gossip a social catastrophe.

Porter took a wife—as neither Lorenz Hart nor Porter's close friend, Noël Coward, ever did. Linda Lee Thomas was a beautiful, charming, and rich divorcée, nine years older than Porter. She would be his closest friend and companion, as well as the hostess who made possible his social life of wit, wealth, and waste.[1] Without her he could never have become the most fashionable, extravagant, and brilliant host of his generation. A party *chez* Porter in the 1920s, especially at the Palazzo Rezzonico in Venice, meant brilliant conversation, company, entertainment (from Cole's songs to Diaghilev's new ballet), decor (their mammoth Red and White Ball of 1925), and extravagance (floating nightclubs on the Grand Canal illuminated by 225,000 candles).

Porter's songs were for the drawing room—delicious public gossip—but never would they offer a peek into a real bedroom. Not even into his own bedroom—or rather, especially not into his own bedroom. Porter developed the unique gift of implying everything while saying nothing. He may not have been less physical, less sexually active, less sensual than Lorenz Hart, but his lyrics suggest that picture. Alec Wilder observes that Porter lyrics "seldom risked or indulged in tenderness or vulnerability.... They often managed to keep at a polite distance from true sentiment..."[2] For Porter, unlike Hart, love (or sex) is an idea, not a sensation. Love is a "thing"— "What Is this Thing Called Love?" "Just One of those Things," "You've Got that Thing," "You Do Something to Me." Or love is an "It"—"Let's Do It," "It's De-lovely," "It's Bad for Me," "Don't Let It Get You Down." Or love is a smart piece of slang—"I Get a Kick Out of You," "Ridin' High," "I've Got You Under My Skin." While for Hart love is a physical kick in the stomach, for Porter love is an abstract "kick" in the imagination, a "high." His imagery is as vague, slippery, and suggestive as Hart's is concrete, specific, and physical. Hart's lyrics are bedroom confessions, Porter's drawing room dish.

Porter's most popular and durable kind of song converted public gossip into musical dish. While Hart's lady was a tramp because she wouldn't dish the dirt with the rest of the girls, Porter's catalog songs dish plenty of dirt. Originally, Porter dished the activities of friends within his own smart circle, as well as the attempts of social climbers to push into that circle. Among those pushy outsiders were a mythical midwestern couple, Mr. and Mrs. S. (for Sonofa) Beech Fitch, about whom Porter and his friend, Elsa Maxwell, invented and planted news items in the Paris *Herald Tribune.* Porter's dishy song about these *nouveaux riches* Fitches eventually pushed its way into *The Gay Divorce.* As he became more and more a theater composer rather than a parlor entertainer, Porter expanded his dish to names in the newspaper columns and fads sweeping the tastes of the nation. Porter wrote camp musical catalogs, parodying the same kinds of items one might see in the headlines of today's supermarket tabloids.

Virtually every Porter show required at least two of these catalog songs—one that dropped names and one that referred to bizarre sexual and social practices. Porter would extend these catalogs to seeming infinity— over four, five, six, or more choruses—never running out of invention, energy, or surprises. And each show would fulfill its promise by delivering two shiny new ones, which seemingly could not equal or top the previous catalogs—but somehow did. Even the least known of these catalog songs are gems of cultural history as societal gossip.

There were two catalog songs for Sophie Tucker in *Leave It to Me.* In "Most Gentlemen Don't Like Love," the sexually wise mama lists the purely predatory habits of male lovers: "a romp and a quickie is all little Dickie means when he mentions romance"; "a pounce in the clover and then when it's over, 'So long and what is your name?'" In "Tomorrow" Tucker parodies the clichés of 1930s social uplift. FDR's nothing to fear but fear itself becomes "there ain't gonna be no sorrow tomorrow": "There'll be no double-crossing, even out in Hollywood"; "You'll even see John L. Lewis with a smile upon his face"; and soldiers "will put war on the fritz and move into the Ritz." The sentiments both parody Irving Berlin's "There's a Lovely Day Tomorrow" and forecast the sappy sunshine song with the same title, "Tomorrow," in *Annie,* four decades later.

There were also two catalog songs for Danny Kaye in *Let's Face It!* (1941). In "Farming" we meet the rich and famous who have taken to the country: Mae West "is at her best in the hay," Monty Woolley "has boll weevils in his beard," Margie Hart is "churning her butter," Elsa Maxwell "got well goosed dehorning her cattle," and George Raft's "bull is beautiful but he's gay!" In "Let's Not Talk About Love" Kaye invents a catalog of conversational subjects to avoid the one that really interests him:

> Let's talk about drugs, let's talk about dope,
> Let's try to picture Paramount minus Bob Hope.

or

Let's speak of Lamarr, that Hedy so fair,
Why does she let Joan Bennett wear all her old hair?

or

Let's check on the veracity of Barrymore's bibacity
And why his drink capacity should get so much publacity,
Let's even have a huddle over Ha'vard Univassity
But let's not talk about love.

Porter's problem was making this chatter amenable to a drawing room as large as a theater and acceptable to a smart set as broad as the entire American public. He suffered a dozen years of Broadway disappointment, beginning with a resounding 1916 flop, *See America First*. Porter had perpetual troubles with censorship and bowdlerization. "Love for Sale" (*The New Yorkers*, 1930) was banned from the radio. Rodgers and Hart had written a song only months earlier about paying for love, "Ten Cents a Dance," with references to pansies and rough guys, to soldiers and sailors and bow-legged tailors, and Ruth Etting sang this specialty number anywhere. However, Porter's prostitute was no dance-hall metaphor but a girl who opens shop on the street and seeks customers to climb the stairs and try her wares. "My Heart Belongs to Daddy" couldn't be played on the radio without a set of sanitized lyrics. Even in the 1953 film of *Kiss Me Kate*, a mere reference to the Kinsey Report in "Too Darn Hot" gets air-brushed to "the latest report." The film is so busy censoring such intellectual references that it overlooks the most blatantly vernacular sexual reference in all of Porter. In "Tom, Dick, and Harry," Bianca informs us that she wants any man whatever. Porter concludes the song with a repetitive one-word coda: Bianca wants a "Dick, Dick, Dick." How do you sing in the upper case?

Porter's most famous difficulties were with one of his most famous songs, "I Get a Kick out of You." The second stanza of the refrain begins, "Some get a kick from cocaine," which Ethel Merman sang without a trace of discomfort in her 1934 Brunswick recording. Some three decades later, Merman's Reprise recording had reformed its sniff: "Some like that perfume from Spain" (which Frank Sinatra, who owned Reprise, always sings). In 1972, a published version of the song substituted, "Some like a bop-type refrain," changing the sniff to a riff that would bore the singer terriff(ically) too. Porter preferred to ravage the song with a jazz riff than a sniff of Spanish perfume. Merman's 1972 album for London, *Merman Sings Merman*, returns to the original sniff of cocaine. It had again become acceptable to mention cocaine in public.

There are two reasons that sniffing perfume from Spain would have driven Porter round the bend. The most obvious is that the best perfume doesn't come from Spain. And Porter knows where the best perfume comes from—as does the wise female alter ego who sings the song. A more subtle reason is that the substitution destroys the song's intellectual structure. Porter has written a song about "getting a kick"—otherwise known as "getting high." How do people "get high" in our (and his) society? One way is liquor—so the first eight bars of the refrain sip champagne. Another is drugs—so the second eight bars sniff cocaine (to rhyme with champagne). The release alters the pattern by removing the dependence on a physical stimulant: getting high just from seeing the beloved nearby (which parallels seeing his "fabulous face" at the end of the verse). The final eight bars of the refrain return to "getting high" with a very literal pun—flying in a plane. You can get high on booze, on drugs, or in a plane (originally in Lindbergh's plane, which Porter changed after the kidnapping). But the best "high" of all is a "mind trip" with the beloved. The substitution of perfume from Spain preserves the rhyming enjambment of whiff with terriff but destroys the idea of the song.

Porter's best songs are built on such ideas, on an intellectual structure that generates the song and organizes its development. Porter could write lengthy catalog songs because his central idea generated a seemingly infinite number of items for the catalog. "Do I Love You, Do I?" (*DuBarry Was a Lady*, 1939), is a catalog of rhetorical questions—doesn't one and one make two? The question about love becomes just one more rhetorical question— perhaps an homage to Porter's favorite songwriter, Irving Berlin, who also wrote a love song of rhetorical questions—"How Deep Is the Ocean?" As Berlin once quipped to Porter, "Anything I can do, you can do better." "At Long Last Love" (*You Never Know*, 1938) is a catalog comparing genuine, valuable cultural objects with their cheap imitations. The singer wonders if his new emotion is real—marble, a new Rolls, Granada—or fake—clay, a used Chevrolet, Asbury Park. Porter drops one of his rare self-references into this catalog—"Will it be Bach that I hear, or just a Cole Porter song?"

"You're the Top" from *Anything Goes* (1934) is a catalog of the culture's most valued objects, artifacts, and institutions—from Shakespeare sonnets to Bendel bonnets, Waldorf salads to Berlin ballads. Porter's unpublished parody of the song trashes the catalog of cultural value but gives more of himself away: "You're the breasts of Venus, you're King Kong's penis, you're self-abuse"; "I'm a eunuch who has just gone through an op."[3] So he *must* be the bottom because he can't be the top. "Anything Goes," the title song, is a catalog of currently fashionable social practices compared to those of our Puritan past—a glimpse of stocking is no longer shocking; authors, who once knew better words, use four-letter words; the smart set attends nudist parties in studios; and (in a rarely heard racist lyric for the London production) ladies fair seek affection "from coons of dark complexion."

One of Porter's best catalogs is his first public hit, "Let's Do It," from his first Broadway hit, *Paris* (1928). Although the song pretends its subject is love—officially titled "Let's Do It, Let's Fall in Love"—its matter is biological not romantic; the clause after the comma merely eased it onto the radio. Porter capitalizes on the linguistic fact that every euphemism for the sex act in English says it without saying it, joining an imprecise multipurpose verb to a nongender pronoun without an antecedent: do it, make it, have it, get it; sometimes with a preposition, get it on (the current American favorite), have it off (its British equivalent). He also capitalizes on the cultural fact that "It," derived from the novels of Elinor Glyn, was a common euphemism for sex in the 1920s, most memorably pinned on Clara Bow, the "It" Girl.

Both the title and the lyric of "Let's Do It" are purely suggestive, saying nothing and everything. The song goes about cataloging all the animals that "do it"—birds and bees (the most elementary metaphors of sex education), romantic sponges, oysters in Oyster Bay, lazy jellyfish, bears in pits, Pekingeses in the Ritz. Porter enlivens the catalog with references to surprising organisms and surprising plays on English sounds and meanings. The song's fixed and familiar structure provides the matrix for every ensuing surprise: "So does every katydid do it" (three declensions of the same verb in six words of a single line); "Moths in your rug do it: what's the use of moth balls?" (though mothballs kill moths, from moth balls come more moths); "giraffes on the sly do it" (ever see a giraffe "on the sly?"); "goldfish in the privacy of bowls do it" (some privacy). Whatever pretense the song makes about "love," its references are entirely reproductive: Siamese twins, shad roe, "sweet guinea pigs do it—buy a couple and wait." While a Lorenz Hart lyric depends on concrete visual imagery—blue rooms, friendly steeples, flying plates—Porter's tool is the abstractness of alliterative sound—cold Cape Cod clams, sentimental centipedes, heavy hippopotami. Such alliteratively suggestive sounds would lead to the "fine finnan haddie" on which a lad is invited to dine in "My Heart Belongs to Daddy."

The difference between Porter and Hart is especially clear in "Looking at You" (*Wake Up and Dream*, 1929). While the title suggests a Hart image—love as a visual, physical blast—Porter's lover does not lose his mental faculties as a result of this sight. Instead, he is inspired to depict the beloved in a series of classical literary conceits. He experiences the "essence and quintessence of joy"; he hears poets tellin' of Helen of Troy. In "You've Got That Thing" (*Fifty Million Frenchmen*, 1929), the beloved has the same sexy "thing" as Eve, Delilah, and Helen. Porter inverts Christian myth in "Experiment" (*Nymph Errant*, 1933), which congratulates Eve for her daring, striving for the apple at the top of the tree, urging us all to pursue that same course of upward mobility. No Fall this! Even Porter's deity comes from the classical world. He refers plurally to the "high gods above":

beginning the verse of "Ours" (*Red, Hot, and Blue!*, 1936); concluding the refrain of "I Loved Him but He Didn't Love Me" (*Wake Up and Dream*); initiating the B section of "Every Time We Say Goodbye" (*The Seven Lively Arts*).

Not surprisingly, many see the literate Porter as more lyricist than composer.[4] He usually began by finding his title for a song, then deducing the lyric from it. "I Get a Kick out of You" is an obvious example. So is "Just One of those Things" (*Jubilee*, 1935), the best song ever written about a one-night stand—great fun but just one of those things. Then Porter designs a melody to support the song's title and the intellectual structure of the lyrics. Although the technique descends directly from Porter's private songs to amuse his friends—the witty lyrics dominating their supporting tunes—less obvious is the brilliant effectiveness of those tunes at punching up both the twists and the meanings of the words.

The tom-tom beat in the release of "You Do Something to Me" not only emphasizes the wonderful rhymes—do do, voodoo, you do—but makes them a mystic incantation. The musical line descends steadily on the sequence of accented beats, suggesting the steady descent into a hypnotic trance. The same punchy syncopation dominates the verse of "You're the Top," mirroring the singer's hesitation about expressing her sentiments, her tendency "to let 'em rest—unexpressed." Like Irving Berlin, Porter, writing both words and music, captures the rhythms and sounds of colloquial speech in musical phrases. Lyricists who write their own tunes are generally more sensitive to the sounds of words than those who write lyrics exclusively. The refrain of "You're the Top" is unsingable without Porter's musical accompaniment. It forces the leaping statement of the song's title to begin on the syncopated off-beat of the first measure, allowing the dominant word, "Top," to fall squarely on the downbeat of the second. The syncopated refrain of "Anything Goes" is itself a mirror of the age—its rhythms, sounds, and spirit suggest the idea that anything indeed goes. And goes. And goes. Then in its release—with the idea that the world has gone mad and the insistent repetitions of "today"—the accented beat shifts to the downbeat of every measure, supported by a musical phrase that climbs the scale in half-steps. In such a song, the musical patterns do not merely support the lyric; they are musical projections of the song's idea.

Porter's most famous song in which music, words, sounds, and idea are perfectly one is "Night and Day." The most striking musical feature of the song is the single repeating G, which dominates it.[5] The G begins the verse with thirty-five consecutive soundings and ends it with eleven; in what may be a deliberate symmetry, Porter also uses the G thirty-five times in the refrain, usually in three-note combinations (for example, the title words, "night and day," often accompany a repeating G). When Porter's melody deserts the G, it adopts his familiar half-step chromatic pattern: ascending in half-step phrases in the verse, descending in half-note steps in the refrain. The song is built on insistent three-beat clusters—equally accented DUM-DUM-DUM. In the verse, there is the BEAT-BEAT-BEAT of the tom-tom, the TICK-TICK-TOCK of a clock, the DRIP-DRIP-DRIP of the raindrops, ending with the transfer of the outside noises to the personal expression of the singer, YOU-YOU-YOU. The triple monosyllables continue in the refrain with the title words and their inversion, DAY-AND-NIGHT. Porter cleverly links the verse to the refrain by making the final three G's of the verse (YOU YOU YOU) identical to the opening three G's of the refrain (NIGHT AND DAY). The refrain is a long one, forty-eight bars, structured A-B-A'-B-C(A")-B', in which the odd release is really a variation on the repeating A motif, and the descending B motif also keeps returning, like the title words and their inversion.

Conceptually, "Night and Day" describes a man possessed by the thought, the memory, the idea, of his beloved. The idea moves from a throbbing sound in the physical universe to an internal pulsing in his brain, under his skin, as much a part of him as the rhythm of his blood driven by his heartbeat. The internal pulse is an insistent three-beat musical pounding of a G, and it refuses to go away—night and day, day and night. The insistent repetitions—of the G, the song's lyric patterns, the three monosyllabic beats, and the descending B section—are all metaphors for the beloved stuck inside the singer's head. The emotion of love has not been translated into a Larry Hart disease based on sight but into a Cole Porter idea based on sound.

This translation of emotion into sound accounts for one of Porter's most familiar and popular kinds of songs, those persistent beguines. "Begin the Beguine" (*Jubilee*) not only introduced our culture to a sensuous new musical sound but to a new word—which Porter first heard as the pidgin-English pronunciation of the word "begin" by a Martinique band leader in Paris. What is nonsense as "begin the begin" becomes romance as "Begin the Beguine." At 108 bars, the song is "the longest popular song ever written."[6] Its length conveys the singer's absorption in and exhaustion from the passionate sounds he is experiencing. For Porter, the Latin surge of the song is another beat-beat-beat of a tom-tom; the pulsing of rhythmic sounds in the air again gets under the skin to enter the bloodstream as a pulse of emotion within. Porter evokes the sensation of the moment not by describing it in images but mirroring it in sounds. After the beguine had begun, Porter began it again and again: "In the Still of the Night" (*Rosalie*, 1937), "I Concentrate on You" (*Broadway Melody of 1940*), "So Near and Yet So Far" (*You'll Never Get Rich*, 1941), "I Love You" (*Mexican Hayride*, 1944), "So in Love" and "Were Thine that Special Face" (both *Kiss Me, Kate*, 1948), "I am in Love" (*Can-Can*, 1953), the title song of *Silk Stockings* (1955), and "Mind If I Make Love to You" (*High Society*, 1956). Two of these beguines were written for Astaire (and "Begin the Beguine" was interpolated in his 1940 *Broadway Melody*), implying their common descent from "Night and Day," that original Porter statement for Astaire of musical sound as rhythmic emotion.

Porter's narrative songs represent an opposite approach to musical composition. Porter is one of the few American composers whose songs can be divided, like poems, as lyric and narrative. Similar to "After the Ball" and other sentimental story songs of the 1890s, wailing of lost virtue or betrayed love, Porter's narrative songs chronicle the lives of very specific characters. Unlike his sentimental predecessors are the kinds of virtues Porter characters lose and their attitudes toward losing them. "Katie Went to Haiti" (*Panama Hattie*, 1940) describes the adventures of an American girl who travels to Haiti, meets one "natie" after another, sticks around to write a travel guide, and dies (three choruses later) at the age of eighty. Her Haitian success derives primarily from her rapport with these local "naties" —whoever they might be. Porter again plays with the suggestive vagueness of verbs like "have" and "knew": Katie knew Haiti and practically all Haiti knew Katie; Katie had her Haiti and practically all Haiti had Katie. Another story song is "But in the Morning, No" (*DuBarry Was a Lady*), a duet in which the singers admit a fondness for all sorts of activities—riding, shooting, boxing, climbing, the breast stroke, double entry (bookkeeping, of course), selling a seat (on the stock market), filling an inside straight, liking third parties (political, that is)—but not in the morning. A delight for Ethel Merman and Bert Lahr, the song falls midway between a Porter narrative song (the singers impersonate delicate aristocrats) and catalog song (ten refrains of comic metaphors about sex that aren't about sex).

Porter's most intriguing narrative song based on a specific character is "Miss Otis Regrets" (1934). The song is a dramatic monologue—like Browning's "My Last Duchess" or "Andrea del Sarto"—not written for a show but on a bet by Porter's friend, Monty Woolley, that no song could ever be written with such a title.[7] Porter won the bet with a dramatic situation: the song is delivered by the butler of the title's Miss Otis— dignified, polite, terribly correct, unmoved by passion. He explains the recent difficulties of his employer as an apology to someone who has come to the Otis manse expecting lunch. The regrettable events of the evening before make it impossible for Miss Otis to keep the appointment. Those events, however, are the stuff of romantic melodrama—the old "Frankie and Johnny" story about a woman whose man done her wrong. Miss Otis drew a gun from under her velvet gown, shot her false lover down, and has been strung up by the lynch mob that dragged her from the jail. With her last gasp she recollects that she will be unable to keep her luncheon date. The contrast between the passionate action of Miss Otis and the dry description of her butler creates the detached irony of a Browning poem as an American song.[8]

Porter invested his creative conception in songs that told stories, not shows that told stories. Like Irving Berlin, he was a songwriter, not a musical dramatist. He didn't much care about the scripts and the shows as a whole. A "score" meant two or three catalog songs, two love ballads, a beguine or two, two rhythm songs, two specialty numbers for the stars, and the usual obligatory numbers for chorus and featured players to fill up an evening. His early shows pulled songs out of the trunk to squeeze them anywhere they might fit. In a final vote for the individual song over the integrity of scores, his will granted explicit permission to take any Porter song from any Porter show and use it in any other. Revivals of Porter shows inevitably do. For Porter, the numbers were the reason for the show—the "fun," the entertaining variety and diversity that gave birth to the American musical show in the first place.

He remained just as committed to the virtuoso performer, the other source of musical "fun." Like Berlin, Porter loved performers and loved to write for them. Porter began writing songs at the age of ten for a performing persona—himself—the sly but dishy little boy at the piano. His first Broadway successes passed out trunk songs to Irene Bordoni, Jessie Matthews, Jack Buchanan, and the like. Beginning with Fred Astaire and *The Gay Divorce* in 1932, Porter wrote songs carefully tailored to the greatest musical performers. One reason "Night and Day" uses a single note eighty-one times is that G was a particularly good note for Astaire. One reason the song uses its insistent rhythms and half-tone modulations is that Astaire was a master of rhythmic punctuation and melodic modulation. Two other Porter songs for *The Gay Divorce*—the ballad, "After You, Who?," and the rhythm song, "I've Got You on My Mind"—were just as carefully tailored to Astaire's rhythmic and vocal precision.[9]

Porter wrote even more consciously for Ethel Merman's vocal instrument and stage persona. Knowing that Merman made her biggest belting sounds on A, B-flat, and C, Porter (like Gershwin before him and Berlin after him) returned repeatedly to these notes as she belted to a climax.[10] Knowing that Merman combined two apparently opposite personality traits—the classy and the brassy—Porter wrote songs that combined the chic and the tough, the lady and the dame. She could pretend to be polite, but she cut through the fake and the phony with a verbal knife when she said what she saw. At some point in every Porter show she'd bark something like, "What the hell is this?" Porter wrote songs just as appreciatively for the throaty malapropisms of Jimmy Durante, the wry casualness of Bob Hope, the prissy nasality of Bert Lahr, the sexual savvy of Sophie Tucker, the speeding gibberish of Danny Kaye, and the gargling lechery of Bobby Clark. Porter would never have won Woolley's bet against "Miss Otis Regrets" without an image of the dry, droll Woolley himself as the song's butler. Woolley's reading of the song in *Night and Day* remains its definitive version.

Two Porter shows are more frequently revived than the others because they hold together better as shows than the others. *Anything Goes* is the best

Ethel Merman's "Blow Gabriel, Blow" in *Anything Goes*

1920s musical of the 1930s. Set on a transatlantic liner, playground of the veddy veddy rich, its original book by Guy Bolton and P. G. Wodehouse (revised by Howard Lindsay and Russell Crouse),[11] the show leaps back two decades to the snappy and joyous Princess Theater. With Ethel Merman in her first and fullest wisecracking role as Reno Sweeney, and with the popular Broadway duo of William Gaxton and Victor Moore to support her with more wisecracks, Porter could write songs for a trio of virtuoso performers. He obliged by writing more memorable songs than for any previous show, carried by the voice and verve of Merman: the cultural critique of the title song; the catalog song to end all catalog songs, "You're the Top"; the mock revivalism of "Blow Gabriel, Blow"; the quintessential Porter of "I Get a Kick out of You"; and the lovely ballad sliding down the half-steps, "All Through the Night." Although the show merely treaded water it kicked up enough splash to run twice as long as any previous Porter show. The last best old-style musical of the kind that began at the Princess, *Anything Goes* is light, fast, flip, hip, with good jokes, comic specialty acts, shrewd cultural observations, and terrific songs, songs, songs.

Like Porter's songs, it swam against the dominant cultural tides. These were the Depression years, after all, and 1934 was among the worst of them. *Anything Goes* hadn't a care in the world; it didn't even take place in the world but in the middle of the Atlantic. Everyone onboard had plenty of dough, and even gangsters were invited to the party. Victor Moore, a mere Public Enemy Number 13, wanted desperately to rise on the FBI's most wanted "charts." If Porter could say "No!" to the theory of the decade's evolving musical theater, he could say "No!" to its serious social concerns as well. And he was not alone. Obviously, not everyone in America stood on a streetcorner with pencils and a tin cup or worried about those who did all through the night and day. Porter was still writing for an elite smart set, wise and witty enough to appreciate his songs. Unlike his private circle of friends a decade earlier, you could invite yourself to this party—just by feeling you belonged there. You didn't need much money. You didn't need to live in New York (just as most subscribers to the *New Yorker* didn't live in New York). You just had to believe that Porter songs spoke to and for you. Many Americans did.

As the nation moved toward war, Porter continued to say "No!" despite the 1937 riding accident that shattered his legs, his health, and, eventually, his spirit. His legs were so badly smashed that he spent the rest of his life enduring great pain and dozens of operations to keep them. His determination, depicted as an act of great personal courage by the same journalists who had earlier depicted his wasteful hedonism, was also a revealing act of great personal vanity. A man without legs didn't cut a very gallant figure, and for the rest of his life they served Porter solely as decoration. He had to be carried into rooms and theaters, then arranged in a casually seated pose, a bit of stage management that caused him terrible embarrassment. He began conversing less and less to fewer and fewer. At his great dinner parties, he would remain silent, forcing others to do the talking, the amusing, while he let his own opinions rest, unexpressed. His sole refuge, his only form of conversation, increasingly became his songs themselves.

His second landmark show came to terms with the musical as a theatrical concept. After a decade of vehicles for Merman and others, Porter began writing shows with clever concepts. The first two didn't quite work. *The Seven Lively Arts*, a 1944 revue, straddled high and low entertainments: songs by Porter, ballets by Stravinsky, jazz by Benny Goodman, comedy by Beatrice Lillie and Bert Lahr. *Around the World* (1946) was a spectacular Mike Todd production (which would become Todd's spectacular film production, *Around the World in 80 Days*, a decade later), written by, directed by, and starring Orson Welles (of all people for a musical). Then Sam and Bella Spewack asked Porter to write songs for a musical based on Shakespeare's *The Taming of the Shrew*. After many doubts Porter agreed. *Kiss Me, Kate* was the second American musical based on Shakespeare, still the best, the longest-running hit Porter ever had. For *Kate* Porter couldn't simply pull witty songs out of the air or out of his trunk; he had to write specifically for *The Taming of the Shrew* and the characters performing it. He adopted the formal strategy of *Show Boat*, *Pal Joey*, and most backstage musicals: onstage performance numbers of the Shakespeare play and off-stage expressions of the performers' feelings.

For the play-within-the-show, Porter songs arose directly from Shakespeare speeches. "I Am Ashamed That Women Are So Simple" is a musical transcription of Katherine's final speech of capitulation, Shakespeare's words set to Porter music, the only Porter melody set to another's lyric. Both "I've Come To Wive It Wealthily in Padua" and "Where Is the Life That Late I Led?" derive from lines in the play, which Porter translates into his favorite form: the catalog. First, Petruchio catalogs the endless faults he is willing to tolerate in a bride, so long as she has money. After he's got her, he catalogs a long list of female sexual specialists in assorted Italian towns, which his marriage prohibits him from visiting.

Offstage, Petruchio and Katherine are Fred Graham and Lilli Vanessi, an estranged married couple of old-time troupers, squabbling as vigorously as the characters they play onstage. For these descendants of the leading man and leading lady of operetta Porter pulled a parody of an old-fashioned operetta waltz from his trunk, "Wunderbar." The schmaltz waltz transports both singers and audience to earlier, youthful days in the theater, when these sorts of songs were sung and heard in every Viennesey operetta. To bring us into the present, Porter writes Fred and Lilli an inevitable beguine, "So In Love," the motif of their former (now rekindled) passion.

The onstage Bianca and Lucentio are offstage Bill Calhoun, with a passion for dice and cards, and Lois Lane, with a passion, like Bianca, for men in general. They descend from the Shakespearean multiplot through the familiar comic and soubrette of their immediate operetta forbears. Porter writes Lois a comic song exactly the obverse of "My Heart Belongs to Daddy." In "Daddy," the singer invites the attention of young, sexy laddies on the sly, always returning to the dependable daddy who treats her so well. In "Always True to You in My Fashion," the singer invites the attentions of wealthy daddies on the sly, always returning to her young, sexy Bill. Porter verbally plays around with Lois's playing around, compiling a lengthy catalog of her various materialistic diversions:

> There's an oil man known as Tex,
> Who is keen to give me checks.
> And his checks, I fear,
> Mean that sex is here
> To stay!
> But I'm always true to you, darlin', in my fashion,
> Yes, I'm always true to you, darlin', in my way.

or

> Mr. Harris, plutocrat,
> Wants to give my cheek a pat.
> If a Harris pat
> Means a Paris hat
> *Bébé!*
> *Mais, Je suis toujours fidèle,* darlin', in my fashion.
> *Oui, Je suis toujours fidèle,* darlin', in my way.

Exactly what way or fashion might that be? The song was among Porter's final lengthy catalogs of sexual dalliance.[12]

Kiss Me, Kate also served two specialty numbers to the featured players. "Another Op'nin', Another Show," is, like Berlin's "No Business Like Show Business," an energetic hymn to the business of putting on shows—a spirited opening number about all opening numbers and all openings of shows (perhaps written as an homage to and in imitation of Berlin). "Brush Up Your Shakespeare" is a Porter catalog of Shakespeare titles, enumerated by two gangsters (stowaways from *Anything Goes*?) who come to collect Bill's gambling debts. The idea for this song, another parodic waltz, is itself Shakespearean—a low-comic dialect number of verbal puns for the modern American equivalents of Shakespeare's cockney clowns. Porter catalogs the ways that a Shakespeare title might prove useful in seducing one's lady fair:

> If she says that her clothes you are mussing,
> What are clothes? *Much Ado about Nussing!*

> or

> If she says your behavior is heinous,
> Kick her right in the *Coriolanus.*

> or

> When your baby is pleading for pleasure,
> Let her sample your *Measure for Measure.*

Like his gangsters, Porter found a clever use for his formal study of Shakespeare and other classical subjects.

Porter's first integrated, new-style book show, like Berlin's *Annie Get Your Gun*, was his most brilliant success, stimulated both by the novelty and the challenge of the task. He followed this first tightly woven show with others that never equaled it in musical, lyrical, or theatrical invention. He returned to Paris, the capital of his hedonistic youth and the setting of his first Broadway success, for two final shows: a nostalgic Paris of the 1890s (*Can-Can*); a politicized Paris of the present (*Silk Stockings*), based on Ernst

Cole Porter poses with his final Broadway score

Lubitsch's 1939 film *Ninotchka*. Both produced Porter hits: "I Love Paris,"
"It's All Right with Me," "All of You." *Silk Stockings* also offered satiric
catalogs of both capitalist decadence, the Hollywood of "Stereophonic
Sound," and Communist decadence, the Russia of "Siberia." After *Silk
Stockings*, Porter summoned his remaining energy for two film scores—*High
Society* (1956) and *Les Girls* (1957)—and a television score—*Aladdin* (1958).
For *High Society*, Porter recycled the great comic catalog song from *DuBarry
Was a Lady*—"Well, Did You Evah?"—a flippant chronicle of social catastro-
phes that serve as boringly polite conversation at chic cocktail parties.

> Have you heard about poor Blanche?
> Got run down by an avalanche.
> Well, did you evah! What a swell party this is.

High Society also yielded the very last Porter hit, "True Love," a
sincerely touching waltz for Bing Crosby, without a trace of Porter mis-
chief. It deliberately evoked the old-fashioned simplicity of George M.
Cohan's sweetly sentimental waltzes. Written in memory of Linda, who
died in 1952, "True Love" was a retrospective return to the time when Cole
and Linda were young—and when Cohan was America's most characteristic
songwriter. Not coincidentally, Porter was Cohan's favorite songwriter
among the generation that succeeded him: like Cohan, it took only one

Porter to write a song. Though it may not be a very memorable Porter song, "True Love" is full of Porter's own memories.

With the continuous pain in his legs and the death of Linda, Porter sank into a morose depression that made him virtually a recluse until his death in 1964. He stopped speaking to everyone; he stopped appearing in public; he even stopped writing songs. The man who had been surrounded by the friends he amused was no longer surrounded, no longer amusing, and no longer amused. Those high gods above no longer smiled down upon him. While they did, he smiled back with a collection of songs that resembled one of his own musical catalogs: an infinite variety of anticipated surprise, always the same, always different.

As Corny as Kansas in August, As Restless as a Willow in a Windstorm

RICHARD RODGERS AND OSCAR HAMMERSTEIN II

If, in Jerome Kern's words, Irving Berlin *is* American popular music, then Oscar Hammerstein II *is* the American musical theater—from his collaboration on *Rose-Marie* in 1924 to his spiritual influence on *Sunday in the Park with George* in 1984. He envisioned a totally unified American music drama in which songs define the characters and drive the narrative, translating Wagner's *Gesamtkunstwerk* into American theater tastes and cultural terms. His stage works would be based not on Germanic myths but on homespun American characters, values, and ideals—combining Wagner's mythic seriousness with good old American fun. He also combined two generations of Hammersteins before him—his grandfather Oscar's productions of grand opera, his uncle Arthur's productions of operettas, and his father Willie's vaudeville shows. After his forty years in the theater, Hammerstein had not only demonstrated a theory but had forced everyone to adopt it. His vision of musical theater triumphed for an obvious reason: it represented the noblest imaginable idea for a show that began in 1866 with some songs, some jokes, and a lot of leg.

Hammerstein was also the premier poet of American musical theater. His lyrics strive for a heightened poetic imagery, based on the ordinary, everyday sensibilities of the characters who produce it. From the sun swimmin' on the rim of a hill in "The Surrey with the Fringe on Top" (*Oklahoma!*, 1943) to the canary yellow sky of "A Cockeyed Optimist" (*South Pacific*, 1949), from the buds bustin' outa bushes of "June Is Bustin' Out All Over" (*Carousel*, 1945) to the snowflakes that stay on the lips and eyelashes of "My Favorite Things" (*The Sound of Music*, 1959), Hammerstein transformed the sights and feelings of everyday American life into a heightened but homespun poetry.

He was also the first modernist of the American musical theater, writing

201

In rehearsal for *South Pacific*: director Joshua Logan, an attentive Richard Rodgers, a dour Oscar Hammerstein

with a conscious command of both the conventions and the history of the art he was crafting. Although it is fashionable to draw a distinction between Hammerstein's "realist" musicals and Stephen Sondheim's "concept" musicals, Hammerstein was the first American to devise a concept for a musical and to write every show within it. His concepts lead directly to Sondheim concepts: figuratively, because Sondheim merely shifts Hammerstein's conceptual emphasis; literally, because Sondheim was not only a Hammerstein admirer but his pupil and *protégé*.

Hammerstein dominates every history of American musical theater published over the last three decades. Ethan Mordden's series of deductions is exemplary: "The musical play is the most significant of all developments in the American musical. *Show Boat* was the first musical play. Hammerstein designed *Show Boat*. That makes him the most significant figure in the musical's history."[1] That significance, however, ignores two corollary losses: the great song hits from Broadway shows (fewer and fewer with every passing season since *Oklahoma!*) and the great top bananas and belting mamas to put them over. Hammerstein's music drama redefined the singer of a song—a specific character living in a specific place at a specific moment in history. While the voice, the I, of a Gershwin, Hart, or Porter lyric is an undefined surrogate for the lyricist himself, the voice, the I, of a Hammerstein lyric is an Oklahoma rancher, or a nurse from Little Rock, or a Victorian British schoolmarm.

Hammerstein's move toward Wagnerian theory demanded a response from Rodgers's music. Songs no longer captured casual moments but great peaks of emotional intensity. An inevitable stage direction in a Hammerstein script describes the music's swelling to "great ecstatic heights," further ecstasized by Robert Russell Bennett's monumental orchestrations. Songs became operatic arias for booming voices or "art songs" for delicate interpreters of *lieder*. The most famous male star of a Rodgers and Hammerstein show, Ezio Pinza, was an opera singer, and the most famous female star of Rodgers and Hammerstein shows, Mary Martin, was capable of singing *lieder*. No belter like Merman, Martin was a head singer with a sweet and willowy but very precise vocal instrument.

Rodgers and Hammerstein scripts also initiated an inescapable pattern: the very long first act, over ninety minutes, and the very brief second act, less than half as long. Their shows do not integrate music and dramatic action so much as music and *character*. Songs introduce characters—their beliefs, values, hopes, intentions—and they depict character interactions— falling in love, arguing each other out of love, feeling empty after the argument. Their songs serve the familiar dramatic functions of exposition (introducing the world of the play and its inhabitants) and complication (chronicling responses to social and emotional problems). The final section of the theatrical pattern—the resolution—is never sung in their shows because it is not singable. Characters perform an action by deed or in

Agnes DeMille's dream ballet for *Oklahoma!*, the first act finale

dialogue: Curly kills Jud in *Oklahoma!*, Billy Bigelow kills himself in *Carousel*, Lt. Cable dies on a spy mission in *South Pacific*. The first act is the long act (and the entertaining act) because all the songs that introduce and complicate characters are in it. To the second act goes the thankless task of getting the plot over with as efficiently as possible. The second act of *Oklahoma!* slots exactly three new songs and three reprises; the second act of *South Pacific* four new songs and two reprises.

Rodgers and Hammerstein shows build to a dramatic and emotional climax at the end of the first act: the great dream ballet of *Oklahoma!*, "Laurey Makes Up her Mind"; Billy's soliloquy in *Carousel*, which leads him to join Jigger's plot to rob Bascombe; Nellie's shattering discovery in *South Pacific* of Emile's previous marriage and interracial children. Although the pattern comes from Rodgers and Hammerstein, it has been adopted by everyone else. The first act of Lerner and Loewe's *My Fair Lady*, one hour and forty-five minutes long, concludes with Eliza's triumph at the ball; the first act of Bernstein-Sondheim-Laurents's *West Side Story*, one hour and thirty-five minutes long, concludes with the choreographed "Rumble" that kills Riff and Bernardo.

To build a first act toward a soaring climax of triumph, pain, or doubt is a good way to get an audience back after intermission; it also increases the danger of disappointing them once you do. The structure runs contrary to the oldest adage of the musical show: build toward "the big finish," the "five-to-eleven number," as it was called when shows began at 8:30. The vaudeville bill always saved its headliners until the very end (like the Busby Berkeley films with their bam-bam-bam finales of three consecutive production numbers). No second act of a Rodgers and Hammerstein show (or most others of the last four decades) is as interesting or entertaining as its first. At best, it economically resolves an interesting story and keeps two terrific musical surprises in reserve: like "Happy Talk" and "Honey Bun" of *South Pacific*.

Although the cliché is that weak musicals run into trouble in the second act, all "integrated" musicals do. The difference between utter failure and resounding success is disguising the difficulty of tying up a complicated plot with very little musical twine. Rodgers and Hammerstein disguise their plot-heavy second acts with a sprinkling of new numbers and reprises plus a terrific production number at or near its very beginning ("The Farmer and the Cowman" for *Oklahoma!*, "A Real Nice Clambake" for *Carousel*, "The Small House of Uncle Thomas" for *The King and I*). Richard Rodgers, aware of the problem, began his work on a show by writing the opening number of the second act.

The Rodgers and Hammerstein shows demonstrate their music-drama idea most convincingly in individual scenes of the first act. The most important and carefully constructed of these scenes is the initial one between the two lovers—Curly and Laurey in *Oklahoma!*, Billy and Julie in *Carousel*, Emile and Nellie in *South Pacific*. In both spirit and method, these scenes descend literally from the first meeting of Magnolia and Gaylord Ravenal in *Show Boat*. Songs are not merely slotted into these scenes but whole scenes are built from interwoven songs, talk, and musical motifs. The songs refuse to stay put in specific spots and slots but seep repeatedly into and through the dialogue. This achievement can be traced to a musical development in the work of Rodgers and a verbal development in the work of Hammerstein.

With Lorenz Hart, Rodgers wrote songs, thirty-two-bar refrains preceded by lovely or intriguing verses. Only an occasional Rodgers and Hart song flaunted a structural innovation—like the haunting "A Ship without a Sail" (*Heads Up!*, 1929), structured A (twelve bars)-B (eight bars)-A' (twelve), or the seventy-six bar "Johnny One Note" (*Babes in Arms*), whose musical extensions permit extended performances of Johnny's big note. With Hammerstein, however, the thirty-two-bar form became a very faint Rodgers skeleton. The essential distinction between verse and refrain disappears: "Out of My Dreams," "What's the Use of Wond'rin'?" and "A Cockeyed Optimist" dispense with the verse altogether. Rodgers regularly extends a refrain's length beyond the basic thirty-two measures with codas, musical interludes between choruses, and other transitional or extensional musical passages. Take, for example, the familiar "There Is Nothin' Like a Dame" (*South Pacific*). Although the song feels like a multichorus catalog of female attractions by a group of comically horny sailors, Rodgers has actually written a single song of precisely 128 measures: A (sixteen bars)-A (sixteen)-B (a four-bar recitative with a torrent of ad-libbed words)-C (the title theme, sixteen bars)-A-B-C-D (a forty-bar coda, listing the "dame's" attractions).

There is no way to alter this structure, to add to it or subtract from it, as with a Cole Porter catalog. The male chorus must sing the entire number in precisely this form, no more and no less.

Rodgers is no longer writing verses and refrains but complex musical structures—arias and recitatives. "Some Enchanted Evening" (*South Pacific*), the single biggest popular hit to come out of any Rodgers and Hammerstein show, is hardly a thirty-two-bar song. It is a precise sixty-bar structure of A (sixteen bars)-A (sixteen)-B (a very odd release of six bars)-A (sixteen)-B' (in which the release becomes a six-bar coda). The song cannot be sung any other way. The "Dual Soliloquy" that precedes it is another odd structure—forty-eight bars, in which every eight-bar section is a variation on an identical musical motif (the "song" is A-A'-A"-A'"-A""-A"""). This musical passage depicts two characters, Nellie and Emile, each submerged in his or her own thoughts (a duet that is really two solos), considering the chances of being accepted by the other.

This "Dual Soliloquy" occupies a central place in the all-important first scene for these two characters. It follows, almost immediately, Nellie's view of her own cheery self—"A Cockeyed Optimist," a forty-bar song without a verse but with a coda. It precedes, almost immediately, Emile's view that life's opportunities must be seized (the sixty-bar "Some Enchanted Evening"). The "Dual Soliloquy" is a forty-eight-bar dramatic transition in which two separate people move toward becoming a unified pair of lovers. The entire drama of their swelling emotions evolves over the 148 measures of the three "songs," each representing a particular point in their progressive emotional journey, each with a radically different musical structure. This is not a love scene with three numbers; it is a scene that moves from getting acquainted to falling in love, whose numbers provide the dramatic transportation.

Rising ecstasy with a sip of cognac: Ezio Pinza and Mary Martin in the "Dual Soliloquy" of *South Pacific*

THEATRE COLLECTION, MUSEUM OF THE CITY OF NEW YORK

Rodgers could not envision this musical dramatization without the sensibilities of Oscar Hammerstein—particularly his ability to translate a character's dialect from the lines of an original play or novel (whether by Lynn Riggs or James Michener) into the lyrics of songs. The problem for Hammerstein, as for every American theater composer, remained how to make characters sing the way they talk. In *Oklahoma!* and *Carousel* rural patterns of American speech—a-worryin' and a-hollerin' and a-scurryin' and a-skeered—skedaddle directly into the songs. Ado Annie "cain't" say no, and her songs burst (or bust) with dialect figures of speech—Nen, Foot! sorta, orta, heared, fergit, turrible, c'n, jist, purty. The New England fishermen of *Carousel*, like the Oklahoma ranchers, sing in their own dialect: "the vittles we et" at the "Real Nice Clambake" were "fitten fer an angels' choir." Hammerstein joins these dialects with images his characters experience in their daily lives: the "bright golden haze on the meadow" and the corn as high as "a elephant's eye" of "Oh, What a Beautiful Mornin'."

Rodgers accompanies these speech patterns with musical patterns that arise from the same personal experience as the dialects. "Oh, What a Beautiful Mornin'" is an old-fashioned waltz with a sixteen-bar verse, structured A-B, and a sixteen-bar refrain, structured A'-A'', whose melody is a variation on the opening motif of the verse. The verse and refrain together form an indivisible thirty-two-bar whole, exactly like Stephen Foster's "Camptown Races" and "Old Black Joe." The implication is that Curly makes up this little waltz extemporaneously, merely improvising his honest, simple feelings in a song inspired by the sights, sounds, and smells of the mornin'. He pours his spontaneous experience into a musical form familiar from the songs of the day, hence credible for him to improvise. Like the Gershwins in *Porgy and Bess*, Rodgers and Hammerstein mirrored the feelings of "simpler folk" with simpler and earlier American song forms.

The most stunning effect of this collaboration is their weaving musical sounds and word sounds into perfect blends of feeling and idea. "The Surrey with the Fringe on Top" was their first (and most dazzling) piece of musical onomatopeia. The song's rhythm mirrors the steady clip-clop-clip-clop of a trotting horse, characterized by five repetitions of a D with five identical quarter notes to begin every line of the refrain. A quarter note becomes the gait of a quarter horse. Hammerstein weds the repeating D's to monosyllables: "chicks and ducks and geese," "watch that fringe and see," "when I drive them high." To conclude the phrase, Rodgers repeats the D once again, this time as a fleeting eighth note, then drops down a note to C, climbs back to the D and jumps up to a G. To these notes, Hammerstein pins multisyllable verbs to emphasize the musical movement—"better scurry," "how it flutters," "steppin' strutters." Rodgers's music "scurries" and "flutters" when Hammerstein's lyric describes scurrying and fluttering.

The same musical-verbal onomatopeia created their Academy Award-winning song, "It Might as Well Be Spring" (*State Fair*, 1945). The singer's listlessness is mirrored by repetitive musical phrases accompanying soft consonants and vowels: "as restless as a willow in a windstorm," dominated by the soft "w"; "as busy as a spider spinning daydreams," dominated by the lazy "s." In the next musical phrase, Rodgers deserts his predictable steps to jump up and down the scale in surprising leaps. Hammerstein accompanies the musical jumps with "jumpy" words in both their sounds and meanings: "as jumpy as a puppet on a string," dominated by the alliterative "p's"; "as giddy as a baby on a swing," dominated by the "y" and the consonants "g," "d," and "b." The meanings and sounds of Hammerstein's words are inseparable from the sounds and feelings of Rodgers's music.[2]

No theater craftsmen constructed these musical-verbal mirrors of dramatic emotion as powerfully or as frequently as Rodgers and Hammerstein. "Many a New Day" (Oklahoma!) is a defiant minuet in which Laurey protests (too much) that she cares not a whit about losing Curly. The rhythmically emphatic beat captures her head's tossing with defiance, accented by every repetitive "many," falling precisely on the downbeat of a measure, and the many "d's" of Hammerstein's lyric which alliterate defiantly—day, dawn, die, do. Laurey is defying no one but herself, her own feelings. "A Wonderful Guy" (South Pacific) is an exuberantly defiant waltz—this time Nellie defies the friends poking fun at her feelings for Emile—with emphatic alliterative sounds on the crashing downbeats: both in the verse ("proud protestations," "person in pants") and refrain ("corny as Kansas"). Rodgers had begun to cherish the waltz, not for its flowing liquidity but for its thumping insistency.

"I'm Gonna Wash that Man Right Outa My Hair" (South Pacific) is a white pastiche of the blues, the only song of its kind Rodgers and Hammerstein ever wrote. Like the blues, its lyric and notes repeat identically three times before moving to a musical and verbal variation on the fourth statement. Like Curly in "Beautiful Mornin'," Nellie is making up a simple song as she goes about her everyday business—washing her hair— the equivalent of singing in the shower. She falls back on a kind of song she's heard often before. What makes her comic lament a white blues is that it lacks any surprising syncopation or mournfully flatted blue notes. A bouncy tune in strict "cut" time, with no unexpected departures from either rhythmic or harmonic regularity, this blues isn't blue. It reflects the way a cockeyed white optimist from Little Rock would sing the blues: revealing her own pervasive racial ignorance by unconsciously turning black blues into white bread.

Hammerstein has cleverly used the canary yellow of Nellie's naiveté to provide a moral commentary about the value and mission of America. As he had done two decades before with Kern and Show Boat, Hammerstein's books with Rodgers mixed thematic invention with operetta convention, contemporary commentary with Operettaland settings. His basic tool remained the double plot of operetta: the romantic love story balanced and paralleled by the comic love story in *Oklahoma!* and *Carousel*, the romantic love story balanced and paralleled by a tragic love story in *South Pacific* and *The King and I*. The multistrand plots carry Hammerstein's moral and political commentary.

In *Oklahoma!* both love stories are triangles in which a "foreigner" invades the romantic territory of true-blooded Americans. Jud Fry stands between Laurey and Curly, just as the comic peddler, Ali Hakim, stands between Will Parker and Ado Annie. Ali, despite his accent, can be assimilated into American society; he belongs in the new state of Oklahoma. Although he is a traveling salesman, that traditional figure of rootless wandering and rampant womanizing, Ali can be very practical when he sees the moonlight shining on the barrel of a father's shotgun. Ali steps out of Will's and Annie's way to marry Gertie and "settle down to run Papa's store" (p. 78).[3] Like Rodgers and Hammerstein's own ancestors with accents, he is one of those immigrants who belongs in America. After all, he is a salesman.

Jud Fry is morally, not geographically, foreign. Physically dirty and slovenly, he collects lewd *Police Gazette* "pitchers" for the walls of his grimy shack. His masturbatory song, "Lonely Room," compares his creepy sexual behavior to that of mice and spiders.[4] Jud's difference is a matter of mind and spirit, not of accent and custom, like Ali Hakim's. Curly frees the new commonwealth of this lurking menace by making a practical response, like Ali, to a weapon—Jud's menacing knife rather than Gertie's father's comic shotgun. Curly's is an act of justifiable resistance to unprovoked attack, consistent with both the spirit and the letter of the law. When the Fed'ral Marshal pronounces Curly's killing a justifiable act of self defense, Hammerstein invokes the very rationale for sending American men from states like Oklahoma overseas to kill the Jud Frys of the world, in 1943 called Nazis.

In later Hammerstein scripts, the obstacle is less personal than ideological, not a specific human being in a triangle but mental and spiritual barriers between the lovers themselves. Julie Jordan and Billy Bigelow of *Carousel*, like Magnolia and Ravenal of *Show Boat*, are psychological opposites— she innocent and well-bred, he a brawlingly powerful sexual animal. Their initial scene of meeting and infatuation is a virtual remake of Hammerstein's 1927 scene, complete with a song about "Make Believe," this time called "If I Loved You." Julie responds to Billy's dynamic sexual energy and he tries to bend to her domesticated demands, but the seeds of dissolution have been planted in this impossible marriage from its beginning. In his lengthy "Soliloquy," the single most consciously operatic passage in any Rodgers and Hammerstein show, Billy undertakes the robbery that leads to his own destruction because he wants to provide materially for his new daughter, the way any proper middle-class father would. His failed robbery of Bascombe, owner of the town's fisheries—its leading citizen, moral dictator, and robber baron—is both a romantic act of political revolution and an illegitimate attack against the law itself, the basis of Hammerstein's civilization. As in *Oklahoma!*, the political debate in *Carousel* is between the legitimate act of defiance and the essential rule of law.

For comic contrast, Julie's friend, Carrie Pipperidge, snares the sensible businessman Mr. Snow, who has planned his entire life even before he lives it. Snow and Carrie grab their materialistic American rainbow but not without a loss of spontaneity and human compassion, not without becoming Bascombes—prudish, moralistic, bourgeois snobs, who pass these values on to their children. Mr. Snow never escapes the literal or metaphoric stench of fish. Although their comic union contrasts with the tragic incompatibility of Julie and Billy, the luckless, incompatible lovers share a passionate intensity that the bloodless, fishy couple lacks.

The dead Billy descends from his eternal home in heaven to observe the graduation, the coming of age, of his daughter, Louise. Like Kim in *Show Boat*, the daughter combines the spirit of both parents, carrying within her that mixture of physical and moral strength into the future where "You'll Never Walk Alone." Unlike Kim, however, Louise can produce no magical resolutions on earth; mortal consequences cannot be avoided and ultimate reconciliations must await immortal reunions. If *Oklahoma!* developed the moral argument for sending American boys overseas, *Carousel* offered consolation to those wives and mothers whose boys would only return in spirit. The meaning lay not in the tragedy of the present but in the hope for a future where no one walks alone.

While *Carousel* interwove tragic main plot and comic subplot, *South Pacific* reverses the two. The wartime *Carousel* suggested that present sacrifice could produce a brighter future; the postwar *South Pacific* warned of present and future dangers if social inequality could not itself be overcome. The main plot initiates a romance between another apparently incompatible couple—the brightly and brashly optimistic American nurse, Nellie Forbush, and the much older but wiser French planter, Emile de Becque. He reads Proust and Anatole France, while she, in his comic butchery of American slang, is a "hick who lives in a stick." He has seen the world and she has seen Little Rock, Arkansas. He has run away to the South Pacific because he once killed a man to defend his rights—the same reason that Americans like Nellie had come to the wartime South Pacific. Nellie can transcend all their differences but one—his former marriage to a Polynesian woman and its result, two "adorable" children who appear Asian not Caucasian. It is she, an American from a Southern state whose laws support segregation, who must overcome her racist assumptions. As in *Oklahoma!* and *Carousel* Hammerstein is testing the idea of law. Of course, Emile *is* as white as she is, but in Nellie's eventually accepting Emile and his children, *South Pacific* looks forward to a wiser racial future. The marriage between Emile and Nellie produces a union of three generations and three continents, of Old World wisdom and New World hope.

The tragic subplot of the show affirms these values. Its look backward to musical dramatizations of interracial East-West conflict—especially *Madame Butterfly*—suggests that looking to the past will produce tragedy in the future. Lt. Joseph Cable is a Mainline Philadelphia Ivy Leaguer who responds to the sensual power of the Polynesian Liat. The crunch comes for this lieutenant, as it does for Puccini-Belasco's Pinkerton, when the act of lust demands the legal sanction of marriage. Cable knows that his value system is artificial, not natural, a result of being badly but "Carefully Taught." But unlike Nellie, he cannot transcend his "education." In this later retelling of *Madame Butterfly*, it is the man who has "sinned" and must be punished by death. It comes, appropriately enough, at the hands of the Japanese, the enemy race his own white nation has come to fight in the South Pacific. Of course, Cable could never have married Liat and taken her home to his Mainline family; it is not Cable himself who is at fault but his "home"—the narrow values of the world that produced him but which he is dying to defend. Unlike the smug and callous Pinkerton, the lieutenant of *South Pacific* is a nice guy, a smart and sensitive Joe; it is his homeland that is wrong and must be taught otherwise. He becomes Hammerstein's sacrificial lamb on the altar of racial equality.

The King and I continues the clash of cultural values. This time neither mainplot nor subplot produces a conciliatory marriage. The king and the schoolmistress he imports from England cannot marry: she is a properly monogamous widow and he is a lustfully polygamous prince. But the sexual energy of their conflicting values—and the complete foreknowledge that their relationship can produce no sexual or romantic resolution—converts their antagonistic but loving companionship into the most intriguing clash of romantic characters in the four shows. While Julie and Billy, Nellie and Emile are clashing metaphors, Anna and the king of Siam are clashing minds, brilliantly equal and witty opponents. While Hammerstein usually let very little of himself into his characters, masking his own views and values behind theirs, the crusty king of Siam is as close to Hammerstein's dour, curmudgeonly self as he ever created.

Unlike earlier jingoistic operettas of cultural antagonism (say, *The Sultan of Sulu*), Hammerstein does not give his representative of Western civilization all the moral ammunition. Although a spokesperson for "democracy"—opposing the Siamese customs of slavery, possessing wives as property, and subservient kowtowing to the king as to a god—the moralistic Anna has forgotten a few historical details. Slavery was originally a British mercantile institution; her visit to Siam in the early 1860s occurs at the very moment of the American Civil War, a historical consequence of British commerce. Nor does Hammerstein admire her sexual squeamishness, and he subjects the symbol of that prudery—the Victorian hoop skirt—to considerable derision. Like Billy Bigelow, the king is an admirably healthy sexual animal—and perhaps Hammerstein lets just a bit more of himself slip out of the closet with the king's sexual attack on Anna's blind propriety.[5] The closest they come to a union is an exuberantly climactic waltz, "Shall We Dance?" a question that returns to the "what if" of "Make Believe" and "If I Loved You." The result of their metaphoric union is, as in every Hammerstein show, a new future with a new law promised by a child. The young prince, a product of the king's tradition and Anna's education, abolishes the law of kowtowing to the king. He does not, however abolish keeping wives as property. Perhaps Hammerstein acknowledges the Marxist argument that in Western democracy monogamous marriage laws also reduce women to property.

If the main plot of *The King and I* is the most crackling of any Rodgers and Hammerstein adaptation, its unhappy subplot is sappy and formulaic. Tuptim, one of the king's many wives, a piece of property he received as a gift from Burma, longs for her true love, Lun Tha. She has been educated in Western ways—well enough to speak Anna's English and to yearn for Anna's romantic monogamy. Her attempt to elope with Lun Tha ends with their executions—like Cable of *South Pacific* and Julie Laverne of *Show Boat*, sacrificed to the misguided mores of a whole culture. Not only do the enslaved lovers "Kiss in a Shadow"; their whole love affair seems a shadowy slave to the Rodgers and Hammerstein formula.

How do Rodgers and Hammerstein inject the variety, the diversity, the "fun" that audiences expect from a musical into these serious-minded shows? With great difficulty. "No girls, no gags, no chance," Michael Todd predicted before the opening of *Oklahoma!*[6] It was easier for *Oklahoma!* than for later Rodgers and Hammerstein scripts to get the gags and the girls into the show. Ado Annie is the classic soubrette, Ali Hakim the classic comic (with a Dutch accent, no less), and Will Parker the comic juvenile. Balancing Laurey's romantic Operettaland yearning to fly "Out of My Dreams" is Annie's comic song of earthly compliance, "I Cain't Say No":

> Fer a while I ack refined and cool,
> A-settin' on the velveteen settee—
> Nen I think of thet ol' golden rule,
> And do fer him whut he would do fer me!

Balancing Curly's poetic sights of the beautiful mornin' are Will Parker's comic sights of "Kansas City":

> With ev'ry kind o' comfort ev'ry house is all complete.
> You c'n walk to privies in the rain an' never wet yer feet!

Balancing Curly and Laurey's romantic "People Will Say We're in Love" is Will and Annie's comic duet, demanding "All er Nothin'":

> If you cain't give me all, give me nuthin'—
> And nuthin's whut you'll git from me!

Agnes DeMille's dream ballet brings to dancing life the French postcards and *Police Gazette* "pitchers" of Jud Fry's girls (as well as Will Parker's comic stripper at the burleecue who went about as fer she could go in "Kansas City").

As the shows move from *Oklahoma!*, they move steadily from not only traditional comic material but even from comic opportunity. The soubrette and comic of *Carousel* are more thematic than funny, and there is no soubrette in *South Pacific*. She has been transformed from the perky gal into the character lady, Bloody Mary, alternately bawdy of speech (parroting sailor slang, like "stingy bastard") and dreamy of song ("Bali Ha'i"). Only the comic, Luther Billis, who does not sing, litters the romantic script with bawdy sailor humor. The subplot romance between Cable and Liat is even more poetically inclined than the mainplot romance between Nellie and Emile; in "Younger than Springtime" Hammerstein's imagery converts Cable's arms into a "pair of birds that burst with song."

South Pacific varies romantic and comic material by translating the differing social backgrounds of the characters into different styles of song: Nellie's upbeat bounce, Emile's romantic wisdom, Bloody Mary's poetry, and American GI humor—whether the longing for dames or Nellie's parody of that longing, "Honey Bun." The comedy of *The King and I* is exclusively confined to the witty script and Jerome Robbins's choreographic parody of *Uncle Tom's Cabin*. This brilliant production number simultaneously alludes to American slavery, Siamese slavery, the parallels between Eastern and Western social oppression, and the oddity of translating Western mores and stories into an alien style of diction and dance.

In building steadily toward a unity of dramatic tone, musical form, and moral statement, the shows of Rodgers and Hammerstein just as steadily sacrificed the variety, the surprises, the virtuoso performance "turns," the witty songs that had brought audiences to American musical shows for a century. Like *Show Boat*, *A Connecticut Yankee*, *Porgy and Bess*, and *Pal Joey*, the four biggest Rodgers and Hammerstein successes were based on source material—two plays, one collection of stories, one novel (that had also been a film). Among their least successful shows were original conceptions: an allegory of Americana small-town life, *Allegro* (1947), and a backstager, *Me and Juliet* (1953). Their successes solidified a trend that they had themselves begun—with different collaborators—in 1927. It became a given that musicals would adapt novels, plays, and, by the mid-1950s, even films that had already been deemed worthy of cultural attention.

The four major Rodgers and Hammerstein shows were as bound to a specific period as they were to the covers of a book. Written between 1943 and 1951, they span the years during and just after World War II. They sought to define exactly what America meant and Americans believed, what its history had been, what moral resources that history provided, what moral lessons of error and inadequacy that history taught, what relationship and responsibility American and Western civilization had to the other sections and peoples of the globe. World War II was global in a way that World War I had never been. The United States, which lay between Europe and Asia, fought in both directions during the same four years. The sequence of Hammerstein shows, from *Oklahoma!* and *Carousel* through *South Pacific* to *The King and I*, suggests a steady expansion of a movement that began in Europe, was formed on both the New England coast and the Western Plains, then crossed the Pacific to less privileged, still enslaved peoples of other races. By 1951, America was fighting yet another war across the Pacific—in Korea, which turned out to be a dress rehearsal for Viet Nam. Though set in an apparent Operettaland, Hammerstein shows were musical debates on the pressing legal and social issues facing the American public and American public policy.

For Hammerstein, voicing the hopes of his generation, America was the beacon of the world, even if that light were sometimes dimmed by a naive optimism, racial prejudice, and sexual prudery. The Rodgers and Hammerstein shows move from the Civil War (the period of *The King and I*) through the 1880s (the period of *Carousel*) and the turn of the century *(Oklahoma!)* to 1943 (the watershed year in the South Pacific and the opening of *Oklahoma!*) and 1951 (when America returned to Southeast Asia). No wonder the United States Navy commissioned Richard Rodgers to write the music for the public telling of World War II—the orchestral score for the documentary television series, *Victory at Sea* (1951). Rodgers had been musicalizing the moral issues of that war for almost a decade. When politicians speak nostalgically of making America "the way she used to be," they are referring less to a reality of what America was than to the vision of what America ought to be in the shows of Rodgers and Hammerstein.

The only other Rodgers and Hammerstein hits came at the end of the decade. *Flower Drum Song* (1958) literally assimilated the exotic East with the modern West, setting the life of San Francisco's Chinatown to American song. Their last show, *The Sound of Music* (1959), was a nostalgic regression. Maria has been hired to educate the Trapp children just as Anna has been hired to teach the Siamese children; Maria and the crusty Baron von Trapp clash with the same willful intensity as Anna and the king of Siam; Maria's innocence, like Julie's and Nellie's, clashes with the baron's worldly and sexual wisdom, like Billy's or Emile's; the show's political backdrop recalls the wartime backdrop of *South Pacific*. *The Sound of Music* also regresses musically—"Climb Every Mountain" is another 4/4 anthem of hope and determination, ripped from the cloth of "You'll Never Walk Alone"; "My Favorite Things" reweaves "Getting to Know You," another interchange between teacher and pupils; "Do Re Mi" whistles a "Happy Tune" with the notes of the musical scale. Rodgers's songs are closer to the simpler structures and spirit of *Oklahoma!* than to the operatic passion and complexity that came later. Written in placid peacetime, between the war in Korea and the war in Viet Nam, the show is too confident that the storms have all been walked through and every mountain climbed.

It is unfashionable to admire this musical show and even more unfashionable to admire Robert Wise's 1965 film,[7] called every parodic name from *The Sound of Muzak* to *The Sound of Mucous*. Wise's film, however, is as good a musical film as there is between 1958 and 1972—the best film version of any Rodgers and Hammerstein show, as good as any film adaptation of a stage musical in the same fifteen years. To understand why requires understanding Broadway's invasion of Hollywood in these same years. Rodgers and Hammerstein converted *Oklahoma!*, *Carousel*, *The King and I*, and *South Pacific* into blockbuster films in rapid order between 1955 and 1958. Models for every filmusical of the next decade, they represent the personal revenge of Broadway creators on a rival entertainment industry that had treated them shabbily two decades earlier. The industry's subtle retaliation was that these films barely lived on the screen and do not survive appreciatively in critical repute.

Richard Rodgers tells the story, with more than a little smug pride, of his triumphant return to Hollywood in 1954 to make *Oklahoma!* He took over Irving Thalberg's private office, the very place where, two decades earlier, he bid his personal goodbye to Thalberg, who did not know (or pretended not to know) who Rodgers was.[8] Hammerstein had equally bad memories of Hollywood in the 1930s—the most discouraging decade of his creative life. Kern had moved to Hollywood, where Hammerstein could never knock out lyrics the way a Lorenz Hart or Ira Gershwin could. Hollywood, which could never get enough of the same old thing, merely expected Kern and Hammerstein to pour old *Show Boat* into new bottles, like Paramount's 1937 *High, Wide, and Handsome*. When Rodgers and Hammerstein returned to Hollywood in triumph, they held all the cards. They personally produced *Oklahoma!* and *South Pacific*, and they firmly controlled the rights, script, and style of the other two.

These are movies made by theater people, not movie people—lacking in visual style, visual interest, even visual beauty (except for an occasional Todd-AO ride in a surrey). They photograph human mouths in motion, while the notes and words (almost literally from the stage scripts) pour out. They are "opera films"—reverential attempts, in a blockbuster era of Hollywood desperation, to hang decorative sights on important music. They reject one of the earliest discoveries of movie musicals—going back to 1929—that space need not remain constant while characters sing. A striking statistic is that *not once* in *Carousel*, *The King and I*, and *South Pacific* does the camera ever desert the singer's space. Only rarely does it even desert a singer's face for the reaction of a listener. The films regress to the leaden visual style of *The Jazz Singer* as a matter of choice not technological limitation. The theory behind the choice must have been that to depart from the lips would distract from the lyrics, from Hammerstein's meanings, images, and sounds.

These four Rodgers and Hammerstein films reject the entire history of the filmusical, especially the powerful relationship of space to music. In *South Pacific* the sailors sing "There Is Nothin' Like a Dame" on what appears to be a real beach: a blue sky blazes overhead, waves roll toward the shore, palm trees offer their leafy shade. The wide CinemaScope frame supplies a vast panorama of visual potential—which Joshua Logan's direction ignores, duplicating the movements and gestures that might have been performed in his stage production (and probably were). Not once during this number does any member of the male chorus *do* anything with this scenery: nobody kicks sand, splashes water, climbs a tree. Nobody even gets wet. The real beach might as well be represented by a painted olio drop; the scenery has no organic relationship to the song. The big surprise on stage was Mary Martin's washing that man right outa her hair with real water: a functional shower is a pretty big deal on a stage. This was also the movie's only use for real water during a musical number. Someone forgot the ocean.

As "opera films," not "real movies," how well does each perform the original script and score with as much visual and cinematic adornment as possible? Twentieth Century-Fox's *The King and I* (1956), directed by Fox's most dependable veteran of musicals, Walter Lang, produced by the movie-wise Charles Brackett, wins this contest hands down. The witty battle of the two characters—their clashing views, values, vision of the world—is genuinely interesting (as it was in the Rex Harrison-Irene Dunne film at Fox a decade earlier). Deborah Kerr and Yul Brynner do more than justice to it. Although the totally studio-bound film (even for the arrival of Anna's ship in Siam's backlot harbor) is as visually heavy as any of the group, the exuberant "Shall We Dance?" spins magnificently within the wide scope frame, and the dazzling "Small House of Uncle Thomas" is the greatest single musical number in any Rodgers and Hammerstein film. Directed, according to rumor, by an uncredited Vincente Minnelli with costumes by Irene Sharaff, the number offers a blazing display of radiant orange and yellow in an abstracted black mental space, a brilliant synthesis of Eastern theatrical convention and Western cinematic dance.

The worst of the lot is *Carousel*, made at the same studio in the same year. The most operatic of Rodgers and Hammerstein's theatrical productions (and Rodgers's own personal favorite), the script is their least dramatic

and most metaphoric—from the pantomimic *Carousel* waltz, to a solilo-
quized aria, to scenes "up above" in heaven. Henry King's direction
captures a styleless visual void—from a *papier maché* forest beside a backlot
lagoon for the interminable initial meeting of Julie and Billy; to a tacky
electric-blue heaven strung with plastic Stars of Bethlehem; to a real beach
where a soliloquizing Billy wanders in thought (but never picks up a
pebble, sifts some sand, or touches a rock). The casting (Gordon MacRae
and Shirley Jones) usually gets the blame for this film (and the allegedly
sexy Bigelow looks pretty potty as MacRae squeezed into a tight striped
sweater). But not even a Frank Sinatra, rumored to have wised up and
walked out at the last minute,[9] would have been able to breathe life into this
script, score, and decor.

South Pacific (1958), though not quite as deadly as *Carousel*, has few
filmusicals to rival it for sheer bad taste. Joshua Logan's sole visual "idea"
for the film was a series of colored filters to convey the poetic imagery of
Hammerstein's lyrics. When Bloody Mary sings of "Bali Ha'i," we watch
Juanita Hall's lips while her face goes fuchsia. The "Enchanted Evening"
turns silver blue, but the faces of the two enchanted lovers, Mitzi Gaynor
and Rossano Brazzi, turn ash gray, something between the color of news-
print and the color of death. And for "A Cockeyed Optimist" the sky (and
everything else) turns a bright canary yellow. A younger Richard Rodgers
had written a parody of conveying emotion by turning colors—"That
Terrific Rainbow" for *Pal Joey*. He must have forgotten it when he produced
the film of *South Pacific*.

Given Hammerstein's highly imagistic lyrics, and their consciously
metaphoric unity with Rodgers's melodies, a Hammerstein film needed
visual imagery to evoke the world of the characters in sights as powerfully
as their words and music do in sounds. Only after Hammerstein's death
could Robert Wise translate his verbal poetry into visual imagery, freely
intercutting images and telescoping space while characters sang. *The Sound
of Music* is a film in which the action is not only set in the Alps and the
characters live in the Alps; Wise makes the Alps live in the characters.
Their lives are inseparable from the scenic surroundings—they ride bicycles
in it, row boats in it, climb trails in it, eat lunch in it. The film draws a
powerful visual contrast between being indoors, in the cramped, dark
confines of the abbey or the von Trapp mansion, and outdoors, where
Maria hears, feels, sees the sound and light of nature's music—and where
she teaches others to hear, see, and sing them. The nature that inspires
Maria's songs also "sings" in the radiance of Wise's images. The film's
score, theme, verbal imagery, and visual imagery are one—sound, space,
and light. The light of that outdoor space inspires the sounds that Maria
makes into music.

Perhaps Maria is too metaphorically perfect for adult belief, and the
children are milked and churned to cutesie-pie butter. But Christopher

Plummer's cranky battles with Julie Andrews ignite the same clash of wit
and wills as the brittle battles between Kerr and Brynner a decade earlier.
The pathetic subplot—teenage Rolf becomes a Nazi, destroying his adolescent romance with Liesl—is as much an absurd understatement as a
predictable Hammerstein formula. The use of singing as a political, not just
a spiritual, metaphor is nonsense: if the Nazis would only sing, the film
implies, if they would hear and make the sound of music as the Trapps do,
they would cease to be Nazis. Bob Fosse's 1972 film of *Cabaret* answered that
chimera with the revelation that the Nazis *did* sing; political values can be
defined not by whether people sing but by what and why they sing.

To make singing itself an act of spiritual, philosophical, and political
commitment is a Hammerstein metaphor that goes back to "Ol' Man River."
As a metaphor, this musicality may have been four decades and four wars
out of date for literate American taste. But the film had more cultural
power in the social climate of 1965 than the show did five years before. In
those five years, a popular and attractive president had been assassinated, a
Caribbean neighbor had become an enemy, blacks were accusing American
society of its persistent racism, and American boys were dying in a
distant place called Viet Nam. Many who stayed home didn't see any
reason for Americans to die there, and said so—loudly. The film of *The Sound
of Music*, like the Rodgers and Hammerstein shows from 1943 to 1951, was
at the center of cultural debate, even if (like the earlier shows) it seemed an
evasion of debate. The film transported a scarred generation of Americans
out of the present's lack of political clarity and social cohesion, back to a
past when Western moral values and American social purpose seemed clear
and coherent. Where and how could clarity and coherency be found again if
not back there—in what America was and what Americans believed in the
battle against the Nazis?

Oscar Hammerstein would have been an influential figure if he had
never written with Richard Rodgers. Co-author of Sigmund Romberg's best
shows (*The Desert Song* and *The New Moon*), Rudolf Friml's best show
(*Rose-Marie*), Kern's best show (*Show Boat*), and supervising producer of
Berlin's best show (*Annie Get Your Gun*), that consistent excellence could
have been no coincidence. Hammerstein's firm conception of what a musical
might and should be stimulated his collaborators to their very best work.

His current cultural reputation is dimmer than it once was. Like David
Belasco of an earlier generation, Hammerstein has suffered the simultaneous
fate of institutionalized reverence and cultural contraction. The four films of
his most important stage works don't capture their theatrical and cultural
vitality. The four original cast recordings, from the era just before high-fidelity
and stereo disks, don't sound very lively four decades later. The work of the
man who began by translating Wagner's music drama into American terms
today seems much more like child's play, much more suitable for children, than
the songs of the poisonously playful Porters, Gershwins, and Harts.

The Bigger the Army and the Navy, The Better the Loving Will Be

WARNERS, PARAMOUNT, UNIVERSAL, AND FOX (1936–1953)

During the richest years of Hollywood history every studio made musicals. For all that activity, few filmusical results were as rich in formal innovation or artistic ingenuity as in the early years of sound or the final years of MGM. The flurry of thinking between 1929 and 1935 that produced the Lubitsch mock-operettas, the Berkeley backstagers, and the Fred&Ginger romances had settled into less fanciful formulas. Movie musicals marked time in the very period when stage musicals made their most extraordinary leaps in formal conception and complexity. Unless you have a real thirst for musicals, any dozen or so between 1936 and 1949 is enough—more than enough—to quench it. Even in the most ordinary of them, a great number or two shines brighter than anything else around it. Filmusicals were still built around numbers, fun songs for fun performers, rather than the music-drama idea of Broadway. By 1950 that idea had crossed the continent to produce Hollywood's richest musical decade—grafting Broadway formal innovation to Hollywood musical fun, the kind of fun that Broadway musicals had steadily surrendered. Until then, Hollywood musicals marched in place while the world marched off to war.

Even before World War II, the studios had formulated the Three Commandments of the Musical: Be Cheap, Fast, and Fun. During the war, the commandments served not only studio policy but national priority. Because musicals were trivial, it was unpatriotic to spend time and money on them. Berkeley's kaleidoscopic infinities and Astaire's metaphoric singularities were idle and wasteful allocations of precious national resources, like manpower (and womanpower) and celluloid. Neither Astaire nor Berkeley returned to them until after the war. On the other hand, musicals provided exactly the kind of entertainment the nation needed in wartime, an American answer to the "white telephone" comedies of life among the chic upper classes and the Operettaland romances that dominated the films of our enemies, Italy and Germany. GIs at the front or on the base needed musicals to take their minds off serious business. Their families at home needed musicals to take their minds off dying sons and husbands. Musicals had always provided songs, jokes, fun, and what GIs called hubba-hubba—legs. White GIs got Betty Grable's; black GIs (drafted in increasing numbers for a segregated army) got Lena Horne's. After the war the studios were no longer certain if Hollywood musicals (not to mention Hollywood itself) had any future at all. Only one studio, MGM, answered the challenge with confidence.

The cheap, fast, fun filmusical came in three essential shapes. The personality vehicle was driven by a famous musical performer or performance team. The personality musical often occupied the middle ground between "real" musicals and comedies sprinkled with a few musical numbers. While some personalities, like Fred Astaire, were famous *because* they were musical performers, others, from the innocent Shirley Temple to the provocative Mae West, were distinctive personalities who were incidentally able to sing and/or dance. Their performance became an extension of personality. With Astaire the performance *was* the personality.

The group musical built a film around a larger and more democratically equal ensemble of performers. As opposed to Berkeley's groups of anonymous "kids," later group musicals featured famous comics, who brought their idiosyncrasies with them to Hollywood from stage, screen, and radio. The personality musical multiplied its personalities into a large group.

Finally, the style musical investigated the meaning and value of musical performance itself, situating it within the traditions of the stage and/or film musical. The definition of style became a comment on and connection to history—whether social history or musical history. The three types had never been mutually exclusive: style musicals could also be personality vehicles (for Fred&Ginger or Maurice and Jeannette) or group musicals (for Berkeley's interchangeable faces). Although hybrids were just as common after 1936, the style musical suffered most, for style seemed the kind of arty luxury that was neither fast, cheap, nor fun.

Warner Bros., famous for the Busby Berkeley style, became especially styleless without him. From 1937, the year of Berkeley's departure, to 1953, the year of Hollywood's collapse, Warner Bros. musicals were the least interesting in Hollywood. Perhaps the only remembered title of the entire fifteen years is the 1942 *Yankee Doodle Dandy* starring James Cagney, directed by Michael Curtiz. Consistent with Warner Bros. "biopics," as *Variety* called them, film biographies of famous European creators like Zola, Madame Curie, and Paul Ehrlich, *Yankee Doodle Dandy* was less a musical than a biopic of a famous American creator and performer, George M. Cohan, in which Cohan performances on stage replaced Curie research in a laboratory. The patriotic verve of Cohan's songs and style, culminating in

"Over There," his musical response to World War I, made him the perfect subject for a wartime musical. Wartime Hollywood often turned back the clock to musical performers at or near the turn of the century, drawing an analogy between the 1917 showbiz response to World War I and the 1941 showbiz response to World War II. Showbiz had simply changed its address from vaudeville house to picture palace. *Yankee Doodle Dandy* transcribes the entire finale of *Little Johnny Jones*, when Cohan sang "Give My Regards to Broadway" for the very first time. The nostalgic recreation suggested that American boys abroad, whether in 1904 or 1942, have always yearned for the "home" of Broadway.

Other Warner Bros. wartime biopics of inspirational Americans included a mythical George Gershwin for *Rhapsody in Blue* (1945) and an even more mythical Cole Porter for *Night and Day* (1946). Since Porter had served (very briefly) in the French Foreign Legion, he became military fodder for patriotic thought. The film alleges he even conceived "Night and Day" in uniform, fifteen years before writing it, listening to the drip drip drip of the raindrops, thinking of Alexis Smith. Again, ace Warner Bros. staffer Michael Curtiz directed the musical propaganda.

Curtiz, born in Hungary, his English coated by a thick accent that only partially obscured the constant stream of profanity that marked his directorial manner, had no particular inclination toward or feeling for musicals. His most famous films included *The Adventures of Robin Hood*, *Angels with Dirty Faces*, *The Private Lives of Elizabeth and Essex*, *The Sea Hawk*, *Casablanca*, and *Mildred Pierce*—vehicles for the great Warner Bros. stars, Errol Flynn, Bogart, Cagney, Bette Davis, with highly atmospheric visual trimmings. Though he knew next to nothing about American song and dance, Warner Bros. also dispatched Curtiz to launch the postwar vehicles of its one musical star, Doris Day: *Romance on the High Seas* (1948) and *My Dream Is Yours* (1949).

Like many musical performers of the war years, Day swung from dance-band vocals into movies. The singing style she found with Les Brown would be the key to her film personality: she sang hot, but with a smile, serving warm vocal mush with a touch of Tabasco. Her song style became her screen style—the sweet ingenue with a touch of the tomboy, the girl next door who was one of the fellas (with a hairstyle to match). She built two decades of film success on the same combination—the musicals at Warner Bros. from 1948 to 1957 and the bedroom comedies (or keep-out-of-the-bedroom comedies) at Universal from 1958 to 1968. Day sailed to Warner Bros. stardom in the Curtiz films on two hit songs (by Sammy Cahn and Jule Styne), which projected both sides of her personality: the breathily romantic, "It's Magic," and its sassy reversal, "Put 'Em in a Box, Tie 'Em with a Ribbon." She wanted the magic of romance, but she was spunky enough to throw its song-lyric clichés into the deep blue sea.

Warner Bros. went further afield for leading musical men to replace Jack

Carson, the studio contract partner of her first two films. She went to
Broadway with Gene Nelson (*Lullaby of Broadway*, 1951), to Paris with Ray
Bolger (*April in Paris*, 1952), to Tin Pan Alley with Danny Thomas (*I'll See
You in My Dreams*, 1952), to turn-of-the-century vaudeville with Gordon
MacRae (*On Moonlight Bay*, 1951; *By the Light of the Silvery Moon*, 1953), and
to the wild west with Howard Keel (*Calamity Jane*, 1953), who had just
returned from there in MGM's *Annie Get Your Gun*. Warners replaced Curtiz
with directors who specialized in musicals: Roy del Ruth, veteran of
musicals at Goldwyn (*Kid Millions*), MGM (*Broadway Melody of 1936*), and
Fox (*On the Avenue*); and David Butler, who directed the first Fox musical,
Sunny Side Up, in 1929. Butler had an enormously long career—over a
decade of Fox musicals for Janet Gaynor, Shirley Temple, Alice Faye, and
Betty Grable, and over a decade of Warner Bros. musicals for Doris Day.
Only Vincente Minnelli directed so many musical films over such a long
career. Butler, no visual stylist like Minnelli, was a master with women
performers—balancing the comedienne with the person, the exotic entertainer with the domestic homebody, the pushy showbiz professional with
the retiring all-American girl. Day and Butler were made for each other.

The only other Warner Bros. musicals that aspired to musical style grew
from another familiar Warner genre. Gangsters shared the neighborhood
with the raucous sounds of American jazz that blared in the smoky gin
joints. Three Warner Bros. films, falling somewhere among biopics, gangster films, and musicals, also fall among Hollywood's best about the making
of jazz music with jazz musicians. *Blues in the Night* (1941) is a musical
biopic of a fictional jazzband leader, *Young Man with a Horn* (1950) a musical
biopic of jazz trumpeter Bix Beiderbecke, and *Pete Kelly's Blues* (1955) drops
jazz vocalists Peggy Lee and Ella Fitzgerald into the battle between gangster
Edmund O'Brien and TV's *Dragnet* cop Jack Webb. As in all Warner Bros.
gangster films, atmosphere, both visual and vocal, is the main ingredient,
and all three directors, Anatole Litvak (noted for films noirs), Curtiz (yet
again), and Jack Webb, built their styles on atmosphere. These films were
more atmosphericals than musicals—in which music was only part of the
atmosphere. An apparent summation of Warner Bros. musicals, *Love Me or
Leave Me* (1955), assembled all the tiles of the studio's musical mosaic: a
biopic of jazz vocalist Ruth Etting, played by Doris Day, the consort of a
gangster, played by James Cagney. The only problem with this Warner
musical is that it was made at MGM. But then *A Star Is Born* of 1954 is the
best MGM musical made at Warners. By the mid-1950s studio labels no
longer guaranteed anything about the product. When the Warner label
meant something, a musical meant either a Warner genre film with music or
Doris Day.

The Paramount label meant musical numbers for powerful personalities.
The styles of the personalities set the styles of the films, many of which
were personality films with only a few musical numbers. Marlene Dietrich

sang a number or two in every film; Mae West sang two or three; the Marx Brothers sang, pianoed, and harped. For Dietrich and West, onstage performance confirmed their power and independence. Their ticket to freedom was economic. As entertainers they could travel and survive anywhere, socially and financially dependent on an audience of men but not on any one man. Finding a man was a matter of romantic choice and sexual taste, not economic necessity. Whether the singing temptress in *Morocco* or the "Hot Voodoo" priestess of animal desire in *Blonde Venus*, whether the provocative storyteller of "I Like a Man What Takes His Time" in *She Done Him Wrong* or the bump-and-grinding "Sister Honky Tonk" of *I'm No Angel*, the musical performances of Dietrich and West were only parenthetic extensions of what they were. For the Marx Brothers the musical extensions were even more parenthetic. Since nothing in their film world made any logical sense, it made no more or less sense to sing a song, play a piano, or pluck a harp.

Even in Paramount musicals, the music itself was parenthetical to what were personality pictures with music. Bing Crosby was the sun of Paramount's musical solar system, and for fifteen years seemingly every Paramount musical revolved about him. If Cole Porter's "Let's Not Talk about Love" tried to imagine Paramount minus Bob Hope, Paramount musicals minus Bing Crosby were even less imaginable. Crosby's planets included the cynically quipping Hope, the sexily saronged Dorothy Lamour, the brash Martha Raye, the brasher Betty Hutton, the brashest Cass Daley, the boozy W. C. Fields, the daffy Mrs. Malaprop, Gracie Allen, and her rational interpreter, George Burns, the oafish Jack Oakie, the world-weary Jack Benny, the snapping Patsy Kelly, the romantic slug, Fred MacMurray, and the romantic stiff, Ray Milland. Casting a musical meant playing Bingo. Paramount spun the talent bin and the first four names to fall out went on the Bingle card. Crosby made sense with anything and everything Paramount put around him—the most comfortable personality in American filmusicals.

The comfort was the personality. Nothing was very serious or important to Crosby—as either a character in a film or an interpreter of a song. He slid through a song the way he slid through life—laid back and hanging loose. Romantic attachments weren't very important and Crosby's romantic ballads, a "Moonlight Becomes You" or "I Surrender Dear," refused to take either love scenes or love songs very seriously. Comic complications weren't very worrisome and Crosby's rhythm numbers never strained themselves with jazzy gymnastics. The songs were the man. Crosby's crooning, the trademark buh-buh-buh-booing that began with "When the Blue of the Night Meets the Gold of the Day," was itself a parody of sexual seduction by romantic singing in the moonlight, already a parody of his own singing style. In contrast to the formal precision of Astaire's song style, Crosby simply opened his mouth to let the words and notes of a song slide out.

Like Astaire, Crosby moved from speech to song without changing gears. His quips often undercut the dire comic catastrophes he faced; you had to be pretty cool to make a joke sitting in a pot of boiling oil surrounded by cannibals. Whatever the catastrophe, Crosby assured Hope that the script wouldn't fail them: they still had five years left on their Paramount contract.

It is tempting to see the relaxed Crosby as a specific response to the 1930s and 1940s—to a Depression at home and a war abroad.[1] Crosby seemed so comforting. Everything would be OK, nothing was very serious, so just lie back and keep cool with a quip and a croon. The Crosby charm and career endured for four decades because it slyly implied that life is always a mess, whatever the current catastrophe. Crosby quipped through Korea, the Cold War, bomb shelters, Viet Nam, political assassinations, and the counterculture—as unimpressed as he had been by the Great Depression and World War II. He was a comic existentialist whose films and style charted a clear course of survival: wait for one mess to end and the next mess to begin. As silly as the plots of his films were, life was no less silly. "Life Is so Peculiar," Crosby crooned in the comparatively late and already self-conscious *Mr. Music* (1950).

Because the "Road" pictures with Hope and Lamour were the most peculiar, they remain the clearest transcripts of Crosby's style (*Road to Singapore*, 1940; *to Zanzibar*, 1941; *to Morocco*, 1942; *to Utopia*, 1945; *to Rio*, 1947; *to Bali*, 1952; *to Hong Kong*, 1962). By mixing mock-exotic Operettaland settings, topical contemporaneity in the Hope and Crosby quips, and Marx Brothers craziness in the disdain for both logical plotting and stylish film art, both the stars and the films make merciless fun of themselves. Hope, Crosby, and Lamour are the Marx Brothers with heart. Other Crosby titles recall the Marx Brothers trademarks of mock-exotica (*Rhythm on the Range*, 1936; *Waikiki Wedding*, 1937) and flippant nonsense (*Dr. Rhythm* and *Sing You Sinners*, 1938).

The directors of these films were not musical specialists but Paramount staffers, many of them veterans of silent comedies: Leo McCarey, Norman Taurog, Frank Tuttle, Victor Schertzinger, Wesley Ruggles (who began as one of Mack Sennett's Keystone Kops). If Warner Bros. musicals were Warner genre pictures with music, Paramount musicals were loony Paramount comedies, like *Million Dollar Legs* (1932), with music—a cross between the wacky nonsense of silent comedy, the verbal jokes of sound comedy, and the singing of musical comedy. Mack Sennett had his own comedy unit on the Paramount lot, and Crosby began there with W. C. Fields. This cross between silent comedy and sound musicals explains the comic menagerie of loons, goons, and baboons that inhabited the Crosby cosmos. No nuttier bunch of clowns— male *and* female—ever worked at any other studio. The films feel less like star vehicles than group musicals for a collection of zany creatures, with Crosby as the zookeeper who inhabits the same cage. Like Mack Sennett's Keystone comedies, the Paramount comedy-musicals were as cheap, trashy, and silly as movies could get.[2] For all their verbal dash and silent slapdash, an occasional musical number is a real gem. In *Dr. Rhythm*, Beatrice Lillie's "Rhythm," written specially for her by Rodgers and Hart, parodies the most famous rhythm songs and singers of the day. In "Small Fry" of *Sing You Sinners*, a delightfully casual Frank Loesser-Hoagy Carmichael rhythm tune, Bing impersonates a hillbilly drunk in whiskers, Fred MacMurray plays his wife in drag, and thirteen-year-old Donald O'Connor smokes, drinks, and womanizes just as good as Pappy Bing.

Paramount made these musicals not for the genteel adult market but for the snappy youth market. It is easy to forget that such television pillars of middle-class middle-age as Crosby, Hope, Martha Raye, Jack Benny, George Burns, and Gracie Allen were ever young or appealed to the young. Those Paramount musicals that didn't go to Tahiti went to college (*College Humor*, 1933; *College Swing*, 1938). Like later youth musicals, they mixed college humor with the popular dances of college kids. Paramount musicals were the swingiest of the Swing Era, and many of their comic personalities came not from the highbrow Broadway stage but from the casual companion of America's dancing youth—radio. Not for nothing were Paramount's all-star revues of the 1930s called *Big Broadcasts* (of 1932, 1936, 1937, and 1938), as opposed to MGM's *Broadway Melodies*.

Paramount swing musicals rocked directly into later generations of inexpensive musicals for the youth market—the Annette Funicello and Frankie Avalon beach-blanket musicals and the Elvis Presley musicals of the late 1950s and early 1960s at Crosby's old studio. Paramount transported Presley to exotic places in films with titles that sounded like Crosby rejects: *Blue Hawaii*, *Viva Las Vegas*, *GI Blues*. If Goldwyn recycled Eddie Cantor as Danny Kaye, Paramount recycled Crosby as Elvis Presley. Elvis, like Bing, was a singer who slid (or writhed, wriggled, and rocked) through life.

Paramount silliness survived the war years by graduating the college kids into the army. Instead of college humor and college swing we got GI humor and GI swing. Instead of the Warner Bros. inspirational biopics of musical Americans, Paramount gave us ordinary, modern-day American guys and gals winning the war and putting on shows—winning the war *by* putting on shows. Instead of Fox's leggy Betty Grable Paramount gave us wacko Betty Hutton, whose vim, verve, and vigor both rallied and mirrored American hope. She was not the sexy little woman that American boys were fighting to save but her perky kid sister. She was loony, like everyone else in Paramount musicals, but she was one determined gal—just like our determined fighting men. She didn't fight but she had fight in her.

The old charity show became the new military show in Paramount's wartime filmusicals—not to raise money but to raise the spirits of our fighting men. The GI show brought the 1929 starstudded revue (with little or less plot) back to filmusicals. Uplifting entertainment for the boys in uniform was more important than a tidy musical narrative, and Paramount musicals never cared much for tidiness anyway. *Star Spangled Rhythm* (1942) threw together Crosby, Hope, Lamour, Veronica Lake, Susan Hayward, Dick Powell, Alan Ladd, Paulette Goddard, Cecil B. DeMille, Arthur Treacher, Eddie "Rochester" Anderson (for the black GIs), and two hit swing songs by Harold Arlen and Johnny Mercer, "That Old Black Magic" and "Hit the Road to Dreamland." *The Fleet's In* (1942) threw together Lamour, Hutton ("Arthur Murray Taught Me Dancing in a Hurry"), Cass Daley, William Holden, the Jimmy Dorsey Orchestra, Helen O'Connell, Bob Eberle, and two more hit songs, "Tangerine" and "I Remember You" (lyrics by Mercer, music by the film's director, Victor Schertzinger). While several Hollywood producers were songwriters (Arthur Freed, B. G. DeSylva, Arthur Schwartz), Schertzinger was the only director who wrote his own songs.

Though Paramount silliness survived the war years, when silliness was patriotic, it did not survive Hollywood's postwar drought, when even silly musicals cost too much in comparison with the silliness that came into the home for free on the tube. When the old Paramount zanies who came from radio departed for TV—Groucho, Burns and Allen, Benny, Raye—Paramount's new zanies, Dean Martin and Jerry Lewis, came from television. Like the Marx Brothers, Martin and Lewis made wacky comedies with a few songs, not musicals. A more domesticated postwar America preferred the girl-next-door of Doris Day to the lout-next-door of Betty Hutton, although Paramount tried to tone her down and budget her up in *The Perils of Pauline* (1947) and *Dream Girl* (1948). Crosby plodded on in more fancy and less fanciful vehicles (*A Connecticut Yankee in King Arthur's Court*, 1949; *Riding High*, 1950) that deserved to lose money and did. Even Crosby defected to television to survive. The loony Paramount musicals that began with Big Broadcasts ended with regular telecasts.

Universal, a minor studio until its postwar rise, took Paramount formulas—often by taking Paramount stars like W. C. Fields and Mae West after Paramount cut them loose. Universal's wartime zanies, Bud Abbott and Lou Costello, fit the Paramount mold and traveled the Paramount road—from radio to cheap wartime comedies with music to television. One of the splashiest untidy wartime revues of the Paramount type was Universal's *Follow the Boys* (1944). Although Universal had just one singing star, soprano Deanna Durbin, attended by adolescent sopranos of both genders, Gloria Jean and Bobby Breen, it could recruit musical entertainers from all over creation to win the war. Universal drafted George Raft for *Follow the Boys* to play Tony West, a theatrical producer who organizes a vaudeville circuit of live entertainers for GI shows. Tony articulates the motto of every wartime musical:

Where there are men in uniform, there will be shows. Show business has come through before and it will again.

Tony comes through all right, but not without the supreme sacrifice. His ship goes down with Tony aboard, traveling to the combat zone, following the boys.

With this slender thread of narrative justification, *Follow the Boys* comes through with the orchestras of Ted Lewis, Charlie Spivak, Tommy Dorsey, and Louis Jordan. The Andrews Sisters sing a medley of their hits. Jeannette MacDonald sings "Beyond the Blue Horizon" and "I'll See You in My Dreams"—as consolation to a blind GI in a hospital who can't see anything at all. While Jeannette offers consoling dreams to the wounded, Dinah Shore assures the healthy others that the girls back home are still waiting: "I'll Get By" and "I'll Walk Alone." For high culture, Vera Zorina dances balletically and Artur Rubinstein plays "Liebestraum." From the movies, Orson Welles, cinema magician, performs magic tricks that refer to the very first film magician, Georges Méliès. He makes Marlene Dietrich disappear, except for her trademark legs, which toddle off by themselves. From vaudeville comes Sophie Tucker to contribute a song of boundless sexual suggestion—"The Bigger the Army and the Navy, the Better the Loving Will Be." There are dog acts and youth acts, Donald O'Connor and Peggy Ryan, for the very youngest GIs, and black acts for the black GIs. When organizing his Victory Caravans of entertainers, Tony West wants blacks to come along—either "singing or cooking." The Delta Rhythm Boys don't have to cook. Their singing of "The House I Live In" is a hymn to ethnic diversity within American unity. The house is a metaphoric America packed with Cohens, Kellys, and Marcellis: "Especially the people—that's America to me."

Follow the Boys is an entertainment mess, as earnest as it is self-serving, maudlin, hackneyed, and (like all those 1929 filmusical revues) interminable. Seeking an entertainment something for everyone, high and low, east and west, black and white, *Follow the Boys* assures us that we *are* all alike, different but the same, one nation, one people of peoples, divisible but indivisible, in contrast to enemies perceived as racial and racist. Its myth of a single America of all the people is *the* musical for America at war.

Twentieth Century-Fox spun variations on a single theme before, during, and after the war: the relation of extraordinary musical performance to normal American life. The one studio that competed with MGM in the quantity and quality of musical production, Fox built its musicals on female performers attended by nonsinging men. In movie after movie, Alice Faye, Betty Grable, Marilyn Monroe, Carmen Miranda, Sonja Henie, and Ethel Merman carried the musical performance while Tyrone Power, Don Ameche, John Payne, and MacDonald Carey smiled encouragement from the pit, the piano bench, or the front row. Only Dan Dailey, who came to Fox in 1947 via MGM, held half the stage and frame with the song-and-dance gal. Conflict in a Fox musical arises from her decision to perform or not to perform—between her onstage career and her offstage aspirations for home and family. Fox musicals depict show folks who either want kids or have kids. The stage itself becomes the obstacle to husband and home, which the woman needs when she grows up, no longer one of the babes in an MGM barn.

In Fox musicals, the stage is a rotten place to catch a husband or raise a family. Showbiz mothers seek shelter from the nomadic life to protect their children—often a Catholic boarding school. Headed by Darryl F. Zanuck since 1935, known in the business as "the non-Jewish studio," Fox musicals are consistently Catholic. Christmas is the key holiday, for no other time of year underlines the inadequacy of showbiz life—parents on the road, living in hotel rooms, separated from their children. The usual answer to familial separation is a house in New Jersey. The showbiz wife makes the decision after some terrible tragedy. In Fox musicals, tragedy means an automobile accident, followed by the drunkeness or amnesia of a lost soul, who drifts away from both showbiz and family as a result. The scars of the accident heal and the lost soul returns for the finale, which forever reunites the literal or metaphoric family onstage.

If showfolk don't live normal lives like normal people, they exude a vital democratic energy in comparison to normal parents, who send their children to snobbish boarding schools and take them to snobbish summer resorts but never take them to shows. The old tension between showfolk and blue noses returns in a new guise in Fox musicals. Showfolk may be vulgar (and Dan Dailey added a vigorous dash of Irish vulgarity to the Fox soup), but they have big hearts. If showbiz drives a terrible wedge between career and family, it also supplies a new and extended family. The society of showfolk becomes a cheery substitute for the conventional warmth of hearth and home at holiday time, an alternative family bringing holiday joy to both parents and children. In the end, the Fox conflict of career and family produces a union of two families—of the normal family unit and the extended spiritual family to which all show people belong.

While MGM musicals descend from the book tradition of weaving song and story, Fox musicals descend from vaudeville. Song-and-dancers in Fox musicals play vaudevillians, and George Jessel, former vaudeville headliner, was a producer of Fox musicals. There are two myths in Fox's view of vaudeville: both a myth of normality and a myth of uniqueness. The normal expectations of American home life are of supreme value (especially after the war when women were expected back at the kitchen stove). But normality needs the extraordinary energy and vitality that all showfolk share. The stage provideth and the stage taketh away.

This myth flew in many variants, most of them written or produced by Lamar Trotti, who was able to dress the same story in perpetually fresh-seeming garments. It could be Trottied out in flashback (*Stormy Weather*, 1943; *Mother Wore Tights*, 1947). It was as applicable to whites, like Betty Grable and Dan Dailey in *Mother Wore Tights*, as to blacks, like Bill Robinson and Lena Horne, in *Stormy Weather*. It was as applicable to Alice Faye (in *Alexander's Ragtime Band*, 1938) as to Sonja Henie (*Second Fiddle*, 1939) as to Betty Grable (*Mother Wore Tights*; *Meet Me After the Show*, 1951) as to Ethel Merman (*There's No Business Like Show Business*, 1954). It was as applicable to the lives of actual performers (*Stormy Weather*; *The Dolly Sisters*, 1945) as to fictional ones (*Sweet Rosie O'Grady*, 1943), as applicable to country folks (*State Fair*, 1945) as city folks (*Wabash Avenue*, 1950).

Fox made the same musical again and again, from *Alexander's Ragtime Band* in 1938 to *There's No Business Like Show Business* in 1954, the bookends of the Fox style and cycle. Both have Irving Berlin scores and Lamar Trotti scripts. Both have Ethel Merman. While in *Alexander's Ragtime Band* she plays the glamorous showbiz outsider who invades the stable family (Marilyn Monroe's role in *There's No Business Like Show Business*), Merman mothers the family in *There's No Business Like Show Business* (Alice Faye's role in *Alexander's Ragtime Band*). While the family is metaphoric in the earlier film—the extended family of Alexander's "band"—it is literal in the later film—the five Donahues. The "family" is tossed by romantic tempests in the earlier film. Singer Alice Faye finds herself between two men, the conductor and the pianist (Tyrone Power and Don Ameche), and the conductor finds himself between two vocalists, Faye and Merman. The familial tempests are domestic in *There's No Business Like Show Business* when the Donohue parents are tossed between their onstage careers and their children's needs. The most difficult son, Donald O'Connor, drinks too much and wanders off to who knows where after Marilyn's rejection (just as Faye does in *Alexander's Ragtime Band* after Power's rejection). *There's No Business Like Show Business* represents the very end of what began sixteen years earlier.

Alexander's Ragtime Band is a historical catalog of twenty-two Irving Berlin songs. Beginning in 1911 with "Alexander's Ragtime Band," moving through the 1920s of "A Pretty Girl Is Like a Melody" and "Blue Skies" to the 1930s of "Heat Wave" and "Easter Parade," it reaches the 1938 present with new Berlin tunes: the rhythmic "Walking Stick," Merman's homage to the hat-and-cane teamwork of Berlin and Astaire, and the lyrical "Now It Can Be Told."[3] What keeps the twenty-seven-year chronicle together is not the attempt to tie some story to the string of songs but to make the songs and musical styles into the chronicle itself. *Alexander's Ragtime Band* is the first filmusical to realize that the history of American popular music is the history of America. Irving Berlin is a historian; to hear his songs is to read that history. Henry King, the film's director, specialized not in Fox musicals but in historical romances. *Alexander's Ragtime Band* is a historical romance with and about music.

The film and songs begin in a polite era, before jazz and ragtime, when

American music and society copied European models. It takes Alexander's band of polite musicians time to learn how to swing the new rhythm of the title tune. Once they do, they take it to low clubs and dance dives that come to vigorous life with the new sound. The music carries Americans to Europe with Berlin hits of World War I: the patriotic strophe, "It's Your Country and My Country," and the comic antistrophe, "Oh, How I Hate To Get Up in the Morning." After the war, the music climbs socially—on stage, radio, movies—ending in a 1938 Carnegie Hall, the home that jazz and classics share. Over twenty-seven years, the actors don't age. Nor do the songs. Ageless, ever fresh and young, the songs are America—a union of past and present, dance dive and concert hall. No previous Hollywood musical demonstrated a closer bond between social history and cultural artifact.

In comparison, *There's No Business Like Show Business*, the end of the Fox line, is more dead and more desperate. With fourteen Berlin songs (only three from *Alexander's Ragtime Band*), a huge CinemaScope frame and budget to match, and six stars from all over the showbiz map, this filmusical had everything—songs, splash, jokes, tears, inspiration, family values, old stars, new stars, borrowed stars, blue stars. From Fox came the charming earthiness of Dan Dailey and the hottest star in Hollywood, Marilyn Monroe. From Broadway came Ethel Merman, fresh from a half-decade with Irving Berlin in *Annie Get Your Gun* and *Call Me Madam*. From pop records came Johnny Ray, "the voice that cried" (but the hands that couldn't keep still). Fox sat Johnny at the piano, hiding his flying hands behind a convenient keyboard. From two decades in showbiz came Donald O'Connor—most familiar in 1953 as co-star of Francis, the Talking Mule, and one of the most popular stars of television's *Colgate Comedy Hour*. Out of nowhere came the fresh young face of Mitzi Gaynor, in her first major film role (although MGM had featured her in low-budget program musicals). The six—count 'em six—big stars stretched across the wide expanse of the CinemaScope frame for the spectacular finale, having finally arrived there by means of every familiar Fox plot device—the family, the Catholic boarding school, the divisive newcomer, the auto accident, the lost soul, the musical reunion. And there was even an uplifting new one—Johnny Ray got the hook by sending him from the stage to a nunnery.

Fox's other Monroe musical of the same year, *Gentlemen Prefer Blondes*, worked less hard and much better. Directed by Howard Hawks, its small screen and brief score (only three songs from the Broadway show, plus two new ones) kept a much tighter comic focus (on Monroe and co-star Jane Russell). Like all Fox musicals it was built around women; like all Hawks comedies it was built on reversals of gender expectations about women—as much a screwball comedy with songs as a musical.[4] In contrast, *There's No Business Like Show Business*, yearning to be as BIG as the MGM musicals of the same period, stretched, padded, and stuffed the Fox formulas beyond their means. Even Walter Lang, Fox's sturdy staff director of musicals, could do little to make it fly or even walk briskly. It was the last oldtime musical at Fox, which would throw its musical life preserver to Rodgers and Hammerstein in 1955.

Between the two poles of *Alexander's Ragtime Band* and *There's No Business Like Show Business* came the same film in black dress, *Stormy Weather* (1943). Like the all-black musicals on Broadway and the all-black *Hallelujah* (1929) at MGM, Fox could solve the "color problem" by eliminating all performers without color. No more impressive collection of black talent had ever been assembled: Bill "Bojangles" Robinson, Lena Horne, Dooley Wilson, Fats Waller, Cab Calloway and his orchestra, blues singer Ada Brown, the perpetually airborne Nicholas Brothers and the arty Katherine Dunham dancers.

This wartime musical was both general propaganda and specific inspiration for black fighting men, depicting the importance of black life and culture to American society as a whole. While the film's early scenes imply that blacks contributed in large numbers to World War I, just as they now contributed to the second war, only a few black battalions of volunteers had actually participated—and without Uncle Sam's express invitation. Historical untruths can be useful to men of whatever color at the front. The pretext for the film is a copy of *Theatre World* magazine, which Bojangles receives on the porch of his Old New Jersey home, surrounded by a passel of black children. The magazine cover informs us it is "Celebrating the Magnificent Contribution of the Colored Race to the Entertainment of the World During the Past Twenty-Five Years." The film becomes cinematic copy of that magazine issue—Fox's musical survey of world events through black musical performance, from 1918 to 1943.

Amazingly—and deliberately—black life and entertainment look no different from white life and entertainment in the Fox films that survey the same turf with the same plot. Bill Robinson and Lena Horne simply replace Dan Dailey and Betty Grable in the conflict of love and career, showbiz and family—Horne "so tightly controlled in her acting that she appeared to be the biggest black bourgeois phony the movies had ever seen."[5] If white American soldiers could fight and die for Betty Grable and a house in a New Jersey suburb, then black American soldiers could fight and die for Lena Horne and a house in some separate but equal New Jersey suburb.

Only rarely does a glimpse of genuine black experience ever spot the sanitized whitewash. The sleazy, smoky dive where Fats Waller plays and sings conveys the power and energy of this music for these people in this setting. Fats sneaks raunchy black slang past white censors who could hear nothing wrong in it: "Been ballin' all my life," Fats says, allegedly describing his music, "and I plan to keep on ballin'." You can bet the GIs, white and black, caught it. Perhaps the censors let them; after all, it was wartime. After the film leaves Waller, its musical numbers take the high white road:

three smooth songs for Lena Horne, including the title tune and "I Can't Give You Anything But Love"; several uninspired tap routines for Bojangles; Cab Calloway's heigh-dee-ho in his trademark white tails; the leaps and splits of the equally tuxedoed Nicholas Brothers; and fancy production numbers, culminating in a Katherine Dunham ballet.

Occasionally, the film reveals its discomfort with what it cannot say and show about blacks in America. In the theaters where black acts perform, the camera deliberately avoids that previously unavoidable image of back-stage musicals—shots of the audience enjoying the show, to remind us we are in a theater and the show is a success.[6] To photograph a theater audience would expose a problem that the film is trying to hide from its own audience, black or white. Is this black show produced for a white audience? (Then how can it be black entertainment? For whom are black entertainments, like this film, produced? What is the difference between the racial composition of the theater audience on the screen and the film audience sitting around you at this moment? And what, therefore, is the reality of racial equality in America?) Is the show produced for a black audience? (Not if it represents a Broadway success.) Is it produced for a fully integrated audience? (No such audience exists in 1943, not even in New York. And what would soldiers and citizens from the South think of it if it did?) Similar to the issue of racial equality itself, the audience within the film must remain invisible, for the film cannot show it—consistent with both the reality of 1943 American society and 1943 wartime propaganda of an undivided nation.

Like *Follow the Boys* and other wartime revues, *Stormy Weather* is earnest but messy, both politically and artistically. Will Bojangles succeed in show business? Will Lena finally agree to marry him? Will the show go on? Will the family go on? Who cares—so let's do another number. Like *Hallelujah*, its black predecessor, *Stormy Weather* seethes with performance energy. Andrew Stone, the film's white director, like King Vidor of *Hallelujah* and James Whale of *Show Boat*, specialized not in movies with music but movies that moved. *Stormy Weather* moves as much as any white musical at Fox and more than most. It certainly moved Arthur Freed at MGM, who found a use for black entertainers like Lena Horne and the Nicholas Brothers, for the expressonistic ballet, and for the conviction that American popular music mirrored the movement of American history.

The stage marriage in *Stormy Weather* also solves the offstage problems of Bill "Bojangles" Robinson and Lena Horne.

14

And Best of All, He's American

ARTHUR FREED AND MGM

From its beginning in 1929 to its collapse in 1960, Arthur Freed *was* the MGM musical. He wrote the lyrics for MGM's first musicals and continued to supply them through the 1930s. He began to produce films as well as lyrics for MGM just before the war. Freed's postwar musical productions were not only the best at MGM but anywhere else in Hollywood. *Singin' in the Rain* was not merely based on Freed lyrics and Nacio Herb Brown tunes; it was a 1952 recapitulation of Freed's two decades at MGM.

For twenty-five years, MGM made three kinds of musicals, whether in prewar black-and-white or postwar color—operettas, barnyards, and backstagers. The most memorable operettas were the prewar cycle for Jeannette MacDonald and Nelson Eddy: *Naughty Marietta* (1935), *Rose Marie* (1936), *Maytime* (1937), *Sweethearts* (1939), and *New Moon* (1940). Adapted from Herbert, Friml, and Romberg stage operettas of a previous generation, salted with new twists of plot and injected with new songs alongside their familiar waltzes and marches, these films consciously poured old theater wine into new movie bottles, linking past with present, American movie prose with idealized Old World romance. Nelson and Jeannette fed on each other's voices, enacting a romance not visual but vocal. For a duet like "Sweethearts" (*Maytime*), the camera sits hypnotically in intimate two shots and close-ups, observing the faces fall in love with the sounds that emanate from them. While Fred&Ginger project the abstract idea of love as physical dance, Nelson and Jeannette project the abstract idea as vocal harmony. While the dance of Fred&Ginger longed to become air, the song of Nelson and Jeannette literally was air, floating unattached to physical body. Although Jeannette drifted to other baritones, like Allan Jones for *The Firefly* (1937), or to other genres, like the historical romance (*San Francisco*, 1936), and Nelson wafted toward Eleanor Powell in *Rosalie* (1937), it was Nelson and Jeannette who made music together, soul mates in ethereal harmony.

After the war MGM still made operettas—produced not by Freed but Joe Pasternak, who brought Deanna Durbin to Universal in the late 1930s and Mario Lanza to MGM a decade later. Lanza was so huge of voice, shape, and schmaltz that he never found his Jeannette. Pasternak tried— Kathryn Grayson (*That Midnight Kiss*, 1949), Ann Blyth (*The Great Caruso*, 1951), Doretta Morrow (*Because You're Mine*, 1952)—then gave up by dubbing Lanza's invisible voice behind Edmund Purdom's lovelier, lankier façade (*The Student Prince*, 1954) or setting Lanza's round presence beside nonmusical co-stars, longer in the tooth (*Serenade*, 1956; *The Seven Hills of Rome*, 1958). Like *The Voice of Firestone* and *The Bell Telephone Hour* on 1950s television, the Lanza filmusicals look back nostalgically to turn-of-the-century America, when the operetta style and sound represented genteel American taste, before Berlin's and Gershwin's pounding on tin.

MGM's ultimate tribute to the operetta was *Deep in My Heart* (1954), an all-star musical homage to Sigmund Romberg. Unlike Victor Herbert and Rudolf Friml, Romberg was more evenly poised between European romance and American showbiz, nineteenth-century music and twentieth-century entertainment. Romberg's career looked as much like Berlin's as Herbert's—a Jewish immigrant who first succeeded in New York then trekked to Hollywood, where he played cards with Ira Gershwin. Some of Romberg's loveliest tunes, like "Lover Come Back to Me" (*New Moon*), were not waltzes but modern 2/4 ballads. If MGM musicals began with Arthur Freed in 1929, they also began with Sigmund Romberg in 1930—the first version of *New Moon* with Lawrence Tibbett and Grace Moore. *Deep in My Heart* closed MGM's operetta circle.

The homespun musicals for Mickey Rooney and Judy Garland were Freed's earliest personal productions. These inexpensive program pictures were spinoffs from Mickey's Andy Hardy series (*Love Finds Andy Hardy*, 1938; *Andy Hardy Meets Debutante*, 1940) into the "Babes" series Mickey and Judy shared (*Babes in Arms*, 1939; *Strike Up the Band*, 1940; *Babes on Broadway*, 1941; *Girl Crazy*, 1943). Known on the MGM lot as barnyard musicals—from that handy old barn where Mickey, Judy, and their friends put on a show—they might just as easily have been called Main Street musicals, where small-town mainstream kids proved they were as talented as uptown main-stage stars.

Not only were Mickey and Judy infectious and vivacious American types who seemingly stepped off a Norman Rockwell magazine cover; they were as gifted a pair of accomplished musicians and dynamic performers as ever shared a bill or frame. Mickey was a spectacular drummer, a deft pianist, a vocalist with infuriatingly brilliant phrasing for a kid, and a dancer who was as agile as he was energetic. Judy had fewer gifts but deeper ones—she moved as well as anyone on a screen and she sang-acted better than anyone ever did, big notes or small, tearful or joyful, up tempo or down. While Shirley Temple was a natural, Mickey and Judy were old pros, pretending to be amateurs or they would have been run out of the small-town plots and Norman Rockwell settings MGM built around them. No youngster who performed as well as they ever stayed in an American small town for very long in the 1930s. Their mothers, like Mama Yule and Mama Gumm, Mickey's and Judy's mothers, had heard of Hollywood.

MGM made equivalents of the barnyard musicals after the war, searching for the magic of Mickey and Judy in low budgets and talented youngsters—Debbie Reynolds, Carleton Carpenter, Mitzi Gaynor, Donald O'Connor. A little musical like *I Love Melvin* (1953) shows how resourceful MGM could try to be with very few resources. The energetic Debbie and Donald try hard—very hard—in skeletal versions of high-budget production numbers. Unlike the war years, 1953 was not a very favorable time for musicals with few resources.

The ultimate MGM barnyard musical was *Summer Stock* (1950), Garland's final film at MGM, a strange mixture of delight and horror, past and present, sorrow and joy. Judy showed up to shoot it on her rare good days between weeks of neurotic collapse. Both her spirits and her weight bounced up and down through the film, even from shot to shot—although she looked sensational for the "Get Happy" climax.[1] While Judy, fully grown (a little too fully grown) still impersonates a fresh farm gal in *Summer Stock*, her partner is no youthful small-town Mickey but the adult Gene Kelly, professional big-town entertainer, not pal but teacher. Kelly and his showbiz chums invade Judy's pastoral world, for the old barn on Judy's farm is just the one they need for their show. While the showfolk learn about the chores and charms of rural life, Judy learns about show business. The most important lesson is about musicals themselves. During the rehearsal of a musical love scene with Kelly, Garland asks him the essential question of every musical: "Why don't they just say it?" Why do they need songs? What does music do? He then sings a love song, "You Wonderful You," and she discovers the answer to her question. The song carries the two of them from conversation to romance, from friendship to love, from prose to poetry. Garland's final film at MGM closed the barn door for good.

The final type of MGM musical was the backstager—Broadway cousin of the barnyard show. Before the war, that meant Eleanor Powell, either within the *Broadway Melody* series (of 1936, 1938, and 1940) or not (*Born to Dance*, 1936; *Honolulu*, 1939; *Lady Be Good*, 1941). With Powell's pyrotechnical tapping, leaping, kicks, and splits at their center, they searched for men to carry the songs, jokes, and plot around her. It wasn't easy. The problem was not just finding her an able dancing partner but a suitable star personality to compensate for the one she lacked. She was the most solitary of filmusical performers—alone and untouchable. The singularity that made her dances so spectacular made the plots around them all the more dismal, meaningless, and irrelevant. MGM paired her most often with the smooth song-and-dancer George Murphy and the alleged clown Buddy Ebsen; they also tried nonsinging James Stewart, big-singing Nelson Eddy, and her only dancing equal, Fred Astaire. Whoever the partner, whatever the plot, whatever the songs, whichever the *Broadway Melody*, Eleanor Powell looks better in compilation films like *That's Entertainment*, which present her sensational numbers without their narrative excuses. More than a dancer or dancing star or dancing woman, Eleanor Powell was a female dancing machine.

Arthur Freed's postwar musicals married the Eleanor Powell backstagers, for which he wrote the lyrics, to the Mickey and Judy barnyards, which he produced. Although he spoke quietly and rarely, Freed recognized both talent and a good idea. He saw his job of producing as making it possible for the talented to exercise their ideas. He also saw the way an MGM backstager might develop: though putting on a show was important, it was less important than the discoveries that show people make about themselves and one another. The show can't go on until the showfolk learn to be plain folks. You couldn't make the performance big time until your heart was as big time as your talent. Freed saw that in the Powell backstagers matters of the mind and heart were mere pretexts and conventions—lacking life, power, or belief. He recognized the internalizing of character in Broadway musicals from *Show Boat* to *Pal Joey* to *Carousel*. He knew that the best prewar filmusicals had also been subtly psychological, whether Lubitsch operettas or Fred&Gingers. On the other hand, Freed accepted the cultural mission and commercial expectation of filmusicals. By trade a songwriter, he could never abandon musical fun for internal drama, songs for scores. How could he make psychologically human filmusicals with great numbers? That was the question.

The answers came from here, there, and everywhere. Historical coincidence provided one. Freed musicals stood at the same intersection that had already been crossed on the other coast—between the fun of great songs and virtuoso performances in past musicals and the dramatic unity of the present's totally integrated book show and score. The Freed musicals explore this very intersection. At the same time, after World War II the entire film industry faced the new competition of television, which successfully mimicked the easy, casual production styles of the movie past. Only by investing more time, care, and money on musical numbers and by deepening the psychological texture of their human portraits could filmusicals gain the dramatic weight that the ordinary television series and sitcom lacked. And by combining color, song, dance, and decor, filmusicals demonstrated sounds, sights, and styles that 1950 television images could only barely suggest.

Another answer came from Freed's old trade of songwriting. While Fox built musicals around performers, Freed built them—directly or indirectly— around songwriters. Direct versions came first—musical biographies of

Eleanor Powell in her characteristic backbend pose: *Born to Dance* and *Broadway Melody of 1936*

Jerome Kern (*Till the Clouds Roll By*, 1946), Rodgers and Hart (*Words and Music*, 1948), and Bert Kollmar and Harry Ruby (*Three Little Words*, 1950). Though Warner Bros. made musical biopics, Freed gave more weight to the music and less to the bio. As they move from Kern to Kollmar and Ruby, they increasingly chronicle the collaborative process of creating not just music but words *and* music. Freed's songwriters were not loners like Cohan and Porter but teams like Rodgers and Hart or Kollmar and Ruby.

These were musicals about teamwork, a fact of creative life that applied equally to songwriting, musicals, and movies. While Warners wove a musical biography around a love story, songwriting *was* the love story in *Three Little Words*. The rift between composer (Fred Astaire) and lyricist (Red Skelton) could only be healed by the setting of three little words, "I love you," to an old trunk tune. The indirect musicals built around songwriters are Freed's three ultimate statements of musical teamwork: George and Ira Gershwin (*An American in Paris*, 1951), Freed himself and Nacio Herb Brown (*Singin' in the Rain*, 1952), Howard Dietz and Arthur Schwartz (*The Band Wagon*, 1953). The songs by these teams provide not only foundations for the musical numbers but convey the spirit and value of a performance tradition, translated and renewed by film.

If Freed wove stylish new scores from old songcloth, he tied himself in knots with original scores: *Yolanda and the Thief* (1945) by Warren and Freed, *The Pirate* (1948) by Cole Porter, *The Belle of New York* (1952) by Warren and Mercer—dull work by very accomplished artisans. The visual styles and performance energy of these films carry them further than their songs. The new songs Freed stitched into the existing score of *On the Town* (1949) were especially embarrassing. Freed assigned Roger Edens, his superb vocal arranger and right-hand man for two decades, to supply replacements for all but three Bernstein originals. Every Edens song for the film ("Prehistoric Man," "Main Street," a vapid title tune, and "You're Awful") is hackwork—the kind of musical garbage that proved the inferiority of Hollywood musicals to Broadway buffs. Freed, who came from the Tin Pan Alley of Gershwin and Berlin, could not understand the songs and sounds of modernist Bernstein. Freed's musical ear lived firmly in the songpast. His musicals were as much in the songpast as they were about it.

One obvious exception, a superb original score for an MGM musical, was *The Wizard of Oz* (1939), by Harold Arlen and E. Y. ("Yip") Harburg. Although Mervyn LeRoy is credited officially as the film's producer, Freed worked closely on it and it worked strongly on him. It was Freed who found Judy Garland in the first place and Freed who wanted Judy Garland as Dorothy. *The Wizard of Oz* was MGM's first color musical, a Color Special that was also about the specialness of color. In *The Wizard of Oz*, color didn't simply mean splashing or smearing color—like the carmine lipstick at Fox—but thinking in color and thinking about color. The colorful score and the color world were allies and extensions of one another.

Since 1929 musicals yearned for color. For a decade, many filmusicals
that lacked the chiaroscura flair of Berkeley or Astaire ended with a color
finale—for no reason except the finale needed a shot of color. Songwriters
supplied musical motivation for an otherwise irrelevant color sequence. The
first lyricist to supply one was Arthur Freed for *Broadway Melody*, "The
Wedding of the Painted Doll." If the doll was painted, she and her retinue
could be painted in colors. The finale of *Show Girl in Hollywood* (1930) asked
us to "Hang onto a Rainbow" and the finale of *Kid Millions* (1934) let us see
the assorted colors of ice cream flavors. Although Irving Berlin provided "I
Used to Be Color Blind" for the dream sequence of Fred&Ginger's *Carefree*,
the disappointing visual results kept it color blind. "Over the Rainbow," the
hit ballad of *The Wizard of Oz*, was one more musical pretext. It became
more than a pretext.

The rainbow region is not only a place of color; it is a place of dreams,
fantasy, magic, and music. As in *Love Me Tonight*, one of the few early
filmusicals Freed admired, to musicalize the world is to magicalize it. To do
it in color is to double magicalize it, to make it the very opposite of the
ordinary, everyday monochrome world—in *The Wizard of Oz* called Kansas.
Other plot motifs cue and key the entire color system—the yellow-brick
road, the emerald city, the ruby-red slippers, the rainbow horse of another
color. Dorothy's white dress shines in this color setting and the inky black
cloak of the Wicked Witch looks doubly dread and drear. Between these two
poles of all colors and no color are the amber, silver, and umber of the
Cowardly Lion, Tin Man, and Scarecrow. The score is as colorful as the
decor: as in *Love Me Tonight*, a delicate blend of discrete songs, "Ding Dong
the Witch is Dead," and running musical motifs, "We're Off to See the
Wizard" or "If I Only Had a Heart" (with its verbal replacements of brain
and nerve).

The lesson of *The Wizard of Oz* was the way color transforms the world
into a special place and a film into a special event. *The Wizard of Oz* was an
ordinary barnyard musical that flew over the rainbow in several senses.
Dorothy's monochrome Kansas barnyard was the same but different in the
color landscape of Oz. Three farmhands become her three magical companions, the neighborhood crone becomes the Wicked Witch, a carnival
huckster becomes a Wizard, and even Dorothy's little dog, Toto, comes
along for the ride, barking the complications that both begin the journey to
Oz and bring her back from it. Color, song, visual motifs, plot, character,
and theme together create a new and special place. Call that place Oz, or
childhood, or dreams, or the imagination. Call it an MGM musical. If *The
Wizard of Oz* assures its audience that, in the end, "There's no place like
home," that we must return to the everyday monochrome of Kansas
normality, it just as strongly assures us that human beings cannot survive
without occasional trips to the color world of dreams, Oz, and musicals.

The color of Oz leads directly to the color of *Meet Me in St. Louis* (1944).

In *Meet Me in St. Louis* both Kansas and Oz have been renamed St. Louis. The black-and-white American world of Kansas has not been transcended but explored to reveal its color. The flight is not out of the world but out of the present. Even Little Dorothy returns in St. Louis, literally as Judy Garland and figuratively as eight-year-old Margaret O'Brien. And Toto too, for the child's name is Tootie. *Meet Me in St. Louis* does not pose an inseparable gap between the two worlds of childhood and adult, imagination and reality, Oz and home, but a continuous terrain to show that those worlds are bridged by the evolving generations of American life.

Given the expense of color filming and the economies of wartime, *Meet Me in St. Louis* had to play an uplifting role in the struggle. St. Louis, born on the frontier and host of a world's fair, becomes a mythical embodiment of American history and culture—its families, seasons, houses with boys next door, holidays like Halloween and Christmas, customs like family dinners, courtship, and engagement parties, technologies like telephones, trolleys, electric light bulbs, and color movies. And its music. The songs of the film are both old and new, historical and current. Wonderful new tunes by Hugh Martin and Ralph Blane ("The Trolley Song," "The Boy Next Door," "Have Yourself a Merry Little Christmas") alternate with old favorites (Kerry Mills's 1903 waltz, "Meet Me in St. Louis, Louie"; "Under the Bamboo Tree," a 1902 "coon song" by black songwriter Bob Cole). In this musical, America's history and values are in its songs as well as its people, in its songs *because* they are in its people. Its songs are its people.

From the color thinking of *The Wizard of Oz* and *Meet Me in St. Louis* arises a stylistic corollary. Color is one—but only one—element of visual style. Visual style can be as important to a filmusical as musical style, the means to harmonize decor with singing and dancing. What the filmusical lacks in musical or dramatic complexity compared to the stage musical it provides in visual complexity. Thinking about visual style meant thinking about space. The best filmusicals seek meaningful spatial contexts for musical performance—as Berkeley, Lubitsch, Mamoulian, and Fred&Ginger did. They are "about" space as much as "about" song and dance. Arthur Freed needed directors who thought about musical performance spatially and about visual space musically. He found not one but three: Vincente Minnelli, Stanley Donen, and Charles Walters. All three came to Hollywood musicals from Broadway—Walters and Donen as dancers, Minnelli as a designer. In their different backgrounds lie different definitions of musicalized space.

Vincente Minnelli was most sensitive to the complex meanings of space. Born into a circus family, he studied painting at Chicago's Art Institute while working as both photographic assistant and window decorator for Marshall Field. Before he was thirty he had become designer and director of the lavish Paramount-Publix stage shows. Minnelli brought his entire background to Freed at MGM. From photography came a sensitivity to the play of light and shadow on photographic objects. From window decoration came the sensitivity to shapes and colors in three-dimensional frames. From his stage shows came flamboyant decor and design. From painting came an analysis of depth, color, and light. And from the circus came comedy with terror, chaos with order, clarity with mystery. Although Minnelli has been tagged with the demeaning label of "colorist,"[2] color was only one of five notes in Minnelli's visual scale: color, light, depth, resonance, and detail.

A student of the French Impressionists who dominated the pictorial style of his youth, he returned often to the visual world of the Impressionists—whether in the ballet of *An American in Paris*, the hotel room of *The Band Wagon*, the nonmusical biography of van Gogh in *Lust for Life* (1956), or the Belle Epoque of *Gigi* (1958). Minnelli was a stickler for details: the precise types and shapes of mirrors, chairs, portraits, tables, pitchers, picture frames, combs, commodes for every place and period; the exact shade of a pair of socks, a glove, a handkerchief, the lining of a dress, or a spray of flowers in a vase. To capture the visual style of a period meant not just finding its light and color but situating characters in rooms with things where people actually lived. Minnelli became a decorator of perfectly historical windows. In *Meet Me in St. Louis* (1944), his first film in color, Minnelli's flights of visual detail carry Freed's exploration of American myth. The decor captures not merely the way a proper American home looked in this period but the way it felt to sit in that kind of room, on that kind of furniture, in that kind of light.

Minnelli asks how a space feels not just how it looks. Much of that feeling comes from its light, without which there can be no movies. The evolution of indoor light, whether pouring through a window or glowing from candles, radiating from oil lamps or glaring from primitive electric bulbs, plays a central role not only in our social history but in the history of visual representation as well. Minnelli knew and felt that history better than any other director of Hollywood musicals. He packed his films with paintings—from either his own or Arthur Freed's private collection—which allude to the history of Western pictorial representation.[3]

Unlike paintings and department-store windows, movies move. Minnelli's movement within his richly articulated spaces was quite unlike anyone's for musical numbers. For Minnelli space is layered, deep, and tangled, concealing surprises which it more and more reveals as the camera pushes inward or pulls back. As opposed to Berkeley's massive pull-backs to infinity, Minnelli pulled his camera back slowly within a limited range, steadily expanding our visual information in constantly shifting planes of perspective. Or he pushed inward, seemingly boring into the very doubts and fears of the character. One not only sees more but understands more by moving the camera. Minnelli situates dancers within entangling forests of decor, then pushes his camera toward them or pulls away as they pierce through the psychological forest or try to escape it. This metaphor for Minnelli's

Judy and Toto looking "Over the Rainbow" in *The Wizard of Oz*; Judy and Tootie (Margaret O'Brien) performing the cakewalk in *Meet Me in St. Louis*

Minnelli's dancing in depth: the ballet from *An American in Paris*

moving camera and decor became literal in *Brigadoon* (1954) when a dancer attempts to flee a forest. Minnelli's layered decor and moving camera are visual correlatives for characters entangled in their thoughts, emotions and cultures—whether Tootie's fright on Halloween in *Meet Me in St. Louis* or Kelly's search for an ever elusive love in the *American in Paris* ballet. The internal drama is projected outward into the visible world of color, space, light, camera movement, and decor. Minnelli is simultaneously Impressionist in his visual palette and Expressionist in his psychological goal.

For Stanley Donen (with or without Gene Kelly as co-director) space is less mysterious but more exuberant. Donen's space does not attack his dancers; his dancers conquer space with their energy. Like Kelly a dancer himself, Donen projects the performer's energy into space, charging space with the energy of dance. Donen's space is centrifugal, hurtling outward from the dancing performer toward the edges of the frame, forcing that frame to move or lose its subject. His most common camera maneuvers are not Minnelli's tracking forward or back but the rushing horizontal tracking shot and the crane shot, up (usually) or down (less frequently).

In *It's Always Fair Weather* (1955), Donen's camera rushes excitedly alongside a celebrating trio of dancing soldiers (Kelly, Dan Dailey, and Michael Kidd), who perpetually threaten to race off frame and leave the camera behind. The horizontal tracks not only keep the dancers on frame but also trap and tap their energy. In *Singin' in the Rain*, the tracking camera mirrors the title song's energetic joy. At that magical moment when Kelly welcomes the rain on his face, already saturated with rapturous song, the camera cranes down and tracks in breathlessly—not Minnelli's camera in terrifying pursuit of a fleeing subject but Donen's joyful mirror of the

The dancing camera for
"Singin' in the Rain":
oblique angles, craning down,
craning up

performance energy that charges the entire frame. When Kelly twirls with his umbrella for the number's big finish—his wide circles traversing the wet street and sidewalks—the camera cranes to a high position so his circular joy fills the frame. Donen's framing of musical numbers is a constant dialogue between performance energy that threatens to break out of the frame and the camera's energy that moves fast enough to prevent it.

Charles Walters, least known of the three, defines space differently. For Walters, space is centripetal, not moving outward from the performer into space but moving inward from the edges of the frame toward the performer. Walters was the MGM director most sensitive to performers and performances. In return, many performers preferred to work with him—especially Judy Garland, who couldn't have made it through *Easter Parade* or *Summer Stock* without him. Astaire, who always focused space on his performance at the center, worked very well with Walters in *Easter Parade*, *The Barkleys of Broadway*, and *The Belle of New York*. While Donen and Minnelli used very active camera strategies for active male performers, Walters was sensitive to women performers who reveal their power not in the way they hurtle through space but in the way they sit still and observe it.

If Minnelli's camera is a pursuer and Donen's a sprinter, Charles Walters's camera is a magnet. When it moves, it keeps the performer as the fixed foot of a compass, traveling around him or her, attracted to the performance as if magnetized or hypnotized. During Garland's wistful "Friendly Star" in *Summer Stock*, Walters's camera performs a quiet and subtle track, moving in a slow semicircle while she sings, keeping her perpetually at the center of the frame, until it comes to rest at an oblique angle that magically unlocks the power of her singing and song. Nor would Leslie Caron's *Lili* (1953) have worked its quiet charm without the sensitive gaze of Walters's transfixed camera. Though Walters may have been Freed's third-stringer, and though Freed may only have assigned him a project after Minnelli and Donen begged off, he was a more comfortable transcriber of musical performance than any first-string director at any other studio.

Of course, they were not the only directors of musicals at MGM. Freed's fourth-stringer was merely Busby Berkeley. Others included George Sidney (for the operettas and plodding Broadway adaptations), Don Weis (for the programmers), Richard Thorpe, and Mervyn LeRoy. MGM was also stocked with every other kind of production talent—cameramen (Robert Gilks, Charles Rosher, Harry Stradling, John Alton), designers (Douglas Shearer, Cedric Gibbons, Cecil Beaton, Preston Ames, Oliver Smith, Henry Greutert, Irene Gibbons, Irene Sharaff), vocal arrangers and orchestrators (Kay Thompson, Conrad Salinger, Lennie Hayton, Johnny Green, Saul Chaplin, Adolph Deutsch, André Previn), and Freed's all-round musical producers, Roger Edens and Lela Simone. The MGM Technicolor musicals were built by a cooperative army of gifted artisans, all contributing to the whole.

In the end, Arthur Freed, the master architect, knew that psychological musicals with great numbers came down both to the production army behind the camera and the performance talent in front of it. No other Hollywood studio ever stocked such a performance stable. There were the pure dancers, Cyd Charisse, Vera-Ellen, Leslie Caron, and Tommy Rall; the singers, Frank Sinatra, Mel Tormé, and Vic Damone; the comics, Red Skelton and Jules Munshin; the soubrettes, Betty Garrett and Virginia O'Brien; the solid all-rounders, June Allison and Van Johnson; and the complete song-and-dancers, Ann Miller and Mickey Rooney. There was the child prodigy, Margaret O'Brien; unlike Shirley Temple at Fox, she balanced childhood innocence with a quirkily precocious imagination. There was the swimming dancer, Esther Williams; unlike Sonja Henie, the skating dancer at Fox, Williams performed beneath the waves rather than atop their frozen surface. There was even a sprinkling of pleasantly nonmusical straight men, Peter Lawford and Tom Drake, like Ray Milland at Paramount and John Payne at Fox. Finally, there were the three headliners, who were like nobody else anywhere: Gene Kelly, Judy Garland, and Fred Astaire, at least one of whom topped the bill of every Freed film. For all his commitment to songs, color, and visual style, Freed never broke the Golden Rule: in musicals performers perform.

The rise of Arthur Freed and the postwar MGM musical can be charted as the rise of a single performer, Gene Kelly, and the fall of another, Judy Garland. It was Kelly, more than any other MGM performer, who rose to the big time by becoming big time in his heart, while Garland just as inexorably fell from it by losing, if not her heart (never her heart), her big time dependability. They intersect at two key points: in Kelly's first film at MGM and Garland's last. In *For Me and My Gal* (1942), Kelly is the uncertain newcomer from Broadway and Garland the veteran of six years in the MGM barnyard at the top of her game. She even tells him: "You'll never make the big time 'cause you're small time in your heart." Although she's right in this film—too right—by *Summer Stock* Kelly is merely on assignment between more important projects, *On the Town* and *An American in Paris*. While he has risen to choreographer-director as well as headliner, Garland was on her way out of the studio and onto the emotional roller coaster that would carry her between neurotic collapse and triumphant comeback for the remainder of her life. Kelly's rise, less fabled and familiar than Judy's fall, was not without stumbling and wandering.

For Me and My Gal was a thoroughly confused and confusing debut. He brought the Broadway louse of *Pal Joey* directly to MGM—a pushy entertainer who will do anything to get ahead. On the eve of World War I, he deliberately breaks his own hand with the lid of a showbiz trunk so he can play the Palace and dodge the draft. This is as small time as you can get in 1942 America. While Judy is big time everywhere—in heart, voice, and style—Gene only looks big time performing beside her. Their duets, staged and shot by Busby Berkeley, are sensational—a depiction of spiritual harmony through performance harmony. Behind them on the wall, as they sing "For Me and My Gal," a sampler proclaims, "Where there's music, there's love." Despite the music, Gene is loveless, "an opportunist, an egotistical actor." Their obligatory postwar onstage reunion, tacked onto the film to make Kelly seem more appealing than a snake, lacks the healing of the Fox finales. *For Me and My Gal* is another of those wartime messes: part terrific song and dance, part inspirational wartime flashback to the vaudeville past, part *Pal Joey*. The big loser was Kelly. You couldn't build a film star on a louse. He didn't know what to do and MGM didn't know what to do with him.

So they sent him down to the minors for seasoning. Movie studios are like baseball franchises, and Kelly's *Take Me Out to the Ball Game* (1949) makes an explicit connection between musicals and baseball. In the filmusical business, the minors were called Columbia—in perpetual need of a partner for Rita Hayworth. The 1944 result was *Cover Girl*, a prestige musical for Columbia, its first in color—with a score by the top names in the business, Jerome Kern and Ira Gershwin, directed by Charles Vidor, produced by lyricist Arthur Schwartz (both of whom would come to MGM). In *Cover Girl* important traits of the Kelly persona first appear. While not an utterly worthless human being, he can still be jealous, spiteful, vain, suspicious, and stubborn. Unlike Astaire, Kelly *can* do something bad. But Kelly can realize his error. Kelly musicals depict his character's psychological growth from error to maturity and understanding, exactly the kind of growth Freed musicals needed. Because his potential for moral understanding must exist all along, he can't be "small time in his heart." He must be big time in his heart but small time at a few low moments.

Cover Girl constructs the first Kelly musical number as a moral debate and psychological struggle, a frantic dance to "Long Ago and Far Away." When Rita wins a cover girl contest for a fashion magazine, Kelly feels both envy and insecurity. How can she love someone so small time, with a little nightclub in Brooklyn, who cannot offer her the Broadway fame and fortune of her wealthy new admirers? Kelly, whose fears are completely of his own making, dances his psychological struggle—a *pas de deux* with his own reflection in double exposure. While Astaire's trick dances with identical selves demonstrate the difference between external appearance and internal conception, Kelly's dance with his own reflection is a morality play, a battle between his character's good and bad selves. The reflection is his own worst angel, who goads his fears and urges him to act on them. The reflection hovers around him on the glass windows of storefronts, transforming an everyday street into an emotional theater. This is a battle he loses, shattering the glass that serves as the screen of his projected debate. He will shatter his relationship with Rita as completely as he shattered that window, and he will pay for it. You can't break windows without paying for them.

Both this musical psychodrama and the upbeat "Make Way for Tomorrow" demonstrate another Kelly trademark. While Astaire seeks a private place, a personal "stage" where he and one other can dance, Kelly takes dancing with him into the everyday world.[4] The result is not Astaire's retreat from the world but Kelly's transformation of the world, converting the ordinary into the marvelous. While ordinary storefronts become psychological mirrors in Kelly's dance debate, those same streets and storefronts become a playground for Kelly, Rita, and Phil Silvers in "Make Way for Tomorrow." Pieces of everyday stuff become imaginative toys—garbage pails and their lids, lampposts, oars on a dock, a mailbox on a corner. And everyday people become sources and subjects of play—a milkman and a drunk. Eventually a cop appears, as he does after Kelly's singin' in the rain, casting the harsh, cold eye of adult normality on this child's play. This Kelly routine might be called street-song *bricolage*.[5] Kelly dances burst out of confining interiors and into the streets—of actual Manhattan in *On the Town* or studio-lot Manhattan on roller skates in *It's Always Fair Weather*—where he spontaneously converts the stuff of the everyday world, anything that comes to hand, into a universe of wondrous objects.

Whatever Kelly did not discover about his screen persona in *Cover Girl* he found when he returned to MGM. In *Anchors Aweigh* (1945), an odd mixture of high art (Kathryn Grayson and José Iturbi) and low entertainment (Kelly and Sinatra), more pieces of the Kelly portrait fit together. Avoiding a uniform in *For Me and My Gal* was a terrible mistake—and not only in losing our wartime sympathies. The military uniform fit him both spiritually and physically. Kelly's manner suggested the buoyant, jaunty American GI of the 1940s, the spirit that won the war, not the one that dodged the draft. It fit him physically because a uniform combines the formal and the casual, the tight and the loose, that Kelly's style and dancing themselves suggest. Unlike Astaire's reed of a body, perfectly encased and showcased, hidden and revealed, by top hat and tails, Kelly's body was a coiled spring, a compact engine of tense muscles, a panther in human form, straining to break its social cages. The Kelly animal seemed both relaxed and powerful, hidden and revealed in a uniform, which became both second skin and social cage. After *Anchors Aweigh*, Kelly wore the uniform again in *On the Town*, *It's Always Fair Weather*, and *Invitation to the Dance* (1956), while he had only just taken it off as *An American in Paris*.

Kelly also looked right in uniform because he was one of a team, one of the guys, and dancing is something Kelly does with his buddies. In *Anchors Aweigh*, he had two buddies—one human, Frank, the crooning Sinatra; one cinematic, Jerry, the cartoon Mouse. In film after film, Kelly dances with his pals—with Jules Munshin and Sinatra in *On the Town* and *Take Me Out to the Ball Game*, with Donald O'Connor in *Singin' in the Rain*, with four GI buddies in the *American in Paris* ballet, with Dan Dailey and Michael Kidd in *It's Always Fair Weather*, and with Jerry the Mouse yet again in *Invitation to the Dance*. Only once, in "The Babbitt and the Bromide" of *The Ziegfeld Follies* (1946) was that buddy Fred Astaire. Why did Freed never pair the two again? Perhaps because Astaire, unlike Kelly, almost never dances with buddies. The rare exceptions are George Murphy in *Broadway Melody of 1940*, Jack Buchanan in *The Band Wagon*, a few hoofs around the block with Bing in *Holiday Inn* and *Blue Skies*, and the duet with Kelly. Either Astaire dances with a woman or he dances alone (even if his solo engages projec-

Buddy dancing: Kelly and Donald O'Connor in "Moses Supposes" of *Singin' in the Rain*

tions or extensions of himself). Dancing with buddies comes from Kelly's buoyant American equality. Astaire doesn't dance with buddies because he hasn't any equals.

What Kelly gains in these buddy dances, he loses in romantic duets, which never have the same meaning, ease, or intimacy as Astaire's. For all of Kelly's aggressively masculine sexuality, he'd rather dance with the guys than the gal. In *Cover Girl*, Kelly's dances with Rita seem rhythmic duels, in which the leading lady merely becomes another buddy. Many of the identical steps with Rita return in Kelly duels with Sinatra or O'Connor. Those duets that are not playful challenges tend toward the balletic *pas de deux*—either figuratively, like "Our Love Is Here to Stay" with Leslie Caron in *An American in Paris*; or literally, like the *pas de deux* in ballets with Caron, Cyd Charisse, and Vera-Ellen, more arty and precious, less sensuous and flowing than Astaire's combination of aesthetic, ballroom and tap. While Kelly projected the idea of love as dancers do on a stage, Astaire projected it as lovers did (or hoped to do) on dance floors. Kelly danced more comfortably with Jerry the Mouse.

Not surprisingly, children and childhood become very important to Kelly. Dancing with a cartoon hero leaps the gap between adult art and child delight. Kelly frequently dances for kids or with kids. In *Living in a Big Way* (1947), his last black-and-white musical, he builds a spectacular routine around children's games (hopscotch, ring-a-round-a-rosie, one-two buckle-my-shoe, one-two-three a-lary) while a crowd of children appreciatively observes his dance play. "I Got Rhythm" in *An American in Paris* is also deliberate and delightful child's play. The closeness to kids emphasizes both virtues and flaws of the Kelly persona—warmhearted, exuberant, and joyful, but also self-centered, mean-spirited, and pouting. Adult experience—learning to live with others, both male and female—helps him grow out of his childishness while preserving his childlike energy and innocence.

If Kelly's dancing is child's play in *Living in a Big Way*, it is also awesome in its sheer athletic difficulty. To delight his child audience, Kelly converts the skeleton of a new house into a circus, walking on its planks high above as if on a high wire, swinging on its ceiling beams as if on a pair of parallel bars, riding its ropes and pulleys as if on a trapeze. The low camera angles, with both air and earth, sky and floor, in the same frame, make it clear that Kelly is really executing these stunts, as difficult as they are dangerous. When Kelly swings from beam to beam high above the earth, then from rooftop to ground for the big finish, he invokes his cinematic ancestors: Harold Lloyd on the clock of *Safety Last*, Chaplin on the high wire of *The Circus*, Keaton on the motorcycle of *Sherlock Jr.*, Douglas Fairbanks leaping from parapets or Johnny Weissmuller swinging from tree to tree. Kelly's stunt dancing embraces two cinema traditions—silent comedy and swashbuckling. Gymnastic clowning literally becomes dancing with Kelly and the Nicholas Brothers in "Be a Clown" of *The*

Pirate. In *Singin' in the Rain*, Kelly's dancing becomes an explicit extension of the Fairbanks tradition when the film-within-the-film changes its style and title from *The Dueling Cavalier* to *The Dancing Cavalier*.

By the 1950 of *Summer Stock*, Kelly was not merely a song-and-dancer in filmusicals but a film persona with a vision of human experience and an attitude toward social experience expressed as singing and dancing. Just as Keaton was Chaplin's opposite as silent clown, moving from different costumes to alternative comic techniques to contrasting visions of experience, Kelly's differences from Astaire move from costume to performance style to personal vision. Kelly sang differently from Astaire—not the precision of Astaire's melodic jumps and rhythmic shifts but a casual, warm, scratchily modest nasality that was as right for his casual clothing as Astaire's vocal precision for his formal wear. While Astaire made everything look easy—spectacular steps looked as simple as walking—Kelly made everything look difficult, devouring enormous chunks of space in leaps, twirls, bucks, and wings. While Astaire's spontaneous invention balanced his external elegance, Kelly's personable informality balanced his overt virtuosity. When Kelly wasn't dancing in military uniform, he was dancing in loafers. It is, of course, impossible to tap dance in loafers; tap shoes, like toe shoes, must be tightly laced. Tap dancing in loafers, like singing in the rain, means dubbing on a soundtrack. But loafers look and feel soft. Kelly needed the softness to balance the blatant brilliance of his technique, which could easily look like showing off—and did in his worst moments and films.

While the appropriate camera strategy for Astaire's dances was unobtrusive observation, respecting his privacy and our privilege of observing it, the appropriate camera strategy for Kelly's dances was demonstratively athletic. The energetic cameras of Minnelli and Donen are as right for Kelly's performance style as the quieter cameras of Mark Sandrich and Charles Walters for Astaire's. The Minnelli camera that races after Kelly in *An American in Paris* strolls with Astaire in *The Band Wagon*.

The contrasting costumes, dancing styles, singing styles, social settings, and camera work of the two performers exactly match their opposite styles of performance—which become views of experience. While Astaire's singularity was a model of American individuality during the Depression, Kelly's sociability was a model of American teamwork during and after the war. If Astaire was not quite of this world, Kelly was very much in and of the world. It seemed both irony and fate when Astaire's Ariel replaced Kelly's injured Caliban for the 1948 *Easter Parade*.

In the second musical to carry Freed's name as producer, the 1940 *Strike Up the Band*, Mickey Rooney offers a sweeping cultural observation: "Look at George Gershwin. His music's as good as Beethoven or Bach. And best of all, he's American." Freed would use Astaire and Kelly to prove Mickey's theorem. They embodied, in opposite ways, Freed's idea of the filmusical: a seamless weave of high art and low entertainment, the elegant European arts and the vital American popular arts, "commercial but with class."[6] In Astaire, art and entertainment met in some mysterious midpoint; Astaire had always been the place where "jazz and ballet merge." In Kelly, art and entertainment were irreconcilable opposites toward which his performances alternately leaned—following both to their absolute ends.

When Gene Kelly observed, both in print and on television, that the *auteur* theory did not apply to musicals,[7] he meant that director alone did not a filmusical make. Kelly's own collaboration with Donen put the idea into practice: Kelly's primary responsibility was blocking and choreography, Donen's camera and decor. What Kelly might have said instead is that a filmusical has many *auteurs*. At MGM, with Arthur Freed's general level of production excellence and the art department's superb visual execution, the three variable *auteurs* for any production were the star performer, the director, and the writers—both script and songwriters. When the performance style of the star, the visual style of the director, and the musical style of the songs met in a narrative package that gave a *consistent meaning* to all three styles, the MGM musical fulfilled Freed's aspiration.

Three late 1940s MGM musicals almost did. *The Pirate* combined Minnelli's visual brilliance and Kelly's swashbuckling bravura with a dogged but drugged Judy Garland and a Porter score both lackluster and meaningless in a film allegedly set in the long ago and far away Caribbean. *Easter Parade* combined the comeback energy of Astaire, the healthiest Garland in years, and a terrific Irving Berlin weave of old and new tunes—with some understandable narrative uncertainty about the substitution of Astaire for Kelly. The freely edited opening number of Kelly and Donen's *On the Town* set a dazzling visual and musical standard that the rest of the film could not sustain. The first MGM musical to put it all together—performer, score, visual style, and cultural meaning—was *An American in Paris* at the turn of the decade. As influential on Hollywood as *Oklahoma!* on Broadway, eight years before, *An American in Paris* was, for Freed, the ultimate proof that Gershwin was as good as Beethoven or Bach; for Minnelli, that a movie musical was as good as a Lautrec or a van Gogh. And best of all, it was American.

15

Mount Hollywood Art School

FIVE FILMS OF
THE FIFTIES

As Gene Kelly concludes his dance on the wet pavement of *Singin' in the Rain*, followed by the cop who interrupts his play, he just happens to splash past a gloomy Victorian house with a large sign on its brick fence: "Mount Hollywood Art School." The sign and house suggest an art exactly opposite *Singin' in the Rain*: serious and sacred, from a "Mount" like a sermon, not a profane Technicolor musical. On the other hand, the sign is a declaration of faith. Arthur Freed, Gene Kelly, Stanley Donen, and the MGM art department, which piped the rain and painted the sign, define the art that Hollywood does best. A song and dance like "Singin' in the Rain" is the summit of Hollywood art—not taught in a musty Victorian manor but at an American school named MGM. The sign declares both the kind of art the film isn't and the kind it is.

Five classic filmusicals of the 1950s wear the same sign—classics because they wear it, proclaiming their confidence and conviction in what they are doing: *An American in Paris, Singin' in the Rain, The Band Wagon, A Star Is Born*, and *Funny Face*. The five have much in common. All are about artists and entertainers—painters, photographers, composers, writers, actors, models, and movie stars. All are set in the commercial capitals of art and entertainment—two in Hollywood, one in New York, one in Paris, one in New York and Paris. Two have music by George Gershwin, three have lyrics by Ira Gershwin; two star Gene Kelly, two star Fred Astaire; two are directed by Vincente Minnelli, two by Stanley Donen. All five are made by MGM personnel—although only three were made by MGM. With the disintegration of Mount Hollywood's premier Art School after 1953, other studios picked up the pieces of scattered MGM talent. The later films are as much about that scattering as anything else.

It is not now fashionable to admire the film that inspired the others. Alan

Jay Lerner's script for *An American in Paris*, which seems loose and meandering, isn't funny; the ballet, which makes little sense in whatever plot the film has, seems pretentious. *An American in Paris* committed the mortal sin for a musical—it won the Academy Award for best picture, the first musical in fifteen years (since MGM's *The Great Ziegfeld*) to do so. For both *auteur* admirers of Minnelli and genre admirers of musicals, the film strains to look art school rather than Hollywood musical.[1]

The ballet, rather than bearing a literal relationship to the plot, is a metaphoric and atmospheric recapitulation of it, as if the events and locations of the film return in visual variation. The plot of *An American in Paris* is itself less a story than a tone poem, an atmosphere and ambience based on the idea of Paris in the American imagination, and the ballet finale is a tone poem within the tone poem. The film travels to the Paris of the Impressionists not to escape from a Hollywood musical but to reveal a broad continuity between Hollywood and Paris, movies and paintings, European schools of art and Mount Hollywood Art School. No other American composer was as right to build this bridge as George Gershwin, who not only wrote the tone poem of the film's title but popular songs, Broadway shows, Hollywood scores, operas, and concerti. This film *must* combine the music of Gershwin, the eye of Minnelli, and the performance of Kelly. Without any one of them, the film would lose its meaning.

The musical numbers, not the plot, carry that meaning. Number for number, no filmusical can rival *An American in Paris* for musical integrity, visual style, and performance energy.[2] Every number relates thematically to the internationalism of musical entertainment or the projecting of internal psychology as pictorial representation. The first number introduces audiences to both themes as well as to newcomer Leslie Caron. Built on "Embraceable You," the number informs us *who* Caron is—she is a French dancer. She doesn't sing, but her dancing is enough to project all the personality she needs. More than enough, for her personality, like the color and musical style of the number, is elusive, constantly changing, the image of an Everywoman ideal for every man.

Like a movie, she is a projection, and we meet her as a projection. While we hear descriptions of her contradictory qualities, we see them projected in a movie mirror. Minnelli and Irene Sharaff become window decorators, draping this MGM window in shifting colors and costumes to match the shifting musical color of the orchestrations. When Lise is vivacious, she dances eight bars of "Embraceable You" as a Charleston—in a white dress, surrounded by blazing red decor, to a brassy jazz beat. When she is studious, she dances eight bars as a minuet—in black tights, surrounded by Renaissance amber decor, performing a split while reading a book, accompanied by baroque woodwinds. Musical coloring, visual coloring, and human coloring become synonymous. What unknown performer ever made a more spectacular debut than Caron in this musical window of color?

The musical-visual imagining occurs literally inside a movie frame, dramatically inside a café mirror's frame, and figuratively as a projection in the minds of those staring at the frame. The projection is shared by a French storyteller, the professional entertainer Henri Borel (Georges Guetary), and his American audience, specifically Adam Cook (Oscar Levant). The projection is framed—and the frame (both of the mirror and the shot) remains constant with every change of color, mood, and music within it. Movies, like paintings, represent a framing, a visual composing, of objects that exist in physical space but mirror the imagination. Music, like painting,

Framings in *An American in Paris*: Lise dances solo in a mirror and with Kelly in a Manet market.

speaks to the imagination—but through the ear. There is a parallel between amber and an oboe, red and a trumpet. All convert an abstract idea—an emotion, a desire, an aspiration—into a physical manifestation. There is no difference between Minnelli's translation of these emotions into frames, between Gershwin's translation of them into songs, and between an Impressionist painter's translation of them into canvases. Frames, colors, musical sound, and dancing performance are simultaneous means to the same end.

In *An American in Paris*, that end is named Lise—and the film's end is in its beginning. What begins as dancing in a mirrored frame will end as dancing in painted frames; what begins as an introduction to an abstract embodiment of love will end as a search for that love. Henri's frame has unknowingly introduced Lise to a friend of the American who will take her away from him. Jerry Mulligan (Kelly) will put her into another frame when he paints her portrait. His moral problem will be what to do with her as a living person, since, unlike the imaginings called movies and paintings, human beings cannot be shared. Because Kelly has climbed from his *Pal Joey* and *For Me and My Gal* gutter, Jerry cannot simply steal her from Henri, who protected her from the Nazis after the death of her parents in the Resistance. Nor can Lise ungratefully reject Henri's gift of life. The moral problem can only be solved when the older man, learning of their love, gives her to Jerry—in a final sharing of a vision.

Adam, the friend between the two rivals, does nothing in the sequence— or film—but quip: a thin disguise for Oscar Levant himself, who built a career on quips. A Jewish intellectual neurotic who alternated between MGM, early TV talk shows where you could say anything, and the loony bin when he said too much, Levant's flippant comments on live television became cultural legends: his fear of *The Loretta Young Show*'s effect on his diabetes; his approval of Marilyn Monroe's marriage to the Jewish Arthur Miller: "Well, she's already got two sets of dishes." The sign of Levant's neurosis is his perpetual cigarette, and Adam Cook manages to smoke three at once in this film, one of which drowns in a cup of coffee. Adam is the traditional comic of musical comedy in an unfamiliar guise—not as comic performer but as cultural oddball, less clown than the spirit of melancholy.[3] The instrument at which Levant excelled—other than his mouth—was the piano. A freeloader in the Gershwin circle, Levant's breathtaking tempi remain superb interpretations of Gershwin's piano music. With Levant, Arthur Freed recycled José Iturbi in a more zany, more American form.

After the projected window of "Embraceable You" come seven more visual-musical projections—five for Kelly, with various companions, and two specialty numbers, one for each buddy. "By Strauss," "I Got Rhythm," and "'S Wonderful" bring Kelly's song and dance to public spaces where he invigorates the world around him. While "By Strauss" descends from the musical style of an older generation, "I Got Rhythm" is a Kelly number

"By Strauss" and "I Got Rhythm." After boys in the foreground observe Kelly's dance with the old woman, she observes Kelly's songplay with them.

with and for kids. While "By Strauss" alludes to European culture, "I Got Rhythm" refers to American movies—from Charlie Chaplin to Hopalong Cassidy. Linking the two numbers is the delicately aged flower seller (Mary Young) with whom Kelly dances "By Strauss" and who becomes a focal observer in "I Got Rhythm," performed in front of her flower stall. Both the café setting of "Strauss" and the flower-stall setting of "Rhythm" return in the ballet—transmuted into a Lautrec café and Manet flowers. The two numbers proclaim the ability of Kelly, of American music, and of American musicals to span generations and cultures—linking things past and passing, American or European, in common enjoyment of cinematic song and dance.

"Tra-la-la" is an indoor duet for a singing and dancing Kelly, accompanied by pal Levant at the piano. This obscure Gershwin song, a parody of love lyrics reduced to an inarticulate la-la-la, expresses Kelly's inarticulate joy after meeting Lise. That joy, punctured by Levant's parodic toying with the tune, transforms the tiny space of Levant's garret into an indoor wonderland. Kelly converts the architecture that confines him—the door jambs, the ceiling, the bulky piano—into his partners, dancing around, among, under, and above them, overwhelming the space with his performance energy and transforming it into another mirror: a projection of his happiness. "'S Wonderful" is an outdoor duet for Kelly and pal Guetary, filling the streets of Paris with their common joy, proclaiming the swonderfulness of their loves. They don't know that they love the same swonderful Lise. The number is not only another metaphoric mirror; it strolls past a street corner where hangs an actual mirror.

"Our Love Is Here to Stay" is Kelly's romantic duet with Caron, out of the world but still in it, beside a backlot Seine on a backlit night, bathed in the ink of Impressionist darkness and golden reflections off the MGM water. As opposed to Fred&Ginger, who reveal their love to each other by dancing, this duet is more a revelation for the audience than the dancers, a projection of their love for us. Their love *is* here to stay; the only question is how will that eternal love overcome the external barriers of history and culture—the war, the death of her parents, her gratitude to the benefactor who is Kelly's friend, and his being an American in Paris, conscious both of American values and Parisian mores.

The two specialty numbers draw a connection between concert music, stage entertainment, and movies. Levant's specialty is his personal dream ballet—a dream concert of Gershwin's *Concerto in F.* Levant turns out to be the only occupant of his fantasy concert hall—piano soloist as well as conductor, tympanist, the entire string section, and the audience screaming "bravo." If the dream suggests the camera tricks of Buster Keaton's *The Playhouse*, in which Buster plays every role on both sides of the footlights, it also demonstrates Minnelli's projection of internal psychology into mirrors of color with looming shadows against an amber ground. At the conclusion of this dream, Levant toasts this projection of success by pulling an iced bottle from his wine bucket—of Coca-Cola. Everything, including his own musical gifts, is a putdown for Levant, the eternal freeloader.

Georges Guetary's "I'll Build a Stairway to Paradise" moves from a fantasy concert hall to an actual music hall. Originally performed in the *George White Scandals of 1922*, both the song and its production style evoke a tradition that links America and Paris, stage and screen, Minnelli and Freed. Guetary sings and dances on and with a staircase, whose steps illuminate on cue as he ascends or descends them, surrounded by showgirls in Ziegfeld plumage as human candelabra. The number evokes the Follies, whether Bergère or Ziegfeld, as well as the three MGM Ziegfeld movies. Though the Ziegfelds, George Whites, and George Gershwins may be gone, their tradition continues in the living art that brings them back to entertainment life—the movies. Minnelli had directed the posthumous 1936 edition of the *Ziegfeld Follies* on Broadway as well as several sequences of Freed's 1946 tribute, *The Ziegfeld Follies*; both Minnelli and Freed, like Levant, had been members of the Gershwin circle. Their common labor of love in *An American in Paris* is nowhere clearer than in the retrospective "Stairway to Paradise."

If the specialty numbers connect concert hall, variety show, and movies, the dream ballet connects paintings, musicals, and movies. It was not the first dream ballet in a film to be sure. Although Freed and Minnelli had tried one with Astaire and Irene Sharaff costumes in *Yolanda and the Thief*, its brilliant translation of psychology into color and movement lacked both musical and visual meaning. The score for Astaire's dance had no particular connection to his dream, his character, or the film; its dreamlike settings looked more like French surrealism of the 1920s than South America of the 1940s. *Yolanda*'s ballet also came too early, midway through the film, like the dream ballet that concludes act one of a Richard Rodgers show.

More like Kelly's "Slaughter on Tenth Avenue" in Freed's *Words and Music*, the *American in Paris* ballet becomes its big finish, in which both musical and visual style share a meaning with the entire film. Although the film is set in a modern Paris, pictured by projecting celluloid on a screen, it is the same Paris so often pictured in oil on canvas. The film that began as motion pictures of Paris landmarks (the Eiffel Tower, the Place de la Concorde) concludes as motion within Impressionist renderings of similar landmarks. The music for those motion pictures had been written by Gershwin, the American who transcended the boundaries between Europe and America, theater and movies, concert hall and music hall. The title of his tone poem is also the title of the movie and its dream ballet.

Kelly searches furtively for an elusive love—symbolized by an intensely red rose. Like the rose, and like Lise in "Embraceable You," the beloved is a projection of the dancer's desire. Only the rose can give color to his imaginative world, for only with the beloved can he dance in a world of Impressionist color. Without her, his world is a black-and-white Kansas, a torn charcoal sketch. The film's dissolving spaces mirror the elusiveness of the beloved—there in his arms, then gone—like the spaces surrounding him. Minnelli's liquid transitions between individual Impressionist settings add cinema's time to painting's space. Shifting light, cinematic dissolves, and, at one point, twirling mirrors create a space that exists nowhere in the physical world, mirroring only the mental world of the imagination.

As he searches for his beloved in this labyrinth, Kelly is tempted by lures that parallel temptations in the film's plot. A quartet of female Furies—two in red, two in white—lure him from his quest, much as Milo (Nina Foch) lures Jerry with her money, the temptation that turns artists into gigolos. Entertainers who make musical movies are as aware of this lure as painters. A parallel quartet of soldier buddies on the prowl lures Kelly with the quest for light amusement, but he deserts them when he catches sight of the beloved. At the end of the ballet, he feels he has lost her forever—just as Jerry feels he has lost Lise. He stands alone, holding only the symbolic rose of his longing, in the black-and-white sketch that began his reverie.

It is remarkable how quickly the film ends after the ballet, without a word of dialogue. Minnelli and Lerner cunningly solve the film's narrative problem *before* the ballet. A brilliant Minnelli camera manuever, following a trail of cigarette smoke to a thoughtfully smoking face, reveals Henri has overheard Jerry's farewell to Lise. This camera revelation, the entire ballet, and the final reunion of Jerry and Lise conclude the film with twenty consecutive minutes of pure visual imagery (like paintings) and music (like musicals). Henri merely need open a taxi door, permitting Lise's flight up a mountain of steps toward the racing Jerry. The painter finally grasps his rose.

The ballet of *An American in Paris*, all sixteen minutes and thirty-seven seconds of it, is the culmination of all the frames, mirrors, and psychological projections that came before, its ultimate representation of picturing the imagination. The ballet, which won the film its Oscar, also set the industry standard: no self-respecting musical could do without one.[4] In *There's No Business Like Show Business*, Donald O'Connor dreams Greek statues to dancing life. In *Daddy Long Legs* (1955), Caron dreams herself and Astaire into an exotic travelogue all over the globe. The dream ballet even dives to the bottom of Esther Williams's pool in *Jupiter's Darling* (1955), where Greek male statues bubble to erotic life. None of them equals the dream ballet of *An American in Paris* in its conceptual relationship to the whole film, its audacity, its demonstration of aggregate talent, and its exercise of Minnelli's eye. That eye not only saw dancing within paintings but dancing through and among paintings in which the paintings themselves dance.

For Freed, Kelly, and Minnelli, the ballet was an American movie renewal of the spirit that produced the paintings and the Gershwin music in the first place. If Gershwin was an American who went to Paris, so did a whole generation of American soldiers. Jerry Mulligan, who came with them, stayed in Paris to paint. The film's dream ballet celebrates a mythic marriage of America and Paris, musicals and paintings. If American soldiers could renew a spent Europe, Gene Kelly and Arthur Freed could renew its traditions by making Impressionist painting into movie dance. The old France of Henri Borel steps aside so the American Jerry Mulligan can marry the young France of Lise. In the final image of the film, large projected letters remind us of a fact we have forgotten: "Made Entirely in Hollywood, U.S.A." *An American in Paris* is a postwar covenant of faith between America and Europe, Hollywood and Paris.

Singin' in the Rain is Hollywood U.S.A. without the Paris drag—much quieter Mount Hollywood Art School, with a single sign rather than a whole ballet. This musical parody merely placed second in the 1982 *Sight and Sound* poll of the best films of all time—a ranking inconceivable in 1952, the year both of the film and the first *Sight and Sound* poll. *Singin' in the Rain* is movieland variation on the art and images of Paris: Hollywood is to Paris as movies are to paintings as Arthur Freed and Nacio Herb Brown are to George and Ira Gershwin. It is prose rather than poetry, images as material processes rather than psychological mirrors, representations as musical performances rather than mental projections. If *An American in Paris* traces the influence of Paris on the art and music of the twentieth century, *Singin' in the Rain* traces the history of MGM musicals.

Set in Hollywood just before and after *The Jazz Singer* of 1927, *Singin' in* the Rain is as much about the coming of musicals to MGM as the conversion of Hollywood to sound. Writers Betty Comden and Adolph Green conjured the coming of sound from the Freed-Brown songs, which authentically evoke both a historical period and its entertainment revolution. Four songs come from MGM's first two musicals, *Broadway Melody* and *The Hollywood Revue of 1929*: "You Were Meant for Me," "Broadway Melody," "The Wedding of the Painted Doll," and "Singin' in the Rain." Every other song, with two exceptions, comes from MGM musicals through the 1930s—"You Are My Lucky Star" and "I've Got a Feelin' You're Foolin'" from *Broadway Melody of 1936*, "Good Mornin'" from *Babes in Arms*, "Would You?" from *San Francisco*. Although "Make 'Em Laugh," Donald O'Connor's specialty number, is a new song, its comic idea comes from "I Love a Mystery" in *Something in the Wind* (1947), its melody and lyrics from Porter's "Be a Clown" in *The Pirate*.[5] Only "Moses Supposes His Toeses Are Roses," written not by Freed and Brown but Comden, Green, and Roger Edens, lacks an MGM predecessor.

Even the choreographic conceptions come from earlier musicals at MGM and elsewhere. Kelly's rain dance is MGM's third. A chorus dances in stage puddles, theatrical lightning, and indoor rain in *The Hollywood Revue of 1929*, while Eleanor Powell and George Murphy dance in park puddles and apparently outdoor rain when "Feeling Like a Million" in *Broadway Melody of 1938*. Maurice Chevalier also danced in and to "The Rhythm of the Rain" in Paramount's 1935 *Folies Bergère*. "Beautiful Girl," originally from MGM's 1932 *Going Hollywood*, suggests both Busby Berkeley, with its montage of kaleidoscopic patterns, and the fashion shows of *Roberta* and *Cover Girl*. "You Were Meant for Me" evokes "Our Love Is Here to Stay," as admittedly electric soundstage light replaces soundstage electricity disguised as moonlight on the Seine.

The "Broadway Melody" ballet capsulizes MGM's entire *Broadway Melody* series in twelve minutes and fifty-seven seconds—built on the "Broadway Melody" refrain of 1929 and the "Broadway Rhythm" vamp of 1936, designed as Expressionist twinkling lights and Art Deco geometrics that recall the decor of previous editions of *Broadway Melody*. Not as deeply psychological as the *American in Paris* ballet, as elusive, evanescent, and analytical of space, light, and color, this later ballet presents a musical myth of Sisyphus. Kelly plays a yokel from the country (like Eleanor Powell in the 1936 *Broadway Melody*) who's "gotta dance" (just as Powell was *Born to Dance*). Pounding on office doors, making the rounds, rising in show biz from sleazy clubs to the glittering Follies, he dances his way to the top of Mount Hollywood-Broadway. Once up there, he finds it a lonely place. The woman of his dreams is a gangster's moll who prefers material tokens to ethereal love. In the end, the dancer remains alone until the cycle begins anew (as it does at the end of *On the Town*); another yokel from the country reminds him that he's "gotta dance." His life

Culmination of the Broadway Melody series—tuxedoes and twinkling Art Deco lights: *Broadway Melody*, *Singin' in the Rain*, (*below*) *Broadway Melody of 1938*

is that dance. And, as opposed to the Fox musicals, that dance is enough.

If the ballet concludes the entire *Broadway Melody* series, it also culminates the film's self-examination of movies. One reason *Singin' in the Rain* could never be interesting as a stage musical (and wasn't) is that it is so much about the practices and procedures of filmmaking. The ballet begins in a studio projection room where Don Lockwood (Kelly) describes for his studio boss, R. F. (Millard Mitchell), the final number of *The Dancing Cavalier*. The blank screen behind him becomes a projection of Don's verbal narration. But no verbal narration could possibly achieve the spatio-temporal transitions and narrative ellipses of this visual projection. This story could not be told without moving images.

The dancer's rise to the top requires just three shots, which record an identical musical passage, whose scoring, staging, and decor become progressively more genteel. Only movies convey temporal processes with three consecutive pieces of time, each an increasingly elaborate variation on the same musical-visual theme. When the dancer spots the woman of his dreams (Cyd Charisse), the crowded casino dissolves into thin air so the pair can dance in a placeless void of pure emotion. Only movies dissolve people and places into thin air, for only movies use a technique named dissolve. Their *pas de deux* is actually a trio—for two human dancers and a fluttering white scarf, twenty-five feet long, soaring above them, trailing behind, wrapped around, a physical extension of their emotion. Only movies can animate a gigantic cloth with some combination of wind and string that is both mechanical trick and pure magic. Only movies can identify a woman's companion by his merely tossing a coin in the air—that most familiar icon of movie gangsters. Only movies can reveal a moral choice by thrusting a bracelet into the frame under the dancer's nose, whose aroma leads her to toss the same kind of coin. Finally, only movies can construct a concrete image in which a dancer soars above the receding Broadway lights below him, to dwarf them with his immensity. The abstract idea cannot take spatio-temporal form without the optical printer.

The virtuoso scarf in *Singin' in the Rain*

No wonder R. F. responds to Lockwood's "description" with a climactic joke that punctures the ballet as a verbal possibility: "Sounds great, but I can't quite visualize it." The ballet is unimaginable as descriptive sound and unvisualizable without movies. The movie has already visualized it for us.

The same battle between musical visualization and verbal description opens the film. At Grauman's Chinese Theatre, the Saint Peter's of 1927 Hollywood, the newest Don Lockwood-Lina Lamont silent epic premieres for its public. A gossip columnist asks Don and Lina to explain the secret of their success to their fans, listening at home to the radio. What those radio listeners hear is very different from what we moviegoers see. Although we see the smiles of both Don and Lina, only Don speaks. While his words intone "Dignity, Always Dignity," the images depict anything but dignity. He speaks of his training at the conservatory and we see him hoofing in a saloon for pennies with Cosmo Brown (Donald O'Connor)—just as Kelly and his brother actually hoofed in Pittsburgh saloons for pennies as kids. He speaks of his early experience in the Theatah, and we see Don and Cosmo in cheap vaudeville, socking across "Fit as a Fiddle and Ready for Love" with gimmick fiddles and fiddle gimmicks. He speaks of dignified acting roles and we see a faceless extra in dangerous and dirty stunts. He speaks of Lina's kind encouragement and we see hate at first sight. Don Lockwood's "rise to the top" is a parody of the Broadway Melody ballet, the same myth, now stripped of its melody by movie images.

Every number in *Singin' in the Rain* restates this paradox of film images and soundtracks: they can either reveal or conceal, work together or at odds. Whenever Lina Lamont "sings" in the frame, the image conceals a lie. Though Lina (Jean Hagen) appears to be singing, her voice really belongs to Kathy Selden (Debbie Reynolds). The film deconstructs Lina's illusion twice. In "Would You?" we observe the step-by-step material process of prerecording a song, dubbing it to another's lip movements, and then seeing it as an illusion of a whole performance on the screen. Ironically, this apparent confession conceals an unrecognized lie: Debbie herself is merely moving her lips to the fuller voice of Betty Royce.[6] Even Kathy Selden is dubbed for this number; Lina Lamont is double dubbed.

Exposing its own technique: lip-synching "Would You?"

In the reprise of "Singin' in the Rain," which returns full circle to Grauman's Chinese, we observe the final destruction of an illusion when Cosmo and R. F. raise the curtain to reveal Kathy Selden's singing behind Lina Lamont's mime. The audience who receives only the words (as on radio) or only the images (as in silent movies) can never be sure about what has been withheld. While the voices of natural human beings are inseparable from their faces, the movies permit exactly this divorce. No wonder this film is about that period when silent movies married radio. And no wonder this film is about a silent movie actress who can mime the movements of speech but cannot talk.

The film's most exuberant numbers just as carefully construct the illusion that the Lina Lamont numbers destroy. "Good Mornin'," "Moses Supposes," and "Make 'Em Laugh" overwhelm indoor space with improvisational dance play, the familiar Kelly method of *bricolage* in which everything on a set becomes a spontaneous dance partner or human extension. "Singin' in the Rain" overwhelms outdoor nature itself with its art. In these four numbers, we get picture and sound, dancing and singing, that have all been generated by Gene, Donald, and Debbie. Those who produce the sounds also produce the steps. But how can Donald O'Connor actually sing while he climbs up or crashes through the *trompe l'oeil* walls? Are those taps we hear on the wet pavement? How do you make tap sounds with loafers in water puddles?

The fact is that these performers don't (and can't) make any of the sounds at the same time that they appear to be making them. "Make 'Em Laugh" is as much *trompe l'oreille* as *trompe l'oeil*. The rain of "Singin' in the Rain" is no more real than the theatrical rain of *The Hollywood Revue of 1929* and the outdoor street no more real than the soundstage sunset of "You Were Meant for Me." It is artificial rain on an indoor set whose sounds have been separately recorded, before and after filming. That the dance appears to take place in nature and that the sounds appear to have been produced at the same time are mere appearances.

Why then is the appearance of Cosmo, Kathy, and Don as performers superior in this film to the appearance of Lina Lamont if all are mere appearances? The answer in *Singin' in the Rain* is that, although all film stars are dependent on the same technology, Cosmo, Kathy, and Don are more aware of and more responsible for the transcribing of their appearances. As whole performers, singer-dancer-actors, they are capable of participating in both visual and vocal transcription, capable of both radio and silent films. The transcriptions that reveal their performance wholeness merely disguise Lina's inadequacy. If *Singin' in the Rain* is about the magic of cinema, it is also about the magic of performance. In a filmusical, only a whole performer is a whole human being.[7] That wholeness is what *The Jazz Singer* revealed about Al Jolson in the first place.

The controlling myth in *Singin' in the Rain* is performance itself.

Performance is a spiritual emanation, carried by the technology of movies, marrying spirit to appearance, as it marries body to voice. The silent Lockwood-Lamont swashbuckling films are artful lies: set in the class-bound Europe of a romantic past that never was, they flee the democratic America of the present.[8] But musicals are performance truths: not escapes from modern America but extensions and expressions of it. The spirit of America resides in its song and dance—the union of physical movement, vocal expression, and emotional energy within the cultural space that movies project. The film's moral journey, like its musical numbers, moves from public lie to performance myth, from a false portrait of love between Don and Lina to a true portrait of love between Don and Kathy, from surface deception offered as truth to a surface image that contains a truth. The final image of the film is both a still billboard and a motion picture frame, an advertisement for a film called *Singin' in the Rain* starring Don Lockwood and Kathy Selden and the final image of a film called *Singin' in the Rain* starring Gene Kelly and Debbie Reynolds.

The Comden and Green script of *Singin' in the Rain* manipulates the same paradox as its numbers—the unstable gap between surface and spirit, deception and truth in movies. The lie of Lina Lamont—who looks like an angel and talks like a witch—is merely the film's most monstrous comic lie. Don Lockwood pretends to love Lina because the fan magazines and the studio press agents want it that way. Kathy Selden pretends she doesn't like movies when she has seen every Lockwood-Lamont opus and wants to break into movies herself. What else would she be doing in Hollywood? They not only pretend to these truths but know they are pretending— which is a form of truth. Performers must separate the public lies necessary for every popular artist from the lying to yourself that makes you "small time in the heart." The final unmasking of Lina's voice is also Don's public confession of the public lies he told to open the film.

While song and dance reveal the spiritual in the material, money reveals only the material. In the ballet, Cyd Charisse is seduced by flipping coins and jewel bracelets. Lina is seduced by the terms of her printed contract. She doesn't know the difference between what she thinks and what fan magazines say she thinks, between genuine and counterfeit feelings, genuine and counterfeit performance. She knows about money: "I have more money than Calvin Coolidge—put t'gither." And she knows about power: "I can syuuue youuuu for the entire styuuuudio," she carefully enunciates to R. F. Although she has learned to mimic proper diction she can never learn to mimic a whole human being, inside or out. In this Hollywood hymn to itself, studios care not about money or power but human performance, fully aware of their responsibilities as manipulators of deceptions—if not fully in control of the most regal deceivers. R. F., whose initials suggest so many Hollywood monsters (including L. B. at this very styuuuudio), is a kindly father figure, easily bullied by his willful children. The beautiful blonde is the Wicked Witch of this West. The only bucket necessary to dissolve her image is the raising of a curtain to expose the screen as a mere screen. This Mount Hollywood Art School is so confident of its control over screened lies and screen truths that it can hang a sign on a set to advertise it.

Within only a year the confidence was gone and the screen had sprung a leak. An air of gloom and doom hangs over *The Band Wagon*—which would account for its lesser popularity. While in *Singin' in the Rain* Mount Hollywood throws open the art school doors, *The Band Wagon* nails them shut, barricading itself against attack, preserving what it can. In *The Band Wagon*, a cycle, a studio, a style, and an entertainment idea are at the end of the line. What exactly happened in a year?

Television was not the only reason people either stayed home or went elsewhere. The American demographic shift to the suburbs had begun, with its mortgage indebtedness for new homes and credit indebtedness for new cars and home appliances. The American recording industry introduced the longplaying record and the electronics industry introduced high-fidelity components to play them. Professional sports, allied with television, expanded and boomed. So did travel and recreation when families wanted to escape television. The consequence was a 50 percent drop in film revenues and 75 percent loss of the film audience between 1948 and 1952. When industries lose revenues they cut costs.

This cutting could only shred the MGM musical, so dependent on the highest standards of technical expertise and production excellence. Although Freed budgets had quadrupled from the first barnyard musicals, which cost about $750,000 to *An American in Paris*, which cost nearly $3 million, his profits kept pace. For fifteen years the usual Freed musical returned 250 percent of its cost. When MGM profits in fiscal 1948–49 fell to less than $1 million, Freed films returned $14 million,[9] underwriting $13 million of MGM duds. By 1953, even the independent Freed unit was not exempt from three MGM policy decisions: massive cutbacks of employees, both talent and technicians; abandoning Technicolor for Eastmancolor; adopting CinemaScope and stereo to compete with the tiny television tube. To convince jittery stockholders that Loews Inc. wasn't kidding, Nicholas Schenck, chairman of the board, forced L. B. Mayer, both the symbol and the reality of the old MGM, out of the company that bore his name. Mayer went out the door just as *Singin' in the Rain* went into production.

Although Freed and Minnelli kept their jobs at MGM, the writing was on the wall. To eliminate technicians meant to eliminate the care and detail on which MGM musicals were built. The careful color system of Jeffrey Cordova's apartment in *The Band Wagon*, for example—the blue hall, red library, green sitting room, and gold parlor—was not simply a lovely way to decorate department-store windows but a communicative way to clarify simultaneous action in different rooms. For Kelly to dance in a world of

Impressionist paintings did not simply mean thinking of some paintings and slapping some paint on a wall. It meant building paintings to enormous three-dimensional sizes and specifications that would permit the movement of people and camera within them. Astaire's famous trick numbers, like dancing on the walls and ceiling of *Royal Wedding*, meant not simply conceiving an Ariel idea, but designing the space and executing the plan so the visual magic would never give its trick away.[10] *The Band Wagon*, which cost about $1 million less than *An American in Paris* and $500,000 less than *Singin' in the Rain*, already shows subtle effects of economies. There is no Astaire trick number in the film, which saves its visual ammunition for a final barrage of musical numbers.

The loss of Technicolor could only bring tears to the eye of a Minnelli. Early Eastmancolor—with cheaper dyes, quicker laboratory procedures, and less demanding shooting requirements—lost in look what it saved in cost. Minnelli knew that painters depended on the brilliance of the oils in their palettes. Like oleomargarine, the wartime necessity that became a postwar economy, and frozen TV dinners, which entered American life at the same time for the same reason, Eastmancolor seemed an easy and economical substitute for the real thing. CinemaScope, on the other hand, seemed not a pale imitation but a barbarous monstrosity. Where, in the history of Western representation, could one find a huge frame of such proportions? The only familiar representational artifacts that resembled the CinemaScope frame's five-to-two shape were the triptych and the dollar bill. Directors less influenced by modern painting came to terms with CinemaScope quickly—like Donen, who recognized the dollar, and Cukor, who recognized the triptych. To see *Brigadoon*, Minnelli's musical after *The Band Wagon*, is to observe the ravages of 1953: shot in pale Eastmancolor and flat CinemaScope; stuck in ponderous studio sets claiming to be the Scottish highlands; adapted from a presold, bankable Broadway hit.

If Comden and Green found one historical context for a catalog of Freed-Brown songs in *Singin' in the Rain*, they found another historical context for a catalog of Howard Dietz-Arthur Schwartz songs in *The Band Wagon*: not the rise of the MGM musical, like *Singin' in the Rain*, but the fall of the MGM musical as mirrored in the fall of Fred Astaire. *The Band Wagon* was the title of the 1931 Fred Astaire show that marked the end of his previous career—the last of his Broadway shows with sister Adele, his last big hit on Broadway. While an earlier Astaire cycle ended with that *Band Wagon*, the next Astaire cycle ends with this *Band Wagon*—and with it the whole Freed cycle of original MGM Technicolor musicals. The songs of that 1931 *Band Wagon* were written by Dietz and Schwartz, just as the songs of the early MGM musicals were written by Freed and Brown. For Comden and Green, *The Band Wagon* and *Singin' in the Rain* were historical bookends—an older Astaire instead of Kelly, an older Broadway entertainment at an end rather than a young Hollywood one at a beginning.

The opening image of *The Band Wagon* under the credits is a top hat and cane—the same as under the credits of the 1935 *Top Hat*. The icons, which immediately announce Astaire, are under glass—in the window of an auction house. Although the window suggests other Minnelli frames, like the café mirror in *An American in Paris*, this frame is motionless, and the lifeless artifacts float unattached to their familiar bearer. The window frame is a display case for relics and the auction house is both a museum and mausoleum of dead artifacts. The hat and cane are of so little use to Astaire (in this film named Tony Hunter) that he is selling them for whatever he can get—suggesting the march of economic history in the sale of formerly valuable assets, like the jewelry of deposed princes. The auction also suggests contemporary Hollywood history, for the 1953 studios had themselves begun to sell off their assets and artifacts. In *The Band Wagon*, no one wants these relics, not even for fifty cents. Tony Hunter, like his icons, is a useless relic—a star of ten or twelve years ago, the Astaire era at RKO, who isn't worth half a 1953 dollar.

The train that carries Tony Hunter out of the Hollywood where he is a relic also carries him back, full circle, to the Broadway where Astaire began. But when he arrives there, he finds little welcome. His song, "By Myself," as he strides beside the train, Minnelli's camera striding beside him, is a powerful statement of the singularity that makes Astaire Astaire— both his loneness and loneliness. That he can sing this song, with this precision, synchronized so carefully to his movement, which is neither dancing nor walking but something between, shows that he's still in a class by himself. But Astaire has grown old (fifty-five to be exact), alone at the end of an entertainment road with no possible successor.

Broadway in 1953 doesn't hold much more hope than Hollywood. If contemporary Hollywood has abandoned its worthless relics, contemporary Broadway has embraced Jeffrey Cordova—director, producer, and star as well as pretentious, egotistical ham. In a neat historical irony, the windbag Cordova is played by that "smarmy British wimp" of the 1930 *Monte Carlo*, Jack Buchanan, who fell on his face at Paramount but picked himself up very nicely in British filmusicals with Elsie Randolph. Like Astaire, Buchanan is an old song-and-dance man. As a matter of ironic fact, Astaire did not introduce his song of singularity, "By Myself," in the 1931 *Band Wagon*. Jack Buchanan did—in Dietz and Schwartz's 1937 revue, *Between the Devil*. *The Band Wagon* is a musical variation on Chaplin's *Limelight*, made just a year earlier. Like Chaplin and Keaton, Buchanan and Astaire participate in a single entertainment tradition that bridges the Atlantic.

In *The Band Wagon*, Jack Buchanan's Cordova stands as Astaire's opposite— the hot theatrical item, very much in tune with today. Embodying the arty entertainment aspirations of both coasts, he could either be a parody of Dore Schary, who had replaced L. B. Mayer at MGM, or Broadway's Rodgers and Hammerstein. Cordova not only plays the devil in a musicalized

Faust; he is also the Mephistopheles who tempts snappy showmen and happy hoofers into the inferno of high art. Like Schary (who would follow Mayer out the MGM door in 1956), Cordova produces shows with messages and meaning. As the Hollywood wits quipped about Schary's disastrous reign at MGM, "He sold his studio for a pot of message." Like Rodgers and Hammerstein, Cordova wants to turn the musical show into a psychological music drama of human and social significance. Against all this arty ammunition, Astaire-Hunter can only stammer that he's just a hoofer who's entertained millions. Although Hunter eventually wins this battle, the film fears that the war is over: the history of cultural taste is on Cordova's side. Tony Hunter *is* an anachronism in 1953.

Like all Freed musicals and all Astaire musicals, *The Band Wagon* believes that high and low, art and entertainment, elite and popular aspirations meet in the American musical. The Impressionist originals in Tony's hotel room, which eventually finance his snappier vision of the show, draw not only a connection to *An American in Paris* but to painters, like Degas, who found art in entertainers. The ultimate hymn to this belief is the new Dietz and Schwartz song for the film, "That's Entertainment," which is to filmusicals what Berlin's "There's No Business Like Show Business" is to the stage.[11] Whether a hot plot teeming with sex, a gay divorcée after her ex, or *Oedipus Rex*, whether a romantic swain after a queen or "some Shakespearean scene (where a ghost and a prince meet and everything ends in mincemeat)," it's all one world of American entertainment. "Hip Hooray, the American way." Dietz's lyrics echo Mickey's theorem in *Strike Up the Band*. What's American? Exactly this kind of movie musical from Mount Hollywood Art School.

Though the number proclaims its belief, the film is less sure of achieving it. It is easy to fall off the wire into the abyss between high seriousness and low fun. Jeffrey Cordova falls off even as he formulates the desire to walk it: "There is no difference between Bill Shakespeare's immortal words and Bill Robinson's immortal feet." Reductive, pat, and phony,

An anthem of belief: Buchanan, Astaire, Fabray, and Levant sing "That's Entertainment."

even his manager reminds him that this sudden inspiration already came to him a week ago in a speech at Princeton. Fred Astaire as Tony Hunter (who isn't invited to speak at Princeton) doesn't reduce the idea to pat phrases because he carries it within him and it comes out in every move he makes. Jeffrey Cordova articulates it better when he casually hoofs up the same stairs he descended during his performance as Oedipus. He doesn't talk the idea but, like Astaire, he dances it. Jeffrey doesn't see any better than Oedipus.

All the film's numbers before the stage performance of "The Band Wagon" are sentimental journeys into Astaire's own past. As he strolls along 42nd Street, the title of the most famous filmusical about putting on a show, he notices the rundown New Amsterdam Theatre—the original home of Ziegfeld's Follies and the 1931 home of Astaire's *Band Wagon*. Like the street itself, the New Amsterdam has become old and shabby. The dance to "A Shine on Your Shoes" in an amusement arcade applies some polish. Movies themselves were born in these very arcades at the turn of the century. Astaire has not only returned to his Broadway roots, but the movies have returned to their amusement roots as electric entertainment machines. Astaire's partner in the number—other than assorted machines of the arcade—is a black shoeshine man (LeRoy Daniels). As in "Bojangles of Harlem" and "Slap That Bass," Astaire draws an explicit connection between black and white song and dance. For its climax, Astaire's shined shoes kick a Mystery Machine to electric life, exactly as his very first kiddie act with Adele climaxed in a blaze of electric light.

"Dancing in the Dark," the hit ballad of the 1931 *Band Wagon*, provides the occasion for Astaire's most beautiful duet since leaving Ginger at RKO. Like "Isn't It a Lovely Day" of *Top Hat*, the dance finds a private stage in a public park. Astaire and Cyd Charisse stroll through a crowd of dancers to seek their own space, moving in rhythm even as they walk, dancing even before the dance begins. Like "Night and Day" of *The Gay Divorcée* and

Return to Fred&Ginger:
Astaire and Cyd Charisse
"Dancing in the Dark"

"They All Laughed" of *Shall We Dance?*, the dance is a conversion, turning a former enemy into a partner, merely because of the way they dance together. Like "Hard to Handle" of *Roberta*, the dance is a conversation, revealing each to the other more articulately than words. If her ballet seems superficially unsuitable to his ballroom-tap-aesthetic (a gender reversal of the clash between Petrov and Linda Keene of *Shall We Dance?*), such subtle differences evaporate in the concrete expression of dance. The same distance between Astaire and Charisse (different styles of dance from different generations) separates Tony Hunter from Gabrielle Gerard. But they can dance together because they both *are* dancers. Despite her name, she, like Hunter (and Petrov) is American; despite her dance style, she, like Hunter, is an entertainer. There is only one world of entertainment for Arthur Freed—and best of all, it's American.

"I Love Louisa," also from the old *Band Wagon*, gathers another fragment of Astaire's past—his comic duos with Adele. Nanette Fabray takes sister Adele's wide-eyed, doll-faced role, Astaire parodies both the German dialect of operettas and his own ethnic origins (Austerlitz was the family name), and Oscar Levant pokes fun from the piano. Like "Dancing in the Dark," "I Love Louisa" produces a reconciliation by reminding performers that entertainment must be infectious, communal fun, spreading from the community of performers to that community called an audience. Laboring under the spell of Cordova's Mephistopheles, the show has become an infernal machine of hellish drudgery. Writers Levant and Fabray, obvious standins for Comden and Green, have not only stopped having fun but have stopped speaking to one another. Levant, neurotic though he be, is the film's artistic conscience. Upon first hearing the idea for a musical about eternal damnation, Levant quips, "That'll leave 'em laughing," recognizing the gap between audience expectation and Cordova pretention. Carried by the spirited singing of "Louisa," Levant travels back to the Freed barnyard musicals for a genuine solution:

> With all this raw talent around here, let's all get together and put on
> a show. Maybe get a barn or something.

Saying it aloud breaks the devil's spell and renews Tony's confidence in what he has known intuitively about entertainment all along.

Only after resolving the conflict between Tony's entertainment and Jeffrey's art can the film serve its climactic dessert of onstage musical numbers—exactly as the Busby Berkeley musicals do. Like *An American in Paris*, *The Band Wagon* sweeps up its narrative dust quickly enough to get on with the show but subtly enough to convince an audience of its psychological credibility. Minnelli, Comden, and Green solve two ticklish problems so cleverly that they both reveal and hide the way to solve such problems.

The first is to make clear that Cordova's "Band Wagon" is a dreadful bomb—but not an irreparable one, given the spirit, talent, and aspirations of its participants. At the dress rehearsal, disaster clearly hangs in the air. Jeffrey's Mephistopheles reigns from on high, above the proceedings. The dance of Charisse and Astaire to "You and the Night and the Music" has been literally dwarfed by his satanic effects: exploding smoke bombs, flashes of fire, and pools of Expressionist light. Minnelli's distant long shots make the dancers invisible. This show has lost its human soul—both the dancers and the dance. Even the singing comes from an invisible off-frame chorus. In Jeffrey Cordova's show everything performs but the performers. His version of "The Band Wagon" is *Faust* after all.

How can Minnelli, Comden, and Green, top this comically disastrous dress rehearsal? How can they show that the New Haven opening was every bit as bad as its rehearsal promised? Musical conventions prepare us for the opposite: the terrible rehearsal redeemed by the glorious performance, whose glory we see in the finished number, an amused audience, and their affirmative applause. To convey Jeffrey's doomed show, the film shows nothing at all of this performance. We watch a wealthy audience, who put up the money for this turkey, stream into the theater expectantly. Then we view three pictorial representations, accompanied by offstage chanting. In the first, travelers depart toward Boecklin's *Isle of the Dead*; in the second, we see a steer's skull, as if baked in the sun of Death Valley; in the third, the frame fills with a turkey-sized egg. The offstage chanting descends into groans and wailing, as if for the Fall of Troy or the blinding of Oedipus. We then view the audience file slowly out of the theater, through the very portals they excitedly entered, as if from a funeral. It is impossible to imagine a more informative, interesting, and delightful way to convey that this show is dead. But it will rise from these ashes like the mythical Phoenix: a new show will hatch from this turkey egg.

The second key moment is Tony Hunter's mutiny, his standing up to Jeffrey and taking charge—but without running him off the ship like Captain Bligh. How does Tony Hunter take charge but keep Jack Buchanan aboard? After performing "I Love Louisa" and hearing Oscar Levant's words, Tony makes a telephone call to Jeffrey's room. He explicitly tells Jeff what's wrong with the show, but asks him to stay aboard as they return to the show's original concept. It is so explicit a speech, so obvious and lengthy an appeal, that Comden, Green, and Minnelli give it a little twist. Only after Tony finishes his breathless monologue does a Minnelli cut reveal that Jeffrey is not at the other end of the telephone line. Tony's declaration has been to a cleaning lady. All seems lost again. Then Minnelli gives us one more twist. Another cut reveals that Jeffrey has been sitting in the room all along, hearing every word of Tony's declaration. This revelation (like Henri's eavesdropping in *An American in Paris*) is so stunning and so magical that it makes whatever follows seem probable.

How exactly did Jeffrey enter this room, whose doors and walls are

Elegant duo in two and three
dimensions: Astaire and Buchanan's
"I Guess I'll Have to Change My Plan"

clearly visible, without anyone seeing him? He could only have entered by
magic. (He is, after all, Mephistopheles.) Or cinema (for these are not solid
walls and doors but sets, mere apparitions, and a camera can leap wherever
it wants). The magical apparition of Jeffrey makes the absolutely impossible
into the perfectly credible. That's entertainment!

So they can get on with the show. And what a show it is: a spectacular
mixture of sight and sound, the visual and the musical. Both Oliver Smith's
sets and Vincente Minnelli's camera play carefully and consciously with the
paradox of cinema spaces, simultaneously two- and three-dimensional. Cyd
Charisse's "New Sun in the Sky" is a blaze of red and gold Impressionist
swirls. Astaire's and Buchanan's duo, "I Guess I'll Have to Change My
Plan," is the most breezily comfortable softshoe duet in film history, set
within a Smith-Minnelli department-store window of pastel stripes for both
walls and floor. "Louisiana Hayride," a specialty rhythm song for Nanette
Fabray and ensemble, begins on a decoratively flat stage set that gallops
magically into apparent motion with the projection of flickering lights on a
motionless hay wagon. Movies, known as the flickers, also bring motion to
still life by the projection of flickering light. "Triplets" is a comic trio for
Buchanan, Fabray, and Astaire as spiteful babies, outfitted with tiny doll
legs. The black ground of their two-dimensional nursery is as visually
clever as it is effective at hiding their adult legs. No less than the paintings of
the *American in Paris* ballet, these stage sets proclaim their origins as painted
drops, then cinemagically transcend them.

The "Girl Hunt Ballet" brings the show to a close by choreographing
Mickey Spillane prose as "Slaughter on Tenth Avenue." Unlike Kelly's
dancing in a world of Impressionist art, Astaire dances in a world of luridly
popular art, close kin to the movies themselves. Unlike other big ballets, the
"Girl Hunt" uses voice-over narration—the comments of parody private-eye
Rod Riley in terse first-person prose that is as usual for the detective novel as
it is right for Astaire. The abstracted cityscapes, Minnelli's color detail, and

Astaire's parodic cool compensate for a less colorful score and less pure dance, five minutes shorter and half as expensive as the ballets of *An American in Paris* and *Singin' in the Rain*. Like the plot of the film, this ballet prefers the low genres of popular fiction and movies—topical, cheap, and contemporary—stylishly converting them into musical-visual art. How do you get Degas and Spillane, *Faust* and *Oedipus Rex*, the Phoenix and the Bounty, a book show and a revue into one little musical? Nothing to it: you make *The Band Wagon* with Fred Astaire.

If *The Band Wagon* is a retrospective history of Fred Astaire, *A Star Is Born* is a retrospective history of Judy Garland: a raw singer with a big heart and a big voice named Esther Blodgett (or Frances Gumm) becomes a star of filmusicals named Vicki Lester (or Judy Garland). Troubles with alcohol in her personal life (not Vicki's but her husband's) threaten her public career. Harold Arlen, who launched Judy's stardom with "Over the Rainbow," launches her comeback with "The Man That Got Away." While the old standard, "I'll Get By," retreats to that wistful Rainbow Judy, "Lose that Long Face" echoes Arlen's "Get Happy" of *Summer Stock*, a clownish urging to forget our troubles, sung by a performer in deep trouble. While its tramp costume suggests "A Couple of Swells," Garland's tramp duet with Astaire in *Easter Parade*, Vicki's instantaneous switch from dressing-room sorrow to on-camera joy mirrors the shift Garland made so often in her deepest periods of MGM misery.[12] Vicki's trunkful of songs for "Born in a Trunk," assembled and arranged by Roger Edens, uses many of the same songs he arranged for Garland's MGM films like *For Me and My Gal* and her triumphant 1951 appearance at the Palace.

Although Vicki Lester is a thin disguise for Judy Garland, *A Star Is Born* also responds to *Singin' in the Rain*. Judy's clown just happens to splash in rain puddles during "Lose that Long Face," and her dance just happens to end when a cop intrudes upon it—as it did for Kelly. *A Star Is Born* begins with the same searchlight hoopla as *Singin' in the Rain*, and ends, like *Singin' in the Rain*, inside the same theater where it began. "Born in a Trunk" is Garland's gotta sing answer to Kelly's "Gotta Dance." While *Singin' in the Rain* is about the joyous birth of the Hollywood musical, *A Star Is Born* is about its troubled middle age. Like *The Band Wagon*, *A Star Is Born* makes specific reference to Hollywood's economic present.

Vicki Lester (or Judy Garland) gives life to her screen world not because she is an image but because she is a performer. The Hollywood "cops" who run studio publicity departments, played with slimy menace by the repellent Jack Carson (still at Warner Bros, but no longer obligated to be funny), don't know the secret of performance that stars, producers, directors, and writers share. The "cops," who believe in graven images, attempt to convert Esther Blodgett into an image named Vicki Lester—a photograph, a singing marionette, a face in a mirror, a painted doll in makeup. But, as in

Quoting Garland history in *A Star Is Born:* "A Couple of Swells" with Astaire in *Easter Parade* becomes "Lose that Long Face."

Singin' in the Rain, performers produce images; images cannot produce performers. Norman Main (James Mason) is the Lina Lamont of *A Star Is Born*—the Hollywood star reduced to a mere image after his performance power has burned out. Norman is the decayed image of decaying Hollywood, a poignant Don Lockwood (or Errol Flynn) who became a sorry drunk rather than a vibrant musical performer. Stars rise and stars fall. Judy Garland had already done both more than once. The life of one star preys parasitically on the decay of another: Vicki Lester can only devour Norman Main. But stardom itself can only devour Vicki Lester (as it did Judy Garland). This sense of decay, in counterpoint to Garland's soaring performance rooted in personal pain, is one reason *A Star is Born* is more wrenching and less amusing than *Singin' in the Rain*.

Another is the ironic insight of George Cukor, who, in two decades at this MGM home, had never directed a musical. Cukor, like all directorial masters, is a master of frames. Those frames present a visual counterpoint between the central subject and the world surrounding him or (more frequently) her. Cukor keeps human personality at the center of his frame but builds historical, psychological, or economic commentary around it with revealing decor. While Minnelli's space pursues performers and Donen's mirrors them, Cukor's space probes them. His shots of single faces are usually two-shots of "conversations" between the figure and a visual world; his two-shots of literal conversations are metaphoric three-shots of two people within one world.

The coming of the wide screen (by whatever Scope or Vision it was hyped) was a boon for Cukor, providing even larger frames for visual counterpoint. While Cukor always preferred lengthy takes to sustain a performance spell,[13] CinemaScope allowed him to sustain them even longer, shooting whole scenes and entire musical numbers without a cut. The lengths allow our observation of framed ironies about which characters are themselves ignorant. *A Star Is Born* (its VistaVision camera managed by Sam Leavitt), is as much *about* the wide screen as it is *in* the wide screen. It is also about the small screen. Television, the ghost at the banquet of *The Band Wagon*, is both seen and heard in *A Star Is Born*, in careful counterpoint to its wide screen.

One example is the key scene when studio head Oliver Niles (Charles Bickford), the film's paternal paralleled to R. F. (Bickford even resembles Millard Mitchell), informs Norman that the studio will not renew his contract. The conversation takes place at night, during a party in Norman's own house, where guests have assembled to watch Norman's latest (and, as it turns out, last) film—*The Black Legion* (close kin to *The Dueling Cavalier*). Directly behind the conversing figures is Norman's extensive gun collection. This conversation will be fatal for Norman. Although his suicide will not use one of these guns (Cukor is too subtle for that), they suggest both danger and fatality. Vicki Lester will play the film's climactic scene, when

she decides to appear in public again after Norman's death, in front of these
same guns—ending the burial that began with this conversation between
Niles and Norman and the guns.

But there is more in this conversational image than the guns behind
them. At the far left of Cukor's wide frame is a flickering black-and-white
television screen—both tiny (in comparison to the film's Scope) and monochromatic (in comparison to the film's color). But that drab little frame has
great power. Niles himself has left the party to watch the fights on TV.
Though he produces movies, he can't escape TV. At the far right of Cukor's
frame is another flickering black-and-white image—*The Black Legion* projected
for Norman's party guests. The conversation between Norman and Niles
takes place at the visual intersection of television and movies; its subject is
their economic and historical intersection in 1954 Hollywood—where Norman will lose his job and, as it turns out, his life. Cukor carefully constructs
an image of, reading from left to right, television, guns, and movies, but
does nothing with his camera to tip his hand. The revealing objects are
"just there."

Television also plays a powerful role in the scene when Vicki Lester
wins her Oscar. The live ceremony is being telecast to viewers at home, for
even movies need TV to publicize its products. In the upper right of the
huge CinemaScope frame is a tiny television monitor's view of the event. At
the lower left, the TV camera slides in and out to record the activities at the
center of the huge frame, while the tiny TV screen in the upper right
immediately transmits them. This visual counterpoint between film and
TV imagery again has meaning. There is an obvious disproportion between
the immense CinemaScope frame in color and the tiny television frame in
black-and-white. Hollywood movies of this era went to great pains to show
the terrible tininess of the TV screen in comparison to the big bright
beautiful film image. But for all its visual weakness, there is something
more flexible and immediate about the TV image. It glides instantly from
long shot to close-up, bringing the viewer close to performers as people,
here and now, making stars into just folks, inviting them into the home as
company. Television reveals the Esther Blodgett in Vicki Lester. Cukor's
framing reveals the cultural disadvantage of film even as it demonstrates its
visual dexterity: big, careful, ornate, distant, and cold. Cukor's film twice
confesses the reason that TV has won the war with movies, even as he
exercises the wonder of movie imagery. Ironically, you won't see either
reference to television on a TV screen, which necessarily lops off the
borders when it adapts wide-screen images for the television rectangle.[14]

Other Cukor images of literal and metaphoric conversation stand out in
A Star Is Born. Several scenes occur outdoors on the terrace of Norman's
beach house, backed by its plate-glass windows. As characters speak, the
windows "speak" behind them, reflecting the roll of the surf. There are a
number of reasons for these pervasive reflections. The most obvious is that

the rolling surf adds motion to still pictures of conversation. This surf also turns out to be the extension and ally of Norman's gun collection indoors on the other side of the glass—for it is in this sea that Norman will end his life. But more important, the restless motion of the surf reflects the restlessness of the characters in these scenes. The rolling sea is a projection of their instability and insecurity. Finally, the surf is a mere illusion, and this metaphoric projection is a literal projection as well. This surf is obviously, upon reflection, no reflection at all but a movie-process sea, superimposed on glass, projected on the blank screens of the windows by an optical printer. This is a scene shot in a studio, not on a beach. It is a Hollywood illusion in a film about Hollywood illusions, a mere trick of framing in a film about framings—whether of wide-screen frames, or publicity photographs, or makeup mirrors.

Such consistent visual motifs contribute to making *A Star Is Born* the most dramatically powerful filmusical of the decade. Cukor's framing also brings the musical numbers to performance life, using the wide screen and the long take as performance spaces for Garland to fill with her hypnotic vocal power. "The Man That Got Away," among the most memorable of all Garland songs (by the Harold Arlen who wrote so many of the others), is shot in a single take, unedited and uninterrupted, of Garland surrounded by musicians, strolling through their space, filling it with her vocal trumpet in answer to their brass trumpets.

There is a key difference in the two different versions of the number that Cukor shot. That difference leads directly to the film's thematic parodox.[15] In the original version, Judy is just one of the musicians, one of a group; their musical instruments engulf her in a visual labyrinth—as the long trumpets, trombones, and clarinets clog the wide frame in visual counterpoint with the vertical singer. She is merely one more musician with one more instrument, the vertical voice rather than horizontal horn in their midst. The setting for this original version is dirtier and dingier, dominated by dusty browns and smoky beiges, redolent of the smell of cold coffee, cheap gin, and stale air, the smoke of more than just tobacco.

In the final version, Judy is the star, dominating the frame, her sight and song only occasionally punctuated by an instrument that pokes into her space. The setting has been cleaned up— dominated by the sharp contrast of light (for Judy) and darkness (for the musicians), inky blue-black and crisp white. This is no casual jam session in which Judy is just one of the gang. She is already a star, and the musicians themselves acknowledge it by playing second horn. While the original version develops the myth of music, a communal celebration of musicianship, the final version develops the myth of stardom, the uniqueness of the solo performer. While the original version would initiate a process that shows her rising from the group to *become* a star, the final version shows her as already a star, merely needing public recognition.

"Born in a Trunk": filmed vaudeville performance by an old vaudeville trouper

Are stars born or made? What does "birth" mean for a star? Aren't stars "born" with the artificial packaging that gives them public life? Is the star of the film's title Esther Blodgett or Vicki Lester? Was Frances Gumm a star when Roger Edens and Arthur Freed first auditioned her? Was Judy Garland still a star after Arthur Freed fired her? Although a star is born with talent, only packaging creates the public figure called a star. The talent is born and the recognition is manufactured and every star is "born" twice—talented as Esther Blodgett and packaged as Vicki Lester. The life of stardom also means to endure personal anguish—as Mrs. Norman Main (or Mrs. Vincente Minnelli).

The lengthy "Born in a Trunk" turns these paradoxes of a star's being into the Big Number about stardom in a film about stardom, a film-within-a-film and an impersonation-within-an-impersonation. The character Vicki Lester impersonates in "Born in a Trunk," like Esther Blodgett and Frances Gumm, is born with star ability but never publicly demonstrates it until after the long hard climb up the ladder of success. Stardom, though born in trunks, climbs into the open on ladders. Deriving from both "Dignity, Always Dignity" and "Broadway Melody," the bookends of *Singin' in the Rain*, "Born in a Trunk" marries the myth of showbiz success to the magic of Garland's vaudeville singing—in the grand MGM style, with Oliver Smith sets and Irene Sharaff costumes, just like the big MGM ballets.

But it fills an odd narrative slot. Like the big ballet of a Richard Rodgers show, it closes a long first act of rising action: the success number that caps Vicki Lester's success. Given the psychological weight and moral darkness of *A Star Is Born*, in a script by playwright Moss Hart, its Big Number appropriately occupies the slot of Broadway's psychological music dramas rather than Hollywood's socko finales.

The Big Number of the second act, which extends the performance power of "The Man That Got Away" and answers the cinematic extravaganza of "Born in a Trunk," is "Somewhere There's a Someone." The oddity of this number is that it *could* have been a Big Number, the kind of material that big musicals always turn into big ballets (as *Daddy Long Legs* does with the same travelogue idea). But it is merely a solo for Garland in her living room. While describing the number she is about to shoot at the studio, Judy performs it for Norman at home without cinematic adornment. It is yet another response to the "Broadway Melody" ballet of *Singin' in the Rain*: a supposedly verbal description of a purely visual concept. It does indeed visualize the number—what else can movies do?—but in a completely different way. Judy transforms a single domestic room into an exotic everywhere all over the globe merely by playing imaginatively with the ordinary objects in this confined space. Squeezing the pillows of her sofa, Judy plays a Paris concertina; wearing a lampshade as a hat, she dances in China; a tiger rug on the floor flies her to Africa; salt and pepper shakers become the maracas of Brazil.

"Somewhere There's a Someone": Judy as a whole movie spectacle in a blank frame

The number raises two questions: Why isn't it a Big Number? Why is it in the film if it isn't a Big Number? The answers are Garland, movies, and performance. Though movies can take you all over the world—to Paris on the MGM backlot by building it, or from West Coast to East by splicing two bits of film—they can also transport you on the power of a performing imagination. Judy Garland is a world in herself, and her performance creates a somewhere as rich as any art director's. While in *The Band Wagon* the stage is a world of entertainment, in *A Star Is Born* the performer is the world of entertainment. Her travelogue ends with a bang, the climactic shootout of movie westerns, illuminated by a flickering projector's pure white light on a blank movie screen (the same screen on which Norman's *Black Legion* flickered and died).

Movies are only flickering shadows of performance energy. Their power comes from the imaginative ability to transform the world (as Chaplin, Disney, Fred Astaire, and Gene Kelly do). "Somewhere There's a Someone" enacts the ideal movie for the ideal audience in the ideal theater—a total performance world of pure imagination for a single audience beloved. In comparison, the ability of movies to roam the world seems pale (as in *This Is Cinerama*, the ultimate travelogue, just two years before). For all of Cukor's visual dexterity, *A Star Is Born* never loses the musical star, its center and subject.

If *A Star Is Born* is a dark response to *Singin' in the Rain*, *Funny Face* is a light response to *An American in Paris*. Once again the setting is Paris (after a stop in New York) and the music is Gershwin (with three new songs by Kay Thompson and Roger Edens). Every other variable has been flipped: Astaire replaces Kelly, Donen replaces Minnelli, photography replaces painting, today's Paris replaces Impressionist yesterday, and actual locations replace backlot renditions. *Funny Face* visits not the Paris of eternal masterpieces like ballets, tone poems, and paintings but the Paris of ephemeral high fashion. The selling of women's clothes is no different from the selling of movies; fashion models are movie stars who stand still. *Funny Face* doesn't want to be better than it is or other than it is; it wants to be just what it is—an Astaire musical with Gershwin songs.

As fashion photographer Dick Avery, Astaire wears a name and a vocation midway between that of photographer Richard Avedon, who shot the fashion photographs for the film, and his own. Fashion photographs, like Astaire movies, sell style, personality, and products to the public, indicating socially favored ways of dressing, standing, looking, and living in contemporary society. Avery photographs a model by becoming her director, helping her exhibit thought and feeling for the viewer, making them visible. Directing the poses and gestures of a model, accompanied by a string quartet, Avery resembles D. W. Griffith on the set of a silent film, using music to evoke the moods of a Lillian Gish. If Avery is the director within the film, Miss Prescott (Kay Thompson), who runs *Quality* magazine, is its studio head. Only in the world of fashion could a woman become a studio head in 1957—a woman of power without a husband, married to her job. Producer Prescott gets the ideas and director Avery shoots them.

The newest bee in Prescott's bonnett is a new model, not just a fresh face (like Rita Hayworth in *Cover Girl*), but a modern woman with a thinking face (as if faces can think). Marian, the professional model in the film, is its Lina Lamont, all surface and no soul, a grotesque parody of human expressiveness without a thought behind the facade. The problem for models is the same as for movie stars—to reveal the inner being through the surface images to which photographs are necessarily confined. What *Quality* needs is not a beautiful face but an odd face, a different face, a funny face. In *Funny Face*, it belongs to Audrey Hepburn.

She is introduced as a woman who thinks, working in a Greenwich Village bookstore, Embryo Concepts. A *Quality* shooting crew crassly invades her shop to use it as the equivalent of a movie set, hoping the empty-headed Marian can appear thoughtful when photographed within decor that signifies thought. Movies too use decor to suggest internal states—just as *Funny Face* uses the Embryo Concepts bookstore to suggest Audrey Hepburn's character in embryo. But Hepburn not only exists in a movie set of books (although this bookshop *is* a movie set of books); she knows what's in the books. She provides a materialist critique of fashion photography—"a chichi and unrealistic approach to economics"—spreading images simply to sell goods, suggesting that life itself consists solely of those material goods. Her embryonic concepts are the foes of fashion, photographs, and movies. Like her bookish setting, she is, in Prescott's description, "movingly dismal." Dressed in black sweater, skirt, and stockings, wrapped in gray jacket and black babushka, she has declared war on color. A stereotypic mid-fifties unisex egghead, even her name, Jo, is not audibly female. Her dreary monochrome outfit, the noncolor of death, looks like a refugee from some foreign "art film" of the decade. While Jo thinks in black and white, the worlds of fashion photography and Hollywood musicals think in color—as Prescott's opening number, "Think Pink," declares. Jo's embryo concepts need coloring.

Every number of *Funny Face* extends its thematic premise (the making of popular images, as in *Singin' in the Rain*) and reflects on its own history (the career and meaning of Fred Astaire, as in *The Band Wagon*). Hepburn's first number, "How Long Has This Been Going On?" reveals that she can emerge from her gray cocoon to become Prescott's color butterfly. Hepburn often emerges from a cocoon—in Broadway's *Gigi* or Hollywood's *Sabrina* and *My Fair Lady*—because she reconciles opposite ideals. Her lovely face *is* a thinking face. Delivered breathlessly with impeccably thoughtful phrasing (carefully coached by Astaire, Thompson, Edens, or some combination of all three), Hepburn sings "How Long Has This Been Going On?" to and with a physical object—a brilliantly colored hat that Marian has left behind in the dark cave of Jo's bookshop. The number not only sustains the visual contrast of color with monochrome but initiates a thematic contrast of indoors and out, of natural and artificial light—the weak, drab light of interiors as opposed to the brilliant sunlight that permits colors to be seen. This film prefers the outdoors—just as it prefers actual Paris locations to studio sets.

Astaire's singing of the title song, which he sang on Broadway exactly thirty years earlier, reveals his own conversion to the modern media of movies and photography. The number demonstrates to both Jo and the audience the way photographs and movies translate faces into images. Parallel to the sound recording of "Would You?" in *Singin' in the Rain*, "Funny Face" documents its own material processes and technology. While Astaire sings of Jo's face he photographs it, develops the negative, frames it for an enlargement, projects it on a screen of photographic paper, and prints it. Like the making of a movie, the song moves from shooting through printing to projection. At its end we see Hepburn's "real" face beside the one that Astaire-Avery has photographed and projected. Except her "real" face is also photographed and projected, for *Funny Face* is a movie and Hepburn is a star. Visually, the number is another ironic combination of monochrome and color, confined to different densities of orange—motivated by the red light of the darkroom but obviously tinted by cinematic filter. Like darkrooms, movie studios use red lights to restrict the entrance of light or noise that destroys takes. If the number's monochrome evokes Astaire at RKO, it also recalls the numbers there that demonstrate an entire process—from getting dressed to playing golf. "Funny Face" simultaneously alludes to three Astaires: on Broadway in 1927, at RKO in 1937, and in this very product of photographic technology in 1957.

This indoor image-making, Jo's screen test, leads directly to stardom in an outdoor photomontage sequence on location, documenting the photographic interplay of art and technology, artifacts and personality. That location is not a dark bookshop but the entire City of Light. The familiar Paris landmarks of the French Impressionists—from the Place de la Concorde to the Place de l'Opéra—are not translated into Minnelli canvases but caught by a contemporary camera, whether Avedon's or Donen's, going about its photographic business. This is the way that color photographs, whether of fashion magazines, travel brochures, or movie travelogues, give life to Paris. Donen draws a parallel between fashion and travel photography when his movie camera becomes a tourist, like Avery, Prescott, and Jo themselves. On the morning of their arrival, they sing "Bonjour Paree" to its famous sights, from the Arc de Triomphe to the Tour Eiffel, their excitement mirrored by Donen's energetic frames (often in widescreen triptychs for the simultaneous depiction of three experiences). Their greeting echoes "How're You?" of *Love Me Tonight*—this time a hello by Ameri-

can visitors (like everyone in the movie house), transported by the technological wonders of wide screen and splitscreen.

During the photomontage sequence depicting the fashion model and
photographer at work, the backgrounds inspire not documentaries of travel
but the telling of stories. The sights of Paris become backdrops for the
moods that Hepburn's face and body are capable of projecting for the
observant camera: from sad like Anna Karenina as she waits in a dreary
Gare de Lyon to majestic like the Winged Victory of Samothrace as she
races down its staircase in the Louvre. The stills are movies in miniature.
Their unity of location, light, framing, color, costume, facial expression,
and physical gesture create coherent images that imply stories and create
characters. The world is not projected as a painter's feeling about a view
but narrated to present a character's feeling in a view, not by applying
pigment to blank canvas but by selecting and arranging materials that the
physical world already offers. The wonder of this photomontage sequence,
call it "An American Fashion Model in Paris," is that while it reveals its own
technological artifice—by showing that photographs are staged, produced
by dyes, and printed by combining color-separation strips—it preserves the
mystery of its results. Like Dziga-Vertov's silent classic, *The Man with the
Movie Camera*, *Funny Face* shows photography to be both mere machinery
and pure magic. Only a central human presence can bring the objective
views to life, for she—whether model or movie star—makes a photograph
empathical.

Empathical? Jo has only agreed to shoot these pictures in Paris because
of a philosophy she wishes to master, empathicalism—which sounds something like existentialism and means something like communicating without
words. Empathicalists make contact merely by empathy—by what the
1950s called intuition and the 1970s called "vibes." The inventor and
founder of empathicalism, Professor Flauster, writes and teaches in Paris—
like all fashionable philosophers. And like all philosophers in all American
movies, Flauster is a phony: he dispenses words to dispense with words,
coins a word to counterfeit not needing words. His real commitment is
self—money, fame, and sex—not empathy with others. The real professor
of empathicalism in the film is Astaire, whose dancing has always been
empathical—an intense communication between beings (whether a partner
or an audience) without words. His song and dance to "Let's Kiss and Make
Up" is an empathicalist textbook. The mere phrasing of the vocal chorus
wins Jo's confidence, the first dance chorus converts his everyday umbrella
into an Astaire cane, and the final dance chorus converts the dancer into a
romantic bullfighter when his ordinary raincoat becomes a matador's cape
and his almost sentient umbrella a sword. Astaire lectures on empathicalism
not by verbalizing it but by doing what he always does—demonstrating
tropes as dance.

Fashion photographs and movies are both empathicalist arts—conveying

"Funny Face": photographic imagery and empathical dancing

mood, feeling, and values without words. The ultimate empathical activity is dancing, and *Funny Face* summarizes its issues in a stunning dance that gathers all its themes. "He Loves and She Loves" is danced by Astaire and Hepburn not in a sound-stage park, like "Isn't It a Lovely Day" or "Dancing in the Dark," but on real grass, with real trees, and real water in a brook, and real swans on the water. It is an empathical synthesis of music, movement, natural imagery, sunlight, color, and cinema technology. In her Embryo bookshop, Jo asks Avery why he doesn't just shoot a tree. "He Loves and She Loves" answers her question: you can't "just" shoot a tree—without knowing the meaning of the tree in that shot. How can the tree be made to speak, empathically, of human emotion? Trees provide the sounding board for "He Loves and She Loves," the resonant backdrop that allows their "music" to be "heard." That is what she learns in Paris and what she learns from Astaire. If Hepburn falls for an Astaire almost sixty, it is because the thoughtful characters she plays perpetually seek older, wiser teachers—Humphrey Bogart, Gary Cooper, Cary Grant.

Unfortunately, *Funny Face* goes on with unnecessary scenes and obligatory numbers after its empathical lesson has been learned: "On How to Be Lovely," a deflation of glamor for Hepburn and Kay Thompson in a stage-set park; "Clap Yo Hands," a parody of holyroller revivalism for Astaire and Thompson. There is no dream ballet or Big Number for a finale—dismissed either by the film's budget or its resolute attachment to commercial art. Avoiding the art school aspiration up Mount Hollywood also leaves the film without a finish. *Funny Face* runs down like a clock, losing the tension of its essential issue: the meaning and value of popular entertainment and musical performance in the first place. By 1957 all Hollywood musicals were either losing or discarding it.

While the fragments of Freed's empire scattered to other studios, the Freed unit crumbled with MGM. After producing thirty-three musicals between 1940 and 1953, he produced seven in the next decade. His last originals, *It's Always Fair Weather* and *Gigi* (1958), documented what had passed and would come to pass. Everyone connected with *Fair Weather* hated it—as did 1955 audiences. *Gigi*, on the other hand, was the most honored filmusical of the decade, winner of more Academy Awards than any previous musical, the biggest grossing film of Freed's career.

It's Always Fair Weather marked the end of the Gene Kelly-Arthur Freed road that began in 1942. The Oscar for the ballet of *An American in Paris* went to Kelly's head rather than his feet. No one could talk to him—and even his pal, Stanley Donen, stopped. Like Kelly himself, *It's Always Fair Weather* often tries too hard to do too much. Comden and Green attempt another retrospective history—this time based on the films of Kelly himself. We have three GIs, as in *On the Town*, and three buddies, as in *An American in Paris* and *Take Me Out to the Ball Game*. One of the GIs wants to paint—just as Jerry Mulligan did. Kelly reverts to the *Pal Joey* louse who will do anything for a buck or a mouse. But he makes his usual discovery in his most memorable number, the film's only memorable tune, "I Like Myself," in a score that even its composer, André Previn, didn't like at all.[16] The morally redeemed Kelly has discovered that he likes himself because there is something in him to like. He glidingly mimes his redemption on roller skates, a skating translation of his singin' in the rain. In regaining his sense of self, Kelly almost redeems the whole film.

Despite its *Fair Weather* title, the film is swamped in a storm of 1950s woes, in and out of Hollywood. All three GI buddies have sold out. A decade earlier, World War II gave both the nation and the Hollywood musical a terrific sense of purpose. In the film's opening number, "March, March," the three buddies rush through the streets of backlot Manhattan to celebrate that sense of 1945 purpose. A distant memory in 1955, their energy has been buried beneath the drive to make a buck—the same shape as the film's CinemaScope frame. Donen and Kelly translate the three GIs, who ripped a ten-dollar bill in three pieces as their pledge to meet ten years later, into the panels of a CinemaScope frame. Whether composing within that frame or splitting it with trick effects, Kelly and Donen remind us that the film, like the frame, is a triptych, united by the almighty dollar.

As can be seen in even the shape of a frame, the film's postwar world has been completely commoditized. Its ultimate vision of selling out is the marriage of advertising to the tiny frame of television—the degraded entertainment of a degraded nation. Even to sing a song means to sell a product. The spirit of song and dance, the very basis of musicals, is imprisoned within a dancing box of detergent (a parody of the tap-dancing package of Old Gold cigarettes on Ted Mack's *Original Amateur Hour*), a pair of commoditized legs beneath a faceless cardboard self. Even the sentimental story of three GIs who meet again ten years later becomes a pretext for advertising—a parody of the televised tearjerker, *This Is Your Life*. The stagy style of Broadway's Dolores Gray, who hosts the televised proceedings with a mixture of saccharine and slime, doesn't make the satire any more tasty (or tasteful). The three buddies, like the movie industry itself, have been as permanently ripped apart as their ten-dollar bill. Perhaps its three ripped pieces are Kelly, Donen, and Freed, who would never again work together. Call *It's Always Fair Weather* the shredding of the old Hollywood by the new America.

Call *Gigi* the swallowing of the old Hollywood by the new Broadway. Freed had always built films with Broadway veterans: from Edens, Minnelli, and Kelly to Oliver Smith, Alan Jay Lerner, and Comden and Green. With *Gigi* Broadway literally took over. When the film ran over budget after location shooting in Paris, requiring massive retakes in Hollywood, Freed steadily surrendered control to Lerner and Loewe, who bought into the production.[17] Like the Rodgers and Hammerstein films of the same period at Fox, the movie is made by Broadway people, not movie people. It even opened in a Broadway playhouse, not a movie house. The Lerner and Loewe score, a wonder for a film score, is also a derivative wonder: *My Fair Lady Goes to Paris*. The Lerner script, a wonder for a film script—balancing the bourgeois moral constraints of movie marriage with the alternative institution of courtesans in Colette's novel—is the same balancing of bourgeois and radical moralities as *My Fair Lady*. Although her elders believe they are molding Gigi into a fit object for sexual stimulation, what they have really fashioned is a fit object for marriage. So many girls in 1950s and 1960s musicals—Gigi, Lise, Jo, Lili, Eliza—receive an education that makes them marriageable women.

For Vincente Minnelli *Gigi* was a return to the Paris of its paintings. As opposed to the sound-stage visions of *An American in Paris*, actual Paris locations produce the painterly visions of *Gigi*—whether a Bois de Boulogne bathed in the golden greens of Seurat or a mirrored Maxim's populated with the faces of Sem. To simply glance at the furnishings of rooms— wallpaper, wall sconces, picture frames, sheet music, water pitchers, crystal goblets—is to note the marriage of Minnelli's eye to Cecil Beaton's meticulous taste.

Gigi was also a return for Chevalier, three decades after his regular filmusical visits to Maxim's in *The Love Parade* and *The Merry Widow*. The Chevalier numbers, "Thank Heaven for Little Girls," "I Remember It Well," and "I'm Glad I'm Not Young Any More," acquire particular meaning from a performer who, like Astaire and Garland, carries his own history of singing such songs in such films. While Chevalier began the cycle of original filmusical conceptions at Paramount, he closes that circle with *Gigi* at MGM.

In *Gigi*, musical performance yields center stage to lines and lyrics. Leslie Caron doesn't even dance—the one musical thing she knows how to do. The film's visual style is bizarrely inconsistent: the minutest details of Belle Epoque Paris clash with MGM soundstage furniture, outdoor sand, sea, and sky with indoor paint and cyclorama.[18] The best one can say of *Gigi* is also the worst: it is the best Broadway musical ever written directly for the screen. As an original musical, *Gigi* reaffirmed what every Hollywood producer, including Arthur Freed, already knew in 1958. Hollywood could not afford to make musicals that weren't Broadway.

From The Horse Right Here to The Rain In Spain

B R O A D W A Y   A N D
H O L L Y W O O D   (1 9 4 8 – 1 9 6 8)

The Rodgers and Hammerstein shows from *Oklahoma!* to *The King and I* confirmed both the conventions and the confidence of the American stage musical. By 1948 producers and audiences knew exactly what a book musical was supposed to be: a romantic drama of conflicting characters, alternately comic and dramatic, based on a literary source, ancient or modern, with at least eighteen musical slots, some sung, some danced, at least twelve in the first act. This formal stability supported two vigorous decades of carefully crafted musical plays. Like the English novel or Italian opera of the nineteenth century, broad cultural agreement about a popular form—the clarity of a musical's conventions, construction, and compact with audiences—allowed many skillful artisans to fit different musical fashions on the common model.

With the question of form so clearly settled, the only remaining issue was style. How do you get that kind of character to sing? As in Rodgers and Hammerstein shows, making a musical meant creating characters rather than constructing an action. If the characters make sense, the action makes sense. And the characters only make sense if their singing makes sense. A song was a projection of character—socially, psychologically, morally, and intellectually. The "voice" of a song no longer came directly from a witty Porter, Hart, or Ira Gershwin, who could be heard in every song of every show by every character. The search for style meant a search for a score—lyrics *and* music appropriate to both the people and the period of the play. A hypothetical musical about Marco Polo could no longer use the "good Jewish music" that Jerome Kern offered Oscar Hammerstein. How would Marco Polo sing? The score that found its stylistic answer created characters who simply couldn't be imagined not singing or singing in any other way.

For two decades composers and writers of musicals roamed the world of books seeking characters who might sing, then musicalizing them in ways that seemed as natural as they were inevitable. From Damon Runyon to George Bernard Shaw, Shakespeare to Cervantes, the tenements of Manhattan to the Stetls of Russia, baseball players to factory workers, Berlin to Wall Street, telephone operators to strippers, perfume salesgirls to taxi dancers, anybody and everybody could find a way to sing of things past, passing, and yet to come. For two decades, the scores of Broadway musicals represented a remarkable blend of individual characterization, a musical style reflecting the social and historical world of the drama, and American popular music. However far the show traveled from contemporary America— whether to a Scottish town of centuries ago or to the Europe of Voltaire— its score never completely left the American cultural present.

Beneath these two decades of fertile musical activity lay the hidden sources of future problems. A shared awareness of clear conventions provides space for the exercise of style, a confidence in the relation of form and content that produces the ages of artistic expression frequently called "classical." Unfortunately, the dependence on firm conventions erases the imaginative interplay between form and style that gave rise to the conventions in the first place. While conventions liberate, clichés freeze. The Gershwins and Rodgers (with either Hart or Hammerstein) drew on the excitement of finding a new form at the same time as creating its style, inventing the conventions while creating the conventions' finest results. The longer the conventions of an artistic form remain stable, the more they narrow expression within them, until some younger generation rejects the conventions altogether. The revolution that blasted the conventions of both the English realistic novel and the Italian romantic opera came in an era of social upheaval surrounding World War I. The revolution that blasted the conventions of the American music drama came in the late 1960s of protest against the war in Viet Nam and the rise of the counterculture. Artistic revolutions proceed from social ones, when stable artistic conventions seem rigid codifications of dead social ideas. Yesterday's romantic rebel becomes tomorrow's AK.

While the form of the American music drama remained stable for two decades, the economics of the theater business did not. As shows cost more and more, tickets cost more and more, with two inevitable consequences: fewer shows and fewer patrons. The same economic woes that hit the movie business after World War II hit the theater business at the same time and for the same reason. Shows had to compete with television and other rivals—especially movies—for the entertainment dollar. On Broadway, the "entertainment dollar" jumped from about three dollars just after the war to ten dollars by 1957 (to twenty dollars by 1967 and forty-five dollars by 1983). While postwar economics hit the movies like a ton of bricks, Broadway was a leaking balloon. The movies had been a booming growth industry for fifty years, while the theater business had been declining steadily since the turn of the century, when the movies first appeared. Economic miseries hit growth industries harder than declining ones. Though Broadway's economic decline was slow and subtle, it could only infect the quality of musical production: fewer shows took fewer chances with fewer unknowns. Economic caution froze artistic conventions into commercial necessities.

Another subtle shift in postwar musicals, with artistic and commercial consequences, was the divorce of America's show music from its pop music—actually, the divorce of its theater music from its dance music. While Broadway shows once came from Tin Pan Alley, Tin Pan Alley had moved from West 28th Street to Motown and Mersey and Nashville. Even by 1943, when Rodgers joined Hammerstein, the period of American popular music that produced the standard jazz and popular repertory had ended, when songs that were once sung or danced on theater stages and movie screens were the songs to which Americans danced offstage and off-screen as well.

Hit songs, the name of the game for Berlin, Gershwin, even Kern, depended on dancing. This style of paired social dancing, in which a male leads his female partner by physical contact, descended from the waltzing couple of the nineteenth century through the two-step of the 1900s to the box step of the 1910s.[1] But the 1980s uncoupled style of rock dancing, of individual motion by nontouching equals, descended from more abandoned, more black, less polite, and less socially acceptable forms—from the shimmy of the 1920s, through the lindy of 1940s swing, to the rock 'n' roll of the 1950s and twist of the 1960s. Broadway musicals chose to have little to do with these sounds in those decades, for the musical patterns and styles that defined character were based on the alternative dancing tradition of engaged pairs.

The divorce of American theater music from its dance music made it more serious and more grand, even as it made it less American and less popular—particularly with the young. The Broadway musical grew steadily older through the 1950s and 1960s, and its audiences grew older with it—in taste and in fact. Broadway shows abandoned their old friends, pop singles and sheet music, for the new LP record, born in 1948. Like operas and symphonies, Broadway shows were recorded as Columbia Masterworks and RCA Red Seals, and the Broadway hills were alive with a sound of music as Masterworky as the recordings. Richard Rodgers deserted the rhythmic bounce of his breezy 2/4 ballads with Lorenz Hart for the sturdy clomp of 4/4 with Hammerstein. "If I Loved You," "You'll Never Walk Alone," "Some Enchanted Evening," "I Have Dreamed," "Something Wonderful," "Love Look Away," "The Sound of Music," and "Climb Every Mountain" are all in 4/4. If Rodgers and Hammerstein songs became simultaneously more dramatic and less danceable, so did every score by every theater composer in the same period. While pop-jazz vocalists and instrumentalists still sing and play Rodgers and Hart, they avoid Rodgers and Hammerstein like the plague.[2] A Gershwin, Porter, or Rodgers and Hart tune preserved its lightness and bounce because, whatever its dramatic statement, it had to be fox-trottable.

An inevitable result was that individual songs from Broadway shows made steadily less impact on the culture as a whole, redefining Broadway as an acquired taste of the adult cultural elite—like opera and symphonic music. Broadway in the 1950s had not totally abandoned its stake in American popular music—and vice versa. "Some Enchanted Evening" (*South Pacific*), "Hey There" (*The Pajama Game*), "Whatever Lola Wants" (*Damn Yankees*), "Standing on the Corner" (*The Most Happy Fella*), "I've Grown Accustomed to Her Face" (*My Fair Lady*), "Tonight" (*West Side Story*), and "Small World" (*Gypsy*), were among the biggest hit songs of the decade on jukeboxes and AM radio. The fifties were also the decade of inventive jazz recordings of Broadway shows, like André Previn-Shelly Manne's classic jazz version of *My Fair Lady*. Since 1970 few Broadway songs make any cultural impression. "Send in the Clowns" (*A Little Night Music*), "What I Did for Love" (*A Chorus Line*), "Memories" (*Cats*), and "I Am What I Am" (*La Cage aux Folles*) are among the few exceptions.

In the two decades from 1948 to 1968 the Broadway musical was a simultaneous site of fertility and contraction, artistic health and commercial decay, creative confidence and progressive cultural withdrawal. Though creators of musical shows ranged wide in search of musical people and places, they remained bound by the formal and cultural expectations for characters and stories that sing. Though the business of Broadway demanded that there be musical shows, it put limits on the kinds of shows they could be. The decade preceding 1958 was more apparently robust, the one after 1958 more obviously sickly.

Two mid-1950s scores by Richard Adler and Jerry Ross were as robust as any. Both *The Pajama Game* (1954) and *Damn Yankees* (1955) brought working-class America to singing life, musicalizing the kinds of characters Americans saw on the contemporary *Honeymooners* or later *All in the Family*. Both define home as a place that could be Archie Bunker's in Queens. Jean Stapleton, who played Archie's Edith, even lived in the neighborhood of *Damn Yankees*. When it leaves that neighborhood, *The Pajama Game* goes to work in a blue-collar garment factory, settling a labor dispute that arises when the union leader falls for the factory's new manager. If *Pajama Game* is blue-collar work (based on Richard Bissell's novel, *7½ Cents*), *Damn Yankees* is blue-collar leisure (based on Douglas Wallop's novel, *The Year the Yankees Lost the Pennant*)—Broadway's only successful musical about baseball. A middle-aged suburbanite sells his soul to the Devil (*Faust* again) to become the slugging star who carries the Washington Senators to a pennant. With dynamic opening numbers in both shows ("Racing with the Clock" and "Six

Months out of Every Year"), agreeable ballads ("Hey There" and "Near to You"), and exciting specialty numbers ("Steam Heat," "Hernando's Hideaway," and "Whatever Lola Wants"), the musical and lyric cadences of Adler and Ross catch the energy of American working-class life. From the creative teams of their shows came major influences on the future of American musicals both on stage and on screen—producer Harold Prince, performer Gwen Verdon, and choreographer Bob Fosse. The premature death of Jerry Ross ended a collaboration that promised more musical views of America's working class.

Meredith Willson carried Broadway back to his own Americana past in *The Music Man* (1957), where con man Harold Hill (Robert Preston) hornswoggles the town of River City, Iowa, into buying marching-band outfits. While he sells them a bill of goods, he loses his heart to Marian Paroo (Barbara Cook), the town librarian. Willson, who wrote the book, music, and lyrics, carefully weaves American musical styles of the Sousa and Cohan era into his score and setting: popular songs of the period, like "Goodnight, Ladies"; the close harmonies of the barbershop quartet; the sentimental waltz, "Goodnight, My Someone," Marian's operetta longing for romance; and the bounciest march heard on Broadway since Romberg, "Seventy-Six Trombones." Hill's march is musically identical to Marian's waltz—but in Sousatime. Whatever the differences in character—Hill is no "White Knight" out of Marian's books—the two belong together because they literally sing the same song (if in the different tempi of their opposing temperaments).

Many musical slots for the score are oddities—a vocal imitation of small-town gossip, "Pick-a-little, Talk-a-little"; Harold Hill's mock-revivalist sermon on pool-playing and other sins of big-city life, "Trouble" (which starts with T, and that rhymes with P, and that stands for pool); and a child's-eye description of a visit to the big city of "Gary, Indiana," a repetitiously inarticulate response to the "Kansas City" of *Oklahoma!* Willson's next visit to the Americana past, *The Unsinkable Molly Brown* (1960), has a score with less historical style but plenty of bounce. A Colorado tomboy pushes her way into snobbish Denver society on mining money, travels on the Titanic, and rescues as many of her fellow passengers as she can. Willson's score is as unsinkable as Molly.

The scores of Jule Styne, who migrated to Broadway from Hollywood, were more blessed in their female stars than their musical styles: Carol Channing in *Gentlemen Prefer Blondes* (1949), based on the Anita Loos novel; Judy Holliday in *Bells Are Ringing* (1956), based on an original Comden and Green script; Ethel Merman in *Gypsy* (1959), based on the memoirs of Gypsy Rose Lee; and Barbra Streisand in *Funny Girl* (1964), based on the life of Fanny Brice. Like Porter and Berlin, Styne could write for stars, a "Diamonds Are a Girl's Best Friend" for Channing or an "Everything's Coming Up Roses" for Merman. And the stars loved him for it.

Although Stephen Sondheim had been hired for *Gypsy*, Merman demanded the experienced Styne. Styne would never have achieved the tonal range and stylistic energy of *Gypsy* without Sondheim as lyricist. Like his mentor Oscar Hammerstein, the young Sondheim stimulated collaborators to their very best work, urging Styne to throw away the throwaways that he so often threw into a score to fill it up. Like *Pal Joey*, the score of *Gypsy* alternated onstage performance numbers in sleazy dives with offstage character numbers in the cheap rooms where they lived. Unlike *Pal Joey*, the louse was no male hoofer but a showbiz mama, pushing her babies up the ladder of success, whether or not they wanted to go. The drive of Styne's music and the snap of Sondheim's lyrics made Ethel Merman's Mama Rose the dynamic dramatic role that topped her seemingly untoppable career.

In a completely different style and sound, Harvey Schmidt and Tom Jones specialized in the nostalgic and whimsical, not the brash and brassy but the shy and charming. *The Fantasticks*, a conscious "little show," like the Princess Theater shows of the teens, began its run in an off-Broadway hole in the wall in 1960 and has remained there for twenty-seven years—the longest continuously running musical in theater history. Based on Edmund Rostand's play *Les Romantiques*, *The Fantasticks* is *Romeo and Juliet* in reverse: two fathers pretend to be at war so their children will defy them and fall in love. With a cast of seven, accompanied only by piano and harp, heavily dependent on mime and presentational staging rather than lavish sets, *The Fantasticks* was also a Broadway musical in reverse. Its informal makeshift, make-do production was perfectly suited to its pleasantly tinkling, casual score.

On the larger Broadway canvas, Jones and Schmidt have fared less well. *I Do! I Do!* (1966), based on Jan de Hartog's play *The Fourposter*, was another combination of nostalgia, charm, and whimsy for a cast of exactly two. But the two were Mary Martin, like Merman in her Broadway sunset, and Robert Preston, before Blake Edwards snatched him up. Built on the entire lifetime of a married couple in and around the fourposter of their bedroom, the show demonstrated, as had *The Fantasticks*, how much could be done with so little.

While Jerry Bock and Sheldon Harnick also traveled to the past, both the musical sound and style were different. *Fiorello!* (1959) returned Broadway audiences to the Depression of New York's reform mayor and *Tenderloin* (1960) to a crusading New York reformer at the turn of the century. In both scores, Jerry Bock's jangling, dissonant tunes and heavily syncopated rhythms support Sheldon Harnick's trickily percussive lyrics (sometimes a bit too tricky) that pound out the relentless rhymes of his speeding words. In *Fiorello!* the lady garment workers cry "Unfair":

> So we sew and sew
> Solely to survive
> So some low so and so
> Can thrive.

296 GERALD MAST

Equally historical but mellower and richer were the Bock and Harnick nostalgia pieces that left "Little Old New York" for the Old World—a graceful prewar Budapest in *She Loves Me* (1963), based on Ernst Lubitsch's film of *The Shop Around the Corner*, and their biggest hit of all, *Fiddler on the Roof* (1964), based on *Tevye the Milkman* of Sholom Aleichem. *She Loves Me* was among the first Broadway musicals based on a Hollywood film (after Harold Rome's *Destry Rides Again* in 1959 and Bob Merrill's *Carnival* in 1961). A sign of the cultural times, movies, no less than novels and plays, provided sources for musicals. *Golden Boy* (1964), *Sweet Charity* (1966), *A Little Night Music* (1973), *Chicago* (1975), *On the Twentieth Century* (1979), *42nd Street* (1980), *Nine* (1981), *La Cage aux Folles* (1983), and *Singin' in the Rain* (1985) would follow. That Broadway shows increasingly cannibalized movies was only one more sign of two musical traditions becoming one.

Fiddler on the Roof was the first Broadway musical to link the Jewish roots of Broadway songwriters with their Yiddish folk roots. For the Jewish Bock and Harnick, and the Jewish Joseph Stein, who adapted *Fiddler's* book from the Yiddish stories, "good Jewish music" was not just a Kern joke but a careful stylistic decision. Of all the Jewish creators of Broadway scores—Kern, Berlin, the Gershwins, Rodgers and Hart or Hammerstein, Lerner and Loewe, Dietz and Schwartz, Comden and Green, Adler and Ross, Stephen Sondheim, Cy Coleman, Leonard Bernstein, Frank Loesser, Marvin Hamlisch—only Bock and Harnick connected Old World Klezmer and New World jazz. Frank Loesser wrote "Sue Me" for a Jewish Nathan Detroit in *Guys and Dolls* (1950), Jerry Herman took Molly Picon to Israel in *Milk and Honey* (1961), Harold Rome went to a Borscht-belt resort in *Wish You Were Here* (1952) and the garment district in *I Can Get It For You Wholesale* (1962). But Bock and Harnick made the connection not only through character and setting but in musical tradition itself, announced by the opening number of *Fiddler on the Roof*, "Tradition." In *Fiddler*, musical tradition and moral tradition are inseparable.

Cy Coleman's scores mirror the energy of contemporary New York. Working frequently with either Dorothy Fields or Carolyn Leigh, Coleman's tunes pound out the driving rhythms of contemporary urban life, wherever and whenever the shows happen to be set. Beginning as both a jazz pianist and popular songwriter (Frank Sinatra's "Witchcraft"), Coleman brings the old spirit of Gershwin's Tin Pan Alley to modern Broadway. Every Coleman show can be predicted to have at least one terrific rhythm song, a driving up-tempo tune or march like "Hey Look Me Over" from *Wildcat* (1961), "I've Got Your Number" from *Little Me* (1963), "Hey Big Spender" from *Sweet Charity*, or "Hey There Good Times" from *I Love My Wife* (1977). Coleman is equally at ease with sweet ballads and waltzes like "Real Live Girl" from *Little Me*, "Our Private World" from *On the Twentieth Century* (1979), or "The Colors of My Life" from *Barnum* (1982). Among the 1960s generation of Broadway composers, Cy Coleman seems most able to bring both the up- and down-tempo styles of the musical past into the present with freshness and originality, without stilted self-consciousness or parodic self-commentary.

Of all creators of Broadway musicals since 1960, no one has been able to write hit songs like Jerry Herman. Like Berlin and Porter, Herman writes both words and music; like them, he is conscious of the way word-sounds fit music-sounds; and like them, he wants hit songs that express a specific character but speak to an entire culture. Herman's hit tunes carry their shows and scores: "Hello Dolly" (1964), "Mame" (1966), and "I Am What I Am" (*La Cage aux Folles*), which could be heard at least once a night in any disco anywhere in the world. In Herman flops—*Dear World* (1969), *Mack and Mabel* (1974)—the tunes thumped hard but never bounced into the cultural ear.

If *Fiddler on the Roof* was the first American musical to make the connection between Broadway music and "good Jewish music," *La Cage aux Folles* makes the first full connection between Broadway creation and the gay sensibility. The "Am" of "I Am What I Am" describes the gay "I" who openly proclaims it. More generally, the song has come to mirror the confidence of an entire younger generation in itself—living life according to its own values, not only willing to live unconventionally but willing to say so publicly. *La Cage aux Folles* is a musical about characters who have come out in a culture that has come out—of whatever kind of closet. Stylistically, Herman doesn't care if everywhere comes out sounding the same—whether turn-of-the-century New York, silent-movie Hollywood, or the South of France. His shows do not have scores so much as songs—interchangeable up-tempo title tunes and treacly waltzes—that seem fished out of some trunk. But he has a very good cultural ear and the trunk a seemingly endless supply of brightness and bounce.

Leonard Bernstein, Frank Loesser, and the team of Alan Jay Lerner and Frederick Loewe, the most distinguished postwar creators of musical plays, were both causes and effects of the musical's vitality in the decade after the war. Bernstein and Loesser took opposite roads only to arrive at a similar place. Like George Gershwin, Bernstein traveled between Broadway house and concert hall; he simply booked the opposite itinerary. A graduate of Harvard in 1939, he studied with some of the major conductors of that generation (Serge Koussevitzky, Dimitri Mitropoulos, Fritz Reiner). Bernstein only migrated to show business after symphonic success: the 1942 premiere of his *Jeremiah* symphony, his 1943 conducting debut with the New York Philharmonic, and his 1943 ballet score, *Fancy Free*. From *Fancy Free* came *On the Town* a year later, expanding the ballet's three sailors on twenty-four-hour leave to a full singing-and-dancing show. Between 1953 and 1957 Bernstein wrote three major scores—two for shows set in contemporary New York, *Wonderful Town* (1953) and *West Side Story* (1957), and one that sailed around the globe in the Operettaland past of Voltaire's *Candide* (1956).

Frank Loesser began with the same musical opportunities as Leonard Bernstein and systematically rejected them. Born in the New York of Gershwin and Berlin, Loesser traveled their self-made, self-taught road. Although his father was a noted accompanist and piano teacher, Loesser, like Ira Gershwin, refused to go near the instrument. Also like Ira he quickly dropped out of the City College of New York. After odd jobs as waiter in the city or bartender in the Catskills, Loesser worked as a lyricist on Tin Pan Alley, and until 1942 he only wrote lyrics. He became head of Hollywood music departments, first at lowly Universal, then in 1936 at lordly Paramount, where he hired first-rate songwriters—Burton Lane, Hoagy Carmichael, Jimmy McHugh, Johnny Mercer—with whom he wrote the lyrics for such hits as "Small Fry," "Two Sleepy People," and "I Got Spurs that Jingle, Jangle, Jingle." Perhaps the patriotic spirit of wartime lured him to the piano. "Praise the Lord and Pass the Ammunition," with words and music by PFC Frank Loesser, sold over two million copies. After the war, Loesser continued to write both words and music in Hollywood, including "A Slow Boat to China" and "Spring Will Be a Little Late this Year." His duet of comic seduction, "Baby It's Cold Outside," won the Academy Award for best song in 1949 (*Neptune's Daughter*), even if it made no sense in an MGM vehicle for Esther Williams and Red Skelton, set in southern California during the summer.

Loesser only moved permanently to Broadway after Hollywood success— with the 1948 *Where's Charley?* for Ray Bolger. Between 1950 and 1961, Loesser, the untrained renegade, wrote three shows with striking affinities to those of the same period by the classically trained Bernstein. Two were set in New York, *Guys and Dolls* (1950) and *How to Succeed in Business Without Really Trying* (1961), and one a world apart in time, place, and style, *The Most Happy Fella* (1956), virtually an Italian opera—by a man who once refused to have anything to do with serious music.

Bernstein's four scores reveal an increasing confidence in his relation to American musical theater. The first two New York shows, with books and lyrics by Comden and Green, seethe with the energy and the myth of the *Town* in both titles. The *Town* shows are mirror images—separated by a decade (like another Comden and Green musical mirror of a decade's passing, *It's Always Fair Weather*). In *On the Town* New York is the great place to visit; in *Wonderful Town* it is the great place to live—for the creative artists and young careerists of Greenwich Village. Bernstein's modernist dissonances and unpredictable rhythms bring the surge of the city to musical life. While the opening number of *On the Town*, "New York, New York," is a musical guidebook to the entire city, from the Bronx that's up to the Battery that's down, the opening number of *Wonderful Town*, "Christopher Street," is a guidebook to a particular neighborhood. Both shows have similarly soaring ballads of affirmation—"Lucky To Be Me" and "It's Love." Both have comic patter songs—"Come Up to My Place," the pushy invitation of a brassy female cabbie, and "A Hundred Ways to Lose a Man," its negation by a brainy female, unable to play soft and dumb. *On the Town* has sadder ballads (for the twenty-four hours must end), "Lonely Town" and "Some Other Time." *Wonderful Town* has better musical parody: the sentimental "Ohio," the bouncy "Wrong Note Rag," and the odd "Conversation Piece," Bernstein's first attempt to mirror verbal conversation as twelve-tone musical composition.

Like Comden and Green's scripts for the *Town* shows, which suggest their experience in writing revues of isolated scenes and sketches, Bernstein's *Town* scores split into clearly demarcated songs and orchestral dance pieces, united by the unmistakable color of the Bernstein sound. His scores for *Candide* and *West Side Story*, however, are totally integrated musical theater conceptions, in which vocal and orchestral music, dialogue, song, and dance are inseparable. *Candide*'s problem as musical theater was that its score was too difficult, brilliantly colored, and complexly orchestrated for performers on a Broadway stage or musicians in a Broadway pit. Its script (originally by Lillian Hellman) was as uncompromising as it was untidy— Candide's relentless journey from belief that all in the world is for the best, through a series of disasters all over the world, to a conviction that the world is a mess best left to its own devices. The only human responsibility is to make one's own garden grow—a pessimistic surrender of political activism in a decade famous for its blacklist, about which Hellman and Bernstein knew only too well. For its successful 1974 revival, Hugh Wheeler tidied and brightened up the book, while Harold Prince shrank operetta silks to presentational leotards, trimming the size and scope of the conception, cast, and orchestra. In making *Candide* manageable, the revival also drained much of its musical color.[3] There was something appropriate (if not inevitable) about its 1982 restaging by the New York City Opera.

Bernstein's score, like the show's script, is a deliberate interplay between operetta and irony, past and present, classical and modernist. While the opening chorus sings "The Best of All Possible Worlds," syncopated rhythms puncture their cheerful statement while chattering strings and squawking winds undercut their apparent harmonies. This dissonant blast of an ascending, two-note cadence in the brass section can be clearly heard, warming up for its tragic reincarnation in "Somewhere" of *West Side Story*. Cunegonde's aria of moral debate between virture and jewelry, "Glitter and Be Gay," is the most brilliant, most demanding, and most difficult piece of virtuoso singing ever required of a Broadway soprano. The glitter of jewelry triumphs in a series of glittering if almost unsingable cadenzas. Even Barbara Cook, the most brilliant Broadway soprano of the decade (or any other?), had understandable difficulties with it on stage, eight shows a week.[4]

Candide's aria of desolation, "It Must Be Me," is, in contrast to Cunegonde's cadenzas, virtually an *a capella* folk song. "Quiet" is a twelve-

Jerome Robbins demonstrates the "*West Side Story* step" to George Chakiris on the set; "The Dance at the Gym" onstage.

tone popular song; "I Am Easily Assimilated" easily assimilates a tango with "good Jewish music;" "Bon Voyage" is another joyful chorus number with odd rhythms and bizarre orchestrations, in which a cheerful populace bids adieu to the show's heroes as they drown. Unlike the *Town* scores, *Candide* is almost entirely vocal, with no obligatory ballet, only a dissonant waltz that introduces us to decadent Paris, the modernist answer to that most lushly romantic of operetta waltzes from *The Merry Widow*. No Broadway score has ever been simultaneously so savage and so ornate.

For the score of *West Side Story*, Bernstein takes his musical colors back to a *Town* no longer wonderful but torn by racial and ethnic strife. In musicalizing *Romeo and Juliet* as a battle of white and Puerto Rican street gangs, Bernstein, lyricist Sondheim, librettist Arthur Laurents, and choreographer Jerome Robbins found another way to invest the Jewish social conscience in topical problems, as Kern and Hammerstein did with "Ol' Man River." Born as *East Side Story*, a battle between Jewish and Catholic families on New York's Lower East Side, *West Side Story* moved crosstown and uptown to find greater social relevance. It allowed Jewish creators to address their own ethnic subjugation while deflecting it to an even more oppressed social group, just as *Show Boat* did. Laurents, whose *Home of the Brave* treated racial and sexual tensions in the American military, created a social context for Bernstein's music, which mirrored the rhythms of modern urban street life.

Jerome Robbins found a style for slum kids to dance to that street music. His choreographic leitmotif—soaring arms opening wide, one arm spreading toward the earth and the other toward the sky, as dancers rise on the ball of one foot—becomes an unforgettable image of reaching for sky and longing for space. The movement reveals that these kids are not fancy free but fancy that one day they might fly free from the social tangle of these very streets. For *West Side Story* Robbins did not plan one big ballet but five: the opening "Prologue" war between the Jets and Sharks, the "Dance at the Gym" which is both a war and a romance, the "Cool" to relax before the big rumble, that "Rumble" to conclude act one, and the "Somewhere" that recapitulates the entire plot—the dream of an ideal someplace destroyed by the same racial hatred as the other place called the West Side. This was not a show with occasional dance. It was a dance show.

It was also a song show, for Sondheim's lyrics found a style for these slum kids to sing words—usually as terse and urgent punctuation of Bernstein's dynamic rhythms. "Something's Coming" is a rhythmic hymn of anticipation, mostly in monosyllables, that snap with percussive onomatopeia:

> With a click,
> With a shock,

> Phone'll jingle,
> Door'll knock.
> Open the latch.

These are words and references that a tenement kid would both know and use. In "Cool," Sondheim fits street slang to the musical cadences of popular song—"stay cool," "stay loose," "easy does it." In "Maria," Sondheim does not multiply images and metaphors for Tony to describe the beloved he has just met. Tony merely says he'll never stop saying Maria, and he isn't kidding. He says her name exactly thirty times in the song, more times than any other beloved has ever been named in any song. The repetition not only is correct dramatically (the boy is overwhelmed by the sight of the something that he knew was coming) and psychologically (he works as a drugstore stockboy, not as a poet). It also shows Sondheim's courage: he doesn't have to show off.

He can show off in other songs—the comic numbers that even a musical tragedy which ends in a death and a dirge needs for variety. "America" combines the rhythms of hispanic street life with ironic lyrics that undercut the Puerto Rico of their origins: Puerto Rico's dirt, poverty, and squalor cannot be forgotten or romanticized. Despite discrimination in New York, America is a comfortable place for Puerto Ricans—with wall-to-wall floors, paved roads for Buicks, electric current, washing machines, and clothes worth washing. Sondheim's ethnic stereotyping is acceptable in dramatic context, for members of an ethnic group have earned the right to poke fun at their own culture.

"Gee Officer Krupke," the show's comic interlude before its final tragedy, is a satiric kids-eye view of confused adult theories of juvenile delinquency. Everybody blames somebody else: judges blame mental problems, psychoanalysts blame unemployment, social workers blame bad kids, and the cops simply want to sweep the streets.

> Dear kindly judge, your hona',
> My parents treat me rough:
> With all the marijuana
> They won't give me a puff.

Bernstein's oom-pah oom-pah tune (a parody of the older generation's tastes) joins Sondheim's argot of tenement life: to earn a buck as a soda jerk "means like be a schmuck."[5] As for Krupke, he can go Krup himself.

In the kids' analysis, adults merely serve their own narrow views and private needs; they don't care about the kids at all. But then the kids don't much care about each other. The "Somewhere" ballet thoroughly destroys the illusion that things might be better elsewhere. There is nowhere else. America (as that song makes clear) is as good as it gets. No combination of American music, dance, dialogue, and lyrics is as disturbing a weave of American musical theater and social disillusion as *West Side Story*.

If Leonard Bernstein composed scores as variations of musical tone within the same color system, Frank Loesser's musical scores adopted the principle of musical opposition. Loesser's *Guys and Dolls* and *Most Happy Fella* depend on multiple layers and levels of musical style. The opening number of *Guys and Dolls*, built on two conflicting songs, sets the style for the show to follow. First, a Damon Runyon trio of Times Square denizens sings a "Fugue for Tinhorns," reading the racing form, doping the ponies, arguing that they've "got the horse right here," a three-part invention of contrapuntal syncopation. Their ragtime fugue is immediately answered by a band of Salvation Army soldiers singing "Follow the Fold," a strict march, like "Onward Christian Soldiers," in the block harmonies of choral hymns. The two songs of the opening number establish a key dramatic opposition: the gamblers, in their natural habitat, sing individualist fugal lines; the invading reformers sing as a group. This musical will be about a lone gambler, Sky Masterson, who falls for a member of the group, the "mission doll" Sarah Brown, Runyon's Times Square answer to *Major Barbara*. In the end, Sky will elicit her individual expression of love and he will join her band to bang the supportive drum.

The two songs also establish the show's conflict of musical styles—a battle between the rhythmic syncopation of jazz and the strict rhythms of nineteenth-century hymns. The missionaries sing sweetly and spiritually: the delicate waltz, "More I Cannot Wish You"; the mission doll's vision of romance, "I'll Know." The tinhorns sing rhythm songs in their gambler's argot: the bouncy little tune, which catalogs all human experience as a pairing of "Guys and Dolls"; the search for a place to hold "The Oldest Established Permanent Floating Crap Game in New York"; the song of anticipation, "Luck Be a Lady," once they find it in the city sewers. Having established the two opposing musical styles, Loesser jumps the gap when the gamblers fulfill an obligation to attend a mission meeting. Nicely Nicely Johnson's specialty solo, "Sit Down, You're Rocking the Boat," is a mock-revivalist confession by a confirmed tinhorn who experiences the power of the almighty in a Jonah-like dream. The ecstasies of singing unite gamblers and missionaries within a single gospel group. Loesser's score, like Runyon's stories, implies that beneath the appearances of social surfaces, gamblers and missionaries alike are members of a single human band—united by song.

To the gamblers and missionaries, Loesser adds a third musical style. As in *Pal Joey*, entertainers inhabit the lowlife world, and two numbers take us to the runway stage of the Hot Box (now there's a name!) for the songs of Miss Adelaide and the Hot Box Girls. The first is a parody of life on the all-American farm, "A Bushel and a Peck"; the second an enactment of mock anger, "Take Back Your Mink," after discovering that a gentleman's expensive gifts were sexual bait, not mere tokens of his esteem. These comic stage numbers—more broadly satiric than the nightclub numbers in *Pal Joey*—suggest the yearning for innocence by those no longer innocent. That yearning leads to two offstage numbers for the Brooklynese Miss Adelaide (Vivian Blaine), a dialect flower of delicate innocence in a world that is not innocent, the lowlife mirror of the "mission doll."

"Adelaide's Lament" is a musical reading of a medical textbook that diagnoses her perpetual cold as psychosomatic. Because her gambler fiancé of fourteen years, Nathan Detroit, refuses to marry her (her aspirations are as pure as her activities are otherwise), Miss Adelaide has caught a cough, la grippe, the postnasal drip. The untutored pronunciation of a barely literate character encounters the tongue-twisting terminology of medical jargon ("psychosomatic symptoms . . . affecting the upper respiratory track," "chronic organic syndromes, toxic or hypertense"). The result is a musical struggle with the meaning and pronunciation of words, a projection of linguistic experience into musical soliloquy. How do you get multisyllabic medical jargon into a comic song for a barely literate nightclub entertainer who has a cold because her boyfriend of fourteen years won't marry her? Nothing to it: you write "Adelaide's Lament."

The duet for Nathan and Adelaide, "Sue Me," is another flavorful weave of singing and conversation, musical structure and verbal rambling, innocence and experience. Like Sky, Nathan wants a doll, not a wife. Adelaide is on the attack ("You promise me this, you promise me that"); Nathan's response is the musical equivalent of a shrug of the shoulders: "So, sue me, sue me, what can you do me?" In a unique combination of talk and song, Loesser makes it possible for Nathan's shoulder shrug to sing in colloquial Jewish phrases: "It's true—so noo?" How do you get Damon Runyon characters to sing? You find verbal-musical patterns that capture the rhythms and argot of their speech and that contrast the harshness of their experience with the core of their innocence.

The Most Happy Fella works in a very different style with a surprisingly similar method. Based on the 1924 Sidney Howard play, *They Knew What They Wanted*, *The Most Happy Fella* follows a middle-aged Italian-American from California's Napa Valley, Tony Esposito, to San Francisco, where he falls for a waitress. He proposes marriage by mail, sending her a photograph of his handsome young foreman, Joey, as bait. When she discovers both Tony's age and duplicity, she has an affair with the Joey whose picture attracted her. She eventually comes to love the older man for his kindness and his passion. Tony converts an ordinary American waitress named Amy into a vision of Italian romance whom he christens Rosabella.

How did Loesser get this story to sing? He becomes a musical chameleon. Recognizing that the essential conflict of the story is between Italian and American life, between the actual Amy and the romantic ideal of Rosabella, Loesser builds a score with two kings of songs. There are

American pop songs for Amy, Joey, her friend Cleo, the inevitable soubrette (created by the wonderful if little known Susan Johnson), and Cleo's inevitable comic beau, Herman; there are Italian songs for Tony, both Pucciniesque arias and folkish tarantellas. Working under the spell of Ezio Pinza in *South Pacific*, Loesser created another Broadway role for an opera singer (literally created for Pinza, the role went to Robert Weede after Pinza's death).

Like Bernstein's *Candide* of the same year, *The Most Happy Fella* displays an astounding range of musical and vocal color. There are more than thirty separate musical slots in the show—in so far as any can be separated at all. Most flow in, through, and over the dialogue: song, talk, and scene are inseparable. The original cast recording was released in two versions—a single LP of eighteen excerpts, and a recording of the entire show on three LP records, the first complete "opera" recording of a Broadway show.[6] The Italian songs soar with their musical richness and passionate intensity. The tarantellas—"Abbondanza" (with the Loesser lyric in Italian), "Sposalizio," and the joyful title tune—feel as exuberantly Italian as "Funiculi, Funicula." The operatic passion of Tony's romantic waltz to "Rosabella," his prayer to his dead "Mama, Mama," and the sublime fullness of "My Heart Is So Full of You" are as close to musical ecstasy as any American songwriter ever attempted.

From these ecstatic heights the show bounces down for three Loesser pop tunes that became hit singles of the fifties: "Standing on the Corner" (the favorite pastime of small-town American males), "Big 'D'" (little a, double l, a, s), and Joey's anthem of wanderlust, "Joey, Joey, Joey." The score is as comfortable with Italian-American immigrants and small-town middle America as was *Guys and Dolls* with Jewish-American lowlife and big-city shyster America. If it weren't for a show which opened six weeks earlier, *The Most Happy Fella* would have been the decade's most impressive theatrical journey to a distant musical style.

That show was *My Fair Lady*, which opened on March 15, 1956, and ran for six years, longer than any previous Broadway musical. Its creators, Alan Jay Lerner and Frederick Loewe, were a very odd couple—which worked particularly well for *My Fair Lady*. Lerner was born in New York with all the advantages: the upper-middle-class Jewish family owned the chain of Lerner dress shops. He was graduated from Harvard in 1940, one year after Leonard Bernstein.[7] "Fritz" Loewe was a literal child of Operettaland, born in Berlin in 1904. His father even played Prince Danilo in the original Berlin cast of *The Merry Widow*. Classically trained in European conservatories, Loewe was the youngest piano soloist ever to appear with the Berlin Philharmonic. Fleeing Hitler's Germany in 1933, Loewe arrived on Broadway to carry American theater music fifty years backward to the era before Tin Pan Alley.

That backward step was exactly what Lerner's flashy lyrics needed, for

Lerner without Loewe overwhelms composers in a cacophonous rush of self-conscious cleverness. Loewe's bouncy marches, schmaltz ballads, and sprightly gavottes tame Lerner's lyrics and make them human. Their shows understandably live in the past—a Scotland of centuries ago in *Brigadoon* (1947), a Mormon pioneer on the western frontier of *Paint Your Wagon* (1951), the Belle Epoque of *Gigi*, the Arthurian Round Table of *Camelot* (1960). *My Fair Lady* marches back to the 1912 London of Bernard Shaw's *Pygmalion*.

How do you get Shaw to sing? In particular, how do you get the Shavian hero—distinguished by his unconventional ideas and brilliant way of phrasing them—to sing? Singing can be a medium for passion, satire, even ironic social observation. But how can it avoid reducing brittle intellect and tart ideas to melodic sugar? The sugar so offended Shaw in *The Chocolate Soldier*, based on his *Arms and the Man*, that the 1908 Oscar Straus operetta was the first and last musical adaptation Shaw permitted during his lifetime. If Shaw hadn't died in 1950, *Pygmalion* could not have become *My Fair Lady*. To avoid the operetta sugar, Lerner and Loewe decided that the Shavian hero doesn't sing. He talk-sings—in Gilbert and Sullivan patter songs (Shavian contemporaries), softened and warmed by lush musical backing. With Higgins's talk-songs, *My Fair Lady* moves seamlessly from Shaw's dialogue, much of which Lerner's script retains, to Lerner and Loewe numbers. Since the flow of Shavian wit is itself a stream of verbal music, Lerner and Loewe simply literalized the musical metaphor.

The apocryphal story has it that Lerner and Loewe originally expected Professor Higgins to sing like a bird, but Rex Harrison croaked like a frog. So they let him talk the songs instead. Anyone who has ever attempted to hum or sing the tunes beneath Higgins's talk-songs will never believe this story. The tunes are unsingable: not even tunes, but oom-pah oom-pah vamps and runs. Most of Higgins's melodies sound as if their composer wore *lederhosen*—and perhaps "Fritz" Loewe did. It was not that Rex Harrison couldn't sing the notes; as if to counter his vocal critics, on the London cast recording he self-consciously sustains as many of them as possible.[8] The talking song of Henry Higgins was the stylistic answer to musicalizing Shavian wit. When Lerner and Loewe repeat the technique—with Louis Jourdan's talk-songs in *Gigi* and Richard Burton's in *Camelot*—they retain their own convention without the powerful dramatic reason for it. These later scores ask not how can a character be made to sing but how can a character be made to talk-sing like Henry Higgins?

Having settled on the Shavian style of Higgins's songs, Lerner and Loewe weave two other levels of musical style into the score—just as Rodgers and Loesser wove multiple musical styles into mirrors of class and character. Eliza, the lowly flower seller whom Higgins turns into a lady, could sing with the conventional fire and passion of operetta and musical heroines. The passionate, full-throated sound of her songs—the longing of "Wouldn't It Be Lovely?" the anger of "Just You Wait, 'Enry 'Iggins," the joy of "I Could Have Danced All Night," the insistence of "Show Me" —contrasts with the dry wit of Higgins's talk-songs. This contrast not only gives the score musical variety and color but embodies the essential dramatic conflict between intellect and emotion. The third musical style belongs to Alfred Doolittle, Eliza's working-class dad, who, like Higgins, is an unconventional moralist—resisting such constraints of middle-class morality as work, sobriety, thrift, and marriage. Lerner and Loewe saw Doolittle as a refugee from the English music hall—literally, since the veteran music-hall performer, Stanley Holloway, created the role. Doolittle's "With a Little Bit of Luck" and "Get Me to the Church on Time" are bouncy, raucous music-hall numbers, oom-pah marches with conventional major harmonies and not a trace of American syncopation. There is theater history as well as dramatic character in this careful score—a weave of Gilbert and Sullivan, German operetta, English music hall, and American musical.

Did Lerner and Loewe successfully musicalize Shaw or did they reduce him to operetta sugar after all? This question (which assumes Shaw's inherent superiority to musicals) was a favorite for critics in 1956. Its answer inevitably carried them to the ending of *My Fair Lady*, in which Eliza returns to Higgins's flat. He, slouched in his favorite chair, hat covering his eyes, asks her where the devil his slippers might be. She "understands" that question as a declaration of love—as declarative as Higgins can manage—and the curtain falls (p. 191).[9] Like all musicals, *My Fair Lady* ends with an apparently romantic resolution—although it is uncertain as to whether the pair will experience a marriage or a menage. *Pygmalion*, however, ends when Eliza informs Higgins that she is going to marry her eminently eligible, hyphenated young suitor, Freddy Eynsford-Hill. After she leaves the Higgins flat, apparently to do so, Higgins exclaims, "Ha ha! Freddy! Freddy!! Ha ha ha ha ha!!!!!" as the curtain falls (p. 89). Shaw even wrote a lengthy epilogue (as he did for so many plays) that depicted Eliza's wretched married life as a language teacher with the empty-headed Freddy. In *My Fair Lady* Higgins conjures up that wretched life in the fuming interlude passages of "I've Grown Accustomed to Her Face."

This supposed difference between *Pygmalion* and *My Fair Lady* should be laid to rest. A key text between the two is the 1938 British film of *Pygmalion*, starring Leslie Howard and Wendy Hiller, co-directed by Howard and Shaw favorite, Anthony Asquith, with the screenplay by Shaw himself. That film ends with the same return of Eliza to Higgins's flat, his same slouch in the chair, same hat over the eyes, and same question about the slippers. Many scenes in the musical (for example, the montage of Eliza's language lessons to "The Rain in Spain Lies Mainly in the Plain") come directly from the 1938 film. Even without that film, one cannot ignore the subtextual implications of Shaw's original. While Higgins and Eliza are explicit opposites in class and temperament, while she is both the statue he creates and the human equal who fights back, such differences and conflicts always look like love in comedies. Theater history and convention prepare audiences to believe that opposites attract: fighting merely proves the attraction between Petruchio and Katherine, Beatrice and Benedick, or Shaw's own Jack Tanner and Ann Whiteside. The romantic ending of *My Fair Lady* makes explicit what *Pygmalion* kept implicit. What do all those "Ha" exclamations of Shaw's curtain line mean in the first place? Shaw was a very shrewd playwright who wrote his explicit romantic denials into his published commentaries, not into his performed plays. In the theater, the unspoken is often more powerful than any utterance.

A much more subtle sugaring of *Pygmalion* occurs in the musical's view of language. In *My Fair Lady*, Higgins's concern for proper pronunciation makes him a crank—crusty and curmudgeonly—whose life is so barren he devotes it to trivia. In American culture, to worship speech is to serve a false god, reversing the order of moral importance between content and style, thought and phrase. Americans like to believe that it doesn't matter how you say something but what you say. For Lerner, Higgins is a comic nut who needs to be straightened out, broadened, humanized by Eliza's passion and sincerity. Lerner and Loewe establish that he is a nut in his first two songs—"Why Can't the English?" (who's he to make such lordly social pronouncements?) and "I'm Just an Ordinary Man" (if he thinks he's ordinary, he doesn't know the meaning of ordinary words). Higgins is so blind he can sing that he will never let a woman in his life—right after he has let her into his house. The Lerner and Loewe score converts Higgins and Eliza into behavioral extremes that suffer from comic blindness, his the result of intellectual affectation and hers of social deprivation. The two meet in a romantic middle. As in so many American musicals, love in *My Fair Lady* crosses the borders of social class.

Higgins was a comic maniac even for Shaw, who was too shrewd a playwright not to make his philosopher kings into comic fools as well. With the intellectual ammunition of Shavian wit, Higgins's comic nearsightedness does not refute a political philosophy but dramatizes it. Higgins's talking songs replace a political philosopher with a witty fool. The Lerner and Loewe score captures Shaw's style even as it fogs his point: that language *does* define human existence and social possibility. The class system is (not was) determined by how people (not just the English) speak. *My Fair Lady* confines this question of speech to the class-bound England of 1912, circumscribed within a society Americans see as distant and foreign.

For Shaw, the difference between a 1912 flower seller and a countess is not birth but education. The countess has been taught a certain style of speech, and because she speaks in that style her existence as a countess is both recognized and confirmed in its noble beauty. If the flower seller is not taught to speak like a countess it must be because her society wishes her to remain a flower seller and wishes to preserve the distinction between flower sellers and countesses. But don't Americans continue to define people—whether in life or in art—by styles of speech? A person who speaks Brooklynese might be cast for Paddy Chayefsky or Millertime but not for the Oval Office or E. F. Hutton. Exactly who in American life is served by the idea that it doesn't matter how you speak, except those who already speak well?

Shaw's *Pygmalion* uses speech to examine the economic consequences of pretending that speech doesn't matter. *My Fair Lady* uses speech as a source of comedic conflict between two opposite human types, ending in the movement of both toward the other. Higgins discovers he has feelings (he's "Grown Accustomed to Her Face") and Eliza discovers she has dignity. In these discoveries, Alfred Doolittle must not be a working-class philosopher but a music-hall eccentric. In *Pygmalion*, when Doolittle agrees to let his unmarried daughter cohabit with a gentleman if he's paid off, it is because he knows that all sexual arrangements—legal or otherwise—are financial. In *My Fair Lady*, it simply reflects Doolittle's jolly contempt for respectability, a deviance which the comic in musical comedy has enjoyed since Kid Conner and Con Kidder of Victor Herbert's *The Red Mill*. In the end, *My Fair Lady* is not a British political comedy about the economics of language but an American musical comedy about love's triumph over the obstacles of social class. What makes it an American musical is not its ending but its score that explicitly defines Higgins and Eliza as the kinds of opposite characters who always fall in love in musicals.

What happens to this most stylish of theater musicals when it moves to the screen? The simple answer is not much. The 1964 film duplicates the show—scene by scene, line by line, number by number, note for note. (Minor exceptions include reversing the order of Doolittle's "Little Bit of Luck" and Higgins's "Ordinary Man.") Rather than cutting numbers, the usual practice of film adaptations, *My Fair Lady* transcribes all twenty-one slots of the show. As with *Gigi*, Lerner and Loewe held all the cards, guaranteeing the reverential transcription of their stage work. And as with *Gigi*, the reverence brought more reverence—another Academy Award for Best Picture. *My Fair Lady* is typical of every transcription of a Broadway "masterpiece" since 1953—only better.

Like the original cast recording of the Broadway show, the film of *My Fair Lady* is a permanent record of an ephemeral event. Shows come and go, but records and movies remain. As a high-budget state-of-the-art transcription of a stage production, supported by both visual and musical taste, in CinemaScope and stereo, *My Fair Lady* is of immense cultural and historical value, even if it were only a transcription of a preexisting work, an "opera film." The substitution of dubbed movie star Audrey Hepburn for musical performer Julie Andrews seemed a terrible mistake to many, especially Broadway buffs, especially with Andrews's screen stardom in *Mary Poppins* of the very same year. The orchestrations for the soundtrack sound tubbier and thumpier, the tempi more leaden, the performances more canned than on the original Broadway cast recording (as they always do on movie soundtracks). For Broadway buffs, the film of *My Fair Lady* was the same as the show—only worse. For movie buffs, the film was too reverential for a "real movie musical"—giving up the clever game between stylized song and credible movie storytelling.[10] Characters sing in *My Fair Lady* while walking through the apparently real world—simply because it is conventional for characters to sing in musicals.

The unique filmic value of *My Fair Lady* lies in its differences from the Broadway original—its star, Audrey Hepburn; its director, George Cukor; and the way that the camera and frame emphasize details of Cecil Beaton's design. Why is Audrey Hepburn in this movie? She can't much sing (as *Funny Face* made clear)—not nearly as well as Julie Andrews, not nearly well enough to produce the passionate full-throated sounds the score requires to reveal Eliza's heart. The easy answer is that Audrey Hepburn is the popular movie star that an expensive film needed to draw audiences to a reverential blockbuster. But the odd parallels between *My Fair Lady* and *Funny Face* reveal Hepburn as more than a generic movie star with commercial power. The kind of star she is, the meaning of her star persona, is far closer to Eliza Doolittle than the Julie Andrews of *Mary Poppins* and *The Sound of Music*.

As in *Funny Face*, Audrey Hepburn begins in black-and-white darkness—in the grimy nighttime streets of Covent Garden—and blooms into color. The monochrome caterpillar becomes a butterfly, the woman who sells flowers becomes a flower. As in *Funny Face*, she is Cinderella, raised from her ashen cinders to capture the hearts of princes at the Embassy Ball. As in *Funny Face*, the older and wiser genie who is her fairy godmother also becomes her prince charming. While in *Funny Face* Hepburn falls for the older Astaire who controls the magic of visual images, in *My Fair Lady* Hepburn falls for the older Harrison who controls the magic of speech. Higgins, no less than Dick Avery, is a maker and polisher of images. The reason for these parallels is not that Cukor and Beaton made a deliberate response to *Funny Face*. (How could they? The script of the film is identical to the stage show.) The reason is that, like Astaire or Kelly, Hepburn brings her own meaning with her to every film: the Cinderella who emerges from a gray pumpkin to fall for the older magician who taught her to make the transformation.

Parallel to the casting of Hepburn as Eliza, George Cukor and Cecil Beaton visually conceive the film as an extended conflict of Art and Nature. Like *Funny Face*, *My Fair Lady* draws a careful visual contrast between indoors and out, monochrome and color, darkness and light. The house of Henry Higgins is the wizard's cave, filled with magic books and magical apparatus. Cukor packs the wide-frame views of Higgins's library with row

My Fair Lady: vocal lessons on stage (Rex Harrison and Julie Andrews) and film (Audrey Hepburn), where the apparatus resembles a movie soundtrack, as a lens stares from behind

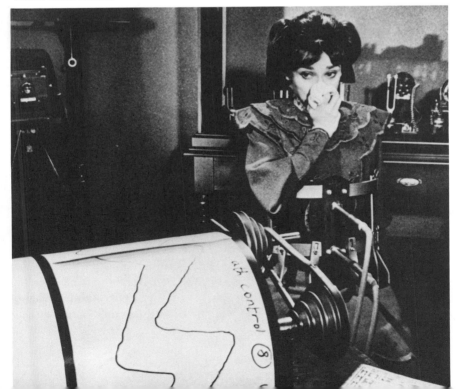

upon infinite row of books, converting Higgins into yet another filmusical Faustus, from whose books come his art.[11] His mechanical devices to aid Eliza's study are both aural and visual. While some record the sounds of her speech and allow them to be played back—like the soundtracks of movies— others allow her to view the way she produces sounds—like the frames of talkies.

Standing silently in the background of Cukor's wide-screen frames are explicit references to the recording of sights and sounds, subtly parallel to the cinema itself. One of the machines that records Eliza's speech produces patterns that resemble a soundtrack, generated in exactly the same way that movies record soundtracks. Directly behind Eliza stands an ancient camera whose lens stares directly into the CinemaScope lens of Harry Stradling's camera, serving no purpose whatever except to connect the events in this story with the invention of the technology that makes film possible. Cukor's cinematic self-references suggest this movie musical as an outgrowth of the technology that produced the vocal machines of Henry Higgins. The art of Higgins leads directly to the art of Cukor. And like the art of Higgins, the movies, whose audiences are composed primarily of Doolittles, are a leveler of class distinctions.

If Higgins's habitat is the cavelike indoors, saturated in deep browns, Eliza's natural habitat is outdoors, blazing with color. For "On the Street Where You Live," Cukor's frames splash the color of a foreground flower into every shot of Eliza and Freddy. The street where she lives is a street of colorful flowers because she is a colorful flower. When Higgins sings of losing Eliza, "I've Grown Accustomed to Her Face," the same street has become drab and autumnal—with gray tree trunks and limbs barren of leaves, brownstone houses devoid of color. Eliza's climactic declaration of mature independence takes place not in the play's parlor but in a Cukor greenhouse, where Eliza waters flowers. Cecil Beaton's clothes for Eliza contain perpetual reminders of flowers in either their colors or patterns. When she returns to the ashen monochrome of Covent Garden wearing her colorful finery, glowing within a drabness she previously matched, the flower she has become no longer matches the soil that produced her.

Covent Garden's fashionable antithesis is the Ascot racetrack, where the "Ascot Gavotte" takes the themes of Art and Nature, monochrome and color into a daytime outdoor world. This time the problem with the garden is not that it is covered by night and poverty but that it is inhabited by people who aren't flowers. Beaton designs exclusively black-and-white costumes, grotesque in shape and ornamentation, for a stiffly formal musical number in an only apparently natural setting. Cukor shoots the number in rigidly motionless formal frames to emphasize the lifeless rigidity of these fashionable folk. This is life become death—crushed not by the social poverty of Covent Garden but by a natural poverty of feeling.

In this visual system, Eliza and Higgins belong together because they represent a marriage of Art and Nature, flower and machine, color and monochrome, Covent Garden and Ascot. They are both "originals." This combination of Hepburn's persona, Cukor's frames, Beaton's design, consistent visual motifs, and artful reminders of cinema itself demonstrate the way that cinematic vision can inject style and meaning into a thoroughly Broadway project. *My Fair Lady* is not an original musical conception for cinema but a theatrical conception brilliantly inflected by cinema values. It is the most one can say for every Hollywood musical between 1958 and 1972: they either added cinematic visual values—editing and atmosphere—to a Broadway property or added one meaningful movie star to a cast of Broadway professionals. *My Fair Lady* did both.

Two other celebrated Academy Award musicals of the period did only the former. *West Side Story* (1961) decorated the Bernstein music and Robbins choreography with wide-screen views of Manhattan streetlife. The prologue, swooping down from the skies into the city streets, is an exhilarating mix of choreography and cutting, stylized movement and realistic decor. The film runs out of visual ideas after its prologue, translating the CinemaScope frame into a stable proscenium arch, within which dances are conceived as purely horizontal, in a relatively flat, open, and static space. The settings of the film retreat from the prologue's challenging mixture of reality and stylization to predictable Expressionist paintings of cityscapes.

Either budget problems, conceptual problems, or the removal of Robbins progressively undermine the film as it rumbles along.[12] The dubbed Maria and Tony—a lifeless Natalie Wood and a wooden Richard Beymer, whose sole talent was the whiteness of his teeth—throw the performance burden on the supporting Anita and Bernardo (veteran performers Rita Moreno and George Chakiris). For all its dance energy, *West Side Story* is another "opera film," resting on the same foundation as the stage show: the dynamic Bernstein music, the audacious Sondheim lyrics, the Robbins choreography, and the novelty of making neorealistic New York street life into song and dance. Whatever its limitations, the movie struck a powerful cultural chord: the first film to sing the spirit of sixties protest against the Krupkes of American life and politics.

Fiddler on the Roof (1971) substitutes the detailed visual atmosphere of a tiny Russian village for the big city of *West Side Story*. In its opening number, "Tradition," lacking the powerful presence of Zero Mostel, who created Tevye on stage, the Norman Jewison images and editing perform a social analysis of the entire Jewish community of Anatevka—cutting freely and rhythmically between the activities of papas, mamas, sons, and daughters. As they go about their daily work, we can clearly see the dust rise from the floor of the barns and we can almost smell the horses, chickens, pigs, and their droppings in the barnyards. This is what cinema does so well—providing social analysis by means of montage and recreating a distant or forgotten way of life in minute visual detail. As the film trudges on for a full three hours, longer than the original show, it seems, like *West Side Story*, more and more tied to its theatrical script, obligated to play all the scenes and do all the numbers, no longer translated into cinema but decorated with cinema.

Jewison's political commentary rests on the metaphoric fiddler of his title: the tenuous position of Jewish life in the Old World, simultaneously settled within its traditions and unsettled within a troubled Europe. Even the traditions of Jewish life are breaking down under the pressure of a twentieth century when young people marry for love not by contract, men and women dance together in public, and social edicts turn former citizens into wandering outcasts. Their expulsion from the little town at the end of the film suggests another departure: not only of those Jews who left for America (and whose descendants would create musicals like this one) but those who went to the Nazi death camps, to disappear, like Anatevka, from the earth.

While atmospheric visual translations of stage hits won Academy Awards, the film musicals that merely added a movie star to a Broadway cast were often more fun. The addition of Doris Day to *The Pajama Game* (1957) at Warner Bros., and the collaboration of stage master George Abbott with film master Stanley Donen, produced not only Day's best musical but the rare Hollywood adaptation that was at least as good as the original. As spokeswoman for the union grievance committee in a pajama factory, Doris Day combined her girl-next-door sweetness with her tough-babe feistiness when she was riled. And there were a lot of grievances at the factory to rile her. Day may not have sung the role better than Broadway veteran Janis Paige, but she sang it as well, filtered through the smile and bounce of her movie-star persona.

Donen's dynamic frames translate the energy of the Adler and Ross score into visual terms. The opening number, "Racing with the Clock," becomes an ecstatic visual race between a speeding song, gliding camera movement, rhythmic cutting on the musical beats, and clever games with camera speed. Day's protest to her fellow workers, "I'm Not at All in Love," is another mixture of musical emotion (she doth protest too much) and camera motion. The comic test, "I'll Never Be Jealous Again," captures the mental movement of the duelling singers in circling tracking shots. In a decade of Hollywood's launderized lyrics, this number refreshingly retains the original's sexual suggestions. "Once a Year Day" takes the energy of the factory outdoors to a park and picnic, mirroring the fun with dynamic interplay between expansive movement and rapid cutting.

This infusion of Broadway material and talent with Hollywood star and visual values was not easily duplicated—even by the same team at the same studio in the very next year. *Damn Yankees* (1958) also added a Warner Bros. star, Tab Hunter, to a complete Broadway package, with directorial responsibility shared by Abbott and Donen. Although critics blamed Hunter for

Mixing Broadway and Hollywood:
Doris Day berates John Raitt
in *The Pajama Game*;
Gwen Verdon vamps Tab
Hunter in *Damn Yankees*.

Leaning toward the future: Gwen Verdon and Bob Fosse dance "Who's Got the Pain" in *Damn Yankees*.

the film's leaden result, the Broadway performers overact up a storm—from the Mephistopheles impersonated by Ray Walston to Gwen Verdon as his witchy accomplice. Whatever Verdon knew about song and dance, Tab Hunter knew about a movie camera, and his sweetly charming Joe Hardy does not sell to the camera but simply allows it to observe him.

The decor of the film is surprisingly flat in comparison to the dynamically deep space of *Pajama Game*'s tree-filled park and machine-filled factory, the camera and choreography surprisingly inert. In "Shoeless Joe from Hannibal Mo" the ballplayers kick up their dancing heels on what purports to be a baseball field. The choreography by Bob Fosse, future directorial master of musicals on both stage and film, ignores the relation of the game to the field on which it is played—the differences between fair and foul, pitcher's mound and home plate, bases and base path, infield and outfield. Fosse's generic choreography looks designed for a Broadway stage, not for a baseball field. Budget may have had something to do with the dull decor and careless detail; Abbott and Donen, who had signed a package deal for both musicals, may have found the money running out of the package. All other differences aside, *The Pajama Game* looks like Donen and *Damn Yankees* does not.

Directorial style almost always accounted for the most vital Hollywood transcriptions. At MGM, Arthur Freed and Vincente Minnelli made their last musical together, *Bells Are Ringing* (1960), reunited with Comden and

Green. Dean Martin joined the Broadway package, replacing Sydney Chaplin, Charlie's eldest son.[13] Adding Martin's star persona to the Judy Holliday vehicle produced another close match of movie star to musical role. As Jeff Moss, a Broadway playwright who's been hitting the bottle harder than the typewriter, Martin fit the public perception of his romance with the grape. Even those who don't care for the liquid Martin style find him charming in this musical.[14] The vivacious answering-service operator Holliday nurses him back to sobriety and success, and the laid back, breezy Martin hoofs with Holliday in casual soft-shoe duets like "Just in Time." In "Drop that Name," Minnelli's eye adds stylish brilliance to a satire of New York's pretentious social elite, a Black-and-White Ball of burlesques and grotesques in answer to *An American in Paris.* Though *Bells Are Ringing* is neither vintage Freed nor vintage Minnelli—cramped by a middle-class present, a CinemaScope frame imprisoned in stageset interiors, and self-conscious disguises for Holliday's shape—it is pleasant enough Holliday and Martin.

The danger of playing mix and match with Hollywod stars and Broadway performers was to find no musical style where the two could meet. Without a Donen or Minnelli the result could be no style whatever—the deadliest sin for a musical, on stage or screen. MGM veteran Charles Walters kept Debbie Reynolds afloat in *The Unsinkable Molly Brown* (1964), as he kept Judy Garland afloat fifteen years earlier. But even MGM veteran George Sidney made a mess with *Bye Bye Birdie* (1963)—one of the worst musicals of the decade (or any other). The least distinctive director of MGM musicals in the glory days, Sidney leaped the stylistic gulfs between the Wild West of *Annie Get Your Gun* (1950), the reverential 1951 *Show Boat*, the 3-D camp of *Kiss Me Kate* (1953), and the cool of Sinatra's *Pal Joey* (1957).

Bye Bye Birdie promised the usual something for everyone: Broadway and TV star Dick Van Dyke, Hollywood teen star Ann-Margret, teen rocker Bobby Rydell, nonsinging movie star Janet Leigh in an absurd black wig, the miscast Broadway dramatic actress Maureen Stapleton, Broadway comedian Paul Lynde, Ed Sullivan himself, a deservedly unknown Jessie Pearson in the title role, and an inexhaustible supply of camera tricks. The original by Charles Strouse and Lee Adams, directed by Gower Champion, was a stylish spoof of topical crazes—teen talk and songs, the drafting of Elvis Presley, the godly Sunday presence of Ed Sullivan. The styleless film buries the spoof in a sarcophagus of overstated bad taste, so desperate to assure us we're having a good time that it smears animated happy faces all over the frame.

Some filmusical messes simply set the Broadway cast and stage scenery in front of a camera and let it run—*Li'l Abner* (1959); *How to Succeed in Business Without Really Trying* (1967). These films saved in gold what they gained in lead. Others melted a lot of gold into a load of lead. *Guys and Dolls*

(1955) combined the always quirky Marlon Brando as gambler Sky Masterson, the always casual Frank Sinatra as the Jewish Nathan Detroit, the dubbed English movie star Jean Simmons (Olivier's Ophelia) as Sarah Brown, and the boffo Broadway comedienne Vivian Blaine as the Adelaide she originated. Produced by Samuel Goldwyn, who always believed that big was best, *Guys and Dolls* was directed by Joseph L. Mankiewicz (who never directed a musical—before or since), fresh from a romp with Brando in *Julius Caesar* and on his way to such lighthearted triumphs as *Suddenly Last Summer* and *Cleopatra*. How could experienced showmen spend so much time and money putting together a package that was so obviously wrong?

Some filmusical projects made sense and were made sensibly. The *Funny Girl* that brought Broadway stardom to Barbara Streisand in 1964, combining her belting voice, Jewish humor, and showbiz chic, brought her film stardom four years later with the same combination, in a solidly directed film by William Wyler. Although Wyler had never directed musicals, like James Whale and Henry King he knew how to make movies. Straining to imitate Mae West, Streisand never came to life under Gene Kelly's direction in *Hello Dolly!* (1969); caked with mascara, not even her eyes could come to life under Vincente Minnelli's direction in the Lerner-Burton Lane flop, *On a Clear Day You Can See Forever* (1970)—after a lovely opening number in a sea of flowers. Streisand did better in Streisand movies than in Broadway adaptations—from her Brice sequel, *Funny Lady* (1973), to *Yentl* (1983), which grafted her own Jewish roots to a musical adaptation of Lower East Side Yiddish theater. In Streisand's 1976 version of *A Star Is Born*, unlike Garland's in 1954, neither her own stardom nor the value of stardom is ever in doubt.

Other filmusicals were made sensibly but made little sense. Mervyn LeRoy, veteran of both *Gold Diggers of 1933* and the 1953 *Rose Marie*, replaced Ethel Merman in *Gypsy* (1962) with foghorn Rosalind Russell, draining the score of its musical color—the primary value of the show in the first place. Veteran Sidney Lumet, noted for neorealist New York film dramas like *12 Angry Men*, *The Pawnbroker*, *Network*, and *Dog Day Afternoon*, slugged through an obligatory film version of *The Wiz* (1978), which proved that rock could be as bland as Victor Herbert. Veteran John Huston, noted for ironic studies of human foibles and failures, from *The Maltese Falcon* and *The Treasure of the Sierra Madre* to *Prizzi's Honor*, slugged through an obligatory film version of *Annie* (1982), which proved that comic strips could be as gray as the classifieds. There was something so *old* about these projects that were supposedly about and for the young—old thinking about old conventions in an old style.

Other musical adaptations tried hard not be sensible and made even less sense. Richard Lester of television commercials and the two Beatles films, *A Hard Day's Night* and *Help!*, struggled mightily to make *A Funny Thing Happened on the Way to the Forum* (1966) as funny as its title and as breezy as the Beatles. While many film buffs admire its funky frenzy, most musical buffs share the opinion of the film's star, Zero Mostel:

> The great thing about the piece on stage was that it was one set, sixteen characters, three houses, and you did it very simply. You go to the movie and there's horses, zebras, peacocks shitting all over the place, your father's moustache, orphans, winos, donkeys with hard-ons . . . [15]

While Lester tries too hard with Sondheim's *Forum*, Broadway director Harold Prince either tries too hard or not at all with Sondheim's *A Little Night Music* (1977). Adding Elizabeth Taylor to the Broadway cast, the film presumably aspired to a mature, Mozartian charm, the musical equivalent of Ingmar Bergman's comedy of youth and age, *Smiles of a Summer Night*, on which the show is based. The result was a precious bore: Taylor looks old enough to play Hermione Gingold. Prince equates film style with relentless cutting, refusing to construct a two-shot and let the camera be.

Joshua Logan, who tinted Rodgers and Hammerstein with filters at Fox, returned to decorate Lerner and Loewe twice. Logan's ponderous *Camelot* (1967) spread Lerner and Loewe's trademark talk-songs to an entire cast of mumblers, supporting the postcard scenery. Logan's *Paint Your Wagon* (1969), with Lee Marvin and Clint Eastwood, who alternately mumble and croak, is as unmusical a musical as has ever been made. Call it *McCabe and Mr. Miller Go to the Spaghetti Western Whorehouse with Laryngitis*. There are few filmusicals to match it for sheer bad taste. Although Logan was an inexhaustible treasure of cinematic bad taste, some credit must also go to Alan Jay Lerner. He spent the two decades after Loewe's retirement pushing collaborators around—whether composers or directors. Lerner's progressive demise is a metaphoric history of both Broadway and Hollywood musicals over the same two decades.

Although movies had been adapting Broadway musicals since the coming of the synchronized soundtrack, only in the late 1950s did Hollywood surrender completely to Broadway. The decades of drought produced the occasional original, so long as the star was English (four for Julie Andrews—*Mary Poppins*, *Thoroughly Modern Millie*, *Darling Lili*, *Star!*—one for Rex Harrison—*Doctor Dolittle*). As the number of musical productions on Broadway also fell steadily, films even hopped aboard near misses or clear flops. While the 1950s were peak years both on Broadway and in Hollywood—from *An American in Paris* to *Funny Face*, from *Guys and Dolls* to *West Side Story*—after 1957 Broadway and Hollywood slid downhill together.

17

The State of the Art, My Friend

M O D E R N I S T   M U S I C A L
M E T A P H O R   O N   S T A G E   A N D
S C R E E N   (1 9 7 0 -   )

In the late 1960s came the American cultural revolution—rising public protest against the war in Viet Nam, the march on Washington, the counterculture's sexual liberation and drug experimentation, the assassinations of Robert Kennedy and Martin Luther King, Jr., Lyndon Johnson's abdication, sit-ins at Berkeley and Columbia, the Grant Park riots during the 1968 Democratic Convention, the Stonewall riot in New York, and a trip to the moon. The bards of popular culture sang this revolution—the Stones, the Doors, Dylan, "Sympathy for the Devil," "Lucy in the Sky with Diamonds," and movies like *The Graduate, Easy Rider, Bonnie and Clyde,* and *2001.* The American musical, a more conservative and retrospective cultural medium than rock music or cult movies, was also on the move— away from stories and toward self-consciousness, away from variants within a stable form and toward an exploration of its forms and its past. The "concept musical" replaced the "realist musical" on both stage and screen.

Although concept musical has become the accepted term, it assumes an opposite—a "realist musical" or "story musical"—as if that opposite were not itself a concept. This older concept, which can be traced from opera to Oscar Hammerstein, reconciled the irreconcilable—internal psychology and singing. A carnival barker sifted through his hopes and a king of Siam mulled over his puzzlement by singing them aloud. Only the vitality of musicals built on this concept hid its paradox for over three decades: that a realistic musical is an oxymoron. To sing thoughts and feelings is necessarily to stylize them. With the steady contraction of new shows within the old concept, the few writers, producers, and directors who stuck with musicals turned to explore the very paradoxes and contradictions in the old concept. How can the stylization of musicals represent *life* at all? How can a song be a projection of internal psychology? Like the modernist move toward

320

self-consciousness in every twentieth-century art, the concept musical explored itself—its forms, its traditions, its variants, its conventions of credibility and style. Songs became less psychological expressions of specific characters than metaphoric comments on personal belief, social custom, or musical tradition. "Modernist musical" or "musical metaphor" describes the new concept better than "concept musical," which simply changed concepts to fit the new cultural times.

The differences between Harold Prince's 1966 stage production of John Kander and Fred Ebb's *Cabaret* and Bob Fosse's 1972 film illustrate the movement from narrative to metaphor. Prince's *Cabaret* straddled the gap between old and new. Like so many backstage musicals, from *Show Boat* to *Guys and Dolls*, from *Top Hat* to *The Band Wagon*, *Cabaret* divides its musical slots between stage numbers and story numbers. The stage numbers create the atmosphere of the Kit Kat Klub, a Berlin cabaret in the period just before Hitler's 1933 triumph. Like Marlene Dietrich's Blue Angel, the Kit Kat Klub is a pleasure palace of absolute amusement where all forms of sensual experience are not only tolerated but celebrated. To enter the Kit Kat Klub was to take refuge from the gathering political storm just outside its doors. But in 1931 Berlin there was no real refuge from that storm. To believe in escape was the evasion that guaranteed Hitler's triumph. Like Germany as a whole, where an entire populace later claimed ignorance of the Nazi death camps, the Kit Kat Klub is an enclosed world where people mind their own business, live their own lives, take their own pleasures. If the Kit Kat is laudable for promoting the opposite social values of a Hitler, it is reprehensible for diverting attention from political responsibility.

Sally Bowles, the free spirit of Christopher Isherwood's *Berlin Stories* on which *Cabaret* is based, embodies this conflict between political blindness and social freedom. Every cabaret number for Sally and the crew at the Kit Kat refers metaphorically to the political climate outside the Klub. "Wilkommen," the opening number for the master of ceremonies (created by Joel Grey), welcomes the theater audience to *Cabaret* as well as an international audience to the Klub. Its three languages (*wilkommen, bienvenue,* welcome) imply that the spirit of the Klub transcends political and linguistic boundaries, catering to an international set of nonconformists, unified by their common amusement tastes. Less than a decade later, the speakers of those languages would be at war. The master of ceremonies sings three other specialty numbers that comment on Weimar's social and sexual politics: "Two Ladies" is a musical *ménage-a-trois*, a parody of alternative sexual tastes; "If You Could See Her" is a romantic duet for man and gorilla, an allusion to the Nazi view of Jews as subhuman; "The Money Song" is a pattering hymn to the power of capital—everyone can be bought. While Sally's "Don't Tell Mama" rejects the traditional parental precepts for every alternative moral code, her ironic title song calls life itself a cabaret, maintaining her political blindness to the end. The show has made it very clear that life in 1931 Weimar Germany is not a cabaret at all.

Joe Masterhoff's script adds plot songs to these metaphoric nightclub numbers, songs of "realistic" character interaction for the usual two lines of action. The romantic leads, Sally and Cliff, the young Englishman who discovers both the joy and the horror of Berlin, sing obligatory romantic solos and duets; the comic couple, Cliff's elderly landlady, Frau Schneider, and her Jewish suitor, Herr Schultz, sing their obligatory comic echo. With Lotte Lenya, the wife of Kurt Weill and the original Jenny in *The Threepenny Opera*, as Frau Schneider, *Cabaret* literally grafted the political metaphor of Brecht to the traditional multiplot of American musical comedy. Both romantic lines in *Cabaret* end by breaking off: Cliff leaves Berlin when Sally's cabaret life offends his rising political conscience; the pragmatic Frau Schneider rejects Herr Schultz for fear of antisemitic attack. Although the plot songs are pleasant enough, they have been written only because 1966 Broadway shows expected those kinds of songs.

But 1972 films did not and Bob Fosse cut them all. Several can be heard as background music on Sally's gramophone, sly reminders of an archaic musical structure that the film had abandoned. Every number in the film but one is a social, political, or sexual metaphor sung on a stage by performers. The film is both more "realistic" (only performers perform) and more metaphoric (every number a social or psychological comment). Even the new song Kander and Ebb wrote for Liza Minnelli, "Maybe This Time," is pure metaphor: her hope for permanent romantic attachment. By cutting between Minnelli's performance of the song in the Klub and Sally's love scene with Cliff (Michael York), Fosse simultaneously mirrors her personal feelings and maintains his metaphoric distance. She does not sing within a love scene but performs in some other literal place and time that has been yoked by editing, the familiar means of cinema metaphor, to this place and time—a musical-visual projection of human thought.[1]

The film also restores suggestions of the Isherwood stories that scared the show's producers. Cliff's homosexuality is an important part of his Berlin experience; Sally is his first (and probably last) heterosexual affair. Though she represents a broadening of Cliff's emotional perspective, she also obscures his moral and political vision. Like the Kit Kat Klub itself, Cliff's sexual education is spiritually revealing and politically blinding. The film replaces the show's cuddly old folks, Schneider and Schultz, with a more disturbing cross-section of German society: a social-climbing opportunist and the Jewish Heiress he woos; an elegantly bisexual count, confident that his elite class can control Hitler as easily as he can balance his own sexual appetites.

His smug blindness is revealed in the film's only number not sung in the Kit Kat Klub: "Tomorrow Belongs to Me." What begins as a serene German folksong chanted by a cherubic youth evolves, like "Deutschland Über Alles," into a ferocious Nazi anthem by an Aryan *Hitlerjunge*. Sung

Performance as metaphor: Liza Minnelli and Joel Grey on the stage of *Cabaret*

outdoors by a cross-section of ordinary German citizens during the day, rather than indoors at night by professional entertainers, building in confidence and intensity, line by line, chorus by chorus, cut by cut, like the Nazi movement itself, "Tomorrow Belongs to Me" is the metaphoric opposite of Sally's songs. It reveals the German social reality in response to the Kit Kat escape, Germany's actual tomorrow as opposed to the Kit Kat Klub's here and now and tonight.

For all its condemnation of Sally's political irresponsibility, the film admires her spontaneity, openness, oddness, her singleminded sensuality, her cockeyed optimism. Converting Isherwood's English Sally into Liza Minnelli's American makes her a 1972 Nellie Forbush. The energy of her nightclub numbers conveys her buoyant spirit as clearly as Nellie's washing that man right outa her hair. Fosse translates her American performance spirit into exuberant dance, dazzling light, brilliant color, and dynamic editing. Like every successful modernist musical, on stage or on screen, the film of *Cabaret* must have it both ways—preserving the fun of musical performance while commenting on a disturbing social phenomenon. Much more clearly than the Broadway show, Fosse's film blames history for the Nazi holocaust—not Sally, not the nightclub, and certainly not singing and dancing. Although there was a socially productive place for Nellie Forbush in the South Pacific of 1943, there was no such place for her in the Berlin of 1931. History wasn't ready for her or her Klub. Minnelli's Sally Bowles is already the counterculture. While in *South Pacific* America is a beacon to the world, slightly dimmed by naiveté, it becomes a follow-spot to the world in *Cabaret*.

If there was theater history in the show's marrying *The Threepenny Opera* to *South Pacific*, there is film history in the film's marrying the American backstagers of Berkeley and Astaire to *The Blue Angel*. Fosse's film begins in black and white, like most 1930s filmusicals, looking into a mirror, a rectangular framing of vision like the movie screen itself, in which the Klub is a distorted reflection. The image focuses itself into discernible life as it bleeds into contemporary color. It is as if the film conjures a new view of the 1930 past from the old materials of monochrome—making the old view less pretty as it becomes more clear, less distant as its images gain the color of the film present. The film of *Cabaret* is not merely a musical about Berlin life in 1930; it is a filmusical about being a filmusical about that life. In reworking the show's weave of onstage numbers and plot numbers as purely metaphoric performances outside the plot that comment on it, Fosse's *Cabaret* was the first modernist filmusical.

Just as Oscar Hammerstein codified the old concept of the story musical, his pupil and protegé, Stephen Sondheim, codified the new concept of the metaphoric musical. A graduate of Williams College, a student of both musical composition with Milton Babbitt and theatrical construction with Hammerstein, Sondheim carefully prepared for a career in musical theater. He spent his early years with words—scripts for *Topper* on television and lyrics for *West Side Story, Gypsy*, and *Do I Hear a Waltz?* (1965), an uncomfortable and literal stepping into Hammerstein's shoes with Richard Rodgers. His first Broadway score, *A Funny Thing Happened on the Way to the Forum* (1962), musicalized the farce of Terence and Plautus as other shows of the decade fit literary properties with an appropriate musical style. Even in its cheery lightness, one can hear Sondheim's trademarks—dissonant brass, odd rhythms, squirrelly tunes, cacophonous orchestrations, and playfully percussive alliteration—"the bong of the bell of the buoy in the bay."

Company (1970) was the first fully modernist musical show—with a Sondheim score, direction by Harold Prince, choreography by Michael Bennett, and a libretto of vignettes by George Furth. The subject of *Company* was, roughly, the perils and poisons of modern marriage—of trying to find permanent company in the modern urban world. Performed on Boris Aronson's gleamingly high-tech modular set that captured the hard shine of trendy New York, Sondheim's throbbing rhythms and dissonant chords captured the feel of the rushing city at work and play. Within that city, we wander with a footloose bachelor, Robert, or Bobby, or Robbie (as his friends variously nickname him) on visits to his coupled friends—newly married, newly divorced, thinking of marriage, thinking of divorce. The

The company of *Company* in the opening "Company" number

THEATRE COLLECTION, MUSEUM OF THE CITY OF NEW YORK

show also observes his three sexual flings—a sensualist, a stewardess, and a kook—as he bounces between affairs and friends. In the end, Robert breaks the pattern when he fails to appear for his annual surprise birthday party. Perhaps he has decided to get married after all, tired of providing company for others. Or perhaps Robert has discovered he needs company—but not with heterosexual couples and female companions. The gay subtext of the show—Sondheim and Furth know about being unmarried men in a coupled world—peeks out of the closet at its conclusion.

The show's title and title song, as ambiguous as its ending, plays on many meanings. *Company* is about company—being with others rather than being alone. It is also about visiting—having and greeting company. And it is a company show, not a star vehicle, for an ensemble of equals. Suspended between a book musical (with a cast of consistent characters and couples) and a revue (a series of vignettes connected only by theme), *Company* also provides company for its audience—the onstage company becomes our company, our circle of friends. A company is also a business, and, consistent with the show's ironies, the partnership that produced it called itself the Company Company. The metaphoric conceptions of modernist musicals begin with their titles.

Given its construction in a thematic circle, Sondheim's score illustrates general states of marriage and mind rather than specific character conflicts. In "The Little Things You Do Together" the cross-section of couples affirms and deplores the quirks that keep them together:

> It's not talk of God and the decade ahead that
> Allows you to get through the worst.
> It's "I do" and "you don't" and "nobody said that"
> And "who brought the subject up first?"
> It's the little things . . .
>
> The concerts you enjoy together,
> Neighbors you annoy together,
> Children you destroy together . . .
>
> It's not so hard to be married.
> It's much the simplest of crimes.
> It's not so hard to be married.
> I've done it three or four times. (pp. 529–31)[2]

"Sorry Grateful" turns these cynical "little things" into a musical contradiction in terms: the sad gladness and empty fullness of married life, the close distance and selfless selfishness of spouses. "Getting Married Today" is a complex contrapuntal trio: a serene soprano booms the idealized sounds of an "O Promise Me," the groom pleads sweetly with his bride, while she, on the edge of nervous collapse, resists with frantic musical chatter:

"we'll both of us be losing our identities—I telephoned my analyst about it and he said to see him Monday, but by Monday I'll be floating in the Hudson, with the other garbage." (p. 545)

How do you sing *that*?

Most songs bristle with the energy of New York on the move. "Another Hundred People" is a restless homage to the endless cycle—both vital and vicious—of New York's perpetual motion, day after day after day, and another hundred people and another hundred people. "The Ladies Who Lunch" is a musical indictment of New York's bored, rich, and chic:

> Another long, exhausting day,
> Another thousand dollars.
> A matinee: A Pinter play,
> Perhaps a piece of Mahler's.

In a bitter twist of self-conscious irony, the lady who scorns these empty ladies, Joanne (Elaine Stritch), is herself one of those who lunch. Her endless rounds of luncheons, concerts, and vodka stingers avoid the most brutal of mortal truths: "Everybody dies." As Levant might quip, that'll leave 'em laughing.

The freedom from a linear plot also allows Sondheim to break free from modern bitterness for dazzlingly lighthearted musical parodies. "You Could Drive a Person Crazy," an attack on Robert's emotional shallowness by the trio of his ladies, parodies the close harmonies of the Andrews Sisters and the "Doo-Wop" of 1950s rock 'n' roll. "Side By Side By Side" is a parody of the soft-shoe duet (Robert is always a third wheel); "What Would We Do Without You?" a parody of the high-stepping chorus line (the outsider keeps couples in chorus). These parodies give the show both musical range and entertainment variety, dressing a metaphor in musical fun, escaping the insistence of modernist sounds for a campy history of popular music and theatrical style.

Follies (1971) extends this contrast between modern musicals and the theatrical past. The theater that once housed the Follies of Dimitri Weissman (Florenz Ziegfeld in disguise) is about to be torn down, a relic of America's cultural past. A final reunion of Follies performers brings that cultural past into the present. Two former Follies girls, best friends in the forties, are now married to the stage-door Johnnies who wooed them (the book's skeleton appropriately comes from MGM's *Ziegfeld Girl*). One has become the rich and famous New York wife of a diplomat, the other the Phoenix housewife of a traveling salesman. While in the past there were hopes for the life ahead, in the present there are only regrets—for the road and the love not taken.

Like Weissman's Follies, like the 1971 musical theater in general, their lives have fallen on bad times. To dramatize the difference between the withered present and the hopeful past, James Goldman's script conjures youthful pairs—ghosts—to play imaginary versions of the married couples in their happy yesterdays. Surrounding these real and ghost couples is a stageful of the past. The Follies stars are living embodiments of theater history, many of them played by former stars of Broadway and Hollywood (Justine Johnston, Ethel Shutta, Mary McCarty, Fifi d'Orsay). When Yvonne De Carlo, a former Hollywood vision of exotica (*Song of Scheherazade*, *Casbah*) sings "I'm Still Here," she states a fact about herself and those on stage with her. She also states a fact for Sondheim about the musical theater: it's still here—barely.

Sondheim builds his score on three kinds of numbers. Modernist songs for the couples—real or ghostly—compare present disillusion with past anticipation ("Waiting for the Girls Upstairs," "Too Many Mornings," "The Road You Didn't Take"). Musical parodies cleverly convert the hopes and fears of the couples—real or ghostly—into Follies-type numbers ("You're Gonna Love Tomorrow," "Losing My Mind," "The Story of Lucy and Jessie"). Finally, the Follies stars of different decades perform conscious parodies of Follies numbers ("Beautiful Girls," "Broadway Baby," "Ah Paree!"). No other Sondheim show conceives and contains so many brilliant parodies—all intrinsic to the thematic comparison of past and present. The parody is Sondheim's musical road to the past.

Like the title of *Company*, *Follies* suggests not only a theater metaphor but a human condition. Human follies are as much the subject of the show as theatrical Follies. But as in *Company* not very much happens amidst all this historical and theatrical metaphor. The curtain in *Follies* comes with the dawn—falling not on an action but an atmosphere. Perhaps the four characters vaguely learn something (as Robert did in *Company*); perhaps they only release their inner pain by singing it aloud as psychodramatic purgation. Spiritual education merely provides the hook for a dazzling array of numbers in which the musical's past invades the theatrical present. Musical theater becomes a metaphor for cultural history: America too was "still here," if in 1971 ruins—like its musical theater.

The interpenetration of past and present and the musical voicing of inner consciousness became Sondheim's two central concerns. *A Little Night Music* (1973) was another move from the present into the past. Set at the turn of the century, Sondheim built every song on the period's dominant musical form—the waltz—an entire score in 3/4 time or some variation on it. Based on Ingmar Bergman's film comedy, *Smiles of a Summer Night*, the show was also a move backward from new concept to old—fitting a linear plot with a musical style, like Sondheim's earlier *Forum*. But this conscious return to Operettaland sought a modern means for singing internal consciousness that would never have occurred to Lehar or Herbert. No less than *Follies*, *A Little Night Music* is haunted by a quartet of ghosts—four figures who do not materially exist but are mental projections of those who do. These musical emanations from Strindberg's chamber plays, like *The Ghost Sonata*, serve as this chamber musical's chamber chorus—singing thoughts and feelings of the characters aloud. Sondheim's musical synthesis of modernist now and harmonious then, of big Broadway show and Mozartian chamber piece—as well as "Send in the Clowns"—made *A Little Night Music* his only Broadway hit after *Company*.

Pacific Overtures (1976) was both more daring and more disappointing for its creators. While *A Little Night Music* traveled across the Atlantic to the operetta past, *Pacific Overtures* travels to the past across the Pacific. Based on Commodore Matthew Perry's opening of Japan to American commerce in 1853 and its economic consequences over the century that followed, *Pacific Overtures* continued the American musical's fascination with the exotic East—from *The Sultan of Sulu* through *The King and I*. Rather than the usual visit of a Western stranger to Eastern culture, *Pacific Overtures* is a metaphoric mixing of Western and Eastern cultures in subject and style. Sondheim's score blends American harmonic patterns with Japanese melodic patterns: a Broadway orchestra in the pit with Kabuki string and percussion instruments on stage. Sondheim's lyrics are a conscious blend of Western wit and the economy of Japanese haiku. Harold Prince's staging blends conventions of Western theater with conventions of Kabuki: a narrator who comments on the action; stylized gestures and makeup; Boris Aronson's settings based on Japanese prints and calligraphy; the use of *oyama* (males who portray the female roles); even traditional Kabuki motifs like the lion dance, the pagoda, and the black-clad invisibility of stage hands. The show's cast of Japanese-American musical performers and Kabuki actors was yet another meeting of West and East, Kabuki and Broadway.

Its title, *Pacific Overtures*, is another of those metaphoric multiplicities that refer not only to Sondheim's musical subject but to making a musical about it. While Perry's visit was an overture to Japan, both an invitation and a demand, it was also an opening of the West to Japan. An overture also marks the opening of a musical, and both *South Pacific* and *Pacific Overtures* are musical consequences of Perry's overture, of Japan's entering American cultural and commercial history. Perry's overture leads directly to the overture of *Pacific Overtures*, played on Japanese instruments. In no other Sondheim show do the multiple levels of metaphoric meaning, theatrical convention, and musical style wrap so tightly around each other.

In a score of brilliantly varied musical colors, one song telescopes the show's ironies. "Say Hello" is a dazzling musical parody to open the second act—where Sondheim (like Richard Rodgers) often slots his biggest, brightest number. The subject of this song is, roughly, the commercial exploitation of Japan by international interests in the decades following Perry's overture. Sondheim constructs a musical montage—distilling a lengthy process into five parodies of musical style, each associated with a particular Western nation (though every performer onstage is Japanese). An American sings a parody of "The Star Spangled Banner" in Sousatime; an Englishman sings a patter parody of Gilbert and Sullivan; a Dutch trader sings a gliding parody of a skater's waltz; a Russian a parody of "The Volga Boatman"; a Frenchman a parody of a music-hall strut in the manner of Maurice Chevalier. Then all five musical motifs weave together in a single musical tapestry. Five singers, representing five national interests, use five parodic musical styles to summarize the binding of Japanese commerce to the West, in a show blending conventions of Kabuki and American musical theater, performed on Broadway entirely by a cast of Japanese!

Sweeney Todd (1979) moves back across the Atlantic to England's Victorian past. Sondheim, Prince, and Hugh Wheeler take their style from a tradition of musical and literary depiction of London low life—from Defoe's *Moll Flanders* and Gay's *The Beggar's Opera* through Dickens, Mr. Hyde, and Jack the Ripper to Brecht's *Threepenny Opera*. *Sweeney Todd* sets itself the task of musicalizing the grim career of a notorious London barber who cut his clients' throats, baking their remains into tasty meat pies prepared by his accomplice, Mrs. Lovett (a name direct from Wycherly—and bubblingly played as Restoration comedy by Angela Lansbury). Sondheim's score again hits its peak in an outrageous parody (this time at the end of Act I). "A Bit of Priest" is Sondheim's ultimate extension and decimation of the waltz—a flowing oom-pah-pah whose subject is the specific taste of various human meats baked into pies. Todd and Lovett skate deliriously over the thin ice of outrageous puns that compare the taste of a pie to the vocation of the human whose flesh provides its filling: a piccolo player's pie tastes piping hot, an actor pie is always overdone, an oily politican pie is always likely to run, a grocer's pie is sure to be green, an admiral's pie is rear, a general's pie can be ordered with or without his privates. No combination of Strauss waltz and Gilbert patter were ever put to a more grotesque theatrical purpose: literalizing the metaphor of life's struggle between the eaters and the et.

While three consecutive Sondheim-Prince shows traveled to the past, *Merrily We Roll Along* (1981) began in the present and rolled into the past. The show's twenty-five-year chronicle of a songwriting team came as close to Sondheim as fiction could. Too close, perhaps. As in *Follies*, youthful hopes evaporate into adult disillusion, material success into spiritual decay: breakdowns and breakups, broken dreams and friendships. As in *Follies*, the history of personal disappointment is a cultural history of American disillusion over the same period—the blasted hopes of a generation that began with the music of Dylan, the launching of Sputnik, and the election of Kennedy. Unlike the ghost couples in *Follies* (or the ghost child in "Someone in a Tree" from *Pacific Overtures*), *Merrily We Roll Along* does not summon ghosts from the past into the present but carries the characters backward into their own pasts. The end of this show is literally in its beginning:

moving steadily backward from 1980 toward the 1955 high-school graduation of the two boys who become successful songwriters as they sell their
souls.

The show trumpets Sondheim's own blasted dreams for the future of
musical theater, where he began with Bernstein in 1957. Its backward
movement is inexorable—no escape, no hope of changing the result.
Dramatic structure never rolls very merrily backwards. As in *Follies* and
Pacific Overtures, the casting of the show was an essential part of its
metaphor: youthful, unknown performers played all the roles, present and
past, adults and youths. The kids become their own ghosts. This unexpected reversal of innocence and experience, like the script's reversal of chronological direction, implied that Sondheim and Prince hoped to float this
theatrical downer on the youthful enthusiasm of a college show. The loss
was professional polish, performance virtuosity, and credible adult satire. A
show might survive a bitterly unpleasant tone, a depressingly analytic
structure, or callow performances—but not all three. The fifteen-year
collaboration of Sondheim and Prince didn't survive it either.

Although *Sunday in the Park with George* (1984) brought Sondheim a new
collaborator, James Lapine, who both wrote the script and staged the show,
Sondheim remained with familiar themes: the relation of past to present
and the relation of artistic creation to cultural history. Sondheim set himself
another audacious conceptual problem: musicalizing Georges Seurat's mammoth painting, "A Sunday Afternoon on the Island of the Grande Jatte."
Although a musical of a painter's life is imaginable, how can an artifact, a
painting, sing? Sondheim's answer draws an extended comparison between paintings and musicals as artifacts—a painting is a show that doesn't
move, composed in pigments rather than in notes. Sondheim's musical
painting bears striking affinities to backstage musicals (like *Pal Joey* and
Cabaret), divided between onstage and offstage numbers. In *Sunday in the
Park with George* we get onpainting and offpainting numbers.

Within the painting, Sondheim creates songs by imagining who its
figures might be and how they might sing—two soldiers, a child with
glasses, a gruff laborer, an old lady (Seurat's mother, perhaps?), a young
woman (Seurat's lover? named Dot?). Even a dog sings his desires. Seurat's
figures become imaginary characters who express themselves in songs—
which is what characters in musicals do. For Sondheim, this is also what
Seurat must have done to paint them in the first place: converting his
models into characters by imagining their inner lives, then externalizing
those thoughts and feelings as "Color and Light." Sondheim's songs are
musical paintings of imaginary mental activity—the "Gossip" of Seurat's
figures, their Sunday thoughts on "The Day Off," their feeling "Hot Up
Here," imprisoned in a painting of a brilliant afternoon on a wall of a
museum. It's always hot for actors on a stage. The total assemblage of
Seurat's individual figures is his whole painting, which is also Sondheim's

whole show; the canvas is the stage where Seurat's characters have been written; the frame of Seurat's painting is congruent with the frame of Sondheim's proscenium arch.

The offpainting numbers make specific connections between the art of Seurat and the art of Sondheim. As a pointillist, Seurat engages the viewer's senses by the application of colored dots to a white canvas. Seurat is a lover of dots—quite literally, since his lover in the show is named Dot. But a composer of musical scores is also a lover of dots—drawing black and white dots on the white spaces of a musical staff to engage the listener's senses as sounds. Seurat's dots must be seen not as individual flecks of color and light but as parts of a symphonic whole, in combination with all the other dots. So too, Sondheim's dots can only be heard in combination—individual notes that become melodic patterns, full chords, individual songs, whole scores, and performed by ensembles of vocal and orchestral musicians. Despite his visual symphony, Seurat was neither understood nor recognized by his own contemporaries. The critics in Sondheim's show find Seurat's work technically brilliant but lacking life, heart, and soul—which is what critics have always said about Sondheim shows.

The second act makes the connection between Sondheim and Seurat, paintings and musicals, even clearer. Set in the present art world, Sondheim constructs his usual conversation between now and then. Seurat's literal descendant is an American modernist sculptor of laser machines that do not reflect color and light but project them. Because his art is mechanical, the sculptor is dependent on collaborators—technicians and engineers—just as composers of musicals are dependent on performers, directors, designers, computers, and stagehands. Because machines are expensive, the artist is also dependent on support from foundations, patrons, and museums—just as Broadway shows need the support of backers and theater owners. In "Putting It Together" and "The State of the Art," the modern artist spins chitchat at cocktail parties, wooing financial backers, just as Broadway shows hold backers' auditions. The title of the sculptor's newest laser work, "Chromolume #7," suggests a piece that is modern, hard, and shiny, aluminum and chrome, more surface than soul, the seventh in a series. Never overlook a Sondheim title. *Sunday in the Park with George* is Sondheim's seventh in a modernist series that began with *Company*—modern, hard, and shiny, if unsentimental, shows. *Sunday in the Park with George* is Sondheim's "Chromolume #7." He can musicalize a painting because he has found theatrical tropes to connect paintings and musicals.

Despite the shine of Sondheim's chromolumes, few justify their making in the usual Broadway terms: they don't make money. The staggering cost of mounting a Broadway musical—as much as $5 million in 1986—means a show must sell out for years at full ticket prices before it can return a penny on its original investment. Sondheim musicals, like laser chromolumes, are expensive. Decor is as essential to their metaphoric meaning as music; if paintings are musical, then musicals are both paintings and projections of light, combining both arts and both acts of *Sunday in the Park with George*. A Sondheim chromolume is a Wagnerian *Gesamtkunstwerk*, a total theatrical universe of sound, color, light, drama, performance, music, and myth. It can't even recoup its costs as a movie since it is so much for and about the stage itself.

Sondheim's chromolumes sacrifice two sources of musical energy on which a Porter or Berlin depended: they lose the power of solo performance in the conceptual forest of the musical metaphor and they lose the fun of individual songs in the unity of entire scores. There have been marvelous performances in Sondheim shows—Elaine Stritch in *Company*, Soon-Teck Oh and Alvin Ing in *Pacific Overtures*, Angela Lansbury in *Sweeney Todd*, Bernadette Peters and Mandy Patinkin in *Sunday in the Park with George*. But chromolumes don't need personality the way a Porter or Berlin needed a Merman. *Sunday in the Park with George* can't even break out of its frame for dazzling Sondheim parodies, its score so successfully pointillist there is only the barest dot of a separable tune in it.[3] Shows desert catchy tunes at their commercial and cultural peril.

It is not difficult to see what was at stake in the bitter contest between *Sunday in the Park* and *La Cage aux Folles* for the 1984 Tony Award. The American musical confronted its own history when two opposite views and periods of musical theater went head to head: the modernist metaphoric conception without tunes which left nobody laughing; the old-fashioned show with laughs, tunes, and legs. Of course, many of its legs were no longer female legs, but male legs pretending. While the old leg shows kicked up the spirits of the tired businessman, exactly which pairs of kicking legs aroused which members of this audience? While its theatrical form might predate *Of Thee I Sing*, the cultural ambiguities of *La Cage aux Folles* were strictly 1984. This play between stable form and cultural twist invigorated musicals for decades.

Beneath the victory of *La Cage aux Folles* lay the suspicion that Sondheim was "killing Broadway." (As if Sondheim had boosted Broadway production costs to $5 million. Wasn't Broadway really killing Sondheim?) Even Seurat's mother in *Sunday in the Park* longs for the old art of the old days. But how else could a Sondheim, schooled by masters of the old days, maintain the excellence and innovation of the old days while extending their tradition? Since 1927 a musical has meant not just songs but a total theatrical conception, an American *Gesamtkunstwerk* of song and dance and visuals. "What makes Sondheim shows so exciting," Ethan Mordden observes, "is their sense of tradition and innovation spliced together."[4] If Sondheim didn't exist, Broadway would invent him.

And what are the alternatives? If not Sondheim, what? One answer since 1970 has been a literal return to the old days—in several different vehicles. The occasional old-style show by Jerry Herman, Cy Coleman, or Kander and Ebb bounces to Broadway on a catchy score, a clever cultural issue, or a star (*Chicago, I Love My Wife, Barnum, La Cage aux Folles*). Not one veteran American composer of these shows is under fifty. Revivals of past hits like *No, No, Nanette, Irene, Oklahoma!, The King and I*, and *Sweet Charity* affirm that postmodernist nostalgia accompanies modernist creation. New revues take to the past on compilations of old songs—*Side By Side By Sondheim, Ain't Misbehavin', Sophisticated Ladies*. New book shows combine old songs with old film plots—*42nd Street, Singin' in the Rain*. Like the Arthur Freed musicals at MGM, these shows begin with a catalog of songs (by the Gershwins, Dubin and Warren, Freed and Brown), which they fit with an appropriate historical milieu. *My One and Only* (1983) was a literal return to the premise that built *An American in Paris* and *Funny Face* on a catalog of Gershwin songs.

A second alternative is the occasional Broadway invasion by the pop, rock, or country music scene—*Godspell, Grease, Pippin, The Wiz, Big River*. While the move of rock to Broadway reforges an old link between theater and popular music, its results are inconsistent. Successful rock and pop creators of one musical rarely return to Broadway with success (Galt McDermott of *Hair*, Jim Jacobs and Warren Casey of *Grease*) or never return at all (Burt Bacharach of *Promises, Promises*, Carole Bayer Sager of *They're Playing Our Song*). The repetitive eight-bar phrases and percussive lyrics of rock songs, so successful at hammering out bursts of youthful passion and energy, don't very well suit mature wit and intellect. Rock musicals are necessarily youth musicals—whether on stage or film. Given its ticket prices, Broadway is not nearly as chummy with the youth market as movies. Successful rock composers, attracted by the prestigious idea of Broadway, want a hit there. But why work so hard on difficult, uncertain projects when you can stay home to turn out sure hits? Conscientious craftsmanship for the musical theater requires a specific commitment to musical theater. Steven Schwartz of *Godspell, Pippin*, and *The Magic Show* is the rare exception who combines rock sounds and rhythms, traditional American song structures, and a commitment to theater.

A pair of theatrical invaders from England whip the sounds of rock music into modernist operas. *Jesus Christ Superstar, Evita, Cats, Starlight Express, Song and Dance, Chess* by Andrew Lloyd Webber and Tim Rice, individually or together, forge links between musical style and cultural myth, adult complexity and youthful enthusiasm, theatrical metaphor and musical fun. They also forge a new link between Broadway and Shaftesbury Avenue, where production costs are lower and theater economies more solid. For Rice and Webber, London's West End has become New Haven, where shows try out before coming into New York. Webber has even bought his own West End theater. The commercial dominance of this British pair suggests a return to that period before Jerome Kern when London's West End dominated Broadway. They also suggest a return to

Irving Berlin's belief in hit songs: Rice and Webber write the hit first, then build a show around it.

The most powerful American compromise between old and new has been the work of Michael Bennett, who began with Prince and Sondheim on *Company*. The rise of the director as a show's prime mover—Bennett, Prince, Tommy Tune, Gower Champion, Bob Fosse—is another sign of its modernist condition. Bennett added heart and glitter to Sondheim's relentless modernity. Although very different in style and subject, one can trace a direct line to Bennett's 1975 *A Chorus Line* from *Hair*, Tom O'Horgan's musical metaphor of six years earlier.[5] Both shows began in Joseph Papp's Shakespeare Festival workshop; both grew improvisationally, on the personal experiences of workshop members. After establishing a general milieu—the counterculture's view of Viet Nam, sex, drugs, and American middle-class mores in *Hair*; auditioning for a Broadway chorus in *A Chorus Line*—both shows spin songs and situations from personal recollections and confessions of the performers. The writers of the score (Galt McDermott, James Rado, and Jerome Ragni of *Hair*; Marvin Hamlisch and Edward Kleban of *A Chorus Line*) did not fit performers into completed songs but found musical and verbal patterns to shape their confessional tales. The songs and vignettes that eventually moved from the workshop to the Broadway stage were those most valid psychologically and most powerful in performance. Workshop members were literally auditioning for *A Chorus Line*; the process of the show's creative evolution was identical to its subject.

With this mix of personal confession and musical form, psychodrama and scripted scene, both shows preserve a balance between modernist metaphor and individual performer—primarily singers in *Hair*, dancers in *A Chorus Line*. Both respected a maxim that the direct historical line from Hammerstein to Sondheim had obscured: in musicals performers perform. Both were as much about performance as they were built on performance. As the shows moved progressively further from the improvisational workshop into commercial institutions—the original Broadway cast, Broadway replacement casts, national and international touring companies, and, ultimately, the movie—they still preserved the power of individual performers and performances. Though the new performers had not suffered the same experiences as the originals, all performers suffer similar ones.

While *Hair* captured the disillusion of the late 1960s, *A Chorus Line* caught the optimism that has come to characterize the late 1970s and 1980s. The performers who audition for these chorus jobs have overcome obstacles that destroy less determined people—broken homes, too little equipment (whether singing voice or "Tits and Ass"), too much equipment (the dancer who is too distinctive), cultural disadvantage (as a black or hispanic ghetto child), cultural prejudice (being gay). The finalists who win the chorus jobs are models of industry, perseverance, and achievement, of American individualism at its best. On the other hand, what they achieve is not stardom

Musical metaphor: people reduced to photos and resumés in *A Chorus Line*

(like Peggy Sawyer in *42nd Street*) but a job in the chorus. They exist to support and surround the star, the "One," who never appears onstage, who is not part of their line or their lives. No less than *Company*, *A Chorus Line* is a company show. Unlike Sondheim's unresolved search for meaningful company, *A Chorus Line* finds it in the sharing of song and dance.

A member of a chorus is both a "One," an individual with personal quirks, feelings, experiences, and one of a group, a harmonious social unit. Dancing in a chorus combines individual urges and social cohesion, doing what one loves to do and does well within a group of equals doing likewise. In its balance of personal expression and social cohesion, *A Chorus Line* formulates the new American dream of the 1980s. We are none of us stars but members of some societal chorus line or other. We exercise our individuality while recognizing our connection. Although the line of masking tape absolutely separates the onstage performer from the audience observer, the mirror that reflects the audience at the show's conclusion leaps the gulf to put us onstage with the dancers. No matter how many games the plodding 1985 Richard Attenborough film found to play with mirrors, it was unable to connect the onstage and offstage choruses so literally. In its balance of One and All, *A Chorus Line* is a musical myth and mirror of our deepest cultural belief.

Although no other modernist musical has touched as deep a chord, Bennett's *Dreamgirls* (1981) dressed another social issue in showbiz terms. The relation of white and black music, white and black performance, has been a motif of American musical theater from the nineteenth-century minstrel shows, through Harrigan and Hart, to *Show Boat* and *Cabin in the Sky*. When American popular music found its style by marrying black sounds to white European patterns, white music found a way to relegate black music to the cultural underground—low bars, whorehouses, cheap entertainments for exclusively black audiences. While American musicals pleaded eloquently for isolated black characters as cultural symbols, like Joe in *Show Boat*, the white-dominated theater and music business determined exactly how many black voices could be heard—like Lena Horne, the one black voice at MGM. Was show business at the forefront of American social change, making white America more comfortable with black experience by exposure to black performance? Or was it a conservative social force, commercially exploiting black performance while buying off isolated black talent with wealth and fame?

These are the questions that *Dreamgirls* consciously raises in its script and score. Its backstage milieu is the rock-music business, the apparent alternative and antagonist to Broadway, where black musical forms were not adapted to thirty-two-bar white tastes but remained true to their original eight-bar patterns of the blues. Or did they? In tracing a Motown singing group resembling the Supremes from its Harlem roots to the national big time, *Dreamgirls* shows that the rock alternative to Broadway was no alternative. Black musicians must still compromise with white tastes to rival the commercial power of white performers. Black singers become "dreamgirls," images of beauty, glitter, and glamour, their sound as sequined as their bodies, to fulfill the expectations of audiences—white and black. The big girl with the big voice and big heart (originated by Jennifer Holliday) will remain a cult star within the separate black underculture. There is no alternative tradition of pure black music, separate from Broadway. The proof is this very show on Broadway, written by white Tom Eyen, directed by white Michael Bennett, about black music in the white world. With a rhythmic black-sounding score (by white Henry Krieger), *Dreamgirls* has it both ways—as dynamic black performance and critique of black performance.

Most filmusicals since 1972 also want to have it the same both ways. The most commercially successful film adaptation of a Broadway musical, Randal Kleiser's 1978 *Grease*, combined both concerns of filmusicals since Fosse's *Cabaret*: dancing youth and the history of musical styles in relation to

American life. From its contemporary disco beginning, *Grease* moves backward into the rock-'n'-roll past, transporting its viewers into the sounds, styles, and dances they would have experienced if they had been born two decades earlier. As in *Alexander's Ragtime Band*, America's popular music is also its cultural history.

For a decade the movie audience has been overwhelmingly a youth market. While young Americans have used movies to get out of the home since the nickelodeons of 1905, out of the world of their parents and into a world of their contemporaries, the proportion of youthful audience members to adults has never been higher than in the 1980s. Many of the adults who still patronize movie theaters like to "think young." The result is the dominance of the youth movie, a "coming of age" in an American *Bildungsroman* where adolescents learn the meaning of adult values and responsibilities—love, friendship, the relation of sexual gratification to a meaningful life, the relation between self and social world. Some of these comings of age occur either with music or through music. And it must be youth music—the rock idiom that convinces the young that the movie speaks to them, for them, and about them.

These musical comings of age are of two basic types, deriving from the oldest division of filmusicals—the star musical and the group musical. John Badham's *Saturday Night Fever* (1977) and Adrian Lyne's *Flashdance* (1983) provide essential statements of the solo or star musical, one for each gender. The male variant for John Travolta features primarily coupled performances (like Fred&Ginger); the female variant for Jennifer Beals features solo dance (like Eleanor Powell). It still seems impossible to find a dancing partner for the female musical star. Ironically, Beals's own second self becomes her partner since she required Marine Jahan to dub her dances.

Both musicals are dance films rather than song-and-dance films: perhaps it would be more accurate to call these rock-dance movies dancicals. The easiest way to achieve musical stylization within narrative credibility is to rely on the social fact that dance is an essential part of youthful experience. In both *Saturday Night Fever* and *Flashdance*, the performers come from the ethnic working classes, dancing descendants of 1955's *Marty*. Coming of age movies for upper-middle-class suburban kids, *Breaking Away*, *Ordinary People*, *Risky Business*, *War Games*, *A Sure Thing* are not dancicals but dialogue films. They perpetuate an American view of class difference, based on mind and body—the upper classes got brains and the lower classes got rhythm.

While dancing provides a terrific high in both *Saturday Night Fever* and *Flashdance*, Tony Manero can only cure his fever by transcending that high. His coming of age means conquering the devotion to dance, both the cause and the effect of his narrow, immature value system. He can only escape his working-class prison into responsible adulthood if he stops dancing like a kid. In *Flashdance* dancing is the means for Alex Owens to escape the working-class prison, the medium in which the mature woman can express herself—if she combines the instinctual rock-dance of the streets with the conventions of classical training. Dancing in both films is a dream—which the male must abandon but the woman must not, for "when you lose your dream you die." Like modernist musicals, *Saturday Night Fever* and *Flashdance* have it both ways—exploiting the energy of dance but keeping it in its social and moral place. While in the 1940s at Twentieth Century-Fox performing made more adult sense for Dan Dailey than for Betty Grable, in the 1980s it makes more adult sense for Jennifer Beals than for John Travolta. Postwar American women belonged in the kitchen; 1980s American women follow their dreams. *Flashdance* can be simultaneously feminist, careerist, and individualist.

The group rock-youth musicals descend from the MGM barnyards and the Berkeley backstagers: musical performance weds personal expression and social cohesion. The essential statement is Alan Parker's (and MGM's) *Fame*, which might be called *Babes on Columbus Avenue* or *Footlight Parade of 1980*. Like Mickey and Judy, the kids of *Fame* are specially gifted and talented; unlike Mickey and Judy, who attend everyperson Small-Town High, the kids of *Fame* attend a special New York school for the gifted and talented. Their curriculum includes speech, song, and dance, chorus and orchestra—the ingredients of musicals themselves. Musical performance summons whites, blacks, and hispanics, gays and straights, dropouts and dreamers, street kids from the ghettoes and white ethnics from middle-class boroughs—as much a mythical cross-section of 1980 urban America diversity as Mickey's and Judy's mythical cross-section of 1940 small-town Americana unity.

The ultimate statement of social harmony is their graduation finale, an official coming of age: "I Sing the Body Electric" combines Walt Whitman's visionary lines with rock rhythms, black gospel with white chorale, symphonic instruments with electronic sounds. As in so many American musicals, performance is the ultimate unifier of here and hereafter. Out of this endlessly rocking cradle come the babes who unite past and future, high and low, sacred and secular, mortal body and electric spirit. In the myth of *Fame*, neither American society nor American musicals need worry about their future as long as talented kids sing and dance together like this. As in *A Chorus Line*, their song is not only of Whitman's Myself but of singing it in chorus.

Adult musicals of the last decade are more sure of past than future. Like musicals on Broadway, Hollywood musicals are stuck in the modernist self-consciousness of their own history and style. As on Broadway, numbers in modernist filmusicals are indirect metaphors for psychological states and thematic issues—although numbers in filmusicals have always been more elusively metaphoric than on the stage, whether a Fred&Ginger duet or a Kelly ballet. Like Freed musicals at MGM, modernist filmusicals are built on old songs: a catalog of pop and rock tunes, from Sophie Tucker's "Some of These Days" to Simon and Garfunkle's "Bye Bye Love" in *All that Jazz*; a catalog of Ellingtonia in *The Cotton Club*. While filmusicals from Astaire to Travolta sought some credible dramatic excuse for musical performance, modernist filmusicals offer neither apology nor explanation. Aware that the tension between musical stylization and narrative credibility is the central problem for every musical, modernist filmusicals burn the bridge between style and story to leap into the gulf of utter artifice.

Bob Fosse's *All That Jazz* (1979) is an American musical version of *8½*—spiritual autobiography as stylized choreography. Like Fosse himself, the protagonist of *All That Jazz*, Joe Gideon (Roy Scheider), is a driven director and choreographer of musical shows and films who suffers a severe heart attack, spending a long convalescence in a hospital. Like Fellini's Marcello, Fosse's Gideon is visited by his own experiences, dreams, and fears. Unlike either Fosse or Marcello, Gideon's visions end in his own musical death. Each number is an extended metaphor for his particular mental or physical condition—in brilliantly stylized, brazenly artificial settings. As in *Cabaret*, Fosse creates a dialectic between the grim story, which goes one way, and the exuberant numbers, which go another. Physical confinement contrasts with the exhilaration of the dances, inner mental processes contrast with their extroverted physicality as numbers.

The film's duality of mind and body, of mental conception and physical execution in space, is mirrored by its stylistic gulf between drab dialogue scenes and flashy musical numbers. Fosse's alter ego can only think in the terms of musical numbers; his very processes of thought are numbers. If *All That Jazz* echoes *8½* it also evokes *Lady in the Dark*, which similarly projected interior mental processes as splashy musical numbers. When Gideon raises his eyes heavenward like Job, he can only imagine God's punishment in showbiz terms: "Don't you like musical comedy?" He can only imagine the death of his own consciousness as a musical number ("Bye Bye Life"). And after his death, his mortal body zipped into a plastic shroud, even his epitaph must be sung—by Ethel Merman, no less: "There's No Business like Show Business." Fosse has lived in musicals and he suspects they will kill him.

Unlike Fosse, Francis Coppola only visits an occasional musical within his careerlong voyage through assorted American genres. His 1968 film of *Finian's Rainbow*, a fanciful 1947 Broadway blast from the left by Fred Saidy, E. Y. "Yip" Harburg and Burton Lane, is a guidebook to other movies and musicals. Coppola packs his film with intrusive references that proclaim the artifices of filmusical style and the tension between credible storytelling and musical convention. The editing of an arrival by train comes directly from *Hallelujah*; a dance with laundry on a clothesline from *Dames*; the aerial floating on that clothing from *Mary Poppins*; the spray of fire hoses on a burning church from *Strike*; the passing of water pails, "Keep the water coming," from *Our Daily Bread*; the use of blackface from two decades of filmusicals between *The Jazz Singer* and *The Jolson Story*. Coppola constructs scenes based entirely on Cole Porter song lyrics or Rodgers and Hammerstein song titles. Fred Astaire (as Finian) is himself a living reference to musical tradition. When Finian raps his shelalagh on a wooden bridge, then taps and twirls his departure, we recognize decades of Astaire twirls for taps and cane. As Finian follows his dream, over Judy Garland's rainbow, we recognize an ascension into the nonmortal ether where Astaire has always dwelt.

Finian's Rainbow plays just as trickily with color and light, two essential filmusical devices. The forest is bathed in a nighttime blue where the glowing gold of leprechaun treasure burns like an amber sun. Old devil moon sparkles on a movie river, brilliant diamonds of shimmering light, to decorate a love duet. However motivated by the plot, Coppola proclaims these effects as tricks of Hollywood light that carry musicals from everyday prose to musical magic. In dedicating itself to exposing the devices of filmusical magic, Coppola merely destroyed the magic, removing the only reason to see this (or any) musical. Unlike Astaire, Coppola is a foreigner to the tongue in which musical is spoken.

The Cotton Club (1984) returns to the limits of credibility and belief in filmusical storytelling, with more attention to colored light and rippling shadow effects. This light shines not in *Finian's* magical forest but at the busy intersection of two familiar though apparently opposite genres—the black musical (like *Stormy Weather*) and the gangster film (like Coppola's *Godfather* movies). The famous Harlem nightclub becomes the film's social center, as nightclubs do in gangster films. The difference in *The Cotton Club* is that the nightclub numbers do not offer brief musical intermissions in a gangster story but split the screen time with the gangsters. Like *Dreamgirls*, *The Cotton Club* explores the paradoxes of black music and performance in white America: a famous nightclub in a black ghetto where the entertainers and music were black (except when written by Harold Arlen and Ted Koehler) but its owners and its audiences white (like the producers and writers of *Hallelujah*, *Stormy Weather*, and *Cabin in the Sky*). Musical performance at the Cotton Club was black expression for white tastes. The black stars were merely servants, relegated to the servant's entrance—like every other black in 1930 white America.

Why are there gangsters in this filmusical? Black musicals and gangster films were contemporaries, simultaneous reflections of American culture in the 1930s. Both film genres presented glossy portraits of ugly cultural phenomena, erasing the ugliness by glamourizing the milieu. The gangster business and show business were also parallel businesses in 1930s American life. While blacks rose from the ghetto in shows, whites rose from the ghetto as gangsters. *The Cotton Club* very carefully spreads ethnic membership in the gangster club among Irish, Jews, Italians, even an Englishman.

While gangster life bought urban immigrant whites power, wealth, women, and glamour, show business bought the same for blacks. While battles for power within gangster life destroyed families and friendships (especially in gangster movies), the struggle for showbiz success also rips black families apart in Coppola's film. Black performers and white audiences at Coppola's Cotton Club were mirror images.

Coppola alternates his focus between the two sides of the mirror, activities outside and inside the Cotton Club, until the finale when he jumps through the looking glass. He intercuts a climactic gangster murder with a climactic musical number (just as he intercut baptism and murder for the climax of *The Godfather*). The rattling taps of Gregory Hines become the rat-a-tats of machine gun bursts in a synesthetic montage of picture and sound. Musical performance finally jumps off the Cotton Club stage and into a purely cinematic Wonderland—a stylized movie set of Grand Central Station that refers to any number of 1932–1934 movies set on trains or in stations: *42nd Street*'s "Shuffle Off to Buffalo," Bing Crosby's *Going Hollywood*, Howard Hawks's *Twentieth Century*. In the end, a credible fiction and its nightclub pretense evaporate into the cinematic ether, like the town of Brigadoon. *The Cotton Club* finale declares itself a mere stylistic display of cutting, staging, and scoring—just a movie, like all those other "just movies" about gangsters and performers of the 1930s. Is Coppola indicting all movies, then and now, for their social evasions or is he guilty of evasion himself? Must movies or musicals necessarily evade? No one seemed to know, and, as with *Finian's Rainbow*, no one seemed to care.[6]

Blake Edwards's *Victor/Victoria* (1982) situates itself more happily at the intersection of genres. It is Cinderella, the most common myth of musicals (like *My Fair Lady* and *The Sound of Music*), in which poor girl gets prince—or King, as he is called in *Victor/Victoria*. It is also a Julie Andrews musical (like *My Fair Lady* and *The Sound of Music*), which is about Julie Andrews as a star (just as the film of *My Fair Lady*, which Andrews didn't make, is about Audrey Hepburn). Andrews, clean-scrubbed and bright-eyed, more girlish than womanly, suspended in cinema between childhood and adulthood, spends more screen time with dolls than guys. Her clear, bright, but thin soprano, which issues from her fresh and cheery visage, suggests the precious, precocious, and passionless. Directed by Andrews's own husband (with, no doubt, a rather different perception of her sexuality), *Victor/Victoria* reduces her supposed sexlessness to absurdity.

By making her a boy, *Victor/Victoria* also becomes a transvestite comedy, like *Twelfth Night* and *Some Like It Hot*, in which boys and girls change clothes and gender to fall in love. Andrews's male impersonation is a traditional "trouser role," much favored by female stars in American musicals of the late nineteenth century. *Victor/Victoria* is also a gangster film, like *Some Like It Hot* and *The Cotton Club*, which mates the most masculine of vocations with the least masculine of performances. And it is a Lubitsch romance, like *Monte Carlo* and *Trouble in Paradise*. Set on a Hollywood soundstage calling itself Paris, it simultaneously refers to Depression hunger and escapes it into Art Deco. Finally, it is a backstager built on nightclub performers, like *The Blue Angel* and *Cabaret*: set in the sexual ambiguity and androgyny of an international between-the-wars smart set. Based on a 1933 German film, *Viktor und Viktoria*, about a transvestite Berliner, the Edwards-Andrews film is literally a Hollywood Frenchification of *Cabaret*.

No less than *The Cotton Club*, *Victor/Victoria* explores the relationship between social stereotypes, movie appearances, and musical conventions. If it can be believed that Andrews is more girl than woman, why not believe she is more boy than woman? Anyone can *see* she is a woman, but in musicals, where people sing and voices carry belief, seeing alone is not believing. As in *Singin' in the Rain*, seeing is believing only when sight and sound sing in synchrony. The behemoth body guard, Bernstein, played by ex-footballer Alex Karras, and the hefty Toddie, played by Robert Preston, Broadway's virile Music Man, *say* they are lovers, so they must be. Karras no more resembles a gay character than one named Bernstein. Of course, being gay or being Jewish isn't a matter of seeing but *being*—except don't movies (and people) operate under the assumption that some people *look* gay or Jewish? Isn't the entire principle of movie casting and characterization based on the principle that people look like what they are?

Surely Cinderella, whom nobody recognized, must have looked some-

Julie Andrews with a new vocal coach (Robert Preston) in *Victor/Victoria*

thing like Cinderella, even when dressed for the ball. The marriage of voice and dress produces a powerful if erroneous impression. Higgins in *My Fair Lady* dresses Eliza's body by changing her voice. Toddie does the obverse in *Victor/Victoria*: changing the interpretation of Victoria's voice by dressing her body. The *travestie* becomes a travesty when the voice can't fit the dress. In the film's finale, Preston reduces an Andrews routine to the absurd, wearing the identical costume (which can't really be identical), performing the identical steps and singing the identical notes (which can't really be identical either), without producing conviction in his womanhood. How could anyone have believed that the lithe performer of that Spanish fandango with that soaring soprano voice was not a woman in the first place?

Musicals and movies play off a contradictory awareness—that things both are and are not what they seem. Unlike *The Cotton Club*, which sees little difference between the cultural clichés of 1934 and 1984, *Victor/Victoria* sees cultural progress since 1934—the black year of Hollywood's Production Code. Like the 1934 *Dames*, *Victor/Victoria* casts the Code as Ezra Ounce. Perhaps its rose-tinted vision of cultural progress explains why *Victor/Victoria* has been one of the few musical hits since 1980 on stage or screen. In the 1980s we can openly acknowledge the ironies of sexual stereotyping on which our movies, musicals, and culture depend. *Victor/Victoria* is a cultural sharing of our acknowledgment, which frees us, in so far as we can be freed at all, from the bondage of images. Having eliminated the Production Code and the images of sexuality it dictated, movies can reconnect with their own pre-1934 past.

Herbert Ross's *Pennies from Heaven* (1981) also reconnects with the past by playing games with cultural belief. Set in the same 1934 as *Victor/Victoria* and the same Depression America as *The Cotton Club*, the Ross film combines Edwards's sexual stereotyping, Fosse's visual dialectic between dialogue scenes and numbers, and Coppola's exploration of fictional conventions. Ross, a dancer and choreographer from the theatrical performance tradition like Fosse, never buries the power of performance beneath visual style. With delightfully animated numbers and a disturbingly cruel narrative, *Pennies from Heaven* is the most exuberantly schizophrenic of modernist filmusicals. Its plot descends inexorably into an inferno of wretched nastiness. A frustrated Chicago music salesman with a frigid wife casually seduces a small-town schoolteacher, who sinks into prostitution. When a blind girl is brutally raped and murdered in the small town, the salesman is executed for a murder he did not commit. The musical numbers bounce through this dismal itinerary without a glance at the grim landscape—dazzling musical homages derived visually from 1930s filmusicals, lip-synched to 1930s hit recordings.

What does the idea of "the thirties" mean to us, fifty years later? What is our memory, our image of that period? For Ross, our images of the decade are plural and contradictory. The thirties meant the Depression—bread lines, farmers in the Dust Bowl, Hoovervilles, bums in boxcars, airless cities, and arid plains. This is the 1930s of movies like *I Was a Fugitive from a Chain Gang*, *Our Daily Bread*, and *You Only Live Once*, of novels like *Studs Lonigan* and *The Grapes of Wrath*, of paintings and photographs by Edward Hopper, Walker Evans, and Ben Shahn. This is the "social realism" of 1930s representation—what we, fifty years later, believe "real life" in the thirties to have looked like.

But the 1930s was also a golden age of movie musicals, and a golden age of recorded music on 78 RPM disks, and a golden age of Broadway shows and songs. These traces have come to stand for the era's "fantasizing escape" from social reality, circularly confirming that grim social realities inevitably require escape. Which of these 1930s is the real representation of actual 1930s experience? How is the "real" 1930s to be represented "realistically"?

These memories of the 1930s play an important role in our cultural debate fifty years later. The thirties was a supposed era of "clean values"—when our sense of decency and social purpose overruled sexual license and personal gain, the opposite of the current "Me Generation" we read about in *Time* magazine. The thirties was when every American small town resembled Mandrake Falls in *Mr Deeds Goes to Town*. *It Happened One Night*, the Hollywood Code, and the Legion of Decency all belonged to 1934, when husbands never wanted to perform odd sexual acts. People in 1934 didn't use words like "ass hole," traveling salesmen in 1934 never talked about getting laid in the back seats of cars. The Walls of Jericho between man and woman never tumbled until they became man and wife. If it didn't happen in 1934 films, it must never have happened in American life. But wasn't this also the Chicago era of Al Capone, John Dillinger, and Pretty Boy Floyd? Where did all those 1930s gangster films come from if not the newspapers? 1934 brought the prohibition of the Production Code even as it ended the Prohibition that served the gangsters so well.

In Arthur Penn's *Bonnie and Clyde*, the Barrow gang escapes from a hard day at the bank by viewing "We're in the Money" from *Gold Diggers of 1933*. *Pennies from Heaven* explores this cultural contradiction—an era of both Busby Berkeley and Clyde Barrow. If the 1930s was a complicated and contradictory decade in American life—like any other—it was the first whose many traces survive so fully and so clearly in the cultural present: as movies, novels, paintings, photographs, recordings, and popular songs. While the myths of history pluck a unitary meaning from each past period, Ross offers an antidote to this creative cultural forgetting. *Pennies from Heaven* shoves the contradictions up against one another, asking us to look at and listen to *all* our memories of that period: Edward Hopper and Busby Berkeley, Bing Crosby and Clyde Barrow, "I Get a Kick Out of You" and "Brother, Can You Spare a Dime?", *Love Before Breakfast* and people without

Pennies from Heaven: from glamorous escape (Steve Martin and Bernadette Peters as Fred&Ginger) to kitchen-sink realism (Martin and Jessica Harper in the kitchen)

breakfast and "The Glory of Love" and "Pennies from Heaven"—the most hopeful of Depression anthems mimed by the picturesque boxcar bum who rape-murders the blind girl. While its "realist" plot scenes derive from the low-key lighting of gangster films and the perspectives of Hopper paintings, the musical numbers of *Pennies from Heaven* represent themselves as 1930s musicals. The same Warner Bros. that produced the gangster films produced the Busby Berkeley musicals. Ken Adam's production design for *Pennies from Heaven* gives us both extrémes of the decade's surviving visual records.

Ross uses lip-synching, the usual bane of filmusicals, in the most creative way since *Singin' in the Rain*—by declaring its patent falsity. Steve Martin is *not* Bing Crosby or Rudy Vallee; even more obviously, he is not one of the Boswell Sisters. Those famous voices also survive in our cultural memory, reminding us that this visual presence is *not* that vocal presence. Lip-synching was an essential if invisible practice of every 1930s musical. How else could mortal movie performers sing so perfectly while they danced so gymnastically? How else could musicals convey fantasies if their musical performance were not as spectacular as it was effortless? The apparent unity of image and song in 1930s musicals was actually two different recordings—one on film, the other on disk—that represented themselves as one. That representational unity was as false as every other—both within the period and in our cultural memory of it.

Lip-synching is the film's metaphor for any false impression of historical unity, derived from an inadequate selection of cultural artifacts. And so the plot goes one grim way and the numbers go merrily another. Even on the gallows the music salesman can quote song titles, as a process-shot rainbow appears in a sky whose lining is not silver and whose clouds have not rolled by. Was this a cheery musical or a gritty realistic drama? The answer, which *Pennies from Heaven* supplies, is that the question doesn't make sense because the opposition it assumes is itself a cultural falsification.

Why didn't they simply sing and dance in this film, like they did in Fred Astaire and Busby Berkeley musicals? Because they didn't simply sing and dance in those films but carefully fit singing and dancing to complex narrative, metaphoric, and visual conceptions. Like lip-synching, the ideas were there even when they were not apparent. For a modern musical to sustain that tradition of conceptual excellence—whether on stage or on screen—means making its creative principles explicit. That is what "the eighties" means as opposed to "the thirties." Film and stage musicals since 1970 have invested themselves in exploring that difference in meaning. No less than this book, they propose a self-conscious history of American shows and films that can't help singin'—and whose singin' is somehow intrinsic both to American life and our view of it.

And Point Me
Toward Tomorrow

F I N A L E

Broadway has been dying for so long that even last decade's flops look good. The Broadway of 1971 that seemed a ruin to Stephen Sondheim in *Follies* seems a palace fifteen years later.[1] The gallows on which Steve Martin spouted song lyrics seems the grave of the Hollywood musical itself. Although Martin rose from the gallows for yet another song, Hollywood hasn't seen a musical hit in half a decade.

Will American shows and films ever stop singin' completely?

In a word, no. The existence of Broadway is an economic imperative in the commercial life of New York City, vital to its corporations and commerce, a major tourist attraction for both American and foreign visitors. Although plays—new or revived—are prestigious necessities, Broadway means musicals. The economic emperors—the Shuberts and Nederlanders who own almost every Broadway and Broadway-type house in America—must fill their theaters. The richest filling will always be musical. No matter what the cost of the gamble, musicals have the best chance to sell the most tickets to the most people for the longest time. Shows will come from London, the Broadway past, the Hollywood past, regional theaters, workshops, song catalogs, off-Broadway, off-off-Broadway. But they will come. Fewer of them, but some.

A musical has always needed an idea for singin' as much as it needed songs to sing. Both the songs and the ideas seem stuck in the past. To sing a thirty-two-bar AABA song is already to visit history. Either the songs come from yesterday—as they do in *Pennies from Heaven*, *My One and Only*, and *Me and My Girl*—or from men over fifty who come from yesterday. Younger audiences seem progressively unwilling to underwrite the terrific costs of these musical trips to yesterday.

348

The place where they sing and dance in the present for young audiences—within clear conventions and shared expectations of musical sounds and structures—is called music video. Like musicals, music videos have two variants: the pure performance video on a stage (like the revue) and the metaphoric, elliptical, or parodic narrative video in the social or natural world (like the book show). Music videos shift the essential entertainment myth from performing to recording, from a nineteenth-century tradition of dynamic performances to a twentieth-century tradition of technological magnification.[2] Where you once got two hours of entertainment with over a dozen musical numbers, two lines of action, and four comics thrown in for fun, now you get one highly polished, very concentrated, rhythmically edited, carefully packaged number. Call it musical inflation. You also used to get more chocolate for a dime than you now get for a dollar. Perhaps one day music videos will evolve into full musicals (like *Krush Groove* and *Purple Rain*) or filmusicals will disappear into music videos. The 1980s dancicals are already a cross between narrative film and rock video.

An opposite hybrid is the English rock opera. A show like Webber and Rice's *Evita* or the Royal Shakespeare Company production of *Les Miserables* is a mammoth amalgam of musical entertainments on both sides of the Atlantic over the last century. Like the spectacular theater productions of the late-nineteenth century that preceded the arrival of movies, these shows feature virtuoso performances by dexterous scenery, usually designed by John Napier. While American musicals have refused to keep in their place throughout this century, bumping against opera on the one side and burlesque on the other, the new rock operas settle the conflict by adopting European opera forms while preserving modern pop-rock sounds. *Les Miserables*, part English and part French in its creation, is even through-sung. With numbers that variously suggest Bizet, the Beatles, the music hall, and Sondheim, *Les Miserables* seems the ultimate musical composite toward which the international pop opera has been tending.

For all their theatrical power, only a limited number of musicals can be built to such an enormous scale. Though the movement of rock opera away from performers and toward visual elaboration mirrors the same movement in American musicals, never before has human performance been so literally dwarfed by the scenic whole. When the production demand for specialness becomes identical to that of opera, the casual connection of musical theater to the cultural present can only be buried. While a Berlin or Porter unconsciously revealed the connection between American music and American cultural history, and a Hammerstein or Sondheim made that connection conscious, the music of these rock operas, like their scenic spectacle, is simply but hugely there. In losing the Americanness of American musicals, the international rock operas lose the connection of popular music to democratic life. The smaller scale British import, *Me and My Girl*, much more successfully translates its attack against the rigidities of social class into the vitality of democratic song and dance. Its script and score are merely five decades old.

American musicals are lost in the past. Although landmark musicals have always explored their origins—from *Show Boat* to *Singin' in the Rain* to *Fiddler on the Roof* to *Follies*—they also built a musical bridge between singin' then and singin' now. The new score was an extension and a renewal of past tradition. It is that past tradition—which combined theatrical conception, musical composition, and performance virtuosity—that is dead. As dead as the clown tradition that produced silent-film comedy. Indeed, they are the same tradition, taking alternate movie paths before and after 1927. Though many 1980s musicals connect the visual styles and fashions of present and past—for example, the punk androgyny of top hats and canes in *My One and Only*—it is the singin' itself that seems isolated from the present by an insurmountable stylistic barrier. The sole connection of musical past and present is to sing the past in the present. Where and how can a new American score find musical renewal that is not merely repetition?

First, perhaps, in rethinking the connection between popular music and performance music, social dancing and staged dance. No less than American musicals, 1980s American popular and dance music explore the eclectic roots of their past. Not only have rock sounds and songs of the last three decades returned to the American cultural present, but there has been an enormous jazz revival.[3] The bards of popular culture encourage young musical tastes to become eclectic: Barbra Streisand sings everything from Schubert to Sondheim, from pap to pop to rock; Bette Midler and Linda Ronstadt move in equally eclectic musical directions. Jazz songwriter-performers like Blossom Dearie, Dave Frishberg, John Pizzarelli, Bob Dorough, and Rupert Holmes combine eclectic musical styles with ironic observations of contemporary cultural pleasures and pursuits. Holmes has moved to Broadway with *The Mystery of Edwin Drood* (1985), the most exciting combination of past and present, old-style music hall and new-style musical score, in years. The high-tech sound systems that have become as necessary for a Broadway show as its scenery have redefined the kind of singer shows require. No longer need the booming voice of a Jolson, Merman, or Pinza rise to the last row of the balcony. The possible styles for a vocal score have not made full use of the sound technology. One answer to the creation of new musicals may be exploring the traditions not just of American musicals but of America's eclectic musical taste.

Another answer may simply be conceiving the musical show or film on a smaller scale. Though the stunning visual production has been obligatory for theater musicals since *The Black Crook* and for filmusicals since *Sunny Side Up*, the extravagant cost of extravaganza has flown higher than its patrons can bear. The casual frivolousness of musical performance has been swallowed by virtuoso scenery and dazzling decor. Can a musical preserve its visual power on a smaller scale? Must brilliantly imaginative visual conceptions cost so much? Singin' in the MGM rain, dancin' in mammoth three-dimensional Impressionist paintings, projecting laser light shows, and collecting decades of Ziegfeld styles no longer justify their costs. Musicals of the future must solve the problem of reducing scale without sacrificing imagination. Rock videos and film dancicals already represent this stylish reduction, as does a new generation of "little" theater musicals—*The Little Shop of Horrors*, *Pump Boys and Dinettes*, *The March of the Falsettoes*, *The Mystery of Edwin Drood*, *Me and My Girl*. Can this reduction be achieved consistently without also reducing the musical to a cheap, "B" genre—like Paramount musicals during World War II?

All it takes is one good idea: one new way to combine song, story, and a vital cultural issue. This book has been a history of those good ideas, the landmark shows and films, writers and composers, directors and performers: *Show Boat*, *Of Thee I Sing*, *Porgy and Bess*, *Pal Joey*, *Oklahoma!*, *My Fair Lady*, *Company*, *The Jazz Singer*, *Monte Carlo*, *Top Hat*, *The Wizard of Oz*, *Meet Me in St. Louis*, *An American in Paris*, *Cabaret*; Kern, Berlin, the Gershwins, Porter, Rodgers and Hart or Hammerstein, Berkeley, Astaire, Garland, Kelly, Freed, Minnelli, Sondheim. Each idea generated dozens and decades of musical shows and films. What might a new good idea be?

Sure of its past, unsure of its future, floating in a modernist present between the overpackaged Scylla of music video and the overblown Charybdis of rock opera, the American musical, whether on stage or screen, whether *Sunday in the Park with George* or *Pennies from Heaven*, tries to stay afloat on its own traditions. Since 1927, the year of both *Show Boat* and *The Jazz Singer*, the Broadway and Hollywood musical vessels have bumped against, grappled with, and jumped aboard one another. Six decades later, they find themselves in the same narrow entertainment strait. They will either sail out of it together or not at all.

Notes

CHAPTER 1

1. Feuer, Jane, *The Hollywood Musical* (Bloomington: Indiana University Press, 1982), p. vii.
2. Erenberg, Lewis A., *Steppin' Out: New York Nightlife and the Transformation of American Culture, 1890–1930* (Chicago: University of Chicago Press, 1984), p. 18.

CHAPTER 2

1. The list would include such names as Dion Boucicault, Bronson Howard, Augustin Daly, William Gillette, Augustus Thomas, Clyde Fitch, Steele MacKaye and his son, Percy MacKaye, David Belasco, and William Vaughn Moody. Current unfamiliarity with their work obscures the cultural power of the theater in the 150 years of its widest social importance and influence. Far more than the novel, which was read privately and more avidly by women than by men, the theater was the major public forum of cultural interchange in the two centuries that saw the rise of the urban bourgeoisie. Regular visits to the theater became the primary way that this rapidly growing class, in both England and America, confirmed and solidified its values.
2. This account of the production of *The Black Crook* is based on Gerald Bordman: *The American Musical Theatre: A Chronicle* (New York: Oxford University Press, 1978), pp. 18–20.
3. This mixed entertainment in *Doctor Faustus* is an embarrassment to English literary scholars; who usually attribute the shenanigans to the low tastes of the groundlings and hack writers other than Marlowe. Although these explanations may be valid, they ignore the theatrical vitality of the comic scenes. Audiences liked their tragedies spiced with comedy, and successful playwrights and playhouse owners gave those audiences what they wanted.
4. The distinction between the two types of Roman comedy—called Old and New—is that the old style was a taut, single-strand farce (often scurrilous or vulgar) and the new was a more romantic multistrand narrative with genteel emotional appeal. Roman comedies that became Shakespearean (*The Comedy of Errors*) or musicals (*A Funny Thing Happened on the Way to the Forum*) might combine two original Roman sources, guaranteeing the double plot of New Comedy. I discuss the

impact of Roman New Comedy on American film comedy in *The Comic Mind: Comedy and the Movies*, rev. ed. (Chicago: University of Chicago Press, 1979), pp. 4–5. Stanley Cavell builds his study of American screwball comedy [*Pursuits of Happiness: The Hollywood Comedy of Remarriage* (Cambridge, Mass: Harvard University Press, 1981)] on the tradition that extends from Roman New Comedy through Shakespeare to Hollywood.

5. For those unfamiliar with it, *The Contrast* was an American adaptation of eighteenth-century British sentimental comedy—which softened the cynical wit and open licentiousness of the earlier Restoration comedies to make them consistent with the mores of the bourgeoisie rather than the court. *The Contrast*, as its title suggests, contrasted the native modesty and simplicity of Americans as opposed to the effete and foppish styles of England. Like Restoration and sentimental comedies, *The Contrast* required a multistrand plot. One can draw a straight line from Elizabethan comedy through Restoration and sentimental comedy to American comedy of the nineteenth century and, finally, to American musical comedy of the twentieth.

6. One wonders what might have happened in Germany if Kurt Weill had not been forced to emigrate to Broadway. The rise of Hitler threw German musical theater back to Wagner and nineteenth-century operetta. It has never recovered its Weimar innovation.

7. The song's title, as both copyrighted and printed in the show's program, was "Paris Is a Paridise for Coons." The misspelling, rather than a deliberate demeaning of the "coon's" inability to use the English language, was probably a play on an internal rhyme: Paree is a pareedise for coons.

8. Among early composers of American theater music, only John Philip Sousa and Reginald De Koven were born in America. De Koven, whose most important work was the 1891 operetta *Robin Hood*, received his musical training in the conservatories of France and Germany.

CHAPTER 3

1. The two words, "refrain" and "chorus," are used interchangeably to describe the thirty-two-bar section because "refrain" has two meanings. On the one hand, it refers to the entire thirty-two-bar structure (including refrain and release). On the other, it refers only to the song's familiar melody in its A sections. This terminological confusion is a result of the American popular song's historical evolution. Older songs, with their brief eight-bar refrains, did not need a term to distinguish the main melody from the release: there was no release, merely a refrain in answer to a verse. Of course, "chorus" has its own ambiguity since it can refer either to the singers or the song.

2. I realize it is difficult to understand song structures merely by reading them on the page. I've chosen familiar songs as examples; if you sing or hum them to yourself, or play any recording of them (vocal or instrumental, straight or jazz), you can hear the construction more clearly.

3. This system of notation, using A and A′ (A prime), can be seen in Alec Wilder's study: *American Popular Song: The Great Innovators 1900–1950* (New York: Oxford University Press, 1972). All further references to Wilder are to this volume.

4. For both the name and the description of this song type, I am indebted to two colleagues at the University of Chicago: Robert Ashenhurst, of the Graduate School of Business, and Irving Kaplansky, formerly of the Department of Mathematics. Ashenhurst refers to this structure as a "Kaplansky Type II," since Kaplansky first noted it after visualizing it in a dream. I have never read a description of it, not even in Alec Wilder's classic study.

5. John Boswell's definitive study, *Christianity, Social Tolerance, and Homosexuality* (Chicago: University of Chicago Press, 1980), provides powerful historical evidence that the social fortunes of Jewish and gay people have been inextricably linked throughout the Christian Era.

6. Charles Belmont Davis, "The Vaudeville Club," *Harper's Weekly* 37 (February 1893), p. 116. Quoted in Erenberg, p. 38.

CHAPTER 4

1. Alec Wilder, for example, invests his entire chapter on Berlin in trying to define a single and consistent Berlin style. He finally gives up.

2. For a discussion of the growth of American cabaret life in the 1910s, see Lewis A. Erenberg, *Steppin' Out: New York Nightlife and the Transformation of American Culture, 1890–1930* (Chicago: University of Chicago Press, 1984), pp. 146–75.

3. Wilder points out the similarity of the two songs but notes they are the only two of this type in Berlin's entire catalog.

4: In Wilder, p. 111.

5. *Betsy* is one of those shows that built a pile of Broadway's brightest talent into a total disaster. Producer Florenz Ziegfeld was so unmoved by the Rodgers and Hart score that he asked Irving Berlin to write "Blue Skies" for its star, Belle Baker. Rodgers and Hart could only grit their teeth when the Berlin interpolation stole whatever attention the show received. The other notable number of the show was also an interpolation: a version of Gershwin's "Rhapsody in Blue" played by Borah Minnevitch and His Harmonica Orchestra.

CHAPTER 5

1. Wilder devotes most of his Kern chapter (pp. 29–90) to analyzing the conflict between Kern's commercial sense, which pulls him toward the American sound, and Kern's European tastes, which pull him the other way.

2. The two standard biographies are Michael Freedland, *Jerome Kern* (London: Robson, 1978), a popularized character portrait of the man and his temperament; and Gerald Bordman, *Jerome Kern: His Life and Music* (New York: Oxford University Press, 1980), a detailed chronicle of Kern's primarily public and creative life.

3. Kern also wrote a new tune to an existing Ira Gershwin lyric, "Put Me to the Test." Originally written by Ira and George for *A Damsel in Distress*, it was cut, then adapted by Kern and Ira Gershwin for *Cover Girl*.

4. So Alec Wilder found it.

5. Wilder is among those who believes *Roberta* a superior score—at least in the density of memorable tunes (particularly with "I Won't Dance" and "Lovely to Look At," added for the movie). As a unified theatrical conception, *Show Boat* is both more ambitious and more successful.

6. Although the copyrighted title of the song uses the dialect contraction "Ol'," the 1927 theater program listed the song as "Old Man River."

7. Hugh Fordin makes the same observation in his brief but informative notes to a collection of Kern songs: *Jerome Kern: The Man and His Music in Story, Picture, and Song* (Santa Monica, Calif: Harms, 1974), p. 173.

CHAPTER 6

1. The British began recording original casts of London musical shows in the 1910s. The first American original cast recording waited for *Oklahoma!* in 1943. The British valued musical shows before Americans did. As the current number of musicals in London's West End indicate, they still do. Surviving recordings of early American shows come from their London productions.

2. Wilder cannot understand the affection for this song (pp. 130–31). Because he studies the scores of songs as musical compositions, he never considers the interplay of words and music. "Fascinating Rhythm" is only interesting in the way its musical-verbal games capture the idea of the song's title—which cannot be seen in the notes on a score.

3. This very famous song had a checkered history. Originally written for *Lady, Be Good* in 1924, from which it was cut, "The Man I Love" was slotted for and subsequently cut from several Gershwin shows of the decade. The song became a hit when the Gershwins' publisher, Max Dreyfus, sent it out on its showless own in 1929. Alec Wilder (p. 130) chronicles its career in detail.

4. Quotations come from the published script of the show, available from Samuel French.

CHAPTER 7

1. The opinion of Mordaunt Hall in the New York *Times*, August 7, 1926.

2. There is confusion about the casting of Jolson in *The Jazz Singer*. George Jessel originated the role on Broadway and had been signed by Warners to film it. Jessel claimed Warners refused to pay him more for singing so he turned down the role. More likely it was the comparison of Jessel's and Jolson's performances in the second Vitaphone program that decided between the two stars: Jolson easily won. Warners also probably wanted and needed a bigger star than Jessel for *The Jazz Singer* experiment. See Harry Geduld, *The Birth of the Talkies* (Bloomington: Indiana University Press, 1975).

3. Although dubbing was uncommon before the 1950s it was not unknown. Dancers like Eleanor Powell, Rita Hayworth, and Vera-Ellen required dubbed singing voices. Unlike Lina Lamont, they were certainly musical performers—if nonsinging ones.

4. In *The Hollywood Musical* (New York: St. Martin's Press, 1981), Ethan Mordden lists the complete works of El Brendel atop his list of the Worst Performances in movie musicals (p. 244).

5. They were such a successful team that Mama Gershwin is rumored to have scolded her sons for not writing successful songs like DeSylva, Brown, and Henderson.

6. Ethan Mordden (*The Hollywood Musical*, pp. 37–38) overpraises the film by overlooking its faults.

7. Both Chaucer and Shakespeare called this the issue of "sovereignty."

8. Mordden's view, p. 38. For Mordden, Buchanan in *Monte Carlo* ranks just below the complete works of El Brendel on his list of Worsts.

9. Some, like Mordden, consider *Applause* both a musical and a masterpiece (*The Hollywood Musical*, pp 40–41). I consider it neither. Although the film occupies the backstage world, it invests very little in its musical numbers—except to generate atmosphere. The film also tries too hard to be a masterpiece to be one.

CHAPTER 8

1. Ziegfeld's only other film, *Glorifying the American Girl*, was a 1929 musical for Paramount that begins as a talent search and ends as a revue.

2. Berkeley directed one film for MGM, *Flying High* (1930), starring Bert Lahr, before settling in with Cantor at Goldwyn.

3. Mark Roth makes an explicit connection between FDR and the Berkeley films in "Some Warners Musicals and the Spirit of the New Deal," collected in *Genre: The Musical* (London: Routledge and Kegan Paul, 1981), edited by Rick Altman, pp.

41–56. For Roth, the mediocrity of Berkeley's "stars"—Dick Powell, Ruby Keeler, Joan Blondell—was powerful proof that if *they* can make it, anybody can.

4. Although written in 1930, the Hollywood Production Code was not implemented as a censorship procedure until 1934. The 1933 and 1934 Berkeley films, increasingly aware of the Code's coming, mock it without violating it. By 1935 even the mockery is gone.

5. Animated films, like Disney's, and experimental films, like Robert Breer's drawn abstractions, Fernand Leger's *Ballet Mécanique*, or Ralph Steiner's H_2O, also translate musical concepts into visual terms. None faced the commercial pressure of making Hollywood genre entertainment.

6. For a detailed analysis of sexist imagery in Berkeley see Lucy Fischer, "The Image of Woman as Image: The Optical Politics of *Dames*," in *Genre: The Musical*, pp. 70–84. For parallels between wet dream and "By a Waterfall," I am indebted to an unpublished 1986 essay, "Busby Berkeley's Wet Dream Ballet," by A. L. Knight, a graduate student at the University of Chicago.

7. The sole survivor of the Ziegfeld-Berkeley tradition in 1980s America is Donn Arden, whose extravaganza revues for Las Vegas showrooms combine spectacular scenic effects with nude show girls. Like Busby Berkeley, Arden's choreographic specialties are the saunter, the smile, and the time-step.

CHAPTER 9

1. Astaire was personally responsible for choreographing every number he danced, worked out in collaboration with his dance director, usually Hermes Pan, and rehearsal pianist, usually Hal Borne. See Arlene Croce's *The Fred Astaire & Ginger Rogers Book* (New York: Outerbridge and Lazard, 1973), pp. 89–96. John Mueller's *Astaire Dancing* (New York: Knopf, 1985) documents many similarly revealing production details.

2. Vincente Minnelli claims (in his memoirs, *I Remember It Well*) that *Yolanda and the Thief* failed because the public could never accept Astaire as a crook.

3. Leo Braudy discusses the search for a perfect dancing partner as Astaire's ultimate quest in *The World in a Frame* (Chicago: University of Chicago Press, 1983). Future references to Braudy are to this discussion.

4. I prefer the compound Fred&Ginger to wordy alternatives (like Fred Astaire-Ginger Rogers film). The ampersand descends from Arlene Croce. She believes Fred&Ginger first became fixed screen deities in "Hard to Handle" of *Roberta*, but they go to Olympus in the earlier "Night and Day" of *The Gay Divorcée*.

5. For a superb discussion of the impact of the Castles on American dance and social styles, see Lewis A. Erenberg, *Steppin' Out*, pp. 158–71. The Castles spread the popularity of social dancing by combining spontaneous expression with social restraint, exuberance with gentility. Jane Feuer (*Hollywood Musical*, pp. 98–99) sees the nostalgic retreat of *The Story of Vernon and Irene Castle* as the somber death knell for Fred&Ginger.

6. Stanley Cavell's *Pursuits of Happiness: The Hollywood Comedy of Remarriage* (Cambridge, Mass.: Harvard University Press, 1981) details the essential motifs of screwball comedy—summed up by the value of having "fun" together.

7. Francis Kornford, Northrop Frye, Frank McConnell, and Stanley Cavell are among those who have paralleled New Comedy with myths of seasonal renewal.

8. Leo Braudy first called their dancing "better than sex" in *The World in a Frame*.

9. This parallels Stanley Cavell's argument in *Pursuits of Happiness* that screwball comedy mimes the myth of modern marriage.

10. There are three spectacular roller-skating solos in American cinema: Chaplin's

in *Modern Times*, Donald O'Connor's in *I Love Melvin* (1953), and Gene Kelly's in *It's Always Fair Weather* (1955). Fred&Ginger give us the only spectacular roller-skating duet.

    11. Astaire plays his own "feelthy piano" for three filmed musical numbers: "I Won't Dance" in *Roberta*, "The Way You Look Tonight" in *Swing Time*, and "I've Got My Eyes on You" in *Broadway Melody of 1940*.

    12. The Eiffel Tower may also represent an in-group joke since it served as RKO's corporate logo.

    13. Film historians have convincingly demonstrated that Edison did not in fact invent movies. In 1937, however, he was popularly believed to have invented them. Hence the film links movies, phonograph, and electricity.

CHAPTER 10

    1. These glimpses into Hart's personal habits come from Richard Rodgers's autobiography, *Musical Stages* (New York: Random House, 1975). All quotations come from that volume.

    2. It is obviously difficult to gather evidence about the private lives of public personalities in America's closeted eras. Although scuttlebutt and insider gossip is an inevitable but questionable source, I have relied on information about New York's gay subculture in the 1930s and 1940s from Jack Richtman, professor of Romantic Languages and Gay Studies at SUNY, Albany.

    3. The collected "Pal Joey" letters and the *Pal Joey* libretto have been published together by the Popular Library (New York, 1976). All page references are to this edition.

    4. A copy of this letter can be found on the record jacket of the 1951 recording of *Pal Joey*, produced for Columbia records by Goddard Lieberson. The show's 1952 Broadway revival followed its success as an LP record.

    5. They have been included, however, in a British recording of a 1980 London revival. They were probably excluded from the Columbia disk because 1951 recording technology limited each side to twenty minutes of music. These parodies, clearly deficient in "gravity" for a historic recording, were easy to cut.

    6. In the key of C that identical note is a G, which repeats in two identical sequences of thirteen quarter notes.

CHAPTER 11

    1. This phrase, "wit, wealth, and waste," is from George Eells's biography of Porter, *The Life that Late He Led* (New York: Putnam, 1967). Because Eells, a very slippery biographer, omits any references to Porter's sexuality and its relationship to his imagination, his study provides a highly questionable psychological portrait.

    2. In *American Popular Song*, p. 223.

    3. See Kimball, Robert, ed. *The Complete Lyrics of Cole Porter* (New York: Knopf, 1983), pp. 120–21.

    4. John Updike's foreword to Kimball's collection of Porter lyrics suggests that Porter would have made a fine poet if he hadn't been seduced by songwriting.

    5. The throbbing note is a G in the key of C, the key signature in the published collection, *Music and Lyrics by Cole Porter: A Treasury of Cole Porter* (New York: Chappel, 1972).

    6. Alec Wilder's description.

    7. Porter and Woolley frequently played this game. Woolley would come up with a title and Porter would write a song to fill it. This would be very good practice for Hollywood. After writing untold versions of title tunes for MGM's

Rosalie, all of which L. B. Mayer rejected, Porter decided he had to write the worst song he could imagine. The result was a big hit.

8. There are very few songs like this in American popular and theater music. The Gershwins' "Sam and Delilah" (*Girl Crazy*) gives us the biblical story from Ethel Merman in the modern guise and dialect of a Wild West buckeroo. In "Eadie Was a Lady" (*Take a Chance*, 1932), by Richard Whiting and Nacio Herb Brown, Merman eulogizes a dead hooker who had "Class with a capital K," as described by her co-workers, Maude and Mabel. In "Guess Who I Saw Today," by Murray Grand and Elisse Boyd (*New Faces of 1952*), a wife, martini in hand, tells her husband the story of discovering his infidelity when she saw him with his new lover earlier that day. Like Porter's, these singing dramatic monologues juxtapose passionate events with detached narration.

9. The only Porter song to make it into Astaire's 1934 film of *The Gay Divorcée* was "Night and Day."

10. Merman was one of the first Broadway singers who "belted" in the manner of a Sophie Tucker, pushing notes out of the chest rather than the head, like operatic singers.

11. The revisions became necessary when a disastrous fire on the *Morro Castle* forced the show to revise its climactic shipwreck. Those revisions were Lindsay and Crouse's first collaboration.

12. The last would be "Nobody's Chasing Me" from *Out of this World* (1950), which returns full circle to the animal activities and imagery of the very first, "Let's Do It."

CHAPTER 12

1. *Broadway Babies*, p. 142.

2. An early Blossom Dearie recording of "It Might as Well Be Spring" on her first Atlantic album—in French!—proves how lifeless it is without Hammerstein's sensitivity to the sounds of English vowels and consonants.

3. All quotations are from the Modern Library edition of *Six Plays by Rodgers and Hammerstein* (New York, 1959). This collection of "plays" represents the only musicals ever published by the prestigious Modern Library series of "Great Books."

4. This song was not included on the Decca original cast recording of the show, the very first cast recording of an American show. Like the parodic numbers of *Pal Joey*, "Lonely Room" was probably considered deficient in tone for such a historic event.

5. Despite the more normal surfaces of Hammerstein's life, he frequented the same kinds of bars and inhabited the same kind of closet as the more flamboyant Porter and desperate Hart. Jack Richtman, professor of Romance Literature and Gay Studies at SUNY, Albany, reports meeting Hammerstein in Upper East Side gay bars during the period of Hammerstein's greatest public popularity. These personal experiences never get into his shows, although the relationship between Anna and the king of Siam is perhaps a very oblique glimpse at a forbidden and impossible love. "We Kiss in a Shadow," also from *The King and I*, opens another crack in the closet door. The song's gay subtext is especially evident when sung by gay men's choruses.

6. Quoted in Mordden, *Broadway Babies*. Todd is the showman whose acumen gave us such stinkeroos as Smell-o-Rama.

7. Ethan Mordden doesn't even mention *The Sound of Music* in either of his books on the Broadway musical. The film, for Mordden, is "neither all that great nor all that horrible," merely a model of Hollywood blockbustership (*The Hollywood Musical*, pp. 203–204).

8. See *Musical Stages* for Rodgers's tales of Hollywood misadventures.
9. Ethan Mordden, *The Hollywood Musical*, p. 199.

CHAPTER 13

1. Ethan Mordden views Crosby this way in *The Hollywood Musical*.
2. I discuss the Sennett style in *The Comic Mind: Comedy and the Movies* (Chicago: University of Chicago Press, rev. ed., 1979).
3. This present telling also foretold the future. "Now It Can Be Told" would evolve melodically into "It Only Happens When I Dance with You" for *Easter Parade*, ten years later.
4. I discuss Hawks in general and *Gentlemen Prefer Blondes* in particular in *Howard Hawks, Storyteller* (New York: Oxford University Press, 1982).
5. According to Donald Bogle in *Toms, Coons, Mulattoes, Mammies, and Bucks: An Interpretive History of Blacks in American Films* (New York: Viking, 1973).
6. See Feuer's (*The Hollywood Musical*, pp. 26–30) superb discussion of the repetitive convention of filming an audience enjoying the musical performance onstage. *Stormy Weather* may be the only Hollywood musical that never does.

CHAPTER 14

1. See Hugh Fordin, *The Movies' Greatest Musicals: Produced in Hollywood USA by the Freed Unit* (New York: Ungar, 1975), for documentation of Garland's perpetual absences throughout the 1940s. All further references to Fordin are to this volume.
2. Ethan Mordden attributes Minnelli's *auteur* status to his reputation as a colorist, a quality he dismisses without exploring (*The Hollywood Musical*, p. 177).
3. Minnelli musicals must be seen in 35 mm prints, projected in theaters. To see them on television—whether telecast or on cassette—may be enjoyable, but you might as well be looking at black-and-white postcards while wearing sunglasses. Even 16mm prints of the films are reduced and, occasionally, faded or duped. Because MGM stuck resolutely with three-strip Technicolor for both film stock and processing until 1953, original 35mm prints of these films still sparkle (even those submitted for copyright to the Library of Congress forty years ago). Most Eastmancolor prints, the cheaper color process adopted in 1953 for economical reasons, have turned red in the Library of Congress vaults.
4. Leo Braudy draws the same contrast between Astaire's and Kelly's performances in *The World in a Frame*.
5. Jane Feuer (*The Hollywood Musical*, pp. 4–6) applies the idea of *bricolage* to musicals, derived from its use in both Lévi-Strauss and Jacques Derrida. In French, a *bricoleur* is a tinkerer, someone who plays with and patches together miscellaneous stuff into a coherent system. *Bricolage* is the act of playing or tinkering with this miscellaneous stuff. Although Feuer observes the common role of *bricolage* in Kelly and Astaire dances, she doesn't note the important difference in the "stuff" they use. Astaire builds numbers on unique, personal, or odd bits of physical material (his own clothing; golf clubs and balls; a magical coat rack). Kelly builds numbers on the ordinary junk of the everyday world.
6. Quoted in Feuer, *The Hollywood Musical*, p. 64. She discusses the general MGM trend (whether in Freed films or those produced by Joe Pasternak) to contrast pop songs with opera sounds.
7. One can read Kelly's claim in Knox, Donald, ed. *The Magic Factory: How MGM Made An American in Paris* (New York: Praeger, 1973). Kelly also made the claim on national television at the 1985 AFI award ceremony to honor him. The *auteur* theory is a pet peeve since, as a performer, he feels demeaned by it. The

theory can, of course, be modified to include performers as *auteurs*. Although all Hollywood films are artistic collaborations, Kelly knows that filmusicals are particularly collaborative.

CHAPTER 15

1. Many *auteur* admirers of Minnelli prefer his dialogue comedies and melodramas to his musicals. *An American in Paris* is like *Lust for Life:* fancy, grand, painterly, appealing to cultured tastes of the Establishment. On the other hand, musical buffs like Ethan Mordden, who loathe the *auteur* formulation, don't like *An American in Paris* either: it isn't "fun" enough. He expects stage musicals to be serious and filmusicals to be fun—and never the twain should meet. For Mordden, *An American in Paris* and *The Band Wagon* are the two most overrated musicals in film history *(The Hollywood Musical*, p. 177). The only thing I find more wrong than this view is his confidence in it. It comes from an inability to see the relationship of visual style to a filmusical—in effect to *see* filmusicals at all.

2. Gene Kelly confirms the conceptual care invested in every number. See Donald Knox, ed., *The Magic Factory.*

3. Ethan Mordden puts Levant up there with El Brendel and Jack Buchanan on his Worst Performances list. The mistake is to consider Levant a performer at all, rather than a zany, onscreen and off.

4. Feuer *(The Hollywood Musical*, pp. 73–76) compares the musical dream ballets of Hollywood to the work of dreams in Freudian theory.

5. Insiders considered "Make 'Em Laugh" neither a variation on "Be a Clown" nor an homage, but out-and-out theft. See Fordin, p. 359.

6. Fordin reveals this little known fact about dubbing Debbie for this one number (p. 358). Feuer *(The Hollywood Musical*, pp. 45–47) also notes that *Singin' in the Rain* destroys the illusion of live performance only to confirm it.

7. Leo Braudy makes a similar point in *The World in a Frame.*

8. I am also indebted to Leo Braudy for this observation.

9. For these figures, see Hugh Fordin.

10. Fordin describes the way they rigged this rotating room (pp. 303–305).

11. Freed specifically asked Dietz and Schwartz for a "There's No Business Like Show Business" (Fordin, p. 403).

12. This switch from sorrow to joy was powerfully demonstrated by an eight-bar reprise, cut from the 1954 release version but restored for the 1983 rerelease.

13. One Cukor take in *Adam's Rib* lasts almost nine minutes, recording Katharine Hepburn's interview of Judy Holliday. This intimate shot with little movement is said to be the longest single take in the history of MGM.

14. Since the mid-1970s film compositions have been "TV safe"—avoiding the edges of the frame for essential information. Because early wide-screen films were weapons in the television war, they consciously constructed frames that TV could never transmit. The 1983 theatrical rerelease of *A Star Is Born* not only restored footage that had never been seen but restored the full frame of Cukor's visual conception that hadn't been seen in three decades. Most people have only seen *A Star Is Born* on a television screen.

15. The original version was shown as a trailer preceding the 1983 rerelease, an overture for the film to follow. The film itself retained the second version of the number.

16. Fordin documents the troubles on this film (pp. 432–36)—the enmity of Kelly and Donen, the dissatisfaction of Previn with his feeble tunes.

17. Fordin is unsure whether Lerner and Loewe bought into the production or bought it altogether. They took over responsibility for finishing the film from Freed,

shooting retakes at MGM (directed by Charles Walters) and assembling the final cut (pp. 489–95). There was so much bitterness during retakes that Lela Simone, the last of Freed's old guard who had worked with him for two decades, left for good.

18. It is very odd for a high taste, big budget, wide-screen musical to look so fake in certain shots. Zsa Zsa Gabor was obviously not skating with Jacques Bergerac; Chevalier and Hermione Gingold clearly sang "I Remember It Well" in an indoor sound stage, not on a Lido terrace. Fordin documents these masquerades. The carelessness, which appalled Cecil Beaton, must be attributed to Broadway people for whom visual detail makes little difference.

CHAPTER 16

1. Lewis Erenberg (*Steppin' Out*, pp. 148–58) notes key differences between the waltz and the new American dances of the 1910s, despite the similarity of their partnering positions. For Erenberg, even the rigid box step permitted subtly spontaneous innovations and casual physical contact. Erenberg would probably see the more abandoned, less structured social dancing of the late twentieth century as an inevitable outgrowth of the style that began early in the century.

2. Jazz vocalists and instrumentalists have never found Rodgers and Hammerstein of much interest. Ella Fitzgerald, for example, made a Rodgers and Hart songbook album (and songbooks for virtually every other major composer of that era—Porter, Berlin, Ellington, Gershwin, Kern, Harold Arlen, Harry Warren, Johnny Mercer) but no Rodgers and Hammerstein songbook.

3. If you have any doubts, just listen to the difference between the two "original" cast recordings. I find the 1974 shoestring revival unlistenable. The 1982 recording of the New York City Opera production is certainly grand enough; it is also stiff and stilted.

4. She sings it flawlessly on the brilliant Columbia 1956 original cast recording. Many of the recordings of this era are so good that both revivals and rerecordings of the shows have difficulty competing with them.

5. You can't hear the rhyme of "buck" and "schmuck" on either the original Broadway cast recording or on the movie soundtrack, which rhyme "dough" and "schmo." The 1985 Bernstein recording of the score, for all its operatic stiffness, restores the original lyric.

6. This is another show whose performances on the Columbia original cast album are so definitive that no revival can compete with it—and few have been attempted.

7. Lerner and Bernstein would hold a very sad reunion in 1976 on *1600 Pennsylvania Avenue*, the absolute bottom of two brilliant careers in the musical theater.

8. The Broadway cast recording of *My Fair Lady* became the biggest selling album in recording history, selling more copies than any previous LP disk. The recording is said to represent the very best performances Rex Harrison and Julie Andrews ever gave. The performances on Columbia's London cast recording are much weaker (they were getting bored and had begun to embroider)—but the recording is in stereo.

9. The scripts of both *Pygmalion* and *My Fair Lady* have been published together by the New American Library (New York, 1975). All page references are to this edition.

10. Ethan Mordden and Jane Feuer clearly define the contrasting views of Broadway and cinema buffs toward this film. For Mordden (*The Hollywood Musical*, p. 202), the film is only valuable for preserving the original stage performances,

watered down by the addition of Hepburn. Feuer never mentions the film at all, not even in her thorough filmography.

11. This is another film that must be seen in the wide-screen version to be fully and truly seen.

12. The myth of this film is that the brilliant choreographer Robbins was undermined by the movie veteran Robert Wise. Wise gets the blame for every inconsistency of the film's style and decor. I can't buy this myth. Robbins never directed a film—before or since—while Wise was a brilliant film editor (merely *Citizen Kane*) who made many wonderfully wise films. *West Side Story* is so visually drab it looks better on television than on the wide screen: the little frame erases the lifeless decor; the frequent intercutting of wide-screen images for television gives the video version more energy than the original.

13. Sydney Chaplin's Broadway success seems unfathomable today. He also created Nicky Arnstein opposite Barbra Streisand's *Funny Girl*. Chaplin could sing a little, dance a little, and play a "real man" at the same time. His Broadway stardom implies the dearth of male musical talent in the period.

14. I prefer Martin in *Bells Are Ringing* to his more heralded performances in *Rio Bravo* and *Some Came Running*.

15. Quoted in Mordden, *The Hollywood Musical*, p. 204.

CHAPTER 17

1. Bruce Kawin would call this number an example of "mindscreen," translating the image on screen into a subjective mental projection. See *Mindscreen: Bergman, Godard, and First-Person Film* (Princeton University Press, 1978).

2. The libretto of *Company* has been published in Stanley Richards, ed. *Great Musicals of the American Theatre*. Volume 1. (Radnor, Pa.: Chilton, 1975). All page references are to this volume.

3. For her 1985 *Broadway Album*, Barbara Streisand took "Putting It Together" from *Sunday in the Park with George* as her initial cut. Her version emphasized the applicability of Sondheim's song to any popular artist. It also emphasized the dependence of the song on brilliant orchestral color.

4. *Broadway Babies*, p. 196. Mordden's discussion of Sondheim's career (pp. 185–96) parallels my own.

5. When *Hair* began at the Public Theatre, its director was Gerald Freedman. O'Horgan projected the workshop concept for the larger Broadway canvas.

6. For the reader who may anticipate a discussion of Coppola's other musical, *One from the Heart* (1982), or Martin Scorsese's *New York, New York* (1977), let me explain, without flogging dead horses, that my discussion would duplicate the observations about *Finian's Rainbow* and *The Cotton Club*. All four films explore conventions of style and belief in filmusicals; all explore the relation of light, music, and decor; all four understand the musical as a film genre rather than a cinematic extension of a lengthy performance tradition. All four are, therefore, unsympathetic toward or ignorant about the power, meaning, and value of musical performance. In their commitment to exploring the conventions of all film genres, Coppola and Scorsese are strangers to the particular power of musicals.

CHAPTER 18

1. Frank Rich makes the same point in the Sunday New York *Times* of September 15, 1985. *Follies* would be an oasis in the Broadway desert of 1985. These increasingly frequent nostalgic looks backward by critics—with revivals of *Merrily We Roll Along*, *Pacific Overtures*, and the RCA recording of *Follies*—ignore their own

2. A film like *Singin' in the Rain* is already aware of the tension between technology and performance, which it resolves firmly in favor of the latter. But the creators of this filmusical (and every other of the period) are all descendants of the nineteenth-century performance tradition, through Broadway, to Hollywood. By the mid-1980s, most performers, composers, and creators of filmusicals and music videos descend from the visual and vocal recording industries.

3. The jazz revival can be seen in recent reissues of classic 1950s and 1960s jazz recordings (on Verve, Capitol, Emarcy) in new jazz labels (Pablo, Concord), and in the establishing of jazz divisions by the mass-market labels. The repetitive eight-bar phrases of rock to which the young dance have dominated popular music for three decades, a full generation. That is a very long time for a dance fashion. A new eclectic fusion of jazz, pop, rock, and cool can be heard in many recent recordings by both jazz and pop artists.

Bibliography

Altman, Rick, ed. *Genre: The Musical: A Reader.* London: Routledge and Kegan Paul, 1981.

Altman, Rick. "The American Film Musical: Paradigmatic Structure and Mediatory Function," in Altman, *Genre*, pp. 197–207.

Anderson, Lindsay. "Minnelli, Kelly, and *An American in Paris*," *Sequence* 14 (1952), pp. 36–38.

Astaire, Fred. *Steps in Time.* New York: Harper, 1959.

Basinger, Jeanine. *Gene Kelly.* New York: Pyramid, 1976.

Belton, John. "The Backstage Musical," *Movie* 24 (Spring 1977), pp. 36–44.

Berlin, Edward A. *Ragtime: A Musical and Cultural History.* Berkeley and Los Angeles: University of California Press, 1980.

Bogle, Donald. *Toms, Coons, Mulattoes, Mammies, and Bucks: An Interpretive History of Blacks in American Films.* New York: Viking, 1973.

Bordman, Gerald. *American Musical Theatre: A Chronicle.* New York: Oxford University Press, 1978.

––––––. *Jerome Kern: His Life and Music.* New York: Oxford University Press, 1980.

Boswell, John. *Christianity, Social Tolerance, and Homosexuality.* Chicago: University of Chicago Press, 1980.

Braudy, Leo. *The World in a Frame.* Chicago: University of Chicago Press, 1982.

Burton, Jack. *The Blue Book of Hollywood Musicals.* Watkins Glen, N.Y.: Century House, 1953.

Casper, Joseph. Andrew. *Vincente Minnelli and the Film Musical.* New York: Barnes, 1977.

Cavell, Stanley. *Pursuits of Happiness: The Hollywood Comedy of Remarriage.* Cambridge, Mass.: Harvard University Press, 1981.

Comolli, Jean-Louis. "Dancing Images," *Cahiers du cinéma in English* 2 (1966), pp. 22–26.

Cook, Jim. "*On a Clear Day You Can See Forever*," *Movie* 24 (Spring 1977), pp. 61–62.

Croce, Arlene. *The Fred Astaire & Ginger Rogers Book.* New York: Outerbridge and Lazard, 1972.

Cutts, John. "On the Bright Side: An Interview with Charles Walters," *Films and Filming* 16 (August 1970), pp. 12–18.

364

Delameter, Jerome. "Busby Berkeley: An American Surrealist," *Wide Angle* 1 (Spring 1976), pp. 30–37.

————. *Dance in the Hollywood Musical.* Ann Arbor: University of Michigan Research Press, 1981.

Dietz, Howard. *Dancing in the Dark.* New York: Quadrangle, 1974.

Druxman, Michael B. *The Musical from Broadway to Hollywood.* New York: Barnes, 1980.

Durgnat, Raymond. "Film Favorites: *Bells Are Ringing,*" *Film Comment* 9 (March-April 1973), pp. 46–50.

Dyer, Richard. "Entertainment and Utopia," in Altman, *Genre,* pp. 175–89.

Edwards, Anne. *Judy Garland: A Biography.* New York: Simon and Schuster, 1974.

Eells, George. *The Life that Late He Led.* New York: Putnam, 1967.

Elsaesser, Thomas. "Vincente Minnelli," in Altman, *Genre,* pp. 11–27.

Engel, Lehman. *The American Musical Theater.* New York: Macmillan, 1967.

Erenberg, Lewis A. *Steppin' Out: New York Nightlife and the Transformation of American Culture, 1890–1930.* Chicago: University of Chicago Press, 1984.

Ewen, David. *The Story of Irving Berlin.* New York: Holt, 1950.

————. *American Popular Songs.* New York: Random House, 1966.

Feuer, Jane. *The Hollywood Musical.* Bloomington: Indiana University Press, 1982.

Fischer, Lucy. "The Image of Woman as Woman: The Optical Politics of *Dames,*" in Altman, *Genre,* pp. 70–84.

Fordin, Hugh. *The Movies' Greatest Musicals: Produced in Hollywood USA by the Freed Unit.* New York: Ungar, 1975.

Frank, Gerold. *Judy.* New York: Harper and Row, 1975.

Freedland, Michael. *Irving Berlin.* New York: Stein and Day, 1974.

————. *Fred Astaire: An Illustrated Biography.* New York: Grossett and Dunlap, 1976.

————. *Jerome Kern.* London: Robson, 1978.

Gardner, Paul. "Bob Fosse," *Action* 9 (May-June 1974), pp. 22–27.

Geduld, Harry. *The Birth of the Talkies.* Bloomington: Indiana University Press, 1975.

Gershwin, Ira. *Lyrics on Several Occasions.* New York: Knopf, 1959.

Giles, Dennis. "Show Making," in Altman, *Genre,* pp. 85–101.

Gilson, René and Brion, Patrick. "Interview with Busby Berkeley," *Cahiers du cinéma in English* 2 (1966), pp. 26–38.

Gottfried, Martin. *Broadway Musicals.* New York: Abrams, 1979.

Green, Stanley. "Hammerstein's Film Career," *Films in Review* 8 (February 1957), pp. 68–77.

————. *Ring Bells! Sing Songs! Broadway Musicals of the 1930s.* New Rochelle, N.Y.: Arlington House, 1971.

————. *The World of Musical Comedy.* New York: Barnes, 1974.

————. *Encyclopedia of the Musical Film.* New York: Oxford University Press, 1981.

————. *Broadway Musicals: Show By Show.* Milwaukee: Hal Leonard, 1985.

Green, Stanley and Goldblatt, Burt, *Starring Fred Astaire.* New York: Dodd, Mead, 1973.

Griffith, Richard. *The Cinema of Gene Kelly.* New York: Museum of Modern Art, 1962.

Hamm, Charles. *Yesterdays: Popular Song in America.* New York: Norton, 1979.

Harmetz, Aljean. *The Making of The Wizard of Oz.* New York: Knopf, 1977.

Harvey, Stephen. "Stanley Donen," *Film Comment* 9 (July-August 1973), pp. 4–9.

————. *Fred Astaire.* New York: Pyramid, 1975.

Hauduroy, Jean-François. "Interview with Comden and Green," *Cahiers du cinéma in English* 2 (1966), pp. 43–50.

Higham, Charles. "George Sidney," *Action* 9 (May-June 1974), pp. 17–21.

Hillier, Jim. "Interview with Stanley Donen," *Movie* 24 (Spring 1977), pp. 26–35.

Hirschorn, Clive. *Gene Kelly: A Biography.* Chicago: Regnery, 1974.

———. *The Hollywood Musical.* New York: Crown, 1981.

Hogue, Peter. "*The Band Wagon,*" *The Velvet Light Trap* 11 (Winter 1974), pp. 33–34.

Jablonski, Edward. *Harold Arlen: Happy with the Blues.* Garden City, N.Y.: Doubleday, 1961.

Jablonski, Edward, and Stewart, D. Lawrence, *The Gershwin Years.* Garden City, N.Y.: Doubleday, 1973.

Johnson, Albert. "Conversation with Roger Edens," *Sight and Sound* 27 (Spring 1958), pp. 179–82.

Kimball, Robert, ed. *The Complete Lyrics of Cole Porter.* New York: Knopf, 1983.

Kimball, Robert, Gill, Brendan, and Feitler, Bea. *Cole.* New York: Holt, 1971.

Kimball, Robert, Simon, Alfred, and Feitler, Bea. *The Gershwins.* New York: Atheneum, 1973.

Knowles, Eleanor. *The Films of Jeannette MacDonald and Nelson Eddy.* New York: Barnes, 1974.

Knox, Donald, ed. *The Magic Factory: How MGM Made An American in Paris.* New York: Praeger, 1973.

Kobal, John. *Gotta Sing, Gotta Dance: A Pictorial History of Film Musicals.* London: Hamlyn, 1971.

Kreuger, Miles, ed. *The Movie Musical from Vitaphone to 42nd Street: As Reprinted in a Great Fan Magazine.* New York: Dover, 1975.

———. *Show Boat: The Story of a Classic American Musical.* New York: Oxford University Press, 1977.

Leonard, Neil. *Jazz and the White Americans: The Acceptance of a New Art Form.* Chicago: University of Chicago Press, 1962.

Lerner, Alan Jay. *On the Street Where I Live.* New York: Norton, 1978.

Levant, Oscar. *The Memoirs of an Amnesiac.* New York: Putnam, 1965.

Lloyd, Peter. "Stanley Donen," *Brighton Film Review* 18 (March 1970), pp. 17–19.

Mariani, John. "Come on with the Rain," *Film Comment* 14 (May–June 1978), pp. 7–12.

Marshall, Michael. *Top Hat & Tails: The Story of Jack Buchanan.* London: Elm Tree, 1978.

Mast, Gerald. *The Comic Mind: Comedy and the Movies*, rev. ed. Chicago: University of Chicago Press, 1979.

———. *Howard Hawks, Storyteller.* New York: Oxford University Press, 1982.

McVay, Douglas. *The Musical Film.* New York: Barnes, 1967.

Milne, Tom. *Mamoulian.* Bloomington: Indiana University Press, 1969.

Minnelli, Vincente (with Hector Arce). *I Remember It Well.* Garden City, N.Y.: Doubleday, 1974.

Mordden, Ethan. *Better Foot Forward: The History of American Musical Theatre.* New York: Grossman, 1976.

———. *The Hollywood Musical.* New York: St. Martin's, 1981.

———. *Broadway Babies: The People Who Made the American Musical.* New York: Oxford University Press, 1983.

Moshier, W. Franklin. *The Alice Faye Movie Book.* New York: A & W Visual Arts, 1974.

Mueller, John. *Astaire Dancing.* New York: Knopf, 1985.

Pechter, William S. "Movie Musicals," *Commentary* (May 1972), pp. 77–81.

Richards, Stanley, ed. *Great Musicals of the American Musical Theatre.* Radnor, Pa.: Chilton, 1975.

Ringgold, Gene and Bodeen, DeWitt. *Chevalier: The Films and Career of Maurice Chevalier.* Secaucus, N.J.: Citadel, 1973.

Rodgers, Richard. *Musical Stages: An Autobiography.* New York: Random House, 1975.

Roth, Mark. "Some Warners Musicals and the Spirit of the New Deal," in Altman, *Genre,* pp. 41–56.

Sarris, Andrew. "Al Jolson," *Film Comment* 13 (September-October 1977), pp. 39–41.

Sennett, Ted. *Hollywood Musicals.* New York: Abrams, 1981.

Shivas, Mark. "Minnelli's Method," *Movie* 1 (June 1962), pp. 17–24.

Smith, Cecil. *Musical Comedy in America.* New York: Theatre Arts, 1950.

Spiegel, Ellen. "Fred and Ginger Meet Van Nest Polglase," *The Velvet Light Trap* 10 (Fall 1973), pp. 17–22.

Springer, John. *All Talking! All Singing! All Dancing!* New York: Citadel, 1966.

Stern, Lee Edward. *The Movie Musical.* New York: Pyramid, 1974.

Sutton, Martin. "Patterns of Meaning in the Musical," in Altman, *Genre,* pp. 190–96.

———. "The Belle of New York," *Movie* 24 (Spring 1977), pp. 54–58.

Taylor, John Russell and Arthur Jackson. *The Hollywood Musical.* New York: McGraw-Hill, 1971.

Thomas, Bob. *Astaire: The Man, The Dancer.* New York: St. Martin's, 1984.

Thomas, Lawrence B. *The MGM Years.* New York: Columbia House, 1971.

Thomas, Tony. *The Films of Gene Kelly: Song and Dance Man.* New York: Citadel, 1974.

———. *Harry Warren and the Hollywood Musical.* Secaucus, N.J.: Citadel, 1975.

Thomas, Tony, and Terry, Jim (with Busby Berkeley). *The Busby Berkeley Book.* New York: A & W Visual Library, 1973.

Todd, A. "From Chaplin to Kelly," *Theater Arts* 35 (August 1951), pp. 50 –51.

Toll, Robert. *Blacking Up: The Minstrel Show in Nineteenth-Century America.* New York: Oxford University Press, 1974.

———. *On with the Show: The First Century of Show Business in America.* New York: Oxford Univerity Press, 1976.

Turim, Maureen. "Gentlemen Consume Blondes," *Wide Angle* 1 (Spring 1976), pp. 68–76.

Vallance, Tom. *The American Musical.* New York: Barnes, 1970.

Vaughn, David. "After the Ball," *Sight and Sound* 26 (Autumn 1956), pp. 89–91.

Wilder, Alec. *American Popular Song: The Great Innovators 1900–1950.* New York: Oxford University Press, 1972.

Williams, Alan. "The Musical Film and Popular Recorded Music," in Altman, *Genre,* pp. 147–58.

Winer, S. " 'Dignity—Always Dignity!': Betty Comden and Adolph Green's Musicals," *The Velvet Light Trap* 11 (Winter 1974), pp. 29–32.

Wodehouse, P. G., and Bolton, Guy. *Bring on the Girls!* New York: Simon and Schuster, 1953.

Woll, Allen L. *Songs from Hollywood Musical Comedies, 1927 to the Present: A Dictionary.* New York: Garland, 1978.

Wood, Robin. "Art and Ideology: Notes on *Silk Stockings,*" in Altman, *Genre,* pp. 57–69.

———. "Never Never Change, Always Gonna Dance," *Film Comment* 15 (September-October 1975), pp. 28–31.

Zadan, Craig. *Sondheim and Company.* New York: Macmillan, 1974.

Index

Smith, Alexis, 221
Smith, Harry B., 51
"Smoke Gets in Your Eyes," 54–55
"So in Love," 192, 197
"So Near and Yet So Far," 162, 192
"Soliloquy," 209, 217
"Some Enchanted Evening," 206, 217, 292, 293
"Some Girls Can Bake a Pie," 79
Some Like It Hot, 343
"Some of these Days," 340
"Some Other Time," 28, 299
"Somebody Loves Me," 74
"Someday My Prince Will Come," 93
"Someone in a Tree," 330
Something in the Wind, 261
"Something Wonderful," 292
"Something's Coming," 301–02
"Somewhere," 299, 301, 302
"Somewhere There's a Someone," 281–82
Sondheim, Stephen, 6, 15, 31, 43, 52, 203, 204, 295, 296, 301, 302, 313, 319, 324–33, 335, 348, 349, 350, 351
Song and Dance, 334
"Song Is You, The," 55
"Song of the Supreme Court Judges, The," 69
"Sonny Boy," 89
"Soon," 173
Soon-Teck-Oh, 333
Sophisticated Ladies, 4, 334
"Sorry Grateful," 326
Sound of Music, The (1959), 59, 170, 201, 214–15
Sound of Music, The (WB, 1965), 215, 217–18, 310, 343
"Sound of Music, The," 292
Sources, 61, 62, 84, 173, 174, 175, 196, 207, 213, 289, 290, 291, 293, 294, 295, 296, 303, 304, 306, 318, 319; *Berlin Stories* (Christopher Isherwood), 321, 322, 324; *Biche au bois, La*, 8; Cervantes, Miguel, 291; Colette, 289; *Comedy of Errors, The*, 173; *8½* (Federico Fellini), 340; Longfellow, Henry Wadsworth, 15; *Faust*, 8–10, 270, 272, 273, 274, 275, 293, 312, 316; Ferber, Edna, 59, 61, 62; *Fourposter, The* (Jan DeHartog), 195; *Freischütz, Der* (Carl Maria von Weber), 8; Loos, Anita, 294; *Matchmaker, The* (Thornton Wilder), 18; Michener, James, 207; *Ninotchka* (Ernst Lubitsch), 199; O'Hara, John, 174, 175, 180; *Pygmalion* (George Bernard Shaw), 291, 306, 307, 308, 309; Riggs, Lynn, 207; *Romantiques, Les* (Edmund Rostand), 295; *Romeo and Juliet*, 295, 301; Runyon, Damon, 291, 302, 304; *7½ Cents* (Richard Bissell), 293; Shaw, George Bernard, 291, 306, 307, 308, 309; *Shop

Around the Corner, The (Ernst Lubitsch), 296; *Smiles of a Summer Night* (Ingmar Bergman), 319, 328; *Song of Myself* (Walt Whitman), 339; "Sunday Afternoon on the Island of the Grande Jatte, A," 331; *Taming of the Shrew, The*, 196, 197; Terence and Palutus, 325; *Tevye the Milkman* (Shalom Aleichem), 296; *They Knew What They Wanted* (Sidney Howard), 304; Twain, Mark, 62, 173; *Uncle Tom's Cabin*, 213; Voltaire, 291; *Viktor und Viktoria*, 343; *Warrior's Husband, The* (Julian Thompson), 173; *Year the Yankees Lost the Pennant, The* (Douglas Wallop), 293
Sousa, John Phillip, 294, 330, 353
Sous les toits de Paris, 110
South Pacific (1949), 4, 6, 15, 59, 61, 77, 201, 204, 205, 206, 208, 209, 210, 211, 212, 213, 214, 215, 293, 305, 324, 329
South Pacific (Twentieth Century-Fox, 1958), 215, 216, 217
Southerners, The, 21
Spatialization, 241–42, 244, 245, 246, 274, 277, 278
    Spatial disorientation and discontinuity, 96, 98, 109, 125, 129, 131, 132, 133, 217, 242, 259, 263
    Spatial stability, 125, 137, 150–51, 216, 277, 279, 313
Spewack, Sam and Bella, 196
Spillane, Mickey, 274, 275
"Sposalizio," 305
"Spring Is Here," 169, 170
"Spring Will Be a Little Late this Year," 298
"Stand and Cheer," 102
"Standing on the Corner," 293, 305
Stapleton, Jean, 293
Stapleton, Maureen, 317
Star Is Born, A (Selznick, 1937), 98
Star Is Born, A (WB, 1954), 86, 222, 253, 275–82
Star Is Born, A (WB, 1976), 318
Star Performer musical, 89, 98, 145, 220, 223, 224, 282, 338, 339
Starlight Express, 334
Star-Spangled Rhythm, 226
State Fair, 170, 207, 229
"State of the Art, The," 332
"Steam Heat," 294
Steamboat Willie, 93
Stein, Joseph, 296
"Steppin' Out with My Baby," 30
Stern, Isaac, 36
"Stereophonic Sound," 199
"Stetson Hat," 121
Stevens, George, 150
Stewart, James, 237
Stone, Andrew, 232